SYMMETRY IN PHYSICS

VOLUME 2: FURTHER APPLICATIONS

SYMMETRY IN PHYSICS

VOLUME 2:

FURTHER APPLICATIONS

J. P. ELLIOTT and P. G. DAWBER

School of Mathematical and Physical Sciences
University of Sussex, Brighton

OXFORD UNIVERSITY PRESS
New York

First published in Great Britain 1979 by
The Macmillan Press Ltd

First published in paperback 1984

Published in the U.S.A. by
Oxford University Press, New York

Library of Congress Cataloging in Publication Data

Elliott, James Philip, 1929–
Symmetry in physics.

Includes bibliographies and index.
CONTENTS: v. 1. Principles and simple applications.
–v. 2. Further applications.
1. Symmetry (Physics) I. Dawber, P. G., joint author. II. Title.
QC174.17.S9E44 530.1′2 79–12055
ISBN 0-19-520455-7 (v. 1)
ISBN 0-19-520456-5 (v. 2)

Printed in Hong Kong

Contents of Volume 1

Contents of Volume 2

Preface to Volume 2

In volume 1 the fundamental role of symmetry was developed and applied to a wide range of problems in classical and quantum physics. In this volume we move on to some more difficult applications and to a more general study of the symmetric and unitary groups, particular cases of which were met in volume 1. These topics would probably only arise at postgraduate level, but would none the less be of interest to the more inquisitive undergraduate.

This volume begins with a further application of the use of 'point groups'—to the motion of electrons in a molecule—and then, in chapter 14, moves away from symmetries with a fixed point to study discrete translations and their applications to crystal structure. The theory of relativity is of profound importance in the philosophy of physics and, when speeds become comparable with that of light, it has practical importance. For all the systems discussed in volume 1 we were able to ignore relativity because the speeds of the particles involved were sufficiently small. Chapter 15 describes the symmetry in four-dimensional space–time which is the origin of relativity theory and discusses its consequences, especially in relation to the classification of elementary particles. The concepts of momentum, energy, mass and spin are interpreted in terms of symmetry using the Lorentz and Poincaré groups and a natural place is found in the theory for particles, like the photon, with zero mass. Chapter 16 is concerned with fields, in contrast to the earlier chapters which dealt with particles or systems of particles. We first describe classical fields, such as the electromagnetic field, using four-dimensional space–time. This is followed by a brief account of the theory of relativistic quantum fields which provides a framework for the creation and annihilation of particles and the existence of antiparticles. Chapters 17 and 18 contain details of two general groups, the 'symmetric' group of all permutations of *n* objects and the 'unitary' group in *N* dimensions, and an intimate relation between these two groups is discussed. Particular cases of these two groups have been met earlier. Chapter 19 describes some unexpected symmetries in two familiar potentials, the Coulomb and the harmonic oscillator potentials, and a number of small, unconnected, but interesting topics are collected into the last chapter.

The text includes worked examples and a selection of problems with solutions. A bibliography of references for further reading is given at the end of each chapter for those who wish either to follow the physical applications into more detail or to study some of the mathematical questions to a greater depth.

As in volume 1, roman type is used for operators and italic type for numbers. Vectors are printed in bold face and four-vectors carry a circumflex.

Brighton, Sussex, 1979

J. P. E.
P. G. D.

13

Electron States in Molecules

In studying the structure of molecules one should strictly consider the motion both of the nuclei of the constituent atoms and of their electrons. However, because of the large mass of the nuclei, relative to that of an electron, one may approximately separate the motions of these two kinds of particle. This 'Born–Oppenheimer' approximation is discussed briefly in section 20.2. For our present purpose we shall be considering the motion of the electrons relative to the nuclei which are assumed to be fixed. Our interest will centre on those molecules for which the arrangement of fixed nuclei is invariant under some point group of symmetry operations. This is precisely the same symmetry group which we used in discussing molecular vibrations in chapter 6. The physical difference between that problem and the present one is that in studying molecular vibrations the electrons were ignored, except in so far as they were responsible for the potential in which the nuclei moved. From the experimental viewpoint the molecular vibrations involve energies of the order of $(10)^{-2}$ eV, whereas the excitation of the electronic motion, which we are about to discuss, requires energies of the order of 1 eV.

Even with the assumption of fixed nuclei the calculation of the electronic wave function is a formidable task—see Eyring *et al.* (1944), Murrell *et al.*

(1970) and Murrell and Harget (1972) in the bibliography—more complex than the calculation of the electronic wave functions of a single atom which we described in chapter 8. We therefore restrict the present discussion to the simple model in which each electron is assumed to move independently in a fixed field due to the nuclei and the other electrons. This is similar to the central field approximation in atoms except that the field now has some point group symmetry instead of being spherical. Having found the single-electron wave functions we can then construct a Slater determinant for the many-electron wave function as described in subsection 8.6.2. One usually refers to a single-particle wave function in the molecule as a 'molecular orbital' to distinguish it from an atomic orbital which refers to a single atom.

13.1 Linear combinations of atomic orbitals (LCAO)

If we consider an electron moving close to one of the nuclei in the molecule it will experience a field which must be quite similar to that in an isolated atom, so that in this region we would expect the wave function to be similar to a free-atom wave function $\phi_{nlm}(\boldsymbol{r}-\boldsymbol{r}_t)$ centred on the nucleus at $\boldsymbol{r}_t$. This leads us to construct wave functions by taking linear combinations of the least-bound atomic orbitals $\phi_{nlm}(\boldsymbol{r}-\boldsymbol{r}_t)$ centred on the different nuclei $\boldsymbol{r}_t$. Such a wave function is called an LCAO molecular orbital. In a simple calculation it is reasonable to assume that only valence electrons are involved in these orbitals, whilst the electrons in the inner full shells of the atoms remain in their unperturbed atomic state. A more complete calculation could include some of these lower energy states and also some of the unoccupied excited states.

The set of atomic orbitals $\phi_{nlm}(\boldsymbol{r}-\boldsymbol{r}_t)$, with n and l fixed and with $\boldsymbol{r}_t$ running over the positions of equivalent nuclei, provides the basis for a representation T of the symmetry group. To see this, we show that the effect of a group operation $\mathrm{T(G}_a)$ on the orbital $\phi_{nlm}(\boldsymbol{r}-\boldsymbol{r}_t)$ is to turn it into another atomic orbital centred on one of the nuclei $\boldsymbol{r}_t$. In detail, using the general definition (3.37) we have

$$\begin{aligned}\mathrm{T}(\mathrm{G}_a)\phi_{nlm}(\boldsymbol{r}-\boldsymbol{r}_t) &= \phi_{nlm}(\mathrm{G}_a^{-1}\boldsymbol{r}-\boldsymbol{r}_t)\\ &= \phi_{nlm}\{\mathrm{G}_a^{-1}(\boldsymbol{r}-\mathrm{G}_a\boldsymbol{r}_t)\}\\ &= \sum_{m'} D^{(l)}_{m'm}(\mathrm{G}_a)\phi_{nlm'}(\boldsymbol{r}-\mathrm{G}_a\boldsymbol{r}_t)\\ &= \sum_{m'} D^{(l)}_{m'm}(\mathrm{G}_a)\phi_{nlm'}(\boldsymbol{r}-\boldsymbol{r}_{t'})\end{aligned} \tag{13.1}$$

where $\boldsymbol{r}_{t'}=\mathrm{G}_a\boldsymbol{r}_t$ and $\mathrm{D}^{(l)}$ is the familiar $(2l+1)$-dimensional irreducible representation of $\mathcal{R}_3$. The representation T will have dimension $(2l+1)N_t$, where N_t is the number of nuclei equivalent to the one at $\boldsymbol{r}_t$.

From general theory we expect an energy eigenstate to transform irreducibly under the symmetry group $\mathcal{G}$, so that we shall be able to label the molecular orbitals by irreducible representation labels of $\mathscr{G}$. To find which labels occur we must reduce the representation T and for this we need to know the character of T which may be deduced from equation (13.1) using an argument like that in section 6.5. From this equation one sees that diagonal matrix elements occur only when $\boldsymbol{r}_t = \boldsymbol{r}_{t'}$, i.e when the nucleus at $\boldsymbol{r}_t$ is unmoved by G_a. The contribution to the character of T from such a nucleus is then simply the character of $D^{(l)}$ which is given from equation (7.42) as

$$\chi^{(l)}(R(\phi)) = \sin(l+\tfrac{1}{2})\phi/\sin\tfrac{1}{2}\phi$$
$$\chi^{(l)}(S(\phi)) = \cos(l+\tfrac{1}{2})\phi/\cos\tfrac{1}{2}\phi \tag{13.2}$$

where $R(\phi)$ is a proper rotation and $S(\phi) = \sigma_h R(\phi) = IR(\phi+\pi)$ is a mirror rotation, in the notation of section 9.1. The characters of the $(2l+1)N_t$-dimensional representation T are then obtained by multiplying these expressions by the number of nuclei left unmoved by the group operation $R(\phi)$ or $S(\phi)$. Once we have the character of T, its reduction is found by using the known table of irreducible characters using the general method of section 4.11.

To construct a molecular orbital $\psi_{nl}^{(\alpha)}(\boldsymbol{r})$ which transforms according to one of the representations $T^{(\alpha)}$ of $\mathscr{G}$ occurring in the above reduction we may use the projection method explained in section 4.19. From equation (4.51) we can construct the un-normalised molecular orbital

$$\psi_{nl}^{(\alpha)}(\boldsymbol{r}) = \sum_a \chi^{(\alpha)*}(G_a)T(G_a)\phi_{nlm}(\boldsymbol{r}-\boldsymbol{r}_t) \tag{13.3}$$

where the sum runs over the group elements G_a and any of the possible values m and $\boldsymbol{r}_t$ may be used.

If a representation $T^{(\alpha)}$ occurs more than once, or if we wish to consider the mixing of different atomic orbital labels nl, then we must form a trial wave function

$$\psi^{(\alpha)}(\boldsymbol{r}) = \sum_{i,n,l} c_{nl}^{(\alpha)i}\psi_{nl}^{(\alpha)i}(\boldsymbol{r}) \tag{13.4}$$

and determine the coefficients $c_{nl}^{(\alpha)i}$ by the variational method. In this sum, the index i distinguishes molecular orbitals when $T^{(\alpha)}$ occurs more than once in the reduction of T. To perform the variational calculation, or even to estimate the relative energies of the single molecular orbitals (13.3) for different α, one must assume some form for the single electron Hamiltonian $H(\boldsymbol{r})$. Since the functions $\psi_{nl}^{(\alpha)i}(\boldsymbol{r})$ are not orthogonal the matrix formulation of this variational problem follows the method of section 5.7. The wave functions and energies for the molecular orbitals with symmetry α are then given by the roots of the matrix equation (5.23); in our present notation,

$$(H^{(\alpha)} - ES^{(\alpha)})\boldsymbol{c}^{(\alpha)} = 0 \tag{13.5}$$

where $\boldsymbol{c}^{(\alpha)}$ is the column vector of coefficients $c_{nl}^{(\alpha)i}$ in equation (13.4). The matrix elements of $H^{(\alpha)}$ and $S^{(\alpha)}$ are given by

$$H^{(\alpha)}_{inl,\,jn'l'} = \int \psi^{(\alpha)i*}_{nl}(\boldsymbol{r})\mathrm{H}\psi^{(\alpha)j}_{n'l'}(\boldsymbol{r})\mathrm{d}\boldsymbol{r}$$

$$S^{(\alpha)}_{inl,\,jn'l'} = \int \psi^{(\alpha)i*}_{nl}(\boldsymbol{r})\psi^{(\alpha)j}_{n'l'}(\boldsymbol{r})\mathrm{d}\boldsymbol{r}$$

Since $\psi^{(\alpha)i}_{nl}(\boldsymbol{r})$ is a known linear combination of atomic orbitals these matrix elements are all given in terms of matrix elements between atomic orbitals. It is usually assumed that the matrix elements of $\mathrm{H}(\boldsymbol{r})$ between atomic orbitals vanish unless the two sites t and t' are identical or nearest neighbours in the molecule. Further assumptions often made are that the diagonal elements are just the single-particle energies in the free atom since the atomic orbitals are well located about a single nucleus and $\mathrm{H}(\boldsymbol{r})$ must approximate the sum of the atomic potentials. Care must be taken in these energy calculations since the atomic orbitals on different sites are not orthogonal. In the simplest approximation, one might assume them to be orthogonal, i.e. $S^{(\alpha)}$ is the unit matrix.

13.2 Examples

To illustrate the techniques developed in the preceding section we will look at two examples. The first will be a hypothetical H_3 molecule with the three hydrogen atoms at the corners of an equilateral triangle and the second will be the water molecule used as an illustration in chapter 6.

H_3 molecule

The H_3 molecule is illustrated in figure 13.1 with the three atoms being labelled by a, b and c. The symmetry group is D_{3h}, but since we shall only be using atomic s-states in our calculation and these have reflection symmetry in the plane we may ignore the horizontal reflection and use just the group D_3.

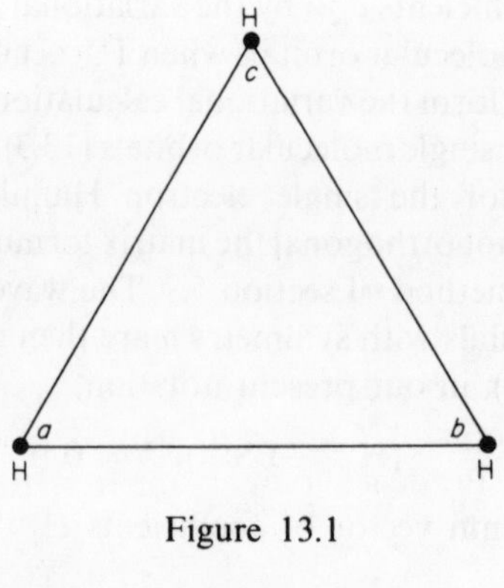

Figure 13.1

The characters are given in table 13.1 together with the character for the three 1*s*-orbitals calculated as outlined above.

Table 13.1

D_3	E	$2C_3$	$3C_2$	
A_1	1	1	1	
A_2	1	1	-1	
E	2	-1	0	
$\chi^{(1s)}$	3	0	1	$= A_1 \dot{+} E$

This reducible representation consists of a singlet A_1 and a doublet E. Thus instead of the three wave functions $\phi_{1s}(a)$, $\phi_{1s}(b)$ and $\phi_{1s}(c)$ we can construct one linear combination $\psi^{(A_1)}$ which transforms like A_1 and a pair $\psi_1^{(E)}$ and $\psi_2^{(E)}$, which transform according to E. Using the projection (13.3), we find

$$\begin{aligned} \psi^{(A_1)} &\propto \{\phi_{1s}(a)+\phi_{1s}(b)+\phi_{1s}(c)\} \\ \psi_1^{(E)} &\propto \{2\phi_{1s}(a)-\phi_{1s}(b)-\phi_{1s}(c)\} \\ \psi_2^{(E)} &\propto \{\phi_{1s}(b)-\phi_{1s}(c)\} \end{aligned} \tag{13.6}$$

In this simple example the irreducible representations occur only once so that no variational calculation is necessary and the states (13.6) are our best one-electron molecular orbitals. The energies of these states in the simplest approximation are then given by

$$E^{(A_1)} = \tfrac{1}{3}(3\varepsilon_{1s}+6\lambda) \qquad = \varepsilon_{1s}+2\lambda$$

$$E_1^{(E)} = E_2^{(E)} = \tfrac{1}{2}(2\varepsilon_{1s}-2\lambda) = \varepsilon_{1s}-\lambda$$

where ε_{1s} is the energy of the free hydrogen 1*s*-orbital and λ is the integral

$$\lambda = \int \phi_{1s}^*(a)\mathrm{H}(\boldsymbol{r})\phi_{1s}(b)\mathrm{d}\boldsymbol{r}$$

The main contribution to this integral is the energy due to the interaction between the electron in the state $\phi_{1s}(a)$ and the nucleus at b and *vice versa*. Since this is due to an attractive force we would expect λ to be negative and hence the totally symmetric state $\psi^{(A_1)}$ to be lowest in energy. Hence, if we put the three electrons into the states (13.6) in a way consistent with the Pauli exclusion principle, the ground state of the molecule will have two electrons with opposite spins in the lowest orbital $\psi^{(A_1)}$ and one electron in one of the degenerate states $\psi^{(E)}$. The total wave function for this state is the Slater determinant constructed from these three functions and since each term in the expansion of the determinant is a product with symmetry $A_1 \times A_1 \times E = E$ it is an E-orbital doublet, the degeneracy arising from the two possible states for the third electron.

H_2O molecule

The symmetry group for the water molecule shown in figure 13.2 is C_{2v}. The hydrogen atoms have one electron each and the oxygen atom has eight electrons in a ground state configuration $1s^2\ 2s^2\ 2p^4$. The atomic orbitals that

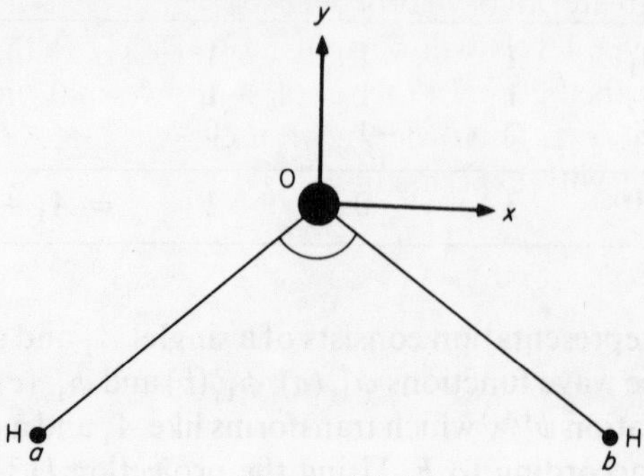

Figure 13.2

we will use are the 1*s*-orbitals on the hydrogen nuclei which we denote $\phi_{1s}(a)$ and $\phi_{1s}(b)$, and the 2*p*-orbitals on the oxygen nucleus, denoted ϕ_{2px}, ϕ_{2py}, ϕ_{2pz}. The atomic 1*s*- and 2*s*-orbitals in oxygen are more tightly bound so we neglect them in this simple calculation. The binding of the 2*p*-orbital in oxygen and the 1*s*-orbital in hydrogen are approximately the same so that we must take account of them both. The character table for the group C_{2v} is shown in table 13.2, together with the characters for the spaces generated by the atomic orbitals. (σ_v denotes a reflection in the plane of the molecule and σ_v' a reflection in the perpendicular plane containing the *y*-axis.)

Table 13.2

C_{2v}	E	C_2	σ_v	σ_v	
A_1	1	1	1	1	
A_2	1	1	−1	−1	
B_1	1	−1	1	−1	
B_2	1	−1	−1	1	
$\chi^{(1s)}$	2	0	2	0	$= A_1 + B_1$
$\chi^{(2p)}$	3	−1	1	1	$= A_1 + B_1 + B_2$

Since all the irreducible representations are one-dimensional it is easy to write down the symmetrised orbitals as

$$\phi_{1s}^{(A_1)} \propto \{\phi_{1s}(a) + \phi_{1s}(b)\}$$

$$\phi_{1s}^{(B_1)} \propto \{\phi_{1s}(a) - \phi_{1s}(b)\}$$

$$\phi_{2p}^{(A_1)} = \phi_{2py}, \qquad \phi_{2p}^{(B_1)} = \phi_{2px}, \qquad \phi_{2p}^{(B_2)} = \phi_{2pz}$$

Since there are two A_1-type orbitals we must allow them to mix. If we denote the free-atom energies of ϕ_{1s} and ϕ_{2p} by ε_{1s} and ε_{2p} then the effect of the mixing will be to produce a pair of A_1-type energies as shown in figure 13.3. In the same way, the two B_1-type orbitals will mix as shown. One may argue qualitatively that, since the bond angle is greater than 90°, the overlap between $\phi_{1s}^{(B_1)}$ and $\phi_{2p}^{(B_1)}$ is greater than that between $\phi_{1s}^{(A_1)}$ and $\phi_{2p}^{(A_1)}$. Hence one expects that the two B_1-type levels will be split more widely than the two A_1-type levels, as shown in the figure. In the simplest approximation, the B_2-level has the free-atom energy ε_{2p}. This ordering of single-particle levels, as shown in the figure, is consistent with experiment.

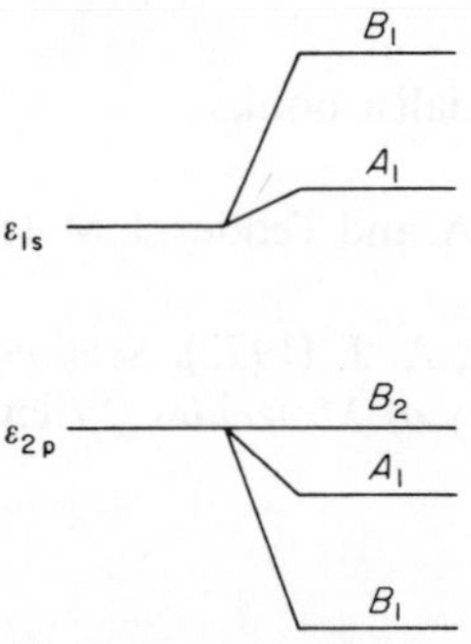

Figure 13.3

To construct the wave function for the water molecule we must now place electrons into these molecular orbitals, building up a Slater determinant. There are six electrons to be placed, two of them coming from the 1*s*-orbits on the hydrogen atoms and four from the 2*p*-orbits in oxygen (recall that the oxygen atom has a configuration of $1s^2\,2s^2\,2p^4$). To describe the molecular ground state we therefore place two electrons (spin up and down) in each of the lowest three levels B_1, A_1 and B_2 of figure 13.3.

13.3 Selection rules for electronic excitations in molecules

Optical absorption can take place when the molecule undergoes a transition from the ground state to an excited state. The simplest excited states can be considered to be single-particle excitations from one occupied molecular orbital to a higher unoccupied one. The energies involved are of the same order of magnitude as in the atomic case so that absorption can be in the visible, infrared or ultraviolet regions of the electromagnetic spectrum. The selection rules governing the transitions can be obtained in the same way as for the levels of an atom in a crystal field, see subsection 9.9.2. In the case of H_2O, because there are two electrons in each orbital, the ground state has A_1 symmetry (like a closed shell). Excited states may be constructed by promoting an electron from the least-bound orbital B_2 into either of the unoccupied A_1 or B_1 orbitals to form states of symmetry B_2 or A_2, respectively, using table 13.2. Only the first of these will be excited by electric dipole transitions since, from the table, the vector representation does not contain A_2.

Bibliography

Eyring, H., Walter, J. and Kimball, G. E. (1944). *Quantum Chemistry* (Wiley, New York)

or one of the more specialist books

Murrell, J. N., Kettle, S. F. A. and Tedder, J. M. (1970). *Valence Theory* (Wiley, New York)

Murrell, J. N. and Harget, A. J. (1972). *Semi-empirical Self-consistent Field Molecular-orbital Theory of Molecules* (Wiley, New York)

Problem

13.1 The methane molecule consists of four hydrogen atoms arranged at the vertices of a regular tetrahedron and a carbon atom at the centre (symmetry group T_d). Show that the four $1s$ atomic orbitals on the hydrogen atoms lead to a singlet and a triplet molecular orbital. Note that the $2s$ and $2p$ atomic orbitals on the carbon atom also lead to a singlet and a triplet of the same symmetries and hence that these will mix to give bonding states.

14

Symmetry in Crystalline Solids

In this chapter we discuss the effects of the translational and rotational symmetry in crystals. The first three sections are concerned with the translational symmetry and section 14.4 discusses in detail how the group theoretical results are used in determining the wave functions for electrons in a crystal. The next three sections sketch briefly how these results can be taken over for various types of elementary excitation in crystals (lattice vibrations, spin waves and excitons), and section 14.8 deals with the selection rules for scattering processes involving the excitations. In the final section we include the effects of the point-group symmetries. There is no attempt in this section to discuss all aspects of space group theory but we give a short description of the nature of the group elements and irreducible representations of the simpler space groups followed by an application to electron states.

14.1 Translational symmetry in crystals

A crystal is formed by arranging atoms or ions in a space lattice defined to be the set of points

$$\boldsymbol{n} = n_1\boldsymbol{a}_1 + n_2\boldsymbol{a}_2 + n_3\boldsymbol{a}_3 \tag{14.1}$$

with n_i integers. The $\boldsymbol{a}_i$ are called primitive translation vectors and must not be coplanar. The parallelepiped defined by $\boldsymbol{a}_1$, $\boldsymbol{a}_2$ and $\boldsymbol{a}_3$ is called the primitive cell. The simplest crystals have just a single atom at each lattice point but more generally an array of atoms with specific relative orientation is associated with each lattice point. Figure 14.1 shows a two-dimensional crystal with two atoms per unit cell.

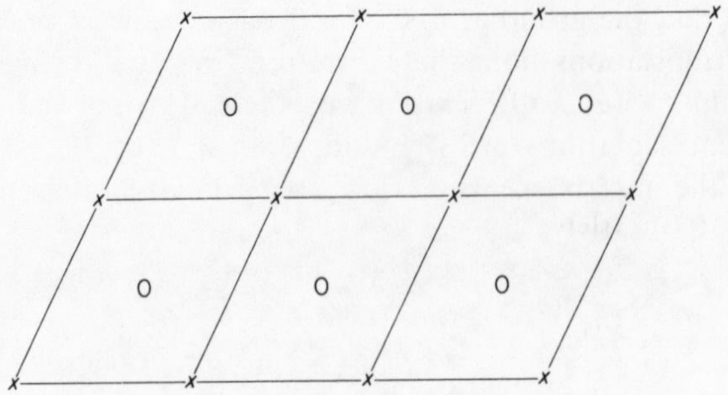

Figure 14.1

As defined by equation (14.1) the space lattice, and consequently the solid, is infinite in extent. In reality a crystal is finite but contains a very large number of atoms $\approx 10^{20}$ per cm^3. Here we will consider only the infinite crystal from which one expects to calculate what are known as the bulk properties of the material, such as conductivity and specific heat. These will be relevant in samples with a small surface to volume ratio, i.e. the number of atoms influenced by the surfaces of the crystal must be small compared with the total number.

The infinite crystal will generally have symmetries which involve rotation but for the moment we consider only the pure translational symmetry described by the group of translation operators $\mathrm{P}(\boldsymbol{n}) \equiv \mathrm{P}(n_1\, n_2\, n_3)$ which displace an arbitrary point $\boldsymbol{r}$ to $\boldsymbol{r}+\boldsymbol{n}$,

$$\mathrm{P}(\boldsymbol{n})\boldsymbol{r} = \boldsymbol{r}+\boldsymbol{n} = \boldsymbol{r}+n_1\boldsymbol{a}_1+n_2\boldsymbol{a}_2+n_3\boldsymbol{a}_3 \tag{14.2}$$

where the primitive translation vectors $\boldsymbol{a}_i$ are fixed and the n_i take integer values. We denote the group by $\mathscr{T}(\boldsymbol{a}_1, \boldsymbol{a}_2, \boldsymbol{a}_3)$ and observe that it has an infinite number of elements.

14.2 The translation group $\mathscr{T}(\boldsymbol{a}_1, \boldsymbol{a}_2, \boldsymbol{a}_3)$

The multiplication rule for translations is easily derived from the defining equation (14.2) since

$$\mathrm{P}(\boldsymbol{m})\,\mathrm{P}(\boldsymbol{n})\,\boldsymbol{r} = \mathrm{P}(\boldsymbol{m})\,(\boldsymbol{r}+\boldsymbol{n}) = \boldsymbol{r}+\boldsymbol{n}+\boldsymbol{m} \qquad (14.3)$$
$$= \boldsymbol{r}+(\boldsymbol{n}+\boldsymbol{m}) = \mathrm{P}(\boldsymbol{n}+\boldsymbol{m})\,\boldsymbol{r}$$

This shows immediately that the group is Abelian and, in particular, the translations along the directions of the three primitive vectors $\boldsymbol{a}_i$ commute with each other so that the group can be considered as a direct product of three subgroups of translations along these directions. We now consider just one of these subgroups $\mathcal{T}(\boldsymbol{a}_1, 0, 0)$. This is an Abelian group and therefore its irreducible representations are one-dimensional. From equation (14.3) it follows that the matrix elements $\mathrm{T}(n_1\,0\,0)$ corresponding to the group elements $\mathrm{P}(n_1\,0\,0)$ satisfy

$$\mathrm{T}(n_1\,0\,0)\quad \mathrm{T}(m_1\,0\,0) = \mathrm{T}(n_1+m_1\,0\,0) \qquad (14.4)$$

Although we use the expression 'matrix element' all these matrices are one-dimensional so that there is only one matrix element. We use the notation $\mathrm{T}(\boldsymbol{n}) \equiv \mathrm{T}(n_1\,n_2\,n_3)$ rather than the cumbersome $\mathrm{T}(\mathrm{P}(\boldsymbol{n}))$ for a representation of the translation group. Given that the matrix element for the identity $\mathrm{P}(0\,0\,0)$ is unity, i.e. $\mathrm{T}(0\,0\,0) = 1$ and defining the constant α by $\alpha = \mathrm{T}(1\,0\,0)$ it follows immediately from equation (14.4) that $\mathrm{T}(n_1\,0\,0) = \alpha^{n_1}$. For T to be a unitary representation α must be a complex number of modulus unity and it is conventional to write $\alpha = \exp(-2\pi i k_1)$, where k_1 is real and serves as a label for the representation

$$\mathrm{T}^{(k_1 0 0)}(n_1\,0\,0) = \exp(-2\pi i k_1 n_1) \qquad (14.5)$$

Since n_1 is always an integer it follows from (14.5) that two representations labelled by k_1 and $k_1' = k_1 + p$ are identical if p is an integer. Thus to describe all unitary irreducible representations, k_1 needs to take any value over an interval of length unity. As we shall see later the obvious interval $0 \leq k_1 < 1$ is not usually the most convenient in three-dimensional problems.

The irreducible representations of the complete group of translations $\mathcal{T}(\boldsymbol{a}_1, \boldsymbol{a}_2, \boldsymbol{a}_3)$ are obtained as direct products of representations of the type (14.5) and are thus one-dimensional and labelled by three parameters k_1, k_2 and k_3 with the explicit form

$$\mathrm{T}^{(\boldsymbol{k})}(\boldsymbol{n}) = \mathrm{T}^{(k_1 0 0)}(n_1\,0\,0)\times \mathrm{T}^{(0 k_2 0)}(0\,n_2\,0)\times \mathrm{T}^{(0 0 k_3)}(0\,0\,n_3)$$
$$= \exp\left[-2\pi i(k_1 n_1 + k_2 n_2 + k_3 n_3)\right] \qquad (14.6)$$

The exponent here has the form of a scalar product but, since the primitive translation vectors $\boldsymbol{a}_i$ are neither orthogonal nor normalised, it is necessary to introduce what is called a 'reciprocal basis' defined by

$$\boldsymbol{b}_1 = \frac{2\pi \boldsymbol{a}_2 \wedge \boldsymbol{a}_3}{\boldsymbol{a}_1 . \boldsymbol{a}_2 \wedge \boldsymbol{a}_3}, \quad \text{etc.} \tag{14.7}$$

before we can write it as a scalar product. The reciprocal basis vectors have the property

$$\boldsymbol{b}_i . \boldsymbol{a}_j = 2\pi \delta_{ij} \tag{14.8}$$

which may also be taken as a definition of the $\boldsymbol{b}_i$. We now define a vector $\boldsymbol{k}$ with components k_i in the basis $\boldsymbol{b}_i$

$$\boldsymbol{k} = k_1 \boldsymbol{b}_1 + k_2 \boldsymbol{b}_2 + k_3 \boldsymbol{b}_3 \tag{14.9}$$

so that

$$\boldsymbol{k} . \boldsymbol{n} = \sum_{ij} k_i n_j \boldsymbol{b}_i . \boldsymbol{a}_j = 2\pi \sum_i k_i n_i \tag{14.10}$$

The irreducible representation matrix element may then be written as

$$\mathrm{T}^{(\boldsymbol{k})}(\boldsymbol{n}) = \exp(-i\boldsymbol{k} . \boldsymbol{n}) \tag{14.11}$$

where $\boldsymbol{n}$ denotes the group element and $\boldsymbol{k}$ labels the irreducible representation.

In one dimension we noted that the representations $k_1 + p$ with p any integer were all the same as the representation k_1 and in three dimensions this will be true for representations obtained by adding integers to any of the k_i. This result is more conveniently expressed if we introduce a 'reciprocal lattice' of points given by the vectors

$$\boldsymbol{K}_{\boldsymbol{m}} = m_1 \boldsymbol{b}_1 + m_2 \boldsymbol{b}_2 + m_3 \boldsymbol{b}_3 \tag{14.12}$$

where the m_i are integers. We now see that the representations $\boldsymbol{k}$ and $\boldsymbol{k} + \boldsymbol{K}_{\boldsymbol{m}}$ are equivalent,

$$\mathrm{T}^{(\boldsymbol{k}+\boldsymbol{K}_{\boldsymbol{m}})}(\boldsymbol{n}) = \exp[-i(\boldsymbol{k} + \boldsymbol{K}_{\boldsymbol{m}}) . \boldsymbol{n}] = \exp(-i\boldsymbol{k} . \boldsymbol{n}) = \mathrm{T}^{(\boldsymbol{k})}(\boldsymbol{n}) \tag{14.13}$$

We conclude this section by deriving the simple rule for constructing product representations of the translation group. Since the irreducible representations of $\mathscr{T}$ are one-dimensional the rule is trivial. The direct product of the representations labelled by $\boldsymbol{k}$ and $\boldsymbol{k}'$ is the representation $\boldsymbol{k} + \boldsymbol{k}'$ since

$$\begin{aligned} \mathrm{T}^{(\boldsymbol{k})}(\boldsymbol{n}) \times \mathrm{T}^{(\boldsymbol{k}')}(\boldsymbol{n}) &= \exp(-i\boldsymbol{k}.\boldsymbol{n}) \exp(-i\boldsymbol{k}'.\boldsymbol{n}) \\ &= \exp[-i(\boldsymbol{k} + \boldsymbol{k}').\boldsymbol{n}] = \mathrm{T}^{(\boldsymbol{k}+\boldsymbol{k}')}(\boldsymbol{n}) \end{aligned} \tag{14.14}$$

However, because of the equivalence noted above we may add a reciprocal lattice vector without changing the result so that

$$\mathrm{T}^{(\boldsymbol{k})} \times \mathrm{T}^{(\boldsymbol{k}')} = \mathrm{T}^{(\boldsymbol{k}+\boldsymbol{k}'+\boldsymbol{K}_{\boldsymbol{m}})} \tag{14.15}$$

14.3   The Brillouin zone and some examples

We have seen that the different representations may be constructed by allowing the parameters k_1, k_2 and k_3 to range over a unit interval. In terms of the vector k this defines a region of space in which k must lie and this region may be visualised by using the reciprocal basis and equation (14.9). If we were to choose the intervals $0 \le k_i < 1$ then the region would be the parallelepiped defined by the reciprocal basis vectors b_1, b_2 and b_3. However it is usually more convenient to choose a region which is as symmetric as possible about the origin, allowing the k_i to be negative. This region is called the 'Brillouin zone' and its boundaries may be defined in terms of the reciprocal lattice given in equation (14.12). The Brillouin zone is defined as being bounded by the planes which bisect normally the vectors joining the origin to all neighbouring reciprocal lattice points.

Some examples of two-dimensional lattices are illustrated in figure 14.2 together with their reciprocal lattices and Brillouin zones. In these two-dimensional examples the vectors b_i are more quickly deduced from the relation (14.8) than from the explicit definition (14.7).

	Simple rectangular	Hexagonal	Face-centred square
Space lattice	a_2 a_1	a_2 a_1	a_2 a_1
Reciprocal lattice and first Brillouin zone (shaded)	b_2 b_1	b_2 b_1	b_2 b_1
	$\lvert b_1 \rvert = 2\pi / \lvert a_1 \rvert$	$\lvert b_1 \rvert = 4\pi / \sqrt{3}\, \lvert a_1 \rvert$	$\lvert b_1 \rvert = 2\sqrt{2}\,\pi / \lvert a_1 \rvert$

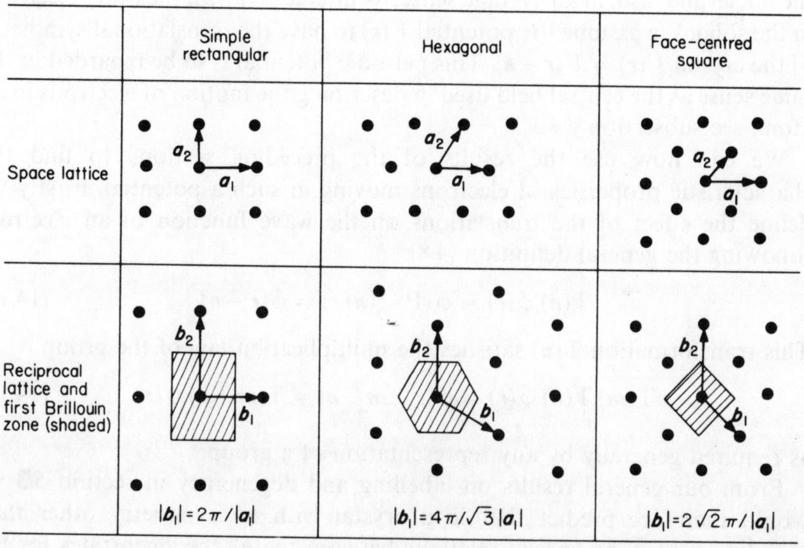

Figure 14.2

One reason for choosing the Brillouin zone rather than any other unit cell is that it demonstrates most easily the point group symmetry of the reciprocal lattice. This is in fact the same as the symmetry of the real space lattice even though these lattices may not be the same. The proof is as follows. The reciprocal lattice vectors $\boldsymbol{K}_m$ defined by equation (14.12) satisfy the equation

$$\exp(i\boldsymbol{K}_m . \boldsymbol{n}) = 1 \qquad (14.16)$$

for all lattice points $\boldsymbol{n}$ and it is easy to show the converse, that any vector which satisfies the condition (14.16) for all $\boldsymbol{n}$ must be a reciprocal lattice vector. If we now take a rotation R_i from the point group which leaves the space lattice invariant then $\mathrm{R}_i^{-1}\boldsymbol{n}$ is also a lattice point so that $\exp(i\boldsymbol{K}_m.\mathrm{R}_i^{-1}\boldsymbol{n}) = 1$. But since the exponent is a scalar product this implies that $\exp(i\mathrm{R}_i\boldsymbol{K}_m.\boldsymbol{n}) = 1$ and hence $\mathrm{R}_i\boldsymbol{K}_m$ is also a reciprocal lattice point. This shows that all reciprocal lattice vectors are taken into reciprocal lattice vectors by any R_i in the group and hence that the reciprocal lattice has the same point-group symmetry as the space lattice.

14.4 Electron states in a periodic potential

The simplest way to treat electrons moving in a crystal is to take an independent electron model where each electron is assumed to move independently in a fixed potential $V(\boldsymbol{r})$, which represents its interaction with the nuclei and also, in an average sense, its interaction with the other electrons in the solid. We assume the potential $V(\boldsymbol{r})$ to have the translational symmetry of the crystal $V(\boldsymbol{r}) = V(\boldsymbol{r}+\boldsymbol{n})$. This periodic potential is to be regarded in the same sense as the central field used in describing the motion of electrons in an atom, see subsection 8.6.1.

We can now use the results of the preceding sections to find the characteristic properties of electrons moving in such a potential. Firstly we define the effect of the translations on the wave function of an electron, following the general definition (4.8):

$$\mathrm{T}(\boldsymbol{n})\,\phi(\boldsymbol{r}) = \phi(\mathrm{P}^{-1}(\boldsymbol{n})\,\boldsymbol{r}) = \phi(\boldsymbol{r}-\boldsymbol{n}) \qquad (14.17)$$

This transformation $\mathrm{T}(\boldsymbol{n})$ satisfies the multiplication law of the group

$$\mathrm{T}(\boldsymbol{m})\,\mathrm{T}(\boldsymbol{n})\,\phi(\boldsymbol{r}) = \phi(\boldsymbol{r}-\boldsymbol{m}-\boldsymbol{n}) = \mathrm{T}(\boldsymbol{m}+\boldsymbol{n})\,\phi(\boldsymbol{r}) \qquad (14.18)$$

as required generally by any representation of a group.

From our general results on labelling and degeneracy in section 5.3 we would therefore predict that in a crystal with no symmetry other than translational (i.e. no special relations between the $\boldsymbol{a}_i$) the eigenstates for the electrons would transform according to the irreducible representations of the translation group, i.e. they would be labelled by a $\boldsymbol{k}$-vector and satisfy the transformation properties

$$\mathrm{T}(\boldsymbol{n})\,\phi^{(\boldsymbol{k})}(\boldsymbol{r}) = \mathrm{T}^{(\boldsymbol{k})}(\boldsymbol{n})\,\phi^{(\boldsymbol{k})}(\boldsymbol{r}) = \exp(-i\boldsymbol{k}.\boldsymbol{n})\,\phi^{(\boldsymbol{k})}(\boldsymbol{r}) \qquad (14.19)$$

so that, using equation (14.17),

$$\phi^{(\boldsymbol{k})}(\boldsymbol{r}-\boldsymbol{n}) = \exp(-i\boldsymbol{k}.\boldsymbol{n})\,\phi^{(\boldsymbol{k})}(\boldsymbol{r}) \qquad (14.20)$$

Also, since the representation $\boldsymbol{k}$ is one-dimensional the eigenstate $\phi^{(\boldsymbol{k})}(\boldsymbol{r})$ would be non-degenerate. The important result (14.20) is the famous 'Bloch theorem' for crystal states. Given the behaviour of the eigenfunction in one cell of the crystal the behaviour in all other cells is determined by the $\boldsymbol{k}$-label and involves a simple phase change. The theorem is often stated in a slightly different form, by writing the eigenfunction (Bloch state) as

$$\phi^{(\boldsymbol{k})}(\boldsymbol{r}) = u_{\boldsymbol{k}}(\boldsymbol{r})\exp(i\boldsymbol{k}.\boldsymbol{r}) \tag{14.21}$$

Substitution into equation (14.20) now shows that the function $u_{\boldsymbol{k}}(\boldsymbol{r})$ defined by equation (14.21) is a periodic function with the periodicity of the space lattice

$$u_{\boldsymbol{k}}(\boldsymbol{r}-\boldsymbol{n}) = u_{\boldsymbol{k}}(\boldsymbol{r}) \tag{14.22}$$

In other words the function $u_{\boldsymbol{k}}(\boldsymbol{r})$ is an invariant with respect to the translation group $\mathcal{T}$.

To find $u_{\boldsymbol{k}}(\boldsymbol{r})$ we must write down the Schrodinger equation for an electron moving in a periodic potential. The Hamiltonian is

$$\mathrm{H} = \frac{\mathrm{p}^2}{2M} + V(\boldsymbol{r}) \tag{14.23}$$

with $V(\boldsymbol{r}) = V(\boldsymbol{r}-\boldsymbol{n})$. Thus, using the form (14.21) for the eigenfunctions $\phi^{(\boldsymbol{k})}(\boldsymbol{r})$, the Schrodinger equation is

$$\left[\frac{-\hbar^2}{2M}\nabla^2 + V(\boldsymbol{r})\right]u_{\boldsymbol{k}}(\boldsymbol{r})\,\exp(i\boldsymbol{k}.\boldsymbol{r}) = \varepsilon(\boldsymbol{k})u_{\boldsymbol{k}}(\boldsymbol{r})\,\exp(i\boldsymbol{k}.\boldsymbol{r}) \tag{14.24}$$

which may be written as

$$\left[\frac{\hbar^2}{2M}(\nabla + i\boldsymbol{k})^2 + \varepsilon(\boldsymbol{k}) - V(\boldsymbol{r})\right]u_{\boldsymbol{k}}(\boldsymbol{r}) = 0 \tag{14.25}$$

Since $u_{\boldsymbol{k}}(\boldsymbol{r})$ is periodic, this differential equation need be solved only within a single unit cell using the periodic boundary condition on $u_{\boldsymbol{k}}(\boldsymbol{r})$ at the edges of the cell. Group theory has thus enabled us to replace a problem for the complete crystal by one for a single cell. For each value of $\boldsymbol{k}$, equation (14.25) will have a set of solutions $\varepsilon_n(\boldsymbol{k})$. We can see immediately from equation (14.25) that as $\boldsymbol{k}$ is slowly varied, the solutions to this differential equation will change continuously showing that the $\varepsilon_n(\boldsymbol{k})$ must be continuous functions of $\boldsymbol{k}$. For each n the energies $\varepsilon_n(\boldsymbol{k})$ are said to form a band since they vary over a limited range of values as we now illustrate.

14.4.1 The nearly-free electron model

We will now discuss the general features of the $\varepsilon(\boldsymbol{k})$ by taking a very simple model for the crystal. This model regards the electrons as being nearly free, treating the periodic potential $V(\boldsymbol{r})$ as a weak perturbation to the free-electron states. Clearly this approximation can only be appropriate for the outermost atomic electrons (valence electrons) which, particularly in a metal, move fairly freely through the crystal. We shall see in the next section that this model is capable of explaining how elements from different sections of the periodic table form metals or insulators.

If we put $V(\boldsymbol{r}) = 0$ it is soon verified that equation (14.25) has solutions of the form

$$u_{\boldsymbol{nk}}(\boldsymbol{r}) = v_c^{-\frac{1}{2}} \exp(i\boldsymbol{K}_{\boldsymbol{n}}.\boldsymbol{r})$$

$$\varepsilon_{\boldsymbol{n}}^0(\boldsymbol{k}) = \frac{\hbar^2}{2M}(\boldsymbol{K}_{\boldsymbol{n}}+\boldsymbol{k})^2 \tag{14.26}$$

where, because of equation (14.16), the periodic boundary conditions are satisfied provided that $\boldsymbol{K}_{\boldsymbol{n}}$ is a reciprocal lattice vector (14.12).

For any fixed $\boldsymbol{k}$ there is therefore one solution for each choice of $\boldsymbol{n}$, i.e. for each choice of the three integers n_1, n_2 and n_3. The 'bands' are then labelled by $\boldsymbol{n}$ although it is sometimes the practice simply to number the bands 1, 2, 3 . . ., starting with the band of lowest energy and progressing upwards consecutively. The constant $v_c^{-\frac{1}{2}}$ is included to make the wave function $u_{\boldsymbol{nk}}(\boldsymbol{r})$ normalised over a unit cell of volume $v_c = |\boldsymbol{a}_1 \wedge \boldsymbol{a}_2 \cdot \boldsymbol{a}_3|$. This is most convenient since, because of the periodicity, most integrals can be reduced to integrals over a unit cell. We notice that the full wave function is

$$\psi_{\boldsymbol{n}}^{(\boldsymbol{k})}(\boldsymbol{r}) = \exp(i\boldsymbol{k}.\boldsymbol{r})u_{\boldsymbol{nk}}(\boldsymbol{r}) = v_c^{-\frac{1}{2}} \exp[i(\boldsymbol{K}_{\boldsymbol{n}}+\boldsymbol{k}).\boldsymbol{r}] \tag{14.27}$$

and equation (14.26) is just the usual expression for the energy of the free-electron plane wave state (14.27). The slightly unusual form of the wave vector is simply a consequence of limiting $\boldsymbol{k}$ to the Brillouin zone.

Figure 14.3 shows a plot versus k of $\varepsilon_n^0(k)$ given by equation (14.26) for a one-dimensional crystal, i.e. atoms arranged along a line with separation a. In this case the single reciprocal basis vector has length $b = 2\pi/a$ and the Brillouin zone boundaries are at $\pm\pi/a$. The figure shows how sections of the single free-electron curve $\varepsilon(k) = \hbar^2k^2/2M$ have been translated by reciprocal lattice vectors into the Brillouin zone.

We now move away from the free-electron limit $V(\boldsymbol{r}) = 0$ and consider the effect of the periodic potential $V(\boldsymbol{r})$ as a perturbation on the free-electron states. Since $V(\boldsymbol{r})$ is invariant under the translation group it will only couple states belonging to the same irreducible representation, i.e. states with the same $\boldsymbol{k}$ vector in the Brillouin zone. The perturbation series for the energy is thus

$$\varepsilon_{\boldsymbol{n}}(\boldsymbol{k}) = \varepsilon_{\boldsymbol{n}}^0(\boldsymbol{k}) + v_c^{-1}\int_{\text{cell}} \exp[-i(\boldsymbol{k}+\boldsymbol{K}_{\boldsymbol{n}}).\boldsymbol{r}]V(\boldsymbol{r})\exp[i(\boldsymbol{k}+\boldsymbol{K}_{\boldsymbol{n}}).\boldsymbol{r}]\mathrm{d}\boldsymbol{r}$$

$$+ v_c^{-2}\sum_{\boldsymbol{m}} \frac{|\int \exp(-i\boldsymbol{K}_{\boldsymbol{m}}.\boldsymbol{r})V(\boldsymbol{r})\exp(i\boldsymbol{K}_{\boldsymbol{n}}.\boldsymbol{r})\mathrm{d}\boldsymbol{r}|^2}{\varepsilon_{\boldsymbol{n}}^0 - \varepsilon_{\boldsymbol{m}}^0} + \ldots \tag{14.28}$$

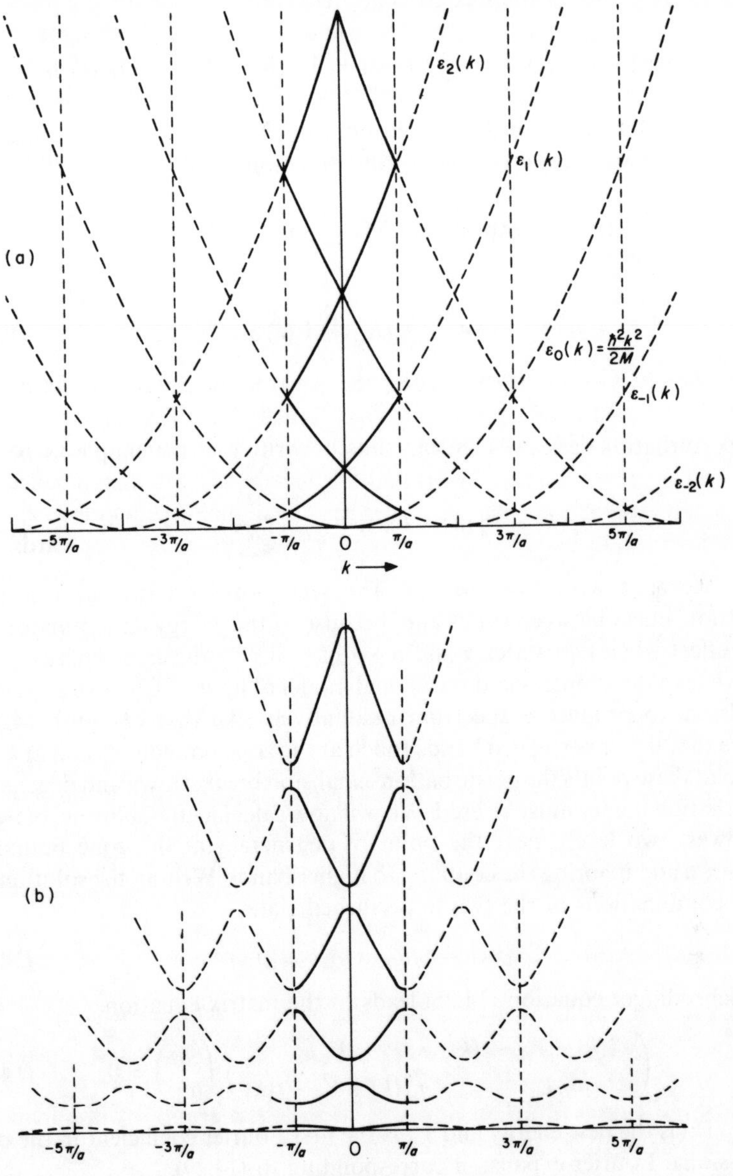

Figure 14.3

where the unperturbed energies $\varepsilon_n^0(\boldsymbol{k})$ are given by equation (14.26). Since the integrals are periodic it is sufficient to restrict the integration to a unit cell, the same region over which the wave functions were normalised. The first-order term is just a constant V_0, equal to the average value of $V(\boldsymbol{r})$. The matrix elements appearing in the second-order term are

$$\int \exp[-i(\boldsymbol{K}_m - \boldsymbol{K}_n).\boldsymbol{r}]V(\boldsymbol{r})\mathrm{d}\boldsymbol{r} = \int \exp(-i\boldsymbol{K}_{m-n}.\boldsymbol{r})V(\boldsymbol{r})\mathrm{d}\boldsymbol{r}$$

and we see that they are just the Fourier coefficients V_{m-n} appearing in a Fourier series expansion of the periodic function $V(\boldsymbol{r})$

$$V(\boldsymbol{r}) = \sum_p \exp(i\boldsymbol{K}_p.\boldsymbol{r})\, V_p$$

$$V_p = v_c^{-1} \int_{\substack{\text{unit}\\ \text{cell}}} \exp(-i\boldsymbol{K}_p.\boldsymbol{r})\, V(\boldsymbol{r})\mathrm{d}\boldsymbol{r} \tag{14.29}$$

The perturbation series (14.28) can thus be written in the simple form

$$\varepsilon_n(\boldsymbol{k}) = \varepsilon_n^0(\boldsymbol{k}) + V_0 + \sum_p \frac{|V_p|^2}{\varepsilon_n^0 - \varepsilon_{n+p}^0} + \ldots \tag{14.30}$$

where we have written $\boldsymbol{p} = \boldsymbol{m} - \boldsymbol{n}$. The second-order term has the usual 'repulsion' effect between states and, because of the energy denominator, has most effect when two states $\boldsymbol{n}$ and $\boldsymbol{n}+\boldsymbol{p}$ have nearly the same energy.

If we take the simple one-dimensional model of figure 14.3(a) we expect the 'repulsion' to produce a spectrum qualitatively like that of figure 14.3(b). Notice that the unperturbed bands touch at the zone boundaries and at $k = 0$ so that at these points the perturbation expansion breaks down and degenerate perturbation theory must be used. We will now calculate the splitting, between the lowest two levels, near the point of degeneracy at the zone boundary $k = -\pi/a$ and ignoring the coupling to higher bands. Writing the solutions as linear combinations of the two unperturbed states

$$u_k(x) = c_0 u_{0k}(x) + c_1 u_{1k}(x) \tag{14.31}$$

the Schrodinger equation (14.25) leads to the matrix equation

$$\begin{pmatrix} \varepsilon_0^0(k) + V_0 - \varepsilon(k) & V_1 \\ V_1 & \varepsilon_1^0(k) + V_0 - \varepsilon(k) \end{pmatrix} \begin{pmatrix} c_0 \\ c_1 \end{pmatrix} = 0 \tag{14.32}$$

where $\varepsilon(k)$ is the new energy and V_1 is the first Fourier coefficient in the one-dimensional Fourier expansion corresponding to (14.29),

$$V_m = \frac{1}{a}\int_0^a \exp(-2\pi imx/a)V(x)\mathrm{d}x \tag{14.33}$$

The solutions are

$$\varepsilon^{\pm}(k) = V_0 + \tfrac{1}{2}[\varepsilon_0^0(k) + \varepsilon_1^0(k)] \pm \tfrac{1}{2}\{[\varepsilon_0^0(k) - \varepsilon_1^0(k)]^2 + 4V_1^2\}^{\frac{1}{2}} \tag{14.34}$$

Away from the zone boundary, where V_1 is small compared with the difference in energies $\varepsilon_0^0(k) - \varepsilon_1^0(k)$, the solutions approach the unperturbed values. At the zone boundary itself $\varepsilon_0^0(k) = \varepsilon_1^0(k)$ and the roots are

$$\varepsilon^{\pm}\left(-\frac{\pi}{a}\right) = \varepsilon_0^0\left(-\frac{\pi}{a}\right) + V_0 \pm |V_1| \tag{14.35}$$

This shows that a 'band gap' appears at the zone boundary with a width $2|V_1|$. A similar calculation for the point of contact between bands labelled n and m would yield a splitting of $2|V_{(n-m)}|$ and the form of these results is illustrated in figure 14.3(b).

This separation of the continuous range of allowed energies in the unperturbed system into bands of allowed energies with gaps containing no electron states is the central result of the theory of electron states in crystals. We will show below how it can give rise to the difference between metals and insulators. Before doing this however we look at the form of the wave functions at the zone boundary. If we take V_1 to be negative, corresponding to an attractive ionic potential at the lattice sites, the solutions to equation (14.32) corresponding to the energies (14.35) are $c_0^{\pm} = \mp c_1^{\pm}$ and hence from equations (14.31) and (14.27)

$$\begin{aligned}\Psi_+^{-\pi/a}(x) &= \frac{1}{(2a)^{\frac{1}{2}}}\exp(-i\pi x/a)\{1 - \exp(2\pi i x/a)\} \\ &= -\left(\frac{2}{a}\right)^{\frac{1}{2}} i \sin\left(\frac{\pi x}{a}\right)\end{aligned} \tag{14.36}$$

and
$$\Psi_-^{-\pi/a}(x) = \left(\frac{2}{a}\right)^{\frac{1}{2}} \cos\left(\frac{\pi x}{a}\right) \tag{14.37}$$

The wave function $\Psi_+^{-\pi/a}(x)$ therefore has a large electron density near $x = \pm a/2$ and consequently midway between lattice points, whereas $\Psi_-^{-\pi/a}(x)$ has a large density at the lattice points and would be expected to have the lower energy which is consistent with equation (14.35).

14.4.2 Metals and insulators

In the last section we found the general behaviour of the $\varepsilon(k)$ curve for a valence electron in a crystal. We now discuss the many-electron ground state which is obtained by putting electrons into these single-electron states, taking care of the Pauli exclusion principle. To do this it is convenient to consider a crystal of finite size so that we can count the number of electrons and the number of states. We shall therefore consider a very large but finite crystal, and the boundary conditions we impose at the surfaces will restrict the values of $\boldsymbol{k}$ which are acceptable for the Bloch states (14.21). The actual choice of boundary conditions will not affect bulk properties and it is usual to use cyclic conditions. We take a crystal with edges parallel to the primitive lattice translations $\boldsymbol{a}_i$ having N_i cells along the edge parallel to $\boldsymbol{a}_i$. The total number of cells is then $N = N_1 N_2 N_3$. The cyclic boundary conditions require the wave functions on opposite edges of the crystal to have the same value so that, for instance

$$\psi(0\,0\,0) = \psi(N_1\,0\,0) = \psi(0\,N_2\,0) = \psi(0\,0\,N_3) \tag{14.38}$$

Using Bloch's theorem (14.21) this means that

$$\exp(2\pi i k_1 N_1) = \exp(2\pi i k_2 N_2) = \exp(2\pi i k_3 N_3) = 1$$

and hence the possible values k_{ip} of k_i are given by $k_{ip} = p/N_i$, with p any integer. The allowed values of $\boldsymbol{k}$ thus form a lattice of points within the reciprocal lattice having N_i points along the unit vector $\boldsymbol{b}_i$ and consequently N points in each unit cell. We must however restrict $\boldsymbol{k}$ to lie in the Brillouin zone which has the same volume as a unit cell, and the above result can be expressed by saying that there are just N allowed values of $\boldsymbol{k}$ uniformly distributed throughout the Brillouin zone for a crystal containing N cells. Since the N_i are very large numbers there will be no real distinction between continuous and discrete values of $\boldsymbol{k}$ when we discuss bulk properties except in so far as it enables us to enumerate the states.

We now return to the one-dimensional crystal of figure 14.3(b) but assume it to be finite with N cells so that there are just N Bloch states corresponding to the N values of k in each of the bands n. We can put two electrons with opposite spin in each of these states so that each band will hold $2N$ electrons. If the atoms of our solid have just one valence electron each, like sodium, then the crystal with N atoms will have N valence electrons which, in the ground state, will occupy the lowest N single-particle states and so only half fill the first band. If, on the other hand, the atoms have two valence electrons the ground state will have all the single-particle states in the first band occupied. On applying an electric field a current can only flow if some electrons can be accelerated and hence move to states with infinitesimally higher energy. For the one-valence electron atoms, such as sodium, this is possible since there are unoccupied electron states immediately above the highest occupied state. We then have a conductor. For atoms with two valence electrons, like magnesium, the band is full and the next available state is at the bottom of the second band so that the minimum energy which can be given to an electron is equal to the band gap $2V_1$. We would therefore expect magnesium to be an insulator. Unfortunately this disagrees with experiment but the reason is that we have used a one-dimensional model. In a three-dimensional calculation we have band gaps at all points on the three-dimensional Brillouin zone boundary but they occur at different energies so that unless the gaps are large there may be no energy region which is always in a band gap. Thus atoms with an even number of electrons which, from the one-dimensional arguments, we would expect to be insulators, are not always so in reality. We can illustrate this effect in two dimensions by drawing the nearly-free electron energy bands from equation (14.26) for a rectangular lattice choosing $\boldsymbol{k}$ to lie first along the x-direction then along the y-direction. The results are plotted in figure 14.4 for the case $a_1 = \frac{3}{2}a_2$

and demonstrate that for this system there will be no gap in energy between the first and second bands since the gaps on the x- and y-boundaries of the Brillouin zone occur at energies $\hbar^2\pi^2/2Ma_1^2$ and $\hbar^2\pi^2/2Ma_2^2$, see problem 14.3, and as shown in the figure this difference is generally large compared with the gaps. The figure also shows how maxima and minima can now occur at points away from the zone boundary or centre where the free-electron curves intersect. Such features are important in considering excitations of electrons from one band to another but we do not discuss this aspect (see Elliott and Gibson, 1974, in the bibliography).

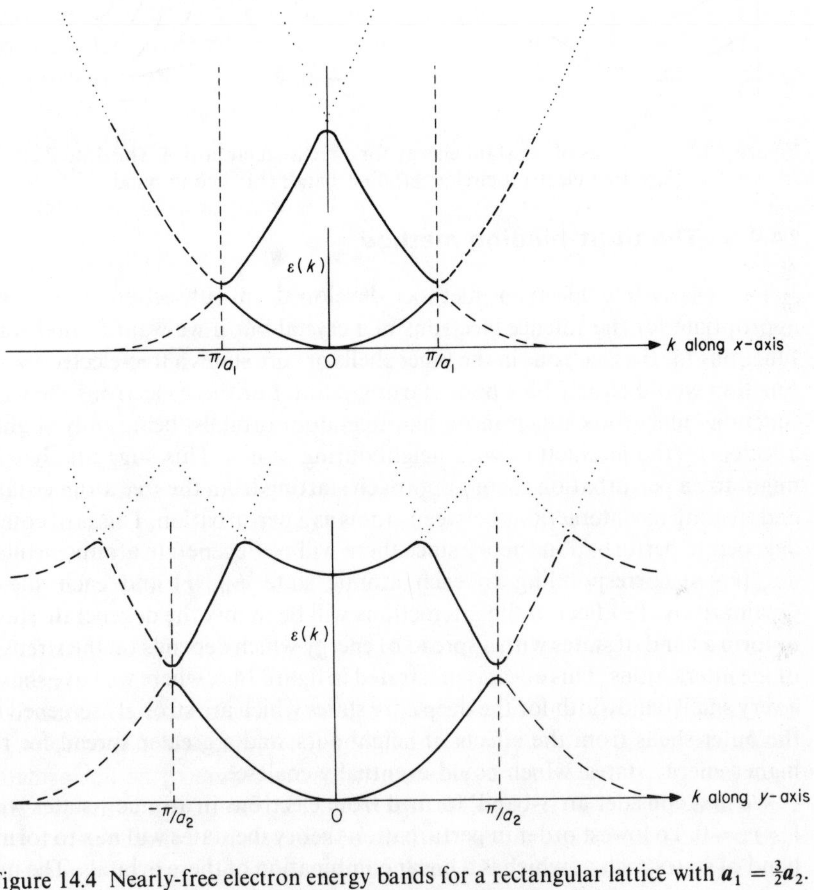

Figure 14.4 Nearly-free electron energy bands for a rectangular lattice with $\boldsymbol{a}_1 = \frac{3}{2}\boldsymbol{a}_2$. The dotted curves are free-electron parabolas

A more complete picture of $\varepsilon(\boldsymbol{k})$ is usually obtained by drawing the contours of constant energy as a two-dimensional diagram in the first Brillouin zone for each band. The first two bands are illustrated in figure 14.5 for the same system as figure 14.4. The contours in figure 14.5 clearly indicate the maxima of figure 14.4 at the points $k_y = \pm\frac{5}{9}\pi/a_2$, $k_x = 0$.

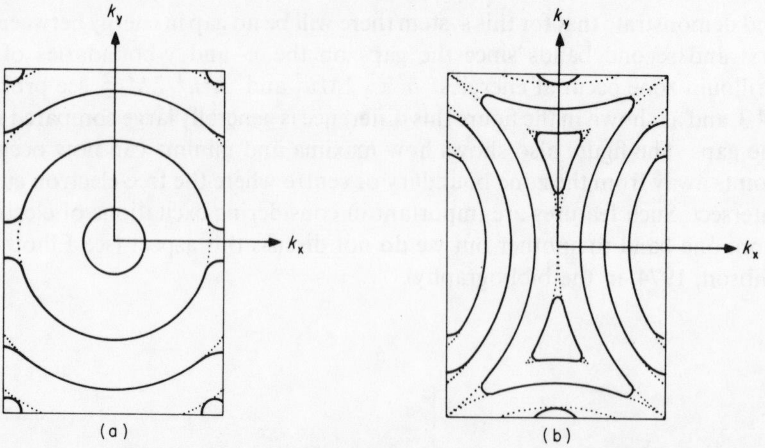

Figure 14.5 Surfaces of constant energy for a rectangular lattice. The dotted curves are free-electron circles: (a) first band; (b) second band

14.4.3 The tight-binding method

The nearly-free electron method developed in subsection 11.4.1 was appropriate for the valence electrons in a crystal but if we want to find wave functions for the electrons in the inner shells or core states a free-electron wave function would clearly be a poor starting point. For these electrons the wave functions must look much more like free-atom orbitals, being only slightly affected by the interaction with neighbouring atoms. This suggests that we might use a perturbation theory approach starting from the free atomic states and treating the interactions between atoms as a perturbation. This is of course degenerate perturbation theory since there will be degenerate atomic orbitals $\phi_{nlm}(\boldsymbol{r}-\boldsymbol{n})$ corresponding to each atomic state $\phi_{nlm}(\boldsymbol{r})$ and each site $\boldsymbol{n}$. Qualitatively the effect of the interactions will be to mix the degenerate states to form a band of states with a spread of energy which depends on the strength of the interactions. This effect is illustrated in figure 14.6, where we have shown a very small bandwidth for the deep core states which are strongly screened by the outer shells from the effects of neighbours, and a greater spread for the higher energy states, which could eventually coalesce.

We first consider an '*s*-band' formed from electrons in atomic *s*-states with $l = m = 0$. To lowest order in perturbation theory the states will mix to form a band of states each of which is a linear combination of these orbitals. The new states must transform according to irreducible representations of the crystal translation group $\mathscr{T}$, i.e. they will be Bloch states labelled by a $\boldsymbol{k}$ vector and can be found by projection (see section 4.19) from an orbital at $\boldsymbol{n} = \boldsymbol{0}$.

$$\begin{aligned}\phi_s^{(\boldsymbol{k})}(\boldsymbol{r}) &\propto \mathrm{P}^{(\boldsymbol{k})}\phi_s(\boldsymbol{r}) \\ &\propto \sum_{\boldsymbol{n}} \exp(i\boldsymbol{k}\,.\,\boldsymbol{n})\phi_s(\boldsymbol{r}-\boldsymbol{n}) \qquad (14.39)\end{aligned}$$

Figure 14.6

We notice that projection from an orbital centred on a different site only changes the overall phase of $\phi_s^{(k)}(r)$ and thus produces the same state.

If the original atomic level is not an *s*-state there will be additional degeneracy corresponding to the allowed values of *m*. In this case we must construct linear combinations of the Bloch states obtained from each orbital *nlm*. We write

$$\phi_{nl}^{(k)}(r) = \sum_m c_m^k \phi_{nlm}^{(k)}(r) \tag{14.40}$$

where

$$\phi_{nlm}^{(k)}(r) = \sum_n \exp(ik.n)\phi_{nlm}(r-n)$$

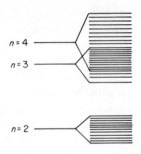

is the Bloch state for orbital m. The coefficients $c_m^{\boldsymbol{k}}$ are generally found by a variational calculation as in section 5.7. In subsection 14.9.2 we show how they may be found from symmetry considerations alone if the crystal has additional point-group symmetry and the vector $\boldsymbol{k}$ points along a symmetry direction.

We can see that the method is analogous to the LCAO method for molecular orbitals discussed in chapter 13, with the irreducible representation label $\boldsymbol{k}$ for the translation group replacing α for the point group. The calculation is less general than that used in chapter 13 in that we have restricted the sum (14.40) to atomic orbitals with a single value of n and l. The method can therefore be extended by taking in more atomic orbitals belonging to atomic states of nearby energy, e.g. states with different values of l but the same principal quantum number n. In this case the variational calculation yields a matrix equation exactly equivalent to equation (13.5).

For the simple Bloch states (14.39) the energy is obtained by evaluating the diagonal matrix element of the one-electron Hamiltonian $\mathrm{H}(\boldsymbol{r})$ in this state,

$$\varepsilon_s(\boldsymbol{k}) = \frac{H_{\boldsymbol{kk}}}{I_{\boldsymbol{kk}}} \tag{14.41}$$

where

$$H_{\boldsymbol{kk}} = \int \phi_s^{(\boldsymbol{k})*}(\boldsymbol{r})\mathrm{H}(\boldsymbol{r})\phi_s^{(\boldsymbol{k})}(\boldsymbol{r})\mathrm{d}\boldsymbol{r}$$

$$I_{\boldsymbol{kk}} = \int \phi_s^{(\boldsymbol{k})*}(\boldsymbol{r})\phi_s^{(\boldsymbol{k})}(\boldsymbol{r})\mathrm{d}\boldsymbol{r}$$

Using the specific form (14.39) of the Bloch functions these expressions can be simplified

$$H_{\boldsymbol{kk}} = \sum_{\boldsymbol{n},\boldsymbol{n}'} \exp[i\boldsymbol{k}.(\boldsymbol{n}-\boldsymbol{n}')] \int \phi_s^*(\boldsymbol{r}-\boldsymbol{n}')\mathrm{H}(\boldsymbol{r})\phi_s(\boldsymbol{r}-\boldsymbol{n})\mathrm{d}\boldsymbol{r}$$

$$= \sum_{\boldsymbol{n},\boldsymbol{n}'} \exp[i\boldsymbol{k}.(\boldsymbol{n}-\boldsymbol{n}')] \int \phi_s^*(\boldsymbol{r}'-\boldsymbol{n}'+\boldsymbol{n})\mathrm{H}(\boldsymbol{r}')\phi_s(\boldsymbol{r}')\mathrm{d}\boldsymbol{r}'$$

where $\boldsymbol{r}' = \boldsymbol{r}-\boldsymbol{n}$ and we have used the fact that $\mathrm{H}(\boldsymbol{r}) = \mathrm{H}(\boldsymbol{r}')$. Introducing $\boldsymbol{p} = \boldsymbol{n}'-\boldsymbol{n}$ as a variable instead of $\boldsymbol{n}'$ gives

$$\mathrm{H}_{\boldsymbol{kk}} = \sum_{\boldsymbol{n},\boldsymbol{p}} \exp(-i\boldsymbol{k}.\boldsymbol{p}) \int \phi_s^*(\boldsymbol{r}-\boldsymbol{p})\mathrm{H}(\boldsymbol{r})\phi_s(\boldsymbol{r})\mathrm{d}\boldsymbol{r}$$

$$= \sum_{\boldsymbol{n},\boldsymbol{p}} \exp(-i\boldsymbol{k}.\boldsymbol{p})H_{\boldsymbol{p}} \tag{14.42}$$

where

$$H_{\boldsymbol{p}} = \int \phi_s^*(\boldsymbol{r}-\boldsymbol{p})\mathrm{H}(\boldsymbol{r})\phi_s(\boldsymbol{r})\mathrm{d}\boldsymbol{r}$$

In the same way we can write

$$I_{kk} = \sum_{n,p} \exp(-i\boldsymbol{k}.\boldsymbol{p}) I_p$$

with
$$I_p = \int \phi_s^*(\boldsymbol{r}-\boldsymbol{p})\, \phi_s(\boldsymbol{r})\, \mathrm{d}\boldsymbol{r} \tag{14.43}$$

The energy given by equation (14.41) can therefore be written

$$\varepsilon_s(\boldsymbol{k}) = \frac{\sum_p \exp(-i\boldsymbol{k}.\boldsymbol{p}) H_p}{\sum_p \exp(-i\boldsymbol{k}.\boldsymbol{p}) I_p} \tag{14.44}$$

To evaluate the integrals H_p and I_p we take the Hamiltonian

$$\mathrm{H}(\boldsymbol{r}) = -\frac{\hbar^2}{2M}\nabla^2 + V(\boldsymbol{r}) \tag{14.45}$$

with $V(\boldsymbol{r})$ the periodic potential and rewrite it as

$$\mathrm{H}(\boldsymbol{r}) = -\frac{\hbar^2}{2M}\nabla^2 + V_{at}(\boldsymbol{r}) + [V(\boldsymbol{r}) - V_{at}(\boldsymbol{r})] \tag{14.46}$$

where $V_{at}(\boldsymbol{r})$ is the central-field potential of the free atom. The first two terms then form the Hamiltonian for a free atom at the origin and the *s*-state wave function is an eigenstate of this Hamiltonian with energy ε_s,

$$\left(\frac{-\hbar^2}{2M}\nabla^2 + V_{at}(\boldsymbol{r})\right)\phi_s(\boldsymbol{r}) = \varepsilon_s\, \phi_s(\boldsymbol{r}) \tag{14.47}$$

Using this equation we can now write the matrix element H_p as

$$H_p = \int \phi_s^*(\boldsymbol{r}-\boldsymbol{p})[\varepsilon_s + V(\boldsymbol{r}) - V_{at}(\boldsymbol{r})]\, \phi_s(\boldsymbol{r})\, \mathrm{d}\boldsymbol{r} \tag{14.48}$$

and equation (14.44) becomes

$$\varepsilon_s(\boldsymbol{k}) = \varepsilon_s + \frac{\sum_p \exp(-i\boldsymbol{k}.\boldsymbol{p}) V_p}{\sum_p \exp(-i\boldsymbol{k}.\boldsymbol{p}) I_p} \tag{14.49}$$

with

$$V_p = \int \phi_s^*\,(\boldsymbol{r}-\boldsymbol{p})[V(\boldsymbol{r}) - V_{at}(\boldsymbol{r})]\, \phi_s(\boldsymbol{r})\, \mathrm{d}\boldsymbol{r} \tag{14.50}$$

The first term on the right-hand side in equation (14.49) is just the free-atom energy level and the second term gives the $\boldsymbol{k}$ dependence which spreads the level into a band. We can see qualitatively how this spreading depends on the unperturbed state in the following way. If $\phi_s(\boldsymbol{r})$ is a deep core state such as a 1s-state, its wave function is very localised so that $I_{\boldsymbol{p}}$ and $V_{\boldsymbol{p}}$ effectively vanish for $\boldsymbol{p}$ not equal to zero because there will be negligible overlap of the wave functions. This means that the second term on the right of equation (14.49) reduces to V_0/I_0 which is independent of $\boldsymbol{k}$ and the bandwidth is zero. For a less deep state a crude approximation might be to neglect the overlap in $I_{\boldsymbol{p}}$ but keep the term in $V_{\boldsymbol{p}}$ for $\boldsymbol{p}$ a nearest neighbour. For a simple cubic crystal, with one atom at each lattice point and for which the three lattice vectors $\boldsymbol{a}_i$ are of equal length a and mutually perpendicular, there are six nearest neighbours $\boldsymbol{p}$. In this case the energy (14.49) is given by

$$\varepsilon_s(\boldsymbol{k}) = \varepsilon_s + V_0 + 2V_1(\cos ak_x + \cos ak_y + \cos ak_z) \qquad (14.51)$$

where V_1 is the value of $V_{\boldsymbol{p}}$ for a nearest-neighbour site (all these will have the same value in a cubic crystal). For a valence electron, several more terms should be kept in both $V_{\boldsymbol{p}}$ and $I_{\boldsymbol{p}}$. The range of values of $\varepsilon_s(\boldsymbol{k})$ as $\boldsymbol{k}$ varies is called the bandwidth and the example given in equation (14.51) is seen to have a bandwidth of $12|V_1|$. To calculate the value of the bandwidth we must, of course, take a model for the periodic potential $V(\boldsymbol{r})$. A simple approximation is to take $V(\boldsymbol{r})$ to be the sum of the atomic potentials $V_{at}(\boldsymbol{r})$, i.e.

$$V(\boldsymbol{r}) = \sum_{\boldsymbol{n}} V_{at}(\boldsymbol{r} - \boldsymbol{n}) \qquad (14.52)$$

With this choice, the shift V_0 is small and negative since the perturbation in equation (14.50) is very small in the central cell where the wave functions $\phi_s(\boldsymbol{r})$ are large, and negative everywhere. For the same reason V_1 is also negative.

In a realistic calculation (see Harrison, 1970 and Ziman, 1972 in the bibliography) of the band structure it is necessary to choose $V(\boldsymbol{r})$ more carefully, since with the above choice the long range nature of the atomic potential would mean that the series (14.49) would converge only very slowly. It is therefore convenient to take $V(\boldsymbol{r})$ to be a sum of localised potentials which are similar to those of a free atom or ion in a small region of atomic size and zero elsewhere. The energies ε_{nl} must then be calculated for these potentials.

14.5 Lattice vibrations

The vibrations of a crystal can be analysed by the methods developed in chapter 6 for molecules. We shall start our discussion with a one-dimensional monatomic model, i.e. identical atoms equally spaced along a line at intervals a. Later, we generalise the results to three dimensions with several atoms per unit cell.

14.5.1 The one-dimensional monatomic lattice

We showed in chapter 6 that the normal modes of vibration must transform according to irreducible representations of the symmetry group which in the present problem means they must be classified by k, and that they can be obtained by projection. Although in this simple problem with identical masses the concept of mass weighting is unnecessary, we none the less use it so that equations from chapter 6 may be taken over directly. The general displacement is given by a vector $\boldsymbol{q}$ in a vector space with dimension equal to the number of atoms. Thus we denote by $\boldsymbol{e}(n)$ a displacement of the nth atom by an amount $M^{-\frac{1}{2}}$ and $\boldsymbol{q} = \sum_n q_n M^{\frac{1}{2}} \boldsymbol{e}(n)$, where q_n is the magnitude of the displacement of the nth atom and M is the mass.

A displacement $\boldsymbol{u}^{(k)}$ with the symmetry k is then obtained by projection from $\boldsymbol{e}(0)$, as in equation (14.39):

$$\begin{aligned} \boldsymbol{u}^{(k)} &= \sum_n \exp(ikna)\,\mathrm{T}(n)\,\boldsymbol{e}(0) \\ &= \sum_n \exp(ikna)\,\boldsymbol{e}(n) \end{aligned} \tag{14.53}$$

In this one-dimensional case, $k = \pm|\boldsymbol{k}| = 2\pi k_1/a$ in the notation of equation (14.9). This equation is analogous to equation (6.34) in the molecular vibration problem.

The displacement $\boldsymbol{u}^{(k)}$ obtained in this way is unique since an identical displacement (apart from a phase factor) would be obtained by projection from a displacement on a different site. This means that $\boldsymbol{u}^{(k)}$ must be a normal displacement and that there is only one normal mode for each k.

The frequency of this normal mode is given by equation (6.35) and follows immediately if we know the form of the potential energy of the crystal for an arbitrary displacement of the atoms. If we take this to have the same form as equation (6.1) allowing q_n to be complex,

$$V = \tfrac{1}{2} \sum_{n,m} B_{nm} q_n^* q_m \tag{14.54}$$

where q_n is the magnitude of the displacement of the nth atom, then equation (6.35) yields

$$\omega_k^2 = \frac{\sum_{n,m} M^{-1} B_{nm} \exp(-ikna)\exp(ikma)}{\sum_{n,m} \exp(-ikna)\exp(ikma)\,\delta_{nm}} \tag{14.55}$$

(Since the displacement $\boldsymbol{u}^{(k)}$ is complex we must use the complex form (3.7) for the scalar products in equation (6.35).) Because of translational invariance the constant B_{nm} can depend only on the difference $n-m$ so that, introducing a variable $p = n-m$ and writing B_p for B_{nm}, we have

$$\begin{aligned} \omega_k^2 &= M^{-1} \sum_n \Big[\sum_p B_p \exp(-ikpa)\Big] \Big/ \sum_n 1 \\ &= M^{-1} \sum_p B_p \exp(-ikpa) \end{aligned} \tag{14.56}$$

A system of this type is the one-dimensional chain of atoms of mass M connected to their nearest neighbours by Hooke's law forces with force constant λ. The potential energy can then be written

$$V = \sum_n \tfrac{1}{2}\lambda(q_n - q_{n-1})^2$$

$$= \tfrac{1}{2}\lambda \sum_n (q_n^2 - 2q_n q_{n-1} + q_{n-1}^2)$$

By changing the dummy variable n in some of the terms this can be written as

$$V = \tfrac{1}{2}\lambda \sum_n (2q_n^2 - q_n q_{n-1} - q_n q_{n+1})$$

so that it has the form of equation (14.54) with $B_{nn} = 2\lambda$, $B_{np} = -\lambda$ for nearest neighbours, and $B_{np} = 0$ for all other pairs. Equation (14.56) now gives

$$\omega_k^2 = \frac{1}{M}[2\lambda - \lambda\exp(-ika) - \lambda\exp(ika)]$$

$$= \frac{2\lambda}{M}(1 - \cos ka)$$

A plot of ω_k^2 against k is shown in figure 14.7. The Brillouin zone boundaries are at $\pm\pi/a$ and the curve shows a great similarity to that of the lowest band of states in the free-electron model. The degeneracy between states with opposite values of k arises from the fact that this particular crystal has a point group with inversion symmetry (see section 14.9).

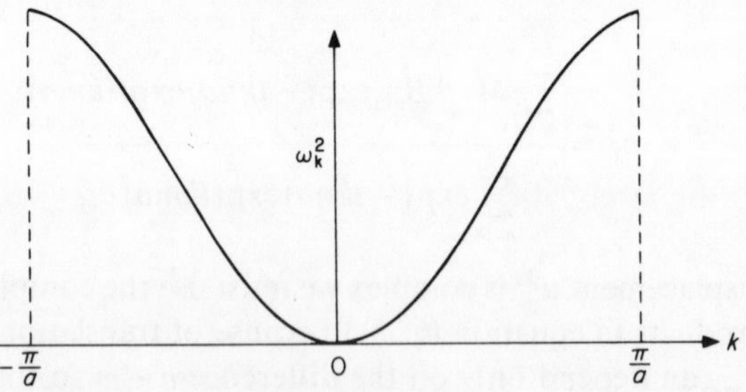

Figure 14.7

The striking difference between these results and those of chapter 6 is that, in the latter, the spectrum of normal mode frequencies was discrete whereas here it is continuous. This arises from our use of an infinite chain. On restriction to a chain of finite length with N atoms, the continuous curve of figure 14.7 would break into N distinct roots corresponding to N equally spaced values of k. In real crystals the number N is so large that the distinction between discrete and continuous spectra is of no consequence.

14.5.2 Three-dimensional crystals with several atoms per unit cell

If we extend the discussion of the previous section to a three-dimensional crystal with a number s of atoms per unit cell we can construct $3s$ orthonormal basis vectors transforming according to the representation $\boldsymbol{k}$ of the translation group $\mathscr{T}$ by projecting on each of the $3s$ linearly independent atomic displacements in a single cell. As in equation (14.53) they have the form

$$\boldsymbol{u}_{ti}^{(\boldsymbol{k})} = \sum_{\boldsymbol{n}} \exp(i\boldsymbol{k}.\boldsymbol{n})\boldsymbol{e}_{ti}(\boldsymbol{n}) \tag{14.57}$$

where $\boldsymbol{e}_{ti}(\boldsymbol{n})$ is a unit displacement, in the mass-weighted sense, of the tth atom in the cell $\boldsymbol{n}$. The suffix $i = x$, y or z specifies the direction of the displacement. The normal modes will be linear combinations of these $3s$ vectors

$$\boldsymbol{u}^{(\boldsymbol{k})} = \sum_{t,i} c_{ti}^{\boldsymbol{k}} \boldsymbol{u}_{ti}^{(\boldsymbol{k})} \tag{14.58}$$

To find the normal frequencies and the coefficients $c_{ti}^{\boldsymbol{k}}$ we follow the method of chapter 6 by diagonalising the $3s \times 3s$ matrix of the potential energy for the displacement (14.58) in the basis (14.57). As an obvious generalisation of equation (14.54) we first write V in terms of the simple coordinates,

$$V = \tfrac{1}{2} \sum_{t,t',i,j,\boldsymbol{n},\boldsymbol{m}} B_{ti\boldsymbol{n},t'j\boldsymbol{m}}\, q_{ti}^{*}(\boldsymbol{n}) q_{t'j}(\boldsymbol{m}) \tag{14.59}$$

where $q_{ti}(\boldsymbol{n})$ is the Cartesian component, in the i-direction, of the displacement of the atom t in the cell $\boldsymbol{n}$. Then from equations (14.57) and (14.58) we see that modes labelled by $\boldsymbol{k}$ have components given by

$$q_{ti}^{\boldsymbol{k}}(\boldsymbol{n}) = c_{ti}^{\boldsymbol{k}} \exp(i\boldsymbol{k}\cdot\boldsymbol{n})/M_t^{\frac{1}{2}}$$

and substituting in equation (14.59) gives the value of V in a mode $\boldsymbol{k}$ as

$$V^{\boldsymbol{k}} = \tfrac{1}{2} \sum_{tt'ij} E_{ti,t'j}^{\boldsymbol{k}} c_{ti}^{\boldsymbol{k}*} c_{t'j}^{\boldsymbol{k}} \Big(\sum_{\boldsymbol{n}} 1\Big)$$

where

$$E_{ti,t'j}^{\boldsymbol{k}} = \frac{1}{(M_t M_{t'})^{\frac{1}{2}}} \sum_{\boldsymbol{p}} B_{ti\boldsymbol{o},t'j\boldsymbol{p}} \exp(-i\boldsymbol{k}.\boldsymbol{p}) \tag{14.60}$$

Here we have written $\boldsymbol{p} = \boldsymbol{n} - \boldsymbol{m}$ and $\boldsymbol{o}$ denotes any fixed cell. It then follows as a generalisation of equation (6.35) that the $\omega_{\boldsymbol{k}}^2$ are eigenvalues of the matrix (14.60).

To show the effect of having more than one atom in the unit cell we consider a one-dimensional chain with two atoms per unit cell and Hooke's law nearest-

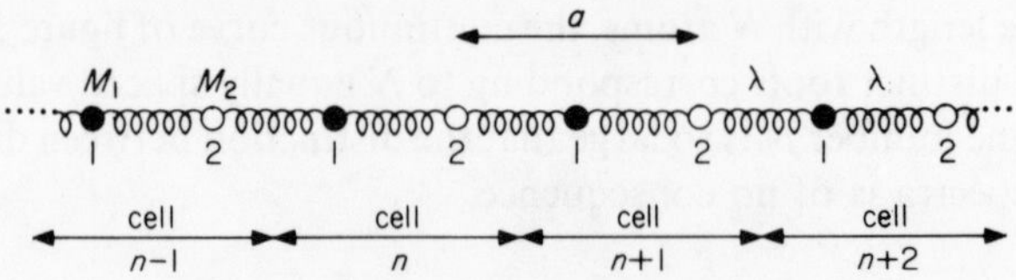

Figure 14.8

neighbour forces, see figure 14.8. The potential energy is

$$V = \tfrac{1}{2}\sum_n \lambda\{[q_2(n)-q_1(n)]^2 + [q_1(n)-q_2(n-1)]^2\}$$

$$= \tfrac{1}{2}\lambda \sum_n [2q_1^2(n) + 2q_2^2(n) - q_2(n)q_1(n) - q_1(n)q_2(n)$$

$$- q_1(n)q_2(n-1) - q_2(n)q_1(n+1)]$$

To get the last equation we have manipulated the dummy variable n. Hence the numbers $B_{to,t'p}$ in the one-dimensional equivalent of equation (14.59) are

$$B_{10,10} = B_{20,20} = 2\lambda$$

$$B_{20,10} = B_{10,20} = B_{10,2-1} = B_{20,11} = -\lambda$$

The roots ω_k^2 of the matrix E are thus found by solving the equation

$$\begin{vmatrix} \dfrac{2\lambda}{M_1} - \omega_k^2 & -\dfrac{\lambda}{(M_1M_2)^{\frac{1}{2}}}[1+\exp(ika)] \\ -\dfrac{\lambda}{(M_1M_2)^{\frac{1}{2}}}[1+\exp(-ika)] & \dfrac{2\lambda}{M_2} - \omega_k^2 \end{vmatrix} = 0$$

$$\text{i.e. } \omega_k^2 = \lambda\left[\left(\frac{1}{M_1}+\frac{1}{M_2}\right) \pm \left\{\left(\frac{1}{M_1}+\frac{1}{M_2}\right)^2 - \frac{2}{M_1M_2}\left(1-\cos ka\right)\right\}^{\frac{1}{2}}\right]$$

Figure 14.9 shows a plot of ω_k^2 as a function of k in the Brillouin zone. Again this curve shows great similarity to the free-electron curves for the lowest two bands. If more atoms are added to the unit cell, more bands are added so that there is always one band for each atom in the unit cell. As k tends to zero, ω_k^2 tends to zero as k^2 and if we quantise the vibration as in chapter 6 the quanta of excitation are called 'phonons'.

In three dimensions the matrix E with elements given by (14.60) will have dimension $3s \times 3s$ so that there are $3s$ roots for each value of $\boldsymbol{k}$. This means that there are 3 bands for each band in figure 14.9. The three lowest bands touch at $\boldsymbol{k} = 0$ and correspond at $\boldsymbol{k} = 0$ to the three translational degrees of freedom, which are not really vibrations.

In crystals with point group symmetries, degeneracies may occur at special points in the Brillouin zone, such as along a line with rotational symmetry. At

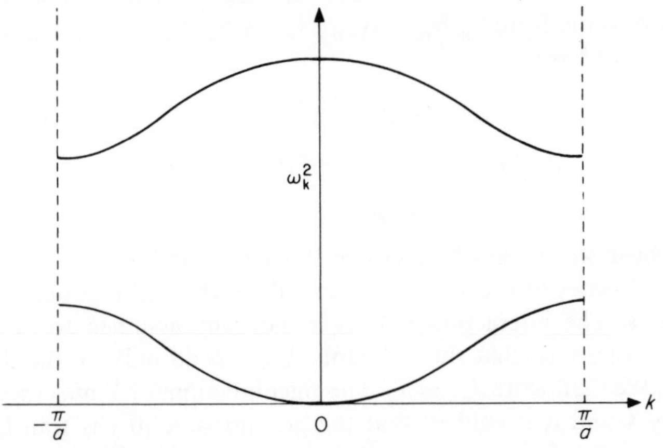

Figure 14.9

such values of $\boldsymbol{k}$ the matrix E can be partially diagonalised by symmetry arguments which we outline in section 14.9.

14.6 Spin waves in ferromagnets

In a simple model of a ferromagnet, the atom at the site $\boldsymbol{n}$ in a crystal has a magnetic moment μ_n and at sufficiently low temperatures (below the Curie point) these moments line up in more or less the same direction so that the crystal has a finite magnetic moment in the absence of any applied field. Experiment shows that the g-factor is very close to 2 so that we can assume that it arises from unpaired spins on the atoms and that the orbital contribution is quenched by the crystal field as described in subsection 9.9.3. Although the origin of the interaction energy is electrostatic, arising from exchange interactions between the electrons, the phenomenon can be discussed in terms of an effective Hamiltonian containing a Heisenberg interaction term

$$V = -\sum_{n,m} J_{nm} \mathbf{S}_n \cdot \mathbf{S}_m \tag{14.61}$$

where $\mathbf{S}_n$ is the spin operator for the atom at site $\boldsymbol{n}$. It is usual to take $J_{nn} = 0$ and J_{nm} positive so that the ground state has all the atomic spins parallel and hence all magnetic moments parallel. In this situation every term $\mathbf{S}_n \cdot \mathbf{S}_m$ takes its maximum value S^2, where S is the value of the atomic spin, and the ground state energy is simply

$$E_0 = -S^2 \sum_{n,m} J_{nm} \tag{14.62}$$

These statements can be justified if we denote the state in which all spins are parallel, in a direction which we choose to call the z-direction, by $|0\rangle$ and write the operator in the form $\mathbf{S}_n.\mathbf{S}_m = \frac{1}{2}(\mathbf{S}_{n+}\mathbf{S}_{m-} + \mathbf{S}_{n-}\mathbf{S}_{m+}) + \mathbf{S}_{nz}S_{mz}$, following (7.35). Then we have

$$\mathbf{S}_{nz}|0\rangle = S|0\rangle$$

and $\qquad \mathbf{S}_{n+}|0\rangle = 0 \qquad$ for all $\boldsymbol{n}$ so that

$$\mathbf{S}_n.\mathbf{S}_m|0\rangle = S^2|0\rangle \tag{14.63}$$

The problem we set ourselves is to find the nature and the energy of the low-lying excited states of the system which will be thermally populated at low temperatures. The interaction (14.61) is naturally assumed to have translational invariance so that the constants J_{nm} depend only on the difference $\boldsymbol{m}-\boldsymbol{n}=\boldsymbol{q}$. We shall write $J_{nm} = J_q$. The eigenfunctions of Vmust therefore be labelled by $\boldsymbol{k}$ and it is evident that the ground state $|0\rangle$ is translationally invariant, with $\boldsymbol{k}=0$. Starting from the ground state $|0\rangle$ with all spins parallel, one may construct many different wave functions with given $\boldsymbol{k}$. Our object here is to construct the low-lying eigenfunctions. Bearing in mind the aligned structure of the ground state one might seek an excited state by turning the spin on a single site $\boldsymbol{p}$ with the lowering operator $\mathbf{S}_{p-}$ and then projecting to produce a state with definite $\boldsymbol{k}$. Such a trial function would be written

$$|\boldsymbol{k}\rangle = \sum_{p} \exp(i\boldsymbol{k}.\boldsymbol{p})\mathbf{S}_{p-}|0\rangle \tag{14.64}$$

and we now show that this is in fact an eigenfunction of V for all $\boldsymbol{k}$. The operator $\mathbf{S}_n.\mathbf{S}_m$ commutes with $\mathbf{S}_p$ unless $\boldsymbol{p}=\boldsymbol{n}$ or $\boldsymbol{m}$, since spin operators on different sites commute. Thus using equation (14.63)

$$\mathbf{S}_n.\mathbf{S}_m|\boldsymbol{k}\rangle = \mathbf{S}^2|\boldsymbol{k}\rangle + \exp(i\boldsymbol{k}.\boldsymbol{n})[(\mathbf{S}_n.\mathbf{S}_m), \mathbf{S}_{n-}]|0\rangle$$
$$+ \exp(i\boldsymbol{k}.\boldsymbol{m})[(\mathbf{S}_n.\mathbf{S}_m), \mathbf{S}_{m-}]|0\rangle$$

and the commutators follow from the familiar commutation relations (7.28) and (7.30) for the spin operators giving

$$[(\mathbf{S}_n.\mathbf{S}_m), \mathbf{S}_{n-}] = \mathbf{S}_{m-}\mathbf{S}_{nz} - \mathbf{S}_{n-}\mathbf{S}_{mz}$$

so long as $\boldsymbol{m} \neq \boldsymbol{n}$. (The case of $\boldsymbol{n}=\boldsymbol{m}$ may be ignored since $J_{nn}=0$.) Putting together these two equations with (14.61) gives

$$\mathrm{V}|\boldsymbol{k}\rangle = -S^2\sum_{n,m} J_{nm}|\boldsymbol{k}\rangle - S\sum_{n,m} J_{nm}\{\exp(i\boldsymbol{k}.\boldsymbol{n})(\mathbf{S}_{m-}-\mathbf{S}_{n-})$$
$$+\exp(i\boldsymbol{k}.\boldsymbol{m})(\mathbf{S}_{n-}-\mathbf{S}_{m-})\}|0\rangle$$

$$= E_0|\boldsymbol{k}\rangle + S\sum_{n,m} J_q\{[1-\exp(i\boldsymbol{k}.\boldsymbol{q})]\exp(i\boldsymbol{k}.\boldsymbol{n})\mathbf{S}_{n-}$$
$$+[1-\exp(-i\boldsymbol{k}.\boldsymbol{q})]\exp(i\boldsymbol{k}.\boldsymbol{m})\mathbf{S}_{m-}\}|0\rangle \text{ where } \boldsymbol{q}=\boldsymbol{m}-\boldsymbol{n}$$

$$= E_0|\boldsymbol{k}\rangle + S\sum_{\boldsymbol{q}} J_{\boldsymbol{q}}[1-\exp(i\boldsymbol{k}.\boldsymbol{q})]|\boldsymbol{k}\rangle$$

$$+ S\sum_{\boldsymbol{q}} J_{\boldsymbol{q}}[1-\exp(-i\boldsymbol{k}.\boldsymbol{q})]|\boldsymbol{k}\rangle$$

$$= E_0|\boldsymbol{k}\rangle + 2S\sum_{\boldsymbol{q}} J_{\boldsymbol{q}}(1-\cos\boldsymbol{k}.\boldsymbol{q})|\boldsymbol{k}\rangle \tag{14.65}$$

This proves that $|\boldsymbol{k}\rangle$ is an eigenstate with an excitation energy of $2S\sum_{\boldsymbol{q}} \mathrm{J}_{\boldsymbol{q}}(1-\cos\boldsymbol{k}.\boldsymbol{q})$, where $\boldsymbol{q}$ runs over all sites relative to a fixed site. For each $\boldsymbol{k}$ we have an excitation of this kind, which is called a 'magnon'. The analogy with the lattice vibration problem of section 14.5 is apparent, with the turning of the spin at a site corresponding to the displacement at that site. Notice that as $\boldsymbol{k}\to 0$ the excitation energy also tends to zero like k^2, so that excitations may be produced at infinitesimally low excitation energy. This contrasts with the finite value which would be found for the expectation value of V in the wave function $\mathrm{S}_{\boldsymbol{p}-}|0\rangle$ in which only the spin at site $\boldsymbol{p}$ is turned. The state $|\boldsymbol{k}\rangle$ corresponding to $\boldsymbol{k}=0$, although having zero excitation, is not identical with the ground state since it is given by $\sum_{\boldsymbol{p}} \mathrm{S}_{\boldsymbol{p}-}|0\rangle$. However the operator $\sum_{\boldsymbol{p}} \mathrm{S}_{\boldsymbol{p}-}$ is the total spin of the system and this corresponds to an infinitesimal rotation of the direction of alignment and does not represent any internal excitation of the system. This degeneracy between states with different directions of magnetisation is inherent in the form of V which is rotationally invariant. In a real crystal, anisotropy would remove this degeneracy and would show up as additional terms in V destroying its rotational invariance.

The operator from equation (14.64) which is usually denoted

$$\mathrm{a}_{\boldsymbol{k}}^{\dagger} = \mathcal{N}\sum_{\boldsymbol{p}} \exp(i\boldsymbol{k}.\boldsymbol{p})\mathrm{S}_{\boldsymbol{p}-}$$

where $\mathcal{N}$ is a normalisation factor, creates a magnon of wave vector $\boldsymbol{k}$. A two-magnon state

$$\psi = \mathrm{a}_{\boldsymbol{k}}^{\dagger}\mathrm{a}_{\boldsymbol{k}}^{\dagger}|0\rangle$$

can then be constructed. This is not quite an exact eigenstate but the error is of the order $1/N$, where N is the number of atoms in the crystal and is large. To the same order of accuracy the magnon creation and annihilation operators obey Bose–Einstein commutation relations (see section 19.1 and subsection 16.3.1) and we can talk about a state in which there are $n_{\boldsymbol{k}}$ magnons with wave vector $\boldsymbol{k}$. Each magnon carries an excitation energy, given in equation (14.65).

14.7 Excitons in insulators (Frenkel excitons)

In a simple insulator such as a rare-gas solid, with no valence electrons, the overlap of atomic wave functions is very small indeed and to a very good approximation the ground state has individual electrons occupying the atomic orbitals on individual atoms. The many-electron wave function is just a product of these orbitals. As in the spin-wave case we might try to construct excited states by raising an electron on one atom to a higher unoccupied orbital in that atom, but again we must use projection to construct a state with definite $\boldsymbol{k}$.

Let ϕ denote the many-electron ground state of an atom and ϕ' the excited state formed from ϕ by exciting one electron into a higher orbital. Thus $\phi_{\boldsymbol{p}}$ and $\phi'_{\boldsymbol{p}}$ refer to such atomic wave functions at site $\boldsymbol{p}$. For the entire crystal we have the corresponding ground state

$$\Psi^0 = \prod_{\boldsymbol{p}} \phi_{\boldsymbol{p}}$$

and for an excitation at site $\boldsymbol{p}$,

$$\Psi_{\boldsymbol{p}} = \phi'_{\boldsymbol{p}} \prod_{\boldsymbol{q} \neq \boldsymbol{p}} \phi_{\boldsymbol{q}} \tag{14.66}$$

The projected state with the correct translational symmetry $\boldsymbol{k}$, called an *exciton*, is then given by

$$\Psi^{(\boldsymbol{k})}_{\text{ex}} = \sum_{\boldsymbol{p}} \exp(i\boldsymbol{k}.\boldsymbol{p})\Psi_{\boldsymbol{p}} \tag{14.67}$$

Note that this differs from the tight-binding model where the states we constructed were one-electron states. An exciton of wave vector $\boldsymbol{k}$ is thus an excitation which propagates through the crystal (but of course does not carry charge). The energy will depend on the $\boldsymbol{k}$ vector, but only to a small extent, and will be approximately equal to the atomic excitation energy.

14.8 Selection rules for scattering

Selection rules for scattering processes in crystals can be derived immediately from the simple relationship (14.15) for the product of representations. For instance if we consider the scattering of an electron in a crystal (electron – phonon scattering) then the probability for scattering from a state of wave vector $\boldsymbol{k}$ to a state of wave vector $\boldsymbol{k}'$ due to the absorption of a phonon of wave vector $\boldsymbol{q}$ will depend on a matrix element which will vanish unless the product representation $\mathrm{T}^{(\boldsymbol{q})} \times \mathrm{T}^{(\boldsymbol{k})}$ contains the representation $\mathrm{T}^{(\boldsymbol{k}')}$. From equation (14.15) this means that

$$\boldsymbol{k}' = \boldsymbol{q} + \boldsymbol{k} + \boldsymbol{K}_{\boldsymbol{m}} \tag{14.68}$$

Scattering with $\boldsymbol{K}_{\boldsymbol{m}} = 0$ is usually called direct and that in which $\boldsymbol{K}_{\boldsymbol{m}} \neq 0$ is called an Umklapp process. Equation (14.68) is often referred to as the conservation of 'crystal momentum'. In a scattering process the energy must also be conserved so that an additional condition is

$$\hbar\omega_{\boldsymbol{q}} + \varepsilon(\boldsymbol{k}) = \varepsilon(\boldsymbol{k}') \tag{14.69}$$

Similar relationships hold for electron – magnon, magnon – phonon, electron – photon, phonon – photon and magnon – exciton scattering.

14.9 Space groups

So far in this chapter we have looked at the consequences of the translational symmetry in crystals. However, the infinite crystal may also be invariant under one of the finite point groups of rotations (proper and improper) about each lattice point which we described in chapter 9. This will occur for example when the primitive lattice vectors $\boldsymbol{a}_i$ are symmetrically placed relative to each other. We now consider the group $\mathscr{G}$ which is obtained by combining the elements $\mathrm{P}(\boldsymbol{n})$ of the translation group $\mathscr{T}$ with the elements R_i of a point group of rotations about a lattice point which we call the origin.

The general group element is written $\{\mathrm{R}_i, \boldsymbol{n}\}$ and is defined by its effect on an arbitrary vector

$$\{\mathrm{R}_i, \boldsymbol{n}\}\boldsymbol{r} = \mathrm{P}(\boldsymbol{n})\mathrm{R}_i\boldsymbol{r} = \mathrm{R}_i\boldsymbol{r} + \boldsymbol{n} \tag{14.70}$$

We can easily verify that these elements satisfy the group postulates by deducing the multiplication law from equation (14.70).

$$\begin{aligned}\{\mathrm{R}_j, \boldsymbol{m}\}\{\mathrm{R}_i, \boldsymbol{n}\}\boldsymbol{r} &= \{\mathrm{R}_j, \boldsymbol{m}\}(\mathrm{R}_i\boldsymbol{r} + \boldsymbol{n}) = \mathrm{R}_j(\mathrm{R}_i\boldsymbol{r} + \boldsymbol{n}) + \boldsymbol{m} \\ &= \mathrm{R}_j\mathrm{R}_i\boldsymbol{r} + \mathrm{R}_j\boldsymbol{n} + \boldsymbol{m} \\ &= \{\mathrm{R}_j\mathrm{R}_i, \mathrm{R}_j\boldsymbol{n} + \boldsymbol{m}\}\boldsymbol{r}\end{aligned}$$

so that $\{\mathrm{R}_j, \boldsymbol{m}\}\{\mathrm{R}_i, \boldsymbol{n}\} = \{\mathrm{R}_j\mathrm{R}_i, \mathrm{R}_j\boldsymbol{n} + \boldsymbol{m}\}$ (14.71)

Because the lattice is invariant under the point group, the vector $\mathrm{R}_j\boldsymbol{n} + \boldsymbol{m}$ gives a lattice point if $\boldsymbol{n}$ and $\boldsymbol{m}$ are lattice points and hence the product (14.71) is contained in the set (14.70).

As a special case of (14.71) we see that rotations and translations do not commute, in fact putting $\boldsymbol{m} = 0$ and $\mathrm{R}_i = \mathrm{E}$ (the identity) we have

$$\mathrm{R}_j\mathrm{P}(\boldsymbol{n}) = \{\mathrm{R}_j, 0\}\{\mathrm{E}, \boldsymbol{n}\} = \{\mathrm{R}_j, \mathrm{R}_j\boldsymbol{n}\} = \mathrm{P}(\mathrm{R}_j\boldsymbol{n})\mathrm{R}_j \tag{14.72}$$

which can also be written as

$$\mathrm{P}(\boldsymbol{n})\mathrm{R}_j = \mathrm{R}_j\mathrm{P}(\mathrm{R}_j^{-1}\boldsymbol{n}) \tag{14.73}$$

Thus the group $\mathscr{G}$ is not a direct product of $\mathscr{T}$ with the point group. As another special case of (14.71) we deduce the inverse

$$\{\mathrm{R}_i, \boldsymbol{n}\}^{-1} = \{\mathrm{R}_i^{-1}, -\mathrm{R}_i^{-1}\boldsymbol{n}\} \tag{14.74}$$

by asking what choice of R_j and $\boldsymbol{m}$ leads to the identity $\{\mathrm{E}, 0\}$ on the right-hand side of (14.71).

Although R_i refers to rotations about a lattice point at the origin, the group $\mathscr{G}$ includes rotations about other points because the product $P(\boldsymbol{n})R_iP(-\boldsymbol{n})$ represents a rotation R_i about the lattice point $\boldsymbol{n}$ (see problem 14.6) rather than the origin. Furthermore, for particular lattices, $\mathscr{G}$ also includes rotations about points other than lattice points. For example, in a two-dimensional square lattice in the xy-plane it is verified that the operation $\{R_z(\pi/2), -\boldsymbol{a}_1\}$ is a rotation $R_z(\pi/2)$ about the point $(\frac{1}{2}, \frac{1}{2}, 0)$ at the centre of a cell. Reflections in planes bisecting the cells may be generated in the same way.

In some crystals there may be additional symmetry operations which are not of the form (14.70). These are the so-called screw-axis and glide-plane transformations which are combinations of translations with rotations in which neither of the separate transformations is a symmetry element. We shall not investigate the larger groups obtained by including such operations but refer the reader to Nussbaum (1966) and Birman (1974)—see the bibliography. This neglect will not invalidate our results but means that in some crystals there will, for example, be further degeneracies unexplained by our discussions. The word 'symorphic' is used to describe the group $\mathscr{G}$ defined above, with 'non-symorphic' referring to the more general space groups with glide-planes or screw-axes.

The inclusion of time-reversal will also enlarge the space groups in much the way that it enlarged the point groups in section 9.8. In particular for magnetic crystals there will be what are known as magnetic space groups in which time-reversal occurs only in conjunction with a rotation or translation and is not itself a symmetry operation. For instance, in many antiferromagnets, translation by a lattice vector must be accompanied by time-reversal to reverse the directions of the spins. We shall not discuss these magnetic space groups any further but a full account may be found in Bradley and Cracknell (1972) in the bibliography to chapter 9.

14.9.1 Irreducible representations of space groups

If we have a representation T of the space group $\mathscr{G}$ then the operator corresponding to the group element $\{R_i, \boldsymbol{n}\}$ is denoted $T(R_i, \boldsymbol{n})$. These operators must satisfy the same relations as the group elements themselves, so that from the definition (14.70) we can write

$$T(R_i, \boldsymbol{n}) = T(\boldsymbol{n})\,T(R_i) \tag{14.75}$$

and in particular from (14.73)

$$T(\boldsymbol{n})\,T(R_i) = T(R_i)\,T(R_i^{-1}\boldsymbol{n}) \tag{14.76}$$

In function space the representation operators are defined in the usual way to satisfy

$$T(R_i, \boldsymbol{n})\,\phi(\boldsymbol{r}) = \phi(\{R_i, \boldsymbol{n}\}^{-1}\boldsymbol{r}) = \phi(R_i^{-1}\boldsymbol{r} - R_i^{-1}\boldsymbol{n}) \tag{14.77}$$

where we have used the result (14.74). We shall be particularly concerned with the effect of group transformations on basis vectors $\boldsymbol{e_k}$ which have been chosen to transform irreducibly with respect to the subgroup of translations $\mathscr{T}$ and hence carry a label $\boldsymbol{k}$. We therefore derive here a few useful results. First, under a simple translation, we have from equation (14.11), by definition of $\boldsymbol{e_k}$,

$$\mathrm{T}(\mathrm{E}, \boldsymbol{n})\boldsymbol{e_k} = \mathrm{T}(\boldsymbol{n})\boldsymbol{e_k} = \mathrm{T}^{(\boldsymbol{k})}(\boldsymbol{n})\boldsymbol{e_k} = \exp(-\mathrm{i}\boldsymbol{k}\,.\,\boldsymbol{n})\boldsymbol{e_k} \tag{14.78}$$

Under a more general transformation $\{\mathrm{R}_i, \boldsymbol{n}\}$ we form the new vector

$$\begin{aligned} \boldsymbol{e}'_{\boldsymbol{k}} = \mathrm{T}(\mathrm{R}_i, \boldsymbol{n})\,\boldsymbol{e_k} &= \mathrm{T}(\boldsymbol{n})\mathrm{T}(\mathrm{R}_i)\boldsymbol{e_k} \\ &= \mathrm{T}(\mathrm{R}_i)\mathrm{T}(\mathrm{R}_i^{-1}\,\boldsymbol{n})\boldsymbol{e_k} \end{aligned}$$

using the result (14.76), and hence

$$\begin{aligned} \boldsymbol{e}'_{\boldsymbol{k}} = \mathrm{T}(\mathrm{R}_i, \boldsymbol{n})\boldsymbol{e_k} &= \exp(-i\boldsymbol{k}\,.\,\mathrm{R}_i^{-1}\,\boldsymbol{n})\mathrm{T}(\mathrm{R}_i)\boldsymbol{e_k} \\ &= \exp(-i\mathrm{R}_i\boldsymbol{k}\,.\,\boldsymbol{n})\mathrm{T}(\mathrm{R}_i)\boldsymbol{e_k} \end{aligned} \tag{14.79}$$

We now consider the effect of a pure translation on this new vector $\boldsymbol{e}'_{\boldsymbol{k}}$

$$\begin{aligned} \mathrm{T}(\mathrm{E}, \boldsymbol{m})\boldsymbol{e}'_{\boldsymbol{k}} = \mathrm{T}(\mathrm{E}, \boldsymbol{m})[\mathrm{T}(\mathrm{R}_i, \boldsymbol{n})\boldsymbol{e_k}] &= \mathrm{T}(\mathrm{R}_i, \boldsymbol{m}+\boldsymbol{n})\boldsymbol{e_k} \\ &= \exp[-i\mathrm{R}_i\boldsymbol{k}\,.\,(\boldsymbol{n}+\boldsymbol{m})]\,\mathrm{T}(\mathrm{R}_i)\boldsymbol{e_k} \\ &= \exp(-i\mathrm{R}_i\boldsymbol{k}\,.\,\boldsymbol{m})[\mathrm{T}(\mathrm{R}_i, \boldsymbol{n})\boldsymbol{e_k}] \\ &= \exp(-i\mathrm{R}_i\,\boldsymbol{k}\,.\,\boldsymbol{m})\boldsymbol{e}'_{\boldsymbol{k}} \end{aligned} \tag{14.80}$$

This last equation shows that the vector $\boldsymbol{e}'_{\boldsymbol{k}}$ transforms irreducibly under the subgroup of translations and belongs to the representation $\mathrm{T}^{(\mathrm{R}_i\boldsymbol{k})}$. (We use the general method given in section 20.3.)

These general results will now be used in constructing and classifying (labelling) the irreducible representations of the space group $\mathscr{G}$. Let L denote the vector space of an irreducible representation. Since the translations form a subgroup $\mathscr{T}$ of $\mathscr{G}$ we are free to choose basis vectors which belong to irreducible representations $\mathrm{T}^{(\boldsymbol{k})}$ of $\mathscr{T}$. Let $\boldsymbol{e_k}$ be such a basis vector. We can then generate a set of vectors by operating on $\boldsymbol{e_k}$ with all the group elements $\mathrm{T}(\mathrm{R}_i, \boldsymbol{n})$. Before continuing the discussion we must make clear that there are two different kinds of vectors involved. There are the vectors $\boldsymbol{k}$ in ordinary three-dimensional space and there are the vectors $\boldsymbol{e_k}$ in the vector space L of the representation. We shall refer to both kinds simply as 'vectors' but it will be clear from the context and from the notation which kind of vector is meant. It is convenient to discuss first the case when $\boldsymbol{k}$ is a vector with no special symmetry, by which we mean that none of the rotations R_i leaves $\boldsymbol{k}$ invariant. In this case, the set of vectors $\boldsymbol{k}_i = \mathrm{R}_i\boldsymbol{k}$ are all different, since if $\boldsymbol{k}_i = \boldsymbol{k}_j$ then $\mathrm{R}_j^{-1}\mathrm{R}_i\boldsymbol{k} = \boldsymbol{k}$ and $\boldsymbol{k}$ would have special symmetry. The set of vectors $\boldsymbol{k}_i$ is called the 'star' of $\boldsymbol{k}$. Hence, from equation (14.80), the set of vectors $\boldsymbol{e}_{\boldsymbol{k}_i} = \mathrm{T}(\mathrm{R}_i)\boldsymbol{e_k}$ in L all belong to different irreducible representations $\mathrm{T}^{(\boldsymbol{k}_i)}$ of $\mathscr{T}$ and are therefore linearly independent. Furthermore, we now show that they form an invariant space and thus provide a representation of $\mathscr{G}$. In other words, the set of vectors $\boldsymbol{e}_{\boldsymbol{k}_i}$ generated from $\boldsymbol{e_k}$ by the action of group *rotations* $\mathrm{T}(\mathrm{R}_i)$ *only*, form a basis for a representation Γ of the complete group $\mathscr{G}$. To do this we calculate the effect of a general transformation $\{R_j, \boldsymbol{m}\}$ on the vector $\boldsymbol{e}_{\boldsymbol{k}_i}$:

$$\begin{aligned} T(R_j, \boldsymbol{m})\boldsymbol{e}_{\boldsymbol{k}_i} &= T(R_j, \boldsymbol{m})T(R_i)\boldsymbol{e}_{\boldsymbol{k}} \\ &= T(R_j R_i, \boldsymbol{m})\boldsymbol{e}_{\boldsymbol{k}} \end{aligned}$$

using equation (14.71). If we call the group element $R_j R_i = R_l$ we can use equation (14.79) and write

$$\begin{aligned} T(R_j, \boldsymbol{m})\boldsymbol{e}_{\boldsymbol{k}_i} &= \exp(-iR_l\boldsymbol{k}.\boldsymbol{m})T(R_l)\boldsymbol{e}_{\boldsymbol{k}} \\ &= \exp(-i\boldsymbol{k}_l.\boldsymbol{m})\boldsymbol{e}_{\boldsymbol{k}_l} \end{aligned} \tag{14.81}$$

where $\boldsymbol{k}_l = R_l\boldsymbol{k} = R_j\boldsymbol{k}_i$. This equation gives the general matrix element for a general group element $\{R_j, \boldsymbol{m}\}$ of $\mathscr{G}$. We note that the dimension of the representation Γ is equal to g, the number of elements in the point group. As in subsection 7.4.2 we can now argue that the set $\boldsymbol{e}_{\boldsymbol{k}_i}$ forms a basis for the space L of the irreducible representation because, if it did not, then the space L would have been reduced. Thus the structure of the irreducible representations of $\mathscr{G}$ is described by the basis vectors $\boldsymbol{e}_{\boldsymbol{k}_i}$ with the matrix elements (14.81). The representation is labelled by an arbitrary vector $\boldsymbol{k}$ and denoted by $\Gamma^{(\boldsymbol{k})}$. There is clearly an equivalence between $\Gamma^{(\boldsymbol{k})}$ and $\Gamma^{(\boldsymbol{k}_i)}$ for any $\boldsymbol{k}_i$ in the star of $\boldsymbol{k}$ and, as with the translation group, there is equivalence if $\boldsymbol{k}$ is replaced by $\boldsymbol{k}+\boldsymbol{K}_n$, where $\boldsymbol{K}_n$ is any reciprocal lattice vector.

If $\boldsymbol{k}$ has special symmetry (e.g. lies on an n-fold rotation axis or in a mirror plane) some of the group elements R_i will leave $\boldsymbol{k}$ invariant. These elements must form a subgroup of the point group and it is called the 'little group' of $\boldsymbol{k}$. If g_l denotes the order of the little group of $\boldsymbol{k}$, and g the order of the point group, then one sees (problem 14.7) that the star of $\boldsymbol{k}$ now contains only g/g_l vectors, which we call $\boldsymbol{k}_p$. In general, there is more than one rotation R with the property $R\boldsymbol{k} = \boldsymbol{k}_p$, for fixed $\boldsymbol{k}$ and $\boldsymbol{k}_p$, but for each $\boldsymbol{k}_p$ we choose just one of these and denote it by H_p. It is easy to show that any rotation may be written $R_i = H_p G_a$, where G_a belongs to the little group.

The irreducible representations of $\mathscr{G}$ will now have a more complicated structure since the vectors $\boldsymbol{e}_{\boldsymbol{k}_i}$ are no longer necessarily linearly independent. The subset of the $\boldsymbol{e}_{\boldsymbol{k}_i}$ for which $\boldsymbol{k}_i = \boldsymbol{k}$, corresponding to elements in the little group, will form a subspace L' of L which is invariant under the little group. Consequently this subspace provides a representation of the little group. Since the little group must itself be one of the point groups its irreducible representations are well known and are denoted by $T^{(\alpha)}$. It can be shown that if L is to give an irreducible representation of the space group, then the representation of the little group given by the subspace L' must be irreducible with respect to the little group. Thus if s_α denotes the dimension of $T^{(\alpha)}$ then there will be a set of s_α linearly independent basis vectors $\boldsymbol{e}^{(\alpha)}_{\boldsymbol{k}\mu}$, where $\mu = 1, 2, \ldots, s_\alpha$, which provide the representation $T^{(\alpha)}$ of the little group and all behave like $T^{(\boldsymbol{k})}$ under translations. By taking elements H_p which lie outside the little group we can now generate a corresponding set of s_α new basis vectors

$e^{(\alpha)}_{k_p\mu}$ for each of the g/g_l vectors k_p in the star. Thus the representation of $\mathscr{G}$ has dimension $s_\alpha g/g_l$ and is denoted by $\Gamma^{(\alpha k)}$.

To construct the representation matrix elements, corresponding to equation (14.81) for the case of special symmetry, we must first write the general rotation in the form $R_i = H_p G_a$, where G_a is an element of the little group and H_p is one of a set of rotations, one for each point in the star, with the property $H_p k = k_p$. Starting from the $e_{k\mu}$ we define the general basis vector by

$$e^{(\alpha)}_{k_p\mu} = T(H_p)e^{(\alpha)}_{k\mu}$$

then

$$\begin{aligned} T(R_j, n)e^{(\alpha)}_{k_p\mu} &= T(n)T(R_j)T(H_p)e^{(\alpha)}_{k\mu} \\ &= T(n)T(H_q)T(G_b)e^{(\alpha)}_{k\mu} \\ &= T(n)\sum_{\mu'} T^{(\alpha)}_{\mu'\mu}(G_b)T(H_q)e^{(\alpha)}_{k\mu'} \\ &= T(n)\sum_{\mu'} T^{(\alpha)}_{\mu'\mu}(G_b)e^{(\alpha)}_{k_q\mu'} \\ &= \exp(-ik_q . n)\sum_{\mu'} T^{(\alpha)}_{\mu'\mu}(G_b)e^{(\alpha)}_{k_q\mu'} \end{aligned}$$

which gives the matrix elements. In deriving this result we have defined H_q and G_b as the factors in the analysis of the rotation $R_j H_p = H_q G_b$ since any rotation can be analysed in this way. The vector k_q is given by $k_q = H_q k$ which is the same as $R_j k_p$ because k is unchanged by G_b. The numbers $T^{(\alpha)}_{\mu'\mu}(G_b)$ are the standard irreducible representation matrices for the little group.

Some examples of 'stars' for two-dimensional lattices are illustrated in figure 14.10 and for a three-dimensional example we take a simple cubic lattice where the Brillouin zone is also a cube of side $2\pi/a$. The point group here is O_h and

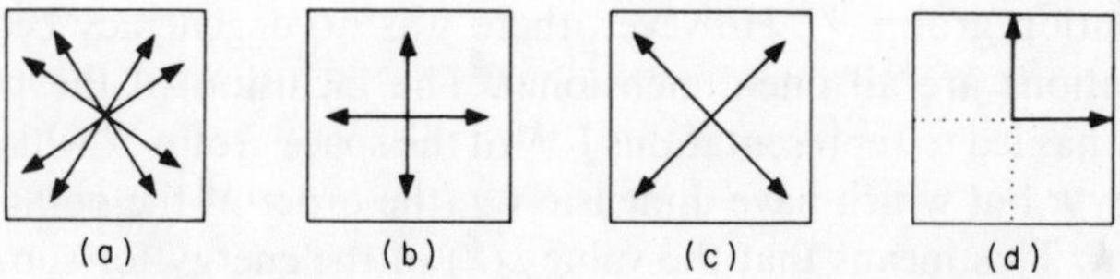

Figure 14.10 Stars of k for a two-dimensional square lattice with symmetry group C_{4v}: (a) general k; (b) k along x-axis; (c) k along square diagonal; (d) k at zone boundary along x-axis

for a general k the star of k will have 48 vectors k_i. The special values of k with symmetry are shown and labelled using the standard solid-state physics notation in figure 14.11. For a general point Δ along the k_x-axis the little group is C_{4v} with 8 elements and the star has 6 points. For the particular point X on the face of the zone, with $k_x = \pi/a$, there is additional symmetry since it is

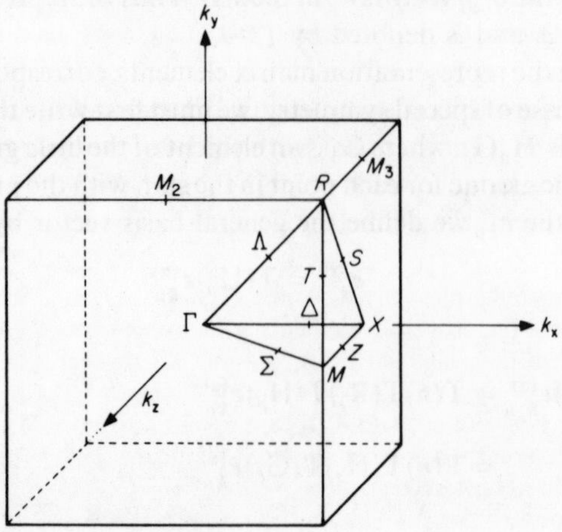

Figure 14.11

equivalent to the $\boldsymbol{k}$-vector with $k_x = -\pi/a$. The little group of X therefore has a reflection plane perpendicular to the x-axis and is D_{4h} with 16 elements. The star of X has thus only 3 points. At the centre Γ of the cube the little group becomes the full cubic group O_h. In a similar way if we proceed from Γ to M along the line ΓM, then at a general point Σ the little group is C_{2v} with four elements and the star of Σ has 12 points. At the special point M, however, all four corners of the cube in the $k_x k_z$-plane are equivalent and the resulting symmetry group is D_{4h} with 16 elements so that the star of M has only three points M, M_2 and M_3 in figure 14.11.

14.9.2 Application to electron states

In section 14.4 we saw how the translational symmetry led to a labelling of the eigenfunctions by $\boldsymbol{k}$ corresponding to the irreducible representation $\mathrm{T}^{(\boldsymbol{k})}$ of the translation group $\mathcal{T}$. However, there was no degeneracy because these representations are all one-dimensional. The inclusion of the point-group symmetry has led to representations $\Gamma^{(\boldsymbol{k})}$ of the space group $\mathcal{G}$ which are again labelled by $\boldsymbol{k}$ but which have dimension g (the order of the point group) for arbitrary $\boldsymbol{k}$. This means that the value $\varepsilon(\boldsymbol{k})$ of the energy for some $\boldsymbol{k}$ will be repeated at all $\boldsymbol{k}_i$ in the star of $\boldsymbol{k}$ or in other words that the constant-energy surfaces when plotted as a function of $\boldsymbol{k}$ will have the full point-group symmetry.

For a vector $\boldsymbol{k}$ with special symmetry the irreducible representation $\Gamma^{(\alpha\boldsymbol{k})}$ has dimension $s_\alpha g/g_l$ giving rise to a degeneracy of the same amount. This corresponds to a degeneracy of order g/g_l due to the number of points in the star and a degeneracy of order s_α at each such point corresponding to the irreducible representation of the little group.

We now consider how we can use these results in a band-structure calculation for the motion of the electrons in a crystal using the tight-binding method of subsection 14.4.3. We shall illustrate the procedure by calculating the form of $\varepsilon(\boldsymbol{k})$ for the bands constructed from atomic p-functions when $\boldsymbol{k}$ lies along the x-axis in a cubic crystal, with the little group C_{4v} of the point Δ in figure 14.11. The character table for this group is shown in table 14.1 and the irreducible representations labelled Δ_1 to Δ_5. The three atomic p-functions

Table 14.1 Character tables for the group C_{4v} at Δ, O_h at Γ and D_{4h} at X, for the common elements (i.e. for the elements which appear in C_{4v}). The irreducible representations are here labelled by Δ_i, Γ_i and X_i, respectively, rather than by the standard notation of appendix A.1 in order to distinguish the representations of the different groups. The groups O_h and D_{4h} are product groups with an S_2 factor so that their representations carry a $\pm$ label. We have only listed the odd parity representations since we are primarily interested in the p-states. The only even parity states to occur belong to the trivial identity representations Γ_1^+ and X_1^+.

C_{4v}	E	C_2	$2C_4$	$2\sigma_v$	$2\sigma_d$
Δ_1	1	1	1	1	1
Δ_2	1	1	1	-1	-1
Δ_3	1	1	-1	1	-1
Δ_4	1	1	-1	-1	1
Δ_5	2	-2	0	0	0
O_h					
Γ_1^-	1	1	1	-1	-1
Γ_2^-	1	1	-1	-1	1
Γ_3^-	2	2	0	-2	0
Γ_4^-	3	-1	1	1	1
Γ_5^-	3	-1	-1	1	-1
D_{4h}					
X_1^-	1	1	1	-1	-1
X_2^-	1	1	1	1	1
X_3^-	1	1	-1	-1	1
X_4^-	1	1	-1	1	-1
X_5^-	2	-2	0	0	0
χ_{vector}	3	-1	1	1	1

transform as the vector representation, see section 5.4, with character given in the last row of the table. This reduces to a sum of Δ_1 and Δ_5 under the little group. Of the three p-functions, p_x belongs to Δ_1 and the pair p_y and p_z belong to Δ_5. (Remember that x is the four-fold axis.) As in equation (14.39) we can construct three Bloch states

$$\phi_q^{(\boldsymbol{k})} = \sum_{\boldsymbol{n}} \exp(i\boldsymbol{k}.\boldsymbol{n})\phi_q(\boldsymbol{r}-\boldsymbol{n}) \qquad (14.82)$$

where $q = x, y$ or z and, for the case being considered with $\boldsymbol{k}$ along the x-axis, they transform in the same way as the *p*-functions under the little group. If these states are now used in a variational calculation, as outlined in section 14.4.3, we may therefore conclude that the states $\phi_y^{(\boldsymbol{k})}$ and $\phi_z^{(\boldsymbol{k})}$ will be degenerate, labelled by the representation $\Gamma^{(\Delta_5 \boldsymbol{k})}$, while $\phi_x^{(\boldsymbol{k})}$ is labelled by $\Gamma^{(\Delta_1 \boldsymbol{k})}$. Because they belong to inequivalent representations these states will not mix.

If we add to the variational calculation the Bloch state $\phi_s^{(\boldsymbol{k})}$ formed from an atomic *s*-state, it will of course have Δ_1 symmetry and therefore mixes with the state $\phi_s^{(\boldsymbol{k})}$. The matrix elements of H in the same nearest-neighbour approximation as equation (14.51) are therefore

$$H_{ss}^{\boldsymbol{k}} = \varepsilon_s + V_{ss}(\mathbf{0}) + 2V_{ss}(0\,0\,a)(2+\cos k_x a)$$
$$H_{sx}^{\boldsymbol{k}} = 2iV_{sx}(a\,0\,0)\sin k_x a$$
$$H_{xx}^{\boldsymbol{k}} = \varepsilon_p + V_{xx}(\mathbf{0}) + 2[2V_{xx}(0\,0\,a) + V_{xx}(a\,0\,0)\cos k_x a]$$
$$H_{yy}^{\boldsymbol{k}} = H_{zz}^{\boldsymbol{k}} = \varepsilon_p + V_{xx}(\mathbf{0}) + 2[V_{xx}(0\,0\,a) + V_{xx}(a\,0\,0) + V_{xx}(0\,0\,a)\cos k_x a]$$

where we have extended the notation of equation (14.51) with, for example,

$$V_{sx}(\boldsymbol{p}) = \int \phi_s^*(\boldsymbol{r}-\boldsymbol{p})[V(\boldsymbol{r}) - V_{at}(\boldsymbol{r})]\phi_x(\boldsymbol{r})\mathrm{d}\boldsymbol{r}$$

and used the fact that

$$V_{xx}(0\,0\,a) = V_{xx}(0\,a\,0) = V_{yy}(a\,0\,0) = V_{yy}(0\,0\,a)$$
$$V_{xx}(a\,0\,0) = V_{yy}(0\,a\,0)$$
$$V_{xx}(\mathbf{0}) = V_{yy}(\mathbf{0})$$
$$V_{sx}(0\,a\,0) = V_{sx}(0\,0\,a) = 0$$

The 2×2 matrix for the mixture of *s*- and *p*-states can now be diagonalised and rather than write out detailed expressions for the energies we have sketched the results in figure 14.12. The figure demonstrates that, as the magnitude of $\boldsymbol{k}$

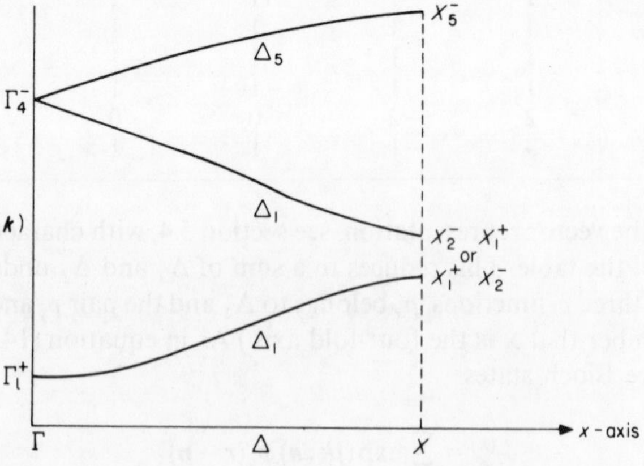

Figure 14.12 Tight-binding energy bands for *s*- and *p*-like atomic states with $\boldsymbol{k}$ along the *x*-axis

tends to zero, the energies for Δ_5 and Δ_1 coalesce and the s and p wave functions are no longer mixed. This additional degeneracy is however to be expected since, at the point Γ, the little group becomes the full octahedral group O_h and the three Bloch functions of equation (14.82) transform according to the irreducible representation Γ_4^- of O_h. The representations Δ_1 and Δ_5 of C_{4v}, which label curves which come together at Γ, may be obtained from the representation Γ_4^- by the process of reduction of Γ_4^- on restriction from O_h to the subgroup C_{4v}, see section 4.18. This connection of Δ_1 and Δ_5 with Γ_4^- is called a compatibility relation. In this way we can also label the irreducible representation at the point X by irreducible representations of the little group at X which is D_{4h} and from the character table we deduce the labels shown in figure 14.12.

14.9.3 Other excitations

All the symmetry properties of $\varepsilon(\boldsymbol{k})$ which we have derived in the previous section for the energy bands of electrons in solids apply to the other excitations discussed in sections 14.5, 14.6 and 14.7. For instance, in a lattice-vibration calculation the three orthogonal atomic displacements at a site transform in the same way as the p-functions, so that the arguments used for the tight-binding bands for p-functions in subsection 14.9.2 can be taken over in calculating the vibrational spectrum of a simple cubic lattice.

Bibliography

For general background reading on the physics of this chapter we suggest one of the following:

Kittel, C. (1971). *Introduction to Solid State Physics* (Wiley, New York)
Elliott, R. J. and Gibson, A. F. (1974). *An Introduction to Solid State Physics and its Applications* (Macmillan, London)
Harrison, W. A. (1970) *Solid State Theory* (McGraw-Hill, New York)

A more advanced treatment is to be found in

Ziman, J. M. (1972). *Principles of the Theory of Solids* (Cambridge University Press)

and for a specialist review on symmetry and electron states in metals see

Nussbaum, A. (1966). *Solid St. Phys.*, **18**, 165

For further reading on space groups see

Birman, J. L. (1974). Theory of space groups and infra-red and Raman lattice processes in insulating crystals, *Handb. Phys.*, **XXV** (2b); Light and matter (1b)

Problems

14.1 Show that the volume of the Brillouin zone is $(2\pi)^3/v_c$, where v_c is the volume of the primitive cell.

14.2 Show that any vector $\boldsymbol{K_m}$ which satisfies equation (14.16) is a reciprocal lattice vector.

14.3 Show that the free-electron parabolas in figure 14.4 are given by

$$\varepsilon^0_{n_1 n_2}(\boldsymbol{k}) = \frac{\hbar^2}{2M}\left\{\left(\frac{2\pi n_1}{a_1}+k_x\right)^2 + \left(\frac{2\pi n_2}{a_2}+k_y\right)^2\right\}$$

where n_1 and n_2 are integers.

14.4 Draw the Brillouin zone for a plane square lattice in two dimensions with symmetry group C_{4v} and mark on it the six kinds of special point where the little group of $\boldsymbol{k}$ is non-trivial. What is the little group at each of these points? Draw up a table of compatibility relations for the irreducible representations for $\boldsymbol{k}$ along the x-direction of figure 14.10 as $k \to 0$ and as $k \to \pi/a$.

14.5 In subsection 14.4.1 we used degenerate perturbation theory to construct the wave functions and hence the energies at the zone boundary for the nearly-free electron model. The fact that the wave functions were odd or even is an example of the states transforming irreducibly under the little group at that point. Consider the two-dimensional square lattice of the previous problem and do a similar calculation using the four degenerate plane waves corresponding to $\boldsymbol{k} = (\pm\pi/a, \pm\pi/a)$. These all have the same reduced $\boldsymbol{k}$ vector which is one of the special points in the zone. The little group at the point is the full symmetry group C_{4v}. By calculating the character of the representation generated by the four equivalent plane waves, show that the degeneracy must be split into a doublet and two singlets and hence use projection operators to construct the eigenstates. Calculate the nearly-free electron energies of these states to first order in $V(\boldsymbol{r})$.

14.6 Show that the product $\mathrm{P}(\boldsymbol{n})\mathrm{R}_i\mathrm{P}(-\boldsymbol{n})$ represents a rotation through the same angle as R_i but about the point $\boldsymbol{n}$.

14.7 Show that if g_l is the order of the little group of $\boldsymbol{k}$ and g is the order of the full point group, then the star of $\boldsymbol{k}$ contains g/g_l vectors.

14.8 Show that the three Bloch functions $\phi^{(\boldsymbol{k})}_q$ of equation (14.82) do, in fact, transform in the same way as atomic p-functions centred at the origin, under operations of the little group.

15

Space and Time

Much of this book has been concerned with symmetries in space. So far as we can tell, space is homogeneous in the sense that an experiment carried out in one laboratory will give the same result as in another and the result will not depend on the direction in which the experiment is set up. This implies that the laws of nature are invariant under translations and rotations and leads to the conservation of linear momentum and angular momentum and all the associated phenomena discussed in earlier chapters. (Within a crystal the positioning of the atoms produces a potential field which lacks these continuous symmetries and is invariant only with respect to finite rotations and translations, as discussed in chapter 14.) Time is also believed to be homogeneous in the sense that an experiment carried out today will give the same result as one carried out tomorrow. This invariance with respect to time translations leads to conservation of energy, a feature which is built into the Schrodinger equation which we have used hitherto as our starting point. The introduction of the theory of relativity by Einstein rested on the idea that space and time possess a deeper homogeneity; that the laws of nature are invariant under a set of transformations (Lorentz) which operate in the four-dimensional 'space' of space and time. The transformations include rotations and translations in both space and time as special cases. The concept of the (rest) mass of a particle has a natural place in this theory and one finds for example that the Schrodinger equation does not satisfy the new invariance. It is necessary to derive a new formulation for both classical and quantum mechanics to incorporate the new invariance. However, the corrections implied by this modification are important only at velocities near that of light, about $3(10)^8$ m/sec. Thus it turns out that for most classical and quantum mechanical applications, including the structure of atoms, molecules and nuclei, the relativistic corrections are small. In this chapter we shall study the groups associated with the Lorentz transformations and see how their representations are related to physical quantities. The improper rotations generated by the inclusion of the space inversion may also be incorporated in the four-dimensional framework along with the time inversion operation.

The concept of four-dimensional space and time is first introduced in section 15.2 where we describe the Lorentz group. Translations in four dimensions are included in section 15.4 leading to the Poincaré group. The improper operations of space and time inversion are included in smaller sections, 15.3, 15.5 and 15.6. Although some indication of the physical significance of the transformations is given in section 15.2 we delay a discussion of the significance of the irreducible representations until the last two sections. The chapter begins in section 15.1 with a discussion of the Euclidean group which combines rotations with translations. This group is concerned entirely with the three space dimensions and in a sense does not belong to the present chapter. Also the physical interest in the Euclidean group is quite small but we include it here for two reasons. Firstly it is very similar to the Poincaré group but somewhat simpler. Secondly, a group isomorphic with the two-dimensional Euclidean group occurs in our study of the Poincaré group and we shall be able to quote from the results of section 15.1. A reader who is anxious to move into four dimensions could defer section 15.1 until he meets this quotation in section 15.4.

15.1 The Euclidean group $\mathscr{E}_3$

We have studied rotations and inversion in some detail in earlier chapters and in chapter 14 we described the symmetry of crystals with respect to finite translations and finite rotations—the 'space groups'. We now study the group of continuous translations and rotations following the procedure used in section 14.9 for the space groups. We stress that the present section is concerned entirely with the three space dimensions.

15.1.1 Translations

First we consider pure translations in one dimension. There is an infinite number of group elements P (ξ) denoting translations along the x-axis $P(\xi)x = x+\xi$, where $-\infty < \xi < \infty$. The multiplication law for the translation group is obviously $P(\xi_1)\, P(\xi_2) = P(\xi_1+\xi_2)$ and it is an Abelian group. In fact the multiplication law is the same as that for the group $\mathscr{R}_2$ (see section 7.3). The irreducible representations are therefore one-dimensional of the form

$$T^{(k)}(\xi) = \exp(-ik\xi) \tag{15.1}$$

with any value of k. There is now no restriction that k should be an integer since there is no periodicity in the variable ξ but k must be real if the representation is to be unitary. The transformation of functions is defined to be

$$\psi'(x) = T(\xi)\psi(x) = \psi(P(-\xi)x) = \psi(x-\xi)$$

following equation (3.37) so that the function $\psi(x) = \exp(ikx)$ transforms like the irreducible representation $T^{(k)}$. Following section 7.3 the infinitesimal operator then takes the form $P_x = -\partial/\partial x$.

The extension to translations in three dimensions is trivial since translations all commute. Thus the three-dimensional translation group is a direct product of three one-dimensional translation groups in x, y and z. The general group element is thus denoted by $P(\rho)$ with the definition

$$P(\rho)\boldsymbol{r} = \boldsymbol{r} + \rho \tag{15.2}$$

where $\boldsymbol{r}$ is a general position vector. Writing $\rho = (\xi, \eta, \zeta)$ there are clearly three parameters and three infinitesimal operators P_x, P_y and P_z which in a space of functions $\psi(\boldsymbol{r})$ are given by $-\partial/\partial x$, $-\partial/\partial y$ and $-\partial/\partial z$. The irreducible representations are obvious generalisations of equation (15.1), being labelled by three numbers k_x, k_y and k_z which form a vector $\boldsymbol{k}$,

$$T^{(\boldsymbol{k})}(\rho) = \exp(-i\boldsymbol{k}.\rho) \tag{15.3}$$

If the Hamiltonian of a quantum system is translationally invariant then the infinitesimal operators P_x, P_y and P_z represent conserved quantities, essentially the three components of the total linear momentum of the system. As they stand, these operators are skew-Hermitian, being the infinitesimal operators of a unitary transformation, but they can be made Hermitian by the inclusion of a factor i. The dimension is also inappropriate for a momentum but this can be put right by including a factor $\hbar$. One actually defines the physical momentum operators p_q by $p_q = i\hbar P_q$. The reason for associating these operators with momentum is that in classical mechanics also the translational invariance of a system leads to the conservation of the total linear momentum, as explained in section 16.1.

Since the irreducible representations of the translation group are one-dimensional this invariance leads to no degeneracy, but simply to the labelling of the eigenfunctions by the representation labels $\boldsymbol{k}$. From the expression given above for $T^{(\boldsymbol{k})}(\rho)$ one sees that the infinitesimal operator P_q has the eigenvalue $-ik_q$ in a state with given $\boldsymbol{k}$. Thus the momentum is given by $\hbar\boldsymbol{k}$. The presence of any potential $V(\boldsymbol{r})$, depending on position $\boldsymbol{r}$, will violate translational symmetry unless V is trivially a constant. Thus for a single particle, translation invariance is relevant if the particle is moving freely. For a system with more than one particle, any internal potential like $V(\boldsymbol{r}_1 - \boldsymbol{r}_2)$ is clearly invariant under translations and thus the total momentum of the system is conserved.

15.1.2 The group operators

The 'Euclidean group' $\mathscr{E}_3$ in three dimensions is formed by the products of the proper rotations $R(\boldsymbol{a})$ and the translations $P(\rho)$. Here $\boldsymbol{a} = (a_x, a_y, a_z)$ denotes the three parameters of the rotation $R(\boldsymbol{a})$ in the notation of section 7.4. The general group element is thus written as $P(\rho)\,R(\boldsymbol{a})$ and its effect on a position vector $\boldsymbol{r}$ is given by

$$P(\rho)R(\boldsymbol{a})\boldsymbol{r} = R(\boldsymbol{a})\boldsymbol{r} + \rho \tag{15.4}$$

using equation (15.2). Notice that rotations and translations do not commute, which is obvious geometrically, and in fact taking the product (15.4) in reverse order we have

$$R(\boldsymbol{a})P(\rho)\boldsymbol{r} = R(\boldsymbol{a})(\boldsymbol{r}+\rho) = R(\boldsymbol{a})\boldsymbol{r} + R(\boldsymbol{a})\rho$$

so that we may conclude that

$$P(\rho)R(\boldsymbol{a}) = R(\boldsymbol{a})P(R^{-1}(\boldsymbol{a})\rho) \tag{15.5}$$

Because of this result it follows that one need only consider group elements of the form $P(\rho)R(\boldsymbol{a})$, since any product in the reverse order may be written in this way using equation (15.5).

Following our general definition (3.37) of the transformation of functions we define the operator $T(\rho, \boldsymbol{a})$ in function space by

$$\begin{aligned} T(\rho, \boldsymbol{a})\psi(\boldsymbol{r}) &= \psi\{[P(\rho)R(\boldsymbol{a})]^{-1}\boldsymbol{r}\} = \psi\{R^{-1}(\boldsymbol{a})P^{-1}(\rho)\boldsymbol{r}\} \\ &= \psi\{R^{-1}(\boldsymbol{a})(\boldsymbol{r}-\rho)\} \end{aligned} \tag{15.6}$$

which is similar to the notation used in section 14.9.

15.1.3 The irreducible representations

Since the rotations and translations do not commute, the group $\mathscr{E}_3$ is not a direct product group so that the labelling of the irreducible representations of $\mathscr{E}_3$ is a non-trivial problem. However, the existence of the translations as an Abelian subgroup enables us to solve this problem following the procedure used in section 14.9 for the space groups.

We use the notation $T(\rho, \boldsymbol{a})$ to denote the representation operator corresponding to the group element $P(\rho)R(\boldsymbol{a})$ and, by definition, the $T(\rho, \boldsymbol{a})$ must satisfy the same multiplication laws as the group elements, i.e. from equation (15.5).

$$T(\rho, \boldsymbol{a}) = T(\rho, 0)T(0, \boldsymbol{a}) = T(0, \boldsymbol{a})T(R^{-1}(\boldsymbol{a})\rho, 0) \tag{15.7}$$

Before constructing the representations of $\mathscr{E}_3$ we need to establish the following property of rotations, namely that any rotation R may be written $R = R_{xy}R_z$ where R_z is a rotation about the z-axis and R_{xy} is a rotation about an axis lying in the xy-plane. To justify this factorisation we define $\boldsymbol{k} = R\boldsymbol{k}_0$, where $\boldsymbol{k}_0$ lies along the z-axis. Now define R_{xy} to be that unique rotation about an axis lying in the xy-plane which carries $\boldsymbol{k}_0$ into $\boldsymbol{k}$, viz. $R_{xy}\boldsymbol{k}_0 = \boldsymbol{k}$. From these definitions we see that

$$R_{xy}^{-1} \ R\boldsymbol{k}_0 = R_{xy}^{-1}\boldsymbol{k} = \boldsymbol{k}_0$$

so that the rotation R_{xy}^{-1} R leaves $\boldsymbol{k}_0$ unmoved and must therefore be a rotation about the z-axis, i.e. $R_{xy}^{-1} R = R_z$ which gives the desired result,

$$R = R_{xy} R_z \tag{15.8}$$

The irreducible representations E of the Euclidean group $\mathscr{E}_3$ may now be generated by a sequence of steps as follows. (See also section 20.3.)

Step (1). Choose basis vectors $|\boldsymbol{k}\rangle$ which belong to irreducible representations $T^{(\boldsymbol{k})}$ of the subgroup of translations so that

$$T(\rho, 0)|\boldsymbol{k}\rangle = \exp(-i\boldsymbol{k}.\rho)|\boldsymbol{k}\rangle \tag{15.9}$$

(It will be more convenient in this chapter to use the notation $|\boldsymbol{k}\rangle$ for a basis vector rather than $\boldsymbol{e}_{\boldsymbol{k}}$ which would be more consistent with section 14.9.)

Step (2) It is now shown that the vector $T(0, \boldsymbol{a})|\boldsymbol{k}\rangle$ transforms like the representation $T^{(R(\boldsymbol{a})\boldsymbol{k})}$ of the subgroup of translations. Using equations (15.7) and (15.9) we have

$$\begin{aligned} T(\rho, 0)(T(0, \boldsymbol{a})|\boldsymbol{k}\rangle) &= T(\rho, \boldsymbol{a})|\boldsymbol{k}\rangle \\ &= T(0, \boldsymbol{a})T(R^{-1}(\boldsymbol{a})\rho, 0)|\boldsymbol{k}\rangle \\ &= T(0, \boldsymbol{a})\exp[-i\boldsymbol{k}.R^{-1}(\boldsymbol{a})\rho]|\boldsymbol{k}\rangle \\ &= \exp[-iR(\boldsymbol{a})\boldsymbol{k}.\rho](T(0, \boldsymbol{a})|\boldsymbol{k}\rangle) \end{aligned} \tag{15.10}$$

which is the desired result. This shows that if the representation E contains a basis vector $|\boldsymbol{k}\rangle$ then it must also contain vectors $|\boldsymbol{k}'\rangle$ for all $\boldsymbol{k}' = R(\boldsymbol{a})\boldsymbol{k}$, i.e. for all $\boldsymbol{k}'$ with $|\boldsymbol{k}'| = |\boldsymbol{k}|$.

Step (3) We now choose a reference direction, usually the z-axis, denoting a vector in this direction by $\boldsymbol{k}_0$, a basis vector which transforms like $T^{(\boldsymbol{k}_0)}$ under translations by $|\boldsymbol{k}_0\rangle$ and a rotation about $\boldsymbol{k}_0$ by $R(\boldsymbol{a}_0)$. As a result of step (2) above, the vector $T(0, \boldsymbol{a}_0)|\boldsymbol{k}_0\rangle$ will also transform like $|\boldsymbol{k}_0\rangle$ under translations because $R(\boldsymbol{a}_0)\boldsymbol{k}_0 = \boldsymbol{k}_0$. Thus the set of basis vectors of E with the same label $\boldsymbol{k}_0$ will form an invariant space under rotations about the z-axis and may therefore be labelled also by the irreducible representations of the group $\mathscr{R}_2$ of rotations about a fixed axis. Thus we may introduce the more detailed notation $|\boldsymbol{k}_0 m\rangle$ in place of $|\boldsymbol{k}_0\rangle$ where m labels the $\mathscr{R}_2$ representation (see section 7.3) and

$$T(0, \boldsymbol{a}_0)|\boldsymbol{k}_0 m\rangle = \exp(-ima_0)|\boldsymbol{k}_0 m\rangle \tag{15.11}$$

Step (4) We are now in a position to construct the representation E. It will be labelled by $|\boldsymbol{k}| = |\boldsymbol{k}_0|$ and m. Starting with a single basis vector $|\boldsymbol{k}_0 m\rangle$ we generate the set

$$|\boldsymbol{k}m\rangle = T(0, \tilde{\boldsymbol{a}}(\boldsymbol{k}))|\boldsymbol{k}_0 m\rangle \tag{15.12}$$

where $\boldsymbol{k}$ is any vector of length $|\boldsymbol{k}_0|$ and $R(\tilde{\boldsymbol{a}}(\boldsymbol{k}))$ is that unique rotation about an axis $\tilde{\boldsymbol{a}}(\boldsymbol{k})$ in the xy-plane which carries $\boldsymbol{k}_0$ into $\boldsymbol{k}$, i.e. $R(\tilde{\boldsymbol{a}}(\boldsymbol{k}))\boldsymbol{k}_0 = \boldsymbol{k}$. We use the tilde on $\tilde{\boldsymbol{a}}$ to signify that this vector lies in the plane perpendicular to $\boldsymbol{k}_0$, i.e. the xy-plane. There is therefore an infinite set of basis vectors $|\boldsymbol{k}m\rangle$ in E which all have the same m and the same length of $\boldsymbol{k}$ but with different directions of $\boldsymbol{k}$. To prove that this set is invariant under the group $\mathscr{E}_3$ we consider the effect of a general operation $T(\rho, \boldsymbol{a})$ on an arbitrary basis vector $|\boldsymbol{k}m\rangle$,

$$\begin{aligned} T(\rho, \boldsymbol{a})|\boldsymbol{k}m\rangle &= T(\rho, 0)T(0, \boldsymbol{a})T(0, \tilde{\boldsymbol{a}}(\boldsymbol{k}))|\boldsymbol{k}_0 m\rangle \\ &= T(\rho, 0)T(0, \tilde{\boldsymbol{a}}(\boldsymbol{k}'))T(0, \boldsymbol{c})|\boldsymbol{k}_0 m\rangle \\ &= T(\rho, 0)T(0, \tilde{\boldsymbol{a}}(\boldsymbol{k}'))\exp(-imc)|\boldsymbol{k}_0 m\rangle \\ &= \exp(-imc)T(\rho, 0)|\boldsymbol{k}'m\rangle \\ &= \exp(-imc)\exp(-i\boldsymbol{k}'.\boldsymbol{\rho})\,|\boldsymbol{k}'m\rangle \end{aligned} \tag{15.13}$$

In deducing this result we have used equation (15.8) for the rotation $R(\boldsymbol{a})R(\tilde{\boldsymbol{a}}(\boldsymbol{k}))$ writing

$$R(\boldsymbol{a})\,R(\tilde{\boldsymbol{a}}(\boldsymbol{k})) = R(\tilde{\boldsymbol{a}}(\boldsymbol{k}'))\,R_z(c) \tag{15.14}$$

which defines the rotations $R(\tilde{a}(\boldsymbol{k}'))$ and $R_z(c)$. The vector $\boldsymbol{k}'$ is defined by $\boldsymbol{k}' = R(\tilde{a}(\boldsymbol{k}'))\boldsymbol{k}_0$ or equivalently by $\boldsymbol{k}' = R(\boldsymbol{a})\boldsymbol{k}$ using equation (15.14). Thus given $\boldsymbol{a}$ and $\boldsymbol{k}$ one can deduce $\boldsymbol{k}'$ and c so that equation (15.13) actually provides the representation matrix elements of E.

By an argument like that used for the group $\mathscr{R}_3$ in subsection 7.4.2 it follows that, if it is to be irreducible, the representation E can have only one basis vector with the labels $|\boldsymbol{k}_0 m\rangle$. Thus the irreducible representations of $\mathscr{E}_3$ are given by equation (15.13). To be definite, we choose a particular axis, the z-axis, in generating the basis vectors but it can be argued quite simply that representations generated by taking $\boldsymbol{k}_0$ in different directions are equivalent so long as $\boldsymbol{k}_0$ has the same length. Thus the direction of $\boldsymbol{k}_0$ is irrelevant in labelling the inequivalent, irreducible representation of $\mathscr{E}_3$ and we use the notation $E^{(|\boldsymbol{k}|,m)}$ for E, where $|\boldsymbol{k}|$ denotes the length of all vectors $\boldsymbol{k}$ appearing in the representation.

As an example of these representations we see that the representation $E^{(|\boldsymbol{k}|,0)}$ may be generated, using equation (15.12) from the function $\exp(i|\boldsymbol{k}|z)$ of position of a single particle. The basis vectors are given by $|\boldsymbol{k}0\rangle = \exp(i\boldsymbol{k}.\boldsymbol{r})$, where $\boldsymbol{k}$ runs over all vectors with fixed length $|\boldsymbol{k}|$. To generate the representations $E^{(|\boldsymbol{k}|,m)}$ one needs to take at least two particles and the function $\exp[i|\boldsymbol{k}|(z_1+z_2)]\ \{(x_1-x_2)+i(y_1-y_2)\}^m$ would suffice for $|\boldsymbol{k}_0 m\rangle$.

The procedure used here in the study of the irreducible representations of $\mathscr{E}_3$ is another example of the general method of 'little groups' used in subsection 14.9.1. Here the little group is the group $\mathscr{R}_2$ which leaves the vector $\boldsymbol{k}_0$ unchanged and the 'star' contains an infinite number of points. This method will be used later in studying the Poincaré group and in fact it is largely for that reason that we have discussed $\mathscr{E}_3$ in detail.

In the particular case $\boldsymbol{k}_0 = 0$ the discussion above will be inappropriate, since no non-zero vectors $\boldsymbol{k}$ can then be formed by step (4). However in this case the representation space is translation invariant and so the irreducible representations are precisely those of the rotation group $\mathscr{R}_3$ described in chapter 7 and we denote them by $E^{(0,j)} \equiv D^{(j)}$. Thus, only for $\boldsymbol{k} = 0$ does the group $\mathscr{E}_3$ have finite-dimensional irreducible representations.

Since $\mathscr{R}_3$ is a subgroup of $\mathscr{E}_3$ it is in principle possible to label the basis vectors of an irreducible representation of $\mathscr{E}_3$ by the $\mathscr{R}_3$ label j. However this is more complicated than the method given above which uses the subgroup of translations. Notice that since translations and rotations do not commute, one cannot use both labels $\boldsymbol{k}$ and j. In quantum mechanics this statement is equivalent to saying that in a system with $\mathscr{E}_3$ symmetry the momentum and the angular momentum are both conserved but since their operators do not commute they may not be measured simultaneously. The choice of basis made for $E^{(|\boldsymbol{k}|,m)}$ corresponds to one in which the momentum is diagonalised together with the angular momentum about the direction of the momentum. Such a basis is sometimes said to be a 'helicity representation'.

15.1.4 The group $\mathscr{E}_2$

In this section we briefly describe the Euclidean group $\mathscr{E}_2$ in two dimensions, not because it is of interest in its own right but because it will be used later, in section 15.4, in constructing irreducible representations of the Poincaré group. Following the steps set out for $\mathscr{E}_3$ we choose basis functions to satisfy the two-dimensional form of equation (15.9). There is then no element but the identity which leaves the two-dimensional vector $\boldsymbol{k}$ invariant. Thus the irreducible representations are labelled simply by $E^{(|\boldsymbol{k}|)}$. An exception occurs when $\boldsymbol{k} = 0$, since all states of the representation are then translation invariant and the group $\mathscr{E}_2$ is effectively restricted to $\mathscr{R}_2$. Thus when $\boldsymbol{k} = 0$ each representation $T^{(m)}$ of $\mathscr{R}_2$ (see subsection 7.3.1) provides a representation of $\mathscr{E}_2$. We denote it by $E^{(0,m)}$ to remind us that $\boldsymbol{k} = 0$.

15.1.5 The physical significance of the Euclidean group $\mathscr{E}_3$

If a Hamiltonian is invariant under the full Euclidean group then by the usual arguments we expect the eigenstates of the system to be labelled by the possible irreducible representations $E^{(|\boldsymbol{k}|,m)}$ and $E^{(0,j)}$ of $\mathscr{E}_3$ and we also expect to find degeneracies. For a physical system to have $\mathscr{E}_3$ symmetry, not only must the Hamiltonian be independent of position, to satisfy translation invariance, but it must also retain rotational invariance. For a single particle this is therefore relevant only for a free particle, with wave function $\exp(i\boldsymbol{k}.\boldsymbol{r})$ and energy $\hbar^2 k^2/2M$. Furthermore this function must correspond to the representation $E^{(|\boldsymbol{k}|,0)}$ as remarked above. The infinite dimensionality of this representation corresponds to the infinite variety of directions of $\boldsymbol{k}$ with given $|\boldsymbol{k}|$, and physically corresponds to the infinity of possible directions of the momentum of a free particle with fixed energy.

The other representations, $E^{(|k|,m)}$ with $m \neq 0$ and $E^{(0,j)}$, cannot be accommodated if we restrict to a single classical particle. For example, $E^{(0,j)}$ would imply a particle at rest but with angular momentum j. For a system of particles the representation $E^{(0,j)}$ has obvious relevance; their centre of mass is at rest but they have an internal angular momentum j. Such a representation, with integer j, would result from a pair of particles interacting through some potential $V(\boldsymbol{r}_1 - \boldsymbol{r}_2)$.

To appreciate fully the relevance of the representation $E^{(|k|,m)}$ when $m \neq 0$ it is helpful to study the infinitesimal operators of $\mathscr{E}_3$ and to construct the Casimir operators (see section 7.5). The six infinitesimal operators are simply the P_x, P_y and P_z for translations and the X_x, X_y and X_z for rotations. The P_q commute among themselves, the commutation relations of the X_q were given in equation (7.25) and those between the P_q and X_q are soon deduced from the multiplication law (15.5), see problem 15.1. The results are

$$[P_q, X_q] = 0, \quad [P_x, X_y] = P_z, \quad [P_y, X_x] = -P_z, \text{ etc} \qquad (15.15)$$

with cyclic rearrangements. The operator $\mathbf{P}^2 = P_x^2 + P_y^2 + P_z^2$ is clearly an invariant and will serve as one Casimir operator and one soon verifies from equation (15.10) that $\mathbf{P}.\mathbf{X}$ also commutes with all P_q and X_q and is therefore a second Casimir operator. (Note that $\mathbf{X}.\mathbf{X}$ is not translation invariant.) The Casimir operators must necessarily be proportional to the unit operator within an irreducible representation and their values in $E^{(|k|,m)}$ are seen to be $-k^2$ and $-km$, respectively. The latter follows quickly by choosing the particular basis vector $|\boldsymbol{k}_0 m\rangle$ and using equation (15.11) for small $\boldsymbol{a}_0$. Physically these two Casimir operators determine the magnitude of the momentum and the component of angular momentum in the direction $\boldsymbol{k}$ of motion. If we use the explicit differential form $P_x = -\partial/\partial x$, etc., with $\mathbf{X} = \boldsymbol{r} \wedge \mathbf{P}$ from equation (7.21), which would be appropriate for the operators relating to a single classical particle, then one sees immediately that $\mathbf{P}.\mathbf{X} = 0$ as expected, implying $m = 0$. Now consider a pair of classical particles so that $P_x = P_{x_1} + P_{x_2} = -\partial/\partial x_1 - \partial/\partial x_2$, etc., and $\mathbf{X} = \boldsymbol{r}_1 \wedge \mathbf{P}_1 + \boldsymbol{r}_2 \wedge \mathbf{P}_2 = \frac{1}{2}(\boldsymbol{r}_1 + \boldsymbol{r}_2) \wedge (\mathbf{P}_1 + \mathbf{P}_2) + \frac{1}{2}(\boldsymbol{r}_1 - \boldsymbol{r}_2) \wedge (\mathbf{P}_1 - \mathbf{P}_2)$. The latter identity simply expresses $\mathbf{X}$ as the sum of an external and an internal part and, on forming the product $\mathbf{P}.\mathbf{X}$, only the internal part survives, giving $\mathbf{P}.\mathbf{X} = \frac{1}{2}(\mathbf{P}_1 + \mathbf{P}_2).(\boldsymbol{r}_1 - \boldsymbol{r}_2) \wedge (\mathbf{P}_1 - \mathbf{P}_2)$. Thus the Casimir operator $\mathbf{P}.\mathbf{X}$ measures the component of internal or relative angular momentum in the direction of motion of the centre of mass of the pair. Within the representation $E^{(|k|,m)}$, all states $|km\rangle$ will have the same magnitude $|\boldsymbol{k}|$ for the total momentum of the pair but the direction of $\boldsymbol{k}$ will vary from state to state. The component of internal angular momentum in the direction $\boldsymbol{k}$ for the state $|km\rangle$ is always m, independent of $\boldsymbol{k}$. For the energy to depend on m the Hamiltonian must contain terms like $\mathbf{P}.\mathbf{X}$ which in physical terms is a scalar product of total momentum and internal angular momentum. Notice that the magnitude of the internal angular momentum plays no part in the representation $E^{(|\boldsymbol{k}|, m)}$ only the projection is relevant. If the internal motion were in a state of internal angular momentum l then the $(2l+1)$ projections $m = l, l-1, \ldots, -l$ would belong to different representations of $\mathscr{E}_3$ and could have different energies. In other words the $\mathscr{R}_3$ symmetry of internal motion is not contained within $\mathscr{E}_3$. (An extension to the Lorentz group, which includes transformations between systems moving with uniform relative velocity, is necessary before the internal angular momentum gains relevance from the point of view of symmetry.)

The discussion in this section has been confined to one or two classical particles, although the extension from two to any number is straightforward. One can of course introduce an intrinsic spin s of a particle in the way described in section 8.4. One does not attempt to define new internal coordinates but this new degree of freedom is confined to the vector space of $2s+1$ states which transform according to $D^{(s)}$ under internal rotations. When at rest, such a particle would trivially belong to the representation $E^{(0,\, s)}$ of $\mathscr{E}_3$ but in motion the significance of s would be lost. As in the case of the internal angular momentum of the pair discussed above, only the spin along the direction of motion has significance in $\mathscr{E}_3$. For a particle with spin s the infinitesimal operator $\mathbf{X}$ is the sum of the usual orbital part $\boldsymbol{r} \wedge \mathbf{P}$ and a spin part $\mathbf{X}_s$ which is defined as a matrix operator in the $(2s+1)$-dimensional spin-space of the particle, as described in section 8.4.

15.1.6 Scalar products and normalisation of basis vectors

This small section may be omitted since it will not be used directly, but we feel it necessary to comment on the fact that the irreducible representations of $\mathscr{E}_3$ have a continuum of basis vectors. Throughout the general discussion of chapter 4 and in all previous applications to physical problems the irreducible representations have had finite dimension and were therefore expressible as finite matrices. Here, for the first time, we have found irreducible representations $E^{(|\boldsymbol{k}|, m)}$ which have a continuous infinity of linearly independent basis vectors $|\boldsymbol{k}m\rangle$ corresponding to different directions of $\boldsymbol{k}$. This situation will occur again for the Poincaré group in section 15.4.

Let us restrict to vectors $|\psi\rangle$ belonging to a particular representation space. Then, in the case of a finite representation, we write

$$|\psi\rangle = \sum_{i=1}^{N} \psi_i |i\rangle \tag{15.16}$$

where $|i\rangle$ denotes a set of linearly independent basis vectors and the ψ_i are numbers. We then define the scalar product of two vectors $|\phi\rangle$ and $|\psi\rangle$ as

$$\langle\phi|\psi\rangle = \sum_{i=1}^{N} \phi_i^* \psi_i \tag{15.17}$$

which implies that

$$\langle i|j\rangle = \delta_{ij} \tag{15.18}$$

A transformation T is unitary, with respect to this definition of scalar product, if $\langle T\phi | T\psi \rangle = \langle \phi | \psi \rangle$ for all $|\phi\rangle$ and $|\psi\rangle$. For a representation like $E^{(|\boldsymbol{k}|, m)}$ with a continuous basis $|\boldsymbol{k}m\rangle$ we write, in place of (15.16),

$$|\psi\rangle = \int \psi(\boldsymbol{k}) |\boldsymbol{k}m\rangle \, d\Omega_{\boldsymbol{k}} \tag{15.19}$$

where the integration runs over all directions of $\boldsymbol{k}$ and $\psi(\boldsymbol{k})$ is a function of direction of $\boldsymbol{k}$. We then define a scalar product as

$$\langle \phi | \psi \rangle = \int \phi^*(\boldsymbol{k}) \psi(\boldsymbol{k}) d\Omega_{\boldsymbol{k}} \tag{15.20}$$

We may now verify that the representation $E^{(|\boldsymbol{k}|, m)}$ given by equation (15.13) is in fact unitary. From equations (15.13) and (15.19)

$$|T\psi\rangle = \int \psi(\boldsymbol{k}) \exp(-imc - i\boldsymbol{k}' . \rho) |\boldsymbol{k}'m\rangle \, d\Omega_{\boldsymbol{k}}$$

$$= \int \psi(R^{-1}\boldsymbol{k}') \exp(-imc - i\boldsymbol{k}' \cdot \rho) |\boldsymbol{k}'m\rangle \, d\Omega_{\boldsymbol{k}'}$$

using the fact that, since $\boldsymbol{k}' = R(\boldsymbol{a})\boldsymbol{k}$ with fixed $\boldsymbol{a}$, the surface integral $d\Omega_{\boldsymbol{k}}$ may be replaced by $d\Omega_{\boldsymbol{k}'}$, i.e. the Jacobian has the value unity. With a change of notation for the integration variable this may now be written as

$$|T\psi\rangle = \int \psi(R^{-1}\boldsymbol{k}) \exp(-imc - i\boldsymbol{k} . \rho) |\boldsymbol{k}m\rangle \, d\Omega_{\boldsymbol{k}}$$

so that comparing with equation (15.19) and using the definition (15.20) of scalar product we have

$$\langle T\phi | T\psi \rangle = \int \phi^*(R^{-1}\boldsymbol{k}) \psi(R^{-1}\boldsymbol{k}) \, d\Omega_{\boldsymbol{k}}$$

$$= \int \phi^*(\boldsymbol{k}) \psi(\boldsymbol{k}) \, d\Omega_{\boldsymbol{k}} = \langle \phi | \psi \rangle$$

The analogue to equation (15.18) may be deduced only if we make use of the Dirac δ-function of the angles of $\boldsymbol{k}'$ and $\boldsymbol{k}$. Notice that the definition of scalar product (15.20) is not quite the same as the integral over all momentum space, since here we keep the magnitude of $\boldsymbol{k}$ fixed.

15.2 The Lorentz group $\mathscr{L}$

Having discussed the way in which rotations and translations come together in the Euclidean group we now temporarily discard translations and study the extension of the rotation group $\mathcal{R}_3$ into four dimensions when time is included. We define the four-dimensional space by associating with each 'event', or happening, a 'point' with four coordinates (x, y, z, ct) which denote the place (x, y, z) and time t of the event, where c is the velocity of light. Thus all four coordinates have the dimension of length. We shall denote the point by a vector $\hat{\boldsymbol{e}} = (x, y, z, ct)$ where $\hat{\boldsymbol{e}}$ is the four-vector from the 'origin' (0, 0, 0, 0) to the point (x, y, z, ct). Remember that an event at the origin in four-space implies an event at the position $x = y = z = 0$ at time $t = 0$.

15.2.1 The Lorentz transformation

In the rotation group $\mathcal{R}_3$ we are interested in vectors $\boldsymbol{r} = (x, y, z)$ in a three-dimensional space and the transformations $\boldsymbol{r}' = \mathrm{R}(\boldsymbol{a})\boldsymbol{r}$ which preserve distance and angle, i.e. which preserve the scalar product $\boldsymbol{r}_1 . \boldsymbol{r}_2 = x_1x_2 + y_1y_2 + z_1z_2$ between any two vectors $\boldsymbol{r}_1$ and $\boldsymbol{r}_2$. In the Lorentz group $\mathscr{L}$ we are interested in vectors $\hat{\boldsymbol{e}} = (x, y, z, ct)$ in a four-dimensional space with real transformations $\hat{\boldsymbol{e}}' = \mathrm{L}\hat{\boldsymbol{e}}$ which preserve the scalar products defined as

$$\hat{\boldsymbol{e}}_1 . \hat{\boldsymbol{e}}_2 = -x_1x_2 - y_1y_2 - z_1z_2 + c^2t_1t_2 \tag{15.21}$$

Such transformations L are called 'Lorentz' transformations and by definition they satisfy the equation

$$\hat{\boldsymbol{e}}'_1 . \hat{\boldsymbol{e}}'_2 = \mathrm{L}\hat{\boldsymbol{e}}_1 . \mathrm{L}\hat{\boldsymbol{e}}_2 = \hat{\boldsymbol{e}}_1 . \hat{\boldsymbol{e}}_2 \tag{15.22}$$

for all vectors $\hat{\boldsymbol{e}}_1$ and $\hat{\boldsymbol{e}}_2$. The notation $\hat{\boldsymbol{e}}$ has been used for a four-vector to distinguish it from a three-vector in ordinary space which would have been written as $\boldsymbol{e}$. We use the simple notation $\hat{\boldsymbol{e}}_1 . \hat{\boldsymbol{e}}_2$ for the four-dimensional scalar product (15.21). The reason why we are interested in such transformation is, quite simply, that one finds from experiment that the laws of physics are invariant with respect to them. The definition (15.21) could have been made with a different sign throughout without any essential change in the transformation but the sign difference between the space and time terms in equation (15.21) is crucial. If the sign of all terms were the same then the group would be $\mathcal{R}_4$ but nature shows no invariance with respect to $\mathcal{R}_4$.

The scalar product of a vector with itself $\hat{\boldsymbol{e}} . \hat{\boldsymbol{e}} = -x^2 - y^2 - z^2 + c^2t^2$ is said to measure the 'length' of the vector, or the 'interval' between events occurring at opposite ends of the vector. The interval is defined as $(\hat{\boldsymbol{e}} . \hat{\boldsymbol{e}})^{\frac{1}{2}}$. Since from the definition (15.21) a scalar product may have either sign it follows that an interval may be real or imaginary. A real interval is called time-like and an imaginary interval is called space-like for obvious reasons. The interval between any two events at $\hat{\boldsymbol{e}}_1$ and $\hat{\boldsymbol{e}}_2$ is similarly defined as $(\hat{\boldsymbol{e}}_1 - \hat{\boldsymbol{e}}_2 . \hat{\boldsymbol{e}}_1 - \hat{\boldsymbol{e}}_2)^{\frac{1}{2}}$ and from equation (15.22) the interval between any two events is unchanged by a Lorentz transformation.

If we define unit vectors $\hat{\boldsymbol{e}}_x, \hat{\boldsymbol{e}}_y, \hat{\boldsymbol{e}}_z, \hat{\boldsymbol{e}}_t$ as (1, 0, 0, 0), etc., then we note, from the definition (15.21) of scalar product, that $\hat{\boldsymbol{e}}_x . \hat{\boldsymbol{e}}_x = -1$, etc., for the space vectors while $\hat{\boldsymbol{e}}_t . \hat{\boldsymbol{e}}_t = 1$. It is convenient to introduce the matrix g with elements defined by $g_{ij} = \hat{e}_i . \hat{e}_j$, where $i = x, y, z$ or t, so that

$$g = \begin{pmatrix} -1 & 0 & 0 & 0 \\ 0 & -1 & 0 & 0 \\ 0 & 0 & -1 & 0 \\ 0 & 0 & 0 & 1 \end{pmatrix}$$

We define the matrix elements L_{ji} of L by the equation

$$\mathrm{L}\hat{e}_i = \sum_j L_{ji} \hat{e}_j$$

so that

$$\hat{e}_j . \mathrm{L}\hat{e}_i = g_{jj} L_{ji}$$

Given an arbitrary vector $\hat{e} = \sum_i e_i \hat{e}_i$ with components e_i then L carries $\hat{e}$ into the new vector

$$\hat{e}' = \mathrm{L}\hat{e} = \sum_{i,j} e_i L_{ji} \hat{e}_j$$

with components $e'_j = \sum_i L_{ji} e_i$. Given a fixed vector $\hat{\varepsilon}$ with components ε_i with respect to the basis $\hat{e}_i$ then its components with respect to the transformed basis $\hat{e}'_j = \mathrm{L}\hat{e}_j$ are given by

$$\bar{\varepsilon}_j = \sum_i (\mathrm{L}^{-1})_{ji} \varepsilon_i = \sum_i g_{ii} L_{ij} g_{jj} \varepsilon_i$$

The defining property (15.22) of the Lorentz transformation leads to the relation

$$g_{ij} = \sum_{k,l} L_{ki} L_{lj} g_{kl}$$

between matrix elements of L which in matrix form is

$$\mathrm{g} = \mathrm{L}^{\dagger}\mathrm{g}\mathrm{L} \qquad (15.23)$$

where $\mathrm{L}^{\dagger}$ denotes the transpose of L. Since $\mathrm{g}^2 = 1$ this implies that $\mathrm{g}\mathrm{L}^{\dagger}\mathrm{g} = \mathrm{L}^{-1}$ which differs from an orthogonal transformation, see section 3.5, through the presence of the matrices g. One can soon verify that L^{-1} is itself a Lorentz transformation and that the set of all L form a group, see problem 15.2.

[Because of the unusual form (15.21) of the scalar product, in which the 'metric' is not the unit matrix, these formulae differ from those given in section 3.7 through the presence of factors g_{ii}. It is possible to avoid the explicit appearance of these factors by defining what are called covariant components e^i for each vector $\hat{e}$ which are defined as $e^i = g_{ii} e_i$. The original set e_i are called the contravariant components. In this way the factors g_{ii} may be absorbed by switching from one set to the other. Thus for example a scalar product takes the form

$$\hat{e}.\hat{f} = \sum_i g_{ii} e_i f_i = \sum_i e^i f_i = \sum_i e_i f^i$$

with the last two expressions involving both covariant and contravariant components but avoiding the g_{ii}. In this book we prefer not to introduce the extra sophistication of having both sets of components and therefore we shall always use the contravariant components e_i denoted by a lower index and transforming according to the equations above.]

Proper and improper transformations

In section 7.4 we distinguished between proper and improper rotations depending on the sign of the determinant. A similar distinction occurs in the Lorentz group but there are now four different types of transformation in the sense that one cannot pass continuously from one type to another. From equation (15.23) we have

$$(\det \mathrm{L})^2 = 1$$

so that one can distinguish between transformations with $\det \mathrm{L} = \pm 1$. Furthermore if we write out equation (15.23) explicitly for the matrix element in the fourth row and fourth column we have

$$-L_{xt}^2 - L_{yt}^2 - L_{zt}^2 + L_{tt}^2 = 1$$

so that

$$L_{tt}^2 = 1 + L_{xt}^2 + L_{yt}^2 + L_{zt}^2$$

Since the L_{ij} are real it follows that $L_{tt}^2 \geqq 1$ and hence the values of L_{tt} can be in either of two separated regions $L_{tt} \geqq 1$ or $L_{tt} \leqq -1$. Thus we have the four types of transformation L distinguished by

(1) $\det \mathrm{L} = 1$, $L_{tt} \geqq 1$ which contains the identity
(2) $\det \mathrm{L} = -1$, $L_{tt} \geqq 1$ which contains the space inversion I
(3) $\det \mathrm{L} = -1$, $L_{tt} \leqq -1$ which contains the time inversion I_t
(4) $\det \mathrm{L} = 1$, $L_{tt} \leqq -1$ which contains the space – time inversion II_t

Transformations of type (1), which are all connected continuously to the identity, are called proper. They form a group which we shall call the 'Lorentz group' $\mathscr{L}$. Extended Lorentz groups may be formed by including either type (2) or type (3) with type (1). We refer to these groups as $\mathscr{L}_s$ and $\mathscr{L}_t$, respectively. Inclusion of all four types gives an even larger group which we denote by $\mathscr{L}_{st}$. The word 'orthochronous' is sometimes used to describe transformations with $L_{tt} \geqq 1$ and the word homogeneous to distinguish all these groups from those which include translations. We shall not use this nomenclature. In this section we confine our attention to the group $\mathscr{L}$.

Pure Lorentz transformations

Before considering the general Lorentz transformation we look at two special cases,

$$\mathrm{R}(\boldsymbol{a}) = \left(\begin{array}{ccc|c} & \mathrm{R}(\boldsymbol{a}) & & 0 \\ & & & 0 \\ & & & 0 \\ \hline 0 & 0 & 0 & 1 \end{array}\right)$$

and

$$\mathrm{Q}_z(b) = \begin{pmatrix} 1 & 0 & 0 & 0 \\ 0 & 1 & 0 & 0 \\ 0 & 0 & \cosh b & -\sinh b \\ 0 & 0 & -\sinh b & \cosh b \end{pmatrix} \tag{15.24}$$

The first of these, written in partitioned form, is simply a rotation, since the condition (15.23) implies that $\mathrm{R}^\dagger \mathrm{R} = 1$ and the time coordinate is unchanged. The second leaves all points in the xy-plane unchanged and is called a pure Lorentz transformation (or 'boost') in the z-direction. It contains a single real parameter b and each value of b in the range $-\infty < b < \infty$ corresponds to a different transformation $\mathrm{Q}_z(b)$. The transformed vector $\hat{\boldsymbol{e}}$ is given by

$$\hat{\boldsymbol{e}}' = \mathrm{Q}_z(b)\hat{\boldsymbol{e}} = (x, y, z \cosh b - ct \sinh b, ct \cosh b - z \sinh b)$$

and the transformation may look a little more familiar if we use the parameter $\beta = \tanh b$ instead of b, so that

$$z' = (z - \beta ct)/(1 - \beta^2)^{\frac{1}{2}}, \quad y' = y, \quad x' = x$$

$$ct' = (ct - \beta z)/(1 - \beta^2)^{\frac{1}{2}} \tag{15.25}$$

(We shall see later that β has the physical significance of a velocity $\beta = v/c$ measured relative to the velocity c of light.) We may clearly define a similar boost transformation in an arbitrary direction defined by a unit 3-vector $\boldsymbol{u}$. The notation $\mathrm{Q}(\boldsymbol{b})$ will be used where $\boldsymbol{b} = b\boldsymbol{u}$ and b defines the magnitude of the boost, as in equation (15.24). The transformed vector $\hat{\boldsymbol{e}}' = \mathrm{Q}(\boldsymbol{b})\hat{\boldsymbol{e}}$ may be deduced as a generalisation from the result for $\mathrm{Q}_z(b)$ and is most easily expressed by giving the space and time components $\boldsymbol{e}'$ and ct' of $\hat{\boldsymbol{e}}'$,

$$\boldsymbol{e}' = \boldsymbol{e} + \{(\cosh b - 1)(\boldsymbol{e}.\boldsymbol{u}) - ct \sinh b\}\boldsymbol{u}$$

$$ct' = ct \cosh b - (\boldsymbol{e}.\boldsymbol{u}) \sinh b \tag{15.26}$$

The 4×4 matrix of Q($\boldsymbol{b}$) may be read off from these equations. For example

$$Q_{xx}(\boldsymbol{b}) = 1 + (\cosh b - 1)u_x^2, \quad Q_{yx}(\boldsymbol{b}) = (\cosh b - 1)u_x u_y,$$

$$Q_{tx}(\boldsymbol{b}) = -u_x \sinh b, \qquad Q_{tt}(\boldsymbol{b}) = \cosh b$$

There is similarity between equation (15.26) and the corresponding expression given for rotations at the beginning of section 7.4.

Since Q($\boldsymbol{b}$) and R($\boldsymbol{a}$) are both Lorentz transformations it follows that their product is also a Lorentz transformation for any $\boldsymbol{a}$ and $\boldsymbol{b}$. Further than this we now show that *any* Lorentz transformation L may be written as such a product. In principle this result is very similar to the factorisation (15.8) of an arbitrary rotation. We first define $\hat{\boldsymbol{e}}_0 = (0, 0, 0, 1)$. Then, for each L we may construct a vector $\hat{\boldsymbol{e}} = \mathrm{L}\hat{\boldsymbol{e}}_0$. From equation (15.26) one sees that there is a unique boost Q($\boldsymbol{b}$) with the property $\mathrm{Q}(\boldsymbol{b})\hat{\boldsymbol{e}}_0 = \hat{\boldsymbol{e}}$. Thus we have

$$\hat{\boldsymbol{e}}_0 = \mathrm{Q}^{-1}(\boldsymbol{b})\hat{\boldsymbol{e}} = \mathrm{Q}^{-1}(\boldsymbol{b})\mathrm{L}\hat{\boldsymbol{e}}_0$$

showing that the product $\mathrm{Q}^{-1}(\boldsymbol{b})\mathrm{L}$ leaves $\hat{\boldsymbol{e}}_0$ invariant and must therefore be a pure rotation. We may therefore write $\mathrm{Q}^{-1}(\boldsymbol{b})\mathrm{L} = \mathrm{R}(\boldsymbol{a})$ so that

$$\mathrm{L} = \mathrm{Q}(\boldsymbol{b})\,\mathrm{R}(\boldsymbol{a}) \tag{15.27}$$

We shall find it convenient to parameterise L in this way by the six parameters needed to define the two three-vectors $\boldsymbol{a}$ and $\boldsymbol{b}$. We note that whereas the magnitudes of the rotation parameters are limited in the usual way $|\boldsymbol{a}| \leqq \pi$, the boost parameters are unlimited. This is clear from equation (15.24) which shows that Q_z satisfies the defining equations of a Lorentz transformation for all b.

15.2.2 The regions of space–time

Before discussing the physical meaning of the Lorentz transformations it is helpful to study their geometrical meaning. It is sufficient to consider a simple boost $\mathrm{Q}_z(b)$ in the z-direction and for this we need to draw only the z and ct-axes as in figure 15.1. Because of the definition $(\hat{\boldsymbol{e}}.\hat{\boldsymbol{e}})^{\frac{1}{2}}$ of 'length', vectors $\hat{\boldsymbol{e}}$ in the (z, ct)-plane with the same length will not lie on circles but on the hyperbolae $-z^2 + c^2t^2 = \hat{\boldsymbol{e}}.\hat{\boldsymbol{e}} = A$, where A is a constant. Since A may take either sign it is convenient to distinguish vectors of the following six types

(1) $\hat{\boldsymbol{e}}.\hat{\boldsymbol{e}} < 0$	called space-like
(2) $\hat{\boldsymbol{e}}.\hat{\boldsymbol{e}} > 0$ with $t > 0$	called future time-like
(3) $\hat{\boldsymbol{e}}.\hat{\boldsymbol{e}} > 0$ with $t < 0$	called past time-like
(4) $\hat{\boldsymbol{e}}.\hat{\boldsymbol{e}} = 0$ with $\hat{\boldsymbol{e}} \neq 0$ and $t > 0$	called future null
(5) $\hat{\boldsymbol{e}}.\hat{\boldsymbol{e}} = 0$ with $\hat{\boldsymbol{e}} \neq 0$ and $t < 0$	called past null
(6) $\hat{\boldsymbol{e}} = 0$	the zero vector

This classification divides space–time into regions as shown in figure 15.1. Space-like and time-like regions are separated by 45° lines of $z = \pm ct$ which

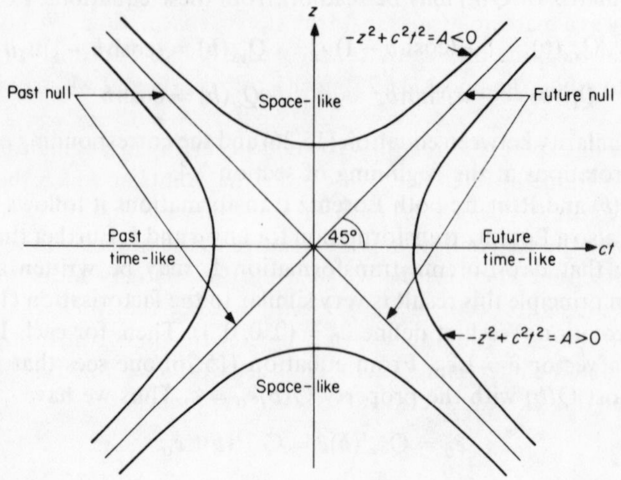

Figure 15.1

contain the null vectors. Notice that a null vector, with $\hat{e}.\hat{e}=0$, does not have all its components zero; this property is restricted to the single zero vector $\hat{e}=0$. Although figure 15.1 is restricted to a single space dimension, the classification is quite general since it is based on the scalar product and the sign of t. In the general case the space-like and time-like regions are separated by what is called the 'light cone', meaning the set of points satisfying $x^2+y^2+z^2=c^2t^2$ and so forming a three-dimensional 'surface' in four-space.

Since a Lorentz transformation preserves the length of a vector it carries a point described by a vector $\hat{e}$ into another point $\hat{e}'$ with the same A, i.e. on the same hyperbola. (One imagines a family of hyperbolae corresponding to different A.) Thus the space-like, time-like, null and zero regions are invariant under Lorentz transformations. Furthermore all six regions remain invariant under the proper Lorentz transformations defined earlier. These do not permit transformation between future and past regions (see problem 15.4). (NB The two-dimensional diagram 15.1 suggests that proper Lorentz transformations cannot connect regions with positive and negative z but this can be achieved in four dimensions with the help of a rotation about one of the other space axes.) One often refers to pictures like figure 15.1 as 'Minkowski diagrams'. An individual at rest with respect to the space axes x, y, z would move parallel to the time axis in the Minkowski diagram while a speed of v relative to the space axes results in a path making an angle $\tan^{-1}(v/c)$ with the time axis. Starting from the origin, with speeds less than that of light, one can reach points in the future time-like region only.

15.2.3 Physical interpretation of the Lorentz transformation

The physical interpretation of the transformation $R(\boldsymbol{a})$ is clear and easy to visualise—it is a rotation. On the other hand we have introduced the boost Q($\boldsymbol{b}$) simply as a mathematical transformation in space–time. We now explain the physical meaning and significance of the boost. For this purpose it is sufficient to study the boost (15.25) in the z-direction and we may use figure 15.1.

Consider an experiment relating to events occurring in a system at rest with respect to a frame of reference. We denote the points at which these events occur by vectors $\hat{\boldsymbol{e}} = (x, y, z, ct)$ in this frame. Suppose that the experiment is repeated with the system now moving, relative to the frame, with velocity $-v$ in the z-direction. Then instinctively, using pre-relativity ideas, one would expect the events to occur at the same times t but that their z-coordinates would have shifted by amounts $-vt$. The later the event, the more it would have shifted in the intervening time t. In other words we might have expected the events in this second experiment to occur at points $\hat{\boldsymbol{e}} = (x, y, z', ct')$, where

$$z' = z - vt, \quad t' = t \tag{15.28}$$

However when the velocity v is comparable with c, the velocity of light, experiment disagrees with these instinctive conclusions—see Muirhead (1973) in the bibliography. The essence of relativity theory, and this agrees with experiment, is the statement that $\hat{e}'$ is obtained from $\hat{e}$ by the Lorentz transformation (15.25), where $\beta = v/c$, rather than by (15.28). Notice however that if $v_{|} \ll c$, a condition which is satisfied in our everyday experiences because of the large value of $c = 2.998(10)^8$ m/sec, then the Lorentz transformation (15.25) reduces to (15.28). It is not therefore too surprising that instinct has failed us. There are a number of startling conclusions from relativity theory which we now bring out by studying three particular cases of the general experiment described above. (We should remark that we could equally well have described the events $\hat{\boldsymbol{e}}'$ as the events $\hat{\boldsymbol{e}}$ as seen by an observer moving with velocity v in the z-direction. The two viewpoints, of the moving system or the moving observer, are both acceptable. We choose to use the former (active) description since it follows our treatment of rotations in which the system is rotated rather than the frame of reference. Most relativity books use the latter (passive) description and we have made our formulae agree with them by using $-v$ rather than v for the velocity of the system.)

(1) Time dilation and the decay of a meson

Consider a meson being produced at the origin $x = y = z = t = 0$ at rest and decaying a time τ later, i.e. at $\hat{\boldsymbol{e}} = (0, 0, 0, \tau)$. This defines a two-event experiment at rest. Now, in the way described generally above, we consider a second experiment in which the meson is produced at the origin with velocity $-v$. According to relativity theory it will decay at the point $\hat{e}'$ given from equation (15.25) by $x' = y' = 0$, $z' = -v\tau(1-\beta^2)^{-\frac{1}{2}}$, $t' = \tau(1-\beta^2)^{-\frac{1}{2}}$. In other words the life of the meson, as measured in the fixed frame, has increased by a factor $(1-\beta^2)^{-\frac{1}{2}}$. This is referred to as the dilation of time and implies that time is not absolute, as one assumed in pre-relativity days. Were it not for this effect the mesons produced by collisions in the upper atmosphere would have decayed long before reaching the surface of the earth. They have speeds close to c so that the factor $(1-\beta^2)^{-\frac{1}{2}}$ is large. Notice however that the 'interval' between the two events, birth and death of the meson, is unaffected by the velocity.

(2) Contraction of rods

The argument in this problem is simplified if we first rearrange equation (15.25) by eliminating t to obtain

$$z' = -\beta ct' + z(1-\beta^2)^{\frac{1}{2}} \tag{15.29}$$

Now consider the difference between the space coordinates of two events at the same time t': $z'_B - z'_A = (z_B - z_A)(1-\beta^2)^{\frac{1}{2}}$. Physically, the same t' means taking a picture of the moving system. Thus if A and B are events marking the ends of a rod then we have shown that the moving rod will have its length contracted by the factor $(1-\beta^2)^{\frac{1}{2}}$, as recorded by the instantaneous picture. We stress that, in our active picture, measurements of position z' and time t' are made in the same, fixed, frame.

(3) Relative velocities and the invariance of the velocity of light

As our third illustration of the consequences of the Lorentz transformation, consider an object moving with uniform velocity $-V$ so that its path in space time is given by $\hat{e} = (0, 0, -Vt, ct)$. Now repeat this experiment but where the object has velocity $-V$ with respect to the system moving with velocity $-v$ relative to the fixed frame. The new path is given from the equations (15.25) by

$$z' = -(V+v)t(1-\beta^2)^{-\frac{1}{2}}$$
$$ct' = (c+vV/c)t(1-\beta^2)^{-\frac{1}{2}}$$

so that $$z'/t' = -(V+v)/(1+vV/c^2)$$

The object therefore moves with a constant speed $V' = (V+v)/(1+vV/c^2)$ with respect to the fixed frame. Thus relative velocities are not simply additive. Furthermore we see that if $V = c$, then $V' = c$, which shows that the velocity of light is the same with respect to all frames of reference. This remarkable result, observed by Michelson and Morley, was one of the earliest experiments which led to the development of relativity theory and is the reason why the velocity of light appears in the Lorentz transformation. One could have defined a Lorentz transformation with any other number for c but it would not have agreed with experiment. It follows from the expression for V' and if V and v are both less than c, then so also is V'. In other words one cannot exceed the velocity of light by superimposing velocities, no matter how close V and v are to c. When one studies relativistic dynamics one finds that an infinite amount of energy would be required to accelerate a particle to precisely the speed of light. Experimental results in high energy particle accelerators are completely consistent with this conclusion. In fact c is an upper limit to the speed of a particle and one sees that the Lorentz transformation has a singularity when $v = c$. There is nevertheless some speculation as to whether it is possible to have objects moving with $v > c$, which remain on the other side of this singularity. The name 'tachyon' has been given to such particles and some of their properties have been discussed theoretically, but so far no evidence has been found for their existence—see Goldhaber and Smith (1975) in the bibliography to chapter 12.

To conclude this section we stress that the statement of Lorentz invariance implies that physical laws are the same in frames moving with uniform relative velocity. The surprise was that the transformation relating motion in two such frames was not what we expected. The term 'Galilean invariance' is used to describe the same statement but when the intuitive transformation (15.28) is used to relate the two frames. Consequently Galilean invariance is valid only for $v \ll c$.

15.2.4 Infinitesimal operators

The Lorentz group $\mathscr{L}$ is a Lie group and we have seen in equation (15.27) that the general element L is defined by six parameters. This number may also be deduced from the fact that a real 4×4 matrix contains 16 parameters and the relation (15.23) between two symmetric 4×4 matrices imposes 10 constraints. To find the infinitesimal matrices we let $\boldsymbol{a}$ and $\boldsymbol{b}$ become small in equation (15.27). Taking the infinitesimal form of $R(\boldsymbol{a})$ from subsection 7.4.1 and that of $Q(\boldsymbol{b})$ from equation (15.26), keeping only first order terms in $\boldsymbol{b}$, we have $L = 1 + \Lambda$ where the infinitesimal matrix Λ is given by

$$\Lambda = \begin{pmatrix} 0 & -a_z & a_y & -b_x \\ a_z & 0 & -a_x & -b_y \\ -a_y & a_x & 0 & -b_z \\ -b_x & -b_y & -b_z & 0 \end{pmatrix} = \sum_{q=x,y,z} (a_q X_q + b_q Y_q) \quad (15.30)$$

where b_q are the three components of the boost vector $\boldsymbol{b}$, the matrices X_q are as defined in equation (7.24) and the matrices Y_q are given by

$$Y_x = \begin{pmatrix} 0 & 0 & 0 & -1 \\ 0 & 0 & 0 & 0 \\ 0 & 0 & 0 & 0 \\ -1 & 0 & 0 & 0 \end{pmatrix}, \quad Y_y = \begin{pmatrix} 0 & 0 & 0 & 0 \\ 0 & 0 & 0 & -1 \\ 0 & 0 & 0 & 0 \\ 0 & -1 & 0 & 0 \end{pmatrix},$$

$$Y_z = \begin{pmatrix} 0 & 0 & 0 & 0 \\ 0 & 0 & 0 & 0 \\ 0 & 0 & 0 & -1 \\ 0 & 0 & -1 & 0 \end{pmatrix} \quad (15.31)$$

These three matrices describe infinitesimal boosts in the three space directions.

The commutation relations of the infinitesimal operators follow from the matrices (15.31)

$$\begin{aligned}
&[X_x, X_y] = X_z \qquad [X_y, X_z] = X_x \qquad [X_z, X_x] = X_y\\
&[Y_x, Y_y] = -X_z \qquad [Y_y, Y_z] = -X_x \qquad [Y_z, Y_x] = -X_y\\
&[X_x, Y_x] = 0 \qquad [X_y, Y_y] = 0 \qquad [X_z, Y_z] = 0 \qquad (15.32)\\
&[X_x, Y_y] = Y_z \qquad [X_y, Y_z] = Y_x \qquad [X_z, Y_x] = Y_y\\
&[X_y, Y_x] = -Y_z \qquad [X_z, Y_y] = -Y_x \qquad [X_x, Y_z] = -Y_y
\end{aligned}$$

We notice that the linear combinations

$$A_q = \tfrac{1}{2}(X_q + iY_q) \quad \text{and} \quad B_q = \tfrac{1}{2}(X_q - iY_q) \qquad (15.33)$$

have much simpler commutation relations

$$\begin{aligned}
&[A_x, A_y] = A_z \qquad [A_y, A_z] = A_x \qquad [A_z, A_x] = A_y\\
&[B_x, B_y] = B_z \qquad [B_y, B_z] = B_x \qquad [B_z, B_x] = B_y
\end{aligned} \qquad (15.34)$$

together with $[A_q, B_{q'}] = 0$ for all q and q'. In other words if we regard the A_q and B_q as the infinitesimal operators they will describe a product group because all A_q commute with all B_q. Furthermore the commutation relations (15.34) of the A_q and B_q separately are precisely those of the group $\mathscr{R}_3$, see equation (7.25). Thus the A_q, B_q describe the infinitesimal operators of the product group $\mathscr{R}_3 \times \mathscr{R}_3$. This does not mean that $\mathscr{L}$ and $\mathscr{R}_3 \times \mathscr{R}_3$ are isomorphic because in $\mathscr{L}$ the X_q and Y_q appear with real coefficients, while in $\mathscr{R}_3 \times \mathscr{R}_3$ it is the A_q and B_q which have real coefficients. However it does enable us to deduce and label the irreducible representation of $\mathscr{L}$ from those of $\mathscr{R}_3 \times \mathscr{R}_3$ because the arguments are based on the algebra of the infinitesimal operators as in section 7.4.

15.2.5 The irreducible representations

We now move away from the basic four-space of the Lorentz group to study representations in more general vector spaces. We shall however use the same notation for the infinitesimal operators, so that whereas in the preceding section A_q and B_q have denoted 4×4 matrices, in the following they will denote the corresponding operators in some vector space which provides the basis of the representation. We know from the general arguments of section 7.1 that the commutators of the infinitesimal operators are the same in all representations and may therefore be taken from equation (15.32).

Since the structure of the irreducible representations $D^{(j)}$ of $\mathscr{R}_3$ was deduced in subsection 7.4.2 entirely from the commutation relations and since the irreducible representations of a product group are labelled by a pair of labels, one for an irreducible representation of each group, it follows that the finite dimensional irreducible representations of the Lorentz group may be labelled by a pair of indices j and j' which take values $0, \frac{1}{2}, 1, \frac{3}{2}, \ldots$, etc., as for $\mathcal{R}_3$. These representations, for which we use the notation $L^{(j,j')}$ have dimension $(2j+1)(2j'+1)$. It may be shown that the representations with j and j' both integers and those with j and j' both half-integers are single valued, but those with one index an integer and the other a half-integer are double valued.

The two indices may be interpreted in terms of the eigenvalues of the two Casimir operators (see section 7.5) $\mathbf{A}^2 = A_x^2 + A_y^2 + A_z^2$ and $\mathbf{B}^2 = B_x^2 + B_y^2 + B_z^2$. Using equation (7.36) and remembering the factor i introduced just before equation (7.26) we have eigenvalues $-j(j+1)$ and $-j'(j'+1)$ for $\mathbf{A}^2$ and $\mathbf{B}^2$. Alternatively, and for convenience later, we may use the two combinations given below

$$\begin{aligned} \mathbf{X}^2 - \mathbf{Y}^2 &= 2(\mathbf{A}^2 + \mathbf{B}^2) \text{ with eigenvalue } -2\{j(j+1) + j'(j'+1)\} \\ \mathbf{X}.\mathbf{Y} &= -i(\mathbf{A}^2 - \mathbf{B}^2) \text{ with eigenvalue } i\{j(j+1) - j'(j'+1)\} \end{aligned} \qquad (15.35)$$

The basis vectors of the representation $L^{(j,j')}$ may be denoted by $e^{jj'}_{mm'}$ where, as in the group $\mathcal{R}_3$, the lower indices $m = j, (j-1), \ldots, -j$ and $m' = j', (j'-1), \ldots, -j'$ denote the eigenvalues of A_z and B_z. Precisely, quoting from subsection 7.3.5 we have

$$A_z e^{jj'}_{mm'} = -ime^{jj'}_{mm'}, \quad B_z e^{jj'}_{mm'} = -im' e^{jj'}_{mm'} \qquad (15.36)$$

The 4×4 Lorentz matrices L must themselves form a single-valued four-dimensional representation which can only be $L^{(\frac{1}{2},\frac{1}{2})}$. To verify this we need only calculate from (15.31) and (7.24) the matrices

$$\mathbf{X}^2 - \mathbf{Y}^2 = \begin{pmatrix} -2 & 0 & 0 & 0 \\ 0 & -2 & 0 & 0 \\ 0 & 0 & -2 & 0 \\ 0 & 0 & 0 & 0 \end{pmatrix} - \begin{pmatrix} 1 & 0 & 0 & 0 \\ 0 & 1 & 0 & 0 \\ 0 & 0 & 1 & 0 \\ 0 & 0 & 0 & 3 \end{pmatrix} = -3$$

and $\quad \mathbf{X}.\mathbf{Y} = 0$

which agrees with the formulae (15.35) when $j = j' = \frac{1}{2}$. One may even go further and deduce the matrices of the operators X_q and Y_q knowing the matrices (see equations (7.40) and (7.39)) of the infinitesimal operators of $\mathcal{R}_3$. Thus for example the matrices (15.31) may be deduced from the $D^{(\frac{1}{2})}$ matrices by a suitable change of basis (see problem 15.5). In particular it is worth noting that $X_z = A_z + B_z$ so that from equation (15.36) the basis vector of $L^{(j,j')}$ labelled by m, m' will be an eigenvector of X_z with eigenvalue $-i(m+m')$ and will transform according to the representation $T^{(m+m')}$ of the group $\mathcal{R}_2$ of physical rotations about the z-axis.

The reduction of products of two irreducible representations of $\mathcal{L}$ is given from the corresponding rule for the rotation group. The result is

$$L^{(j_1,j_1')} \times L^{(j_2,j_2')} = \sum_{J,J'} L^{(J,J')} \qquad (15.37)$$

where $|j_1 - j_2| \leqq J \leqq (j_1 + j_2)$ and $|j'_1 - j'_2| \leqq J' \leqq (j'_1 + j'_2)$.

The physical rotation group $\mathscr{R}_3$ is a subgroup of the Lorentz group $\mathscr{L}$ and hence $L^{(j,j')}$ must reduce into a sum of irreducible representations $D^{(J)}$ on restriction from $\mathscr{L}$ to $\mathscr{R}_3$. The rule is

$$L^{(j,j')} = \dot{\sum_{|j-j'| \leqq J \leqq (j+j')}} D^{(J)} \tag{15.38}$$

which may be derived simply in two steps. First we note from equation (15.37) that

$$L^{(j,0)} \times L^{(0,j')} = L^{(j,j')}$$

But in the representation $L^{(j,0)}$ we must have $B_q = 0$ so that $X_q = A_q$. Hence for rotations $L^{(j,0)} \equiv D^{(j)}$. In the same way $L^{(0,j')} \equiv D^{(j')}$, so far as rotations are concerned, and this gives the desired result (15.38) using equation (7.44). As an example of this result we have

$$L^{(\frac{1}{2},\frac{1}{2})} = D^{(1)} \dot{+} D^{(0)}$$

which is to be expected since the 4×4 Lorentz matrices themselves give the representation $L^{(\frac{1}{2},\frac{1}{2})}$ and the four-space breaks up into the three-space components, which transform like $D^{(1)}$, and the time component which is rotation invariant.

We should also notice that whereas for the group $\mathscr{R}_3$ the complex conjugate of a representation $D^{(j)}$ is equivalent to $D^{(j)}$ with a change of basis $e^*_m = (-1)^{j-m} e_{-m}$ in the notation of subsection 7.4.2 (see also section 7.7), the complex conjugate of $L^{(j,j')}$ is equivalent to $L^{(j',j)}$, a distinct representation. Thus $L^{(j,j')}$ is equivalent to its complex conjugate only when $j = j'$. The justification for this statement comes directly from equation (15.33) but we must be careful to distinguish the operator A_q in the complex conjugate representation which we denote by $(A_q)^*$ from the complex conjugate A^*_q of the operator A_q. Now, in the complex conjugate representation, X_q and Y_q are replaced by X^*_q and Y^*_q so that

$$(A_q)^* = X^*_q + iY^*_q = (X_q - iY_q)^* = B^*_q$$

Since the representations $D^{(j)}$ of $\mathscr{R}_3$ are self-conjugate this implies an interchange of j and j'.

Notice also that the representations $L^{(j,j')}$ are not unitary. To be unitary, the infinitesimal operators must be skew-Hermitian, i.e. have pure imaginary eigenvalues. But we have seen, in discussing $\mathscr{R}_3$ in section 7.4, that A_q and B_q are skew-Hermitian so that from equation (15.33) X_q is skew-Hermitian but Y_q is Hermitian. Thus no matter what basis we choose, these finite-dimensional irreducible representations of the Lorentz group are not unitary. The identity representation $L^{(0,0)} = 1$ is naturally an exception to this result.

15.3 The Lorentz group with space inversions $\mathscr{L}_s$

The addition of the space inversion I to the rotation group $\mathscr{R}_3$ was a trivial process. The inversion commutes with rotations, leading to the product group $O_3 = \mathscr{R}_3 \times S_2$ (see section 7.4) and the irreducible representations of O_3 are labelled by the pair of labels j, π, where $\pi = \pm$ is the parity.

The addition of the space inversion I to the Lorentz group $\mathscr{L}$ is not so simple because I does not commute with the Lorentz transformations. However from the separation (15.27) of an arbitrary L into a rotation $\mathrm{R}(\boldsymbol{a})$ and a boost $\mathrm{Q}(\boldsymbol{b})$ we need only concern ourselves with the products of I with boosts. For the particular boost $\mathrm{Q}_z(b)$ one sees from the matrix (15.24) and the matrix

$$\mathrm{I} = \begin{pmatrix} -1 & 0 & 0 & 0 \\ 0 & -1 & 0 & 0 \\ 0 & 0 & -1 & 0 \\ 0 & 0 & 0 & 1 \end{pmatrix} \tag{15.39}$$

that $\mathrm{IQ}_z(b) = \mathrm{Q}_z(-b)\mathrm{I}$, and it is clear that this will be true for any direction in place of z. Thus $\mathrm{IQ}(\boldsymbol{b}) = \mathrm{Q}(-\boldsymbol{b})\mathrm{I}$ or in other words $\mathrm{IQ}(\boldsymbol{b})\mathrm{I} = \mathrm{Q}(-\boldsymbol{b})$ showing that I simply changes the direction of the boost, a result which might have been expected. In terms of infinitesimals this means that

$$\mathrm{IX}_q = \mathrm{X}_q\mathrm{I}, \qquad \mathrm{IY}_q = -\mathrm{Y}_q\mathrm{I} \tag{15.40}$$

so that

$$\mathrm{A}_q\mathrm{I} = \mathrm{IB}_q \quad \text{and} \quad \mathrm{B}_q\mathrm{I} = \mathrm{IA}_q \tag{15.41a}$$

which implies that

$$\mathrm{A}^2\mathrm{I} = \mathrm{IB}^2 \quad \text{and} \quad \mathrm{B}^2\mathrm{I} = \mathrm{IA}^2 \tag{15.41b}$$

The structure and labelling of the irreducible representations of the group $\mathscr{L}_s$ may now be deduced quite simply from these multiplication laws which are of course valid not only in the 4×4 matrices but in all representations. As in the preceding section, we still use the same notation A_q, etc., to denote both the infinitesimal 4×4 matrices and the corresponding operators in a general representation. However, in line with the notation of section 4.1, we use the notation T(I) for the transformations induced by the inversion operator I in a general representation space.

Let us denote the basis vectors of an irreducible representation $\mathrm{L}^{(j,j')}$ of $\mathscr{L}$ by $\boldsymbol{e}^{jj'}_{mm'}$ with $m = j, (j-1), \ldots, -j$, $m' = j', (j'-1), \ldots, -j'$. Then using (15.41)

$$\mathbf{A}^2[\mathrm{T(I)}\boldsymbol{e}^{jj'}_{mm'}] = \mathrm{T(I)}\mathbf{B}^2\boldsymbol{e}^{jj'}_{mm'} = -j'(j'+1)[\mathrm{T(I)}\boldsymbol{e}^{jj'}_{mm'}]$$

while

$$\mathbf{B}^2[\mathrm{T(I)}\boldsymbol{e}^{jj'}_{mm'}] = -j(j+1)[\mathrm{T(I)}\boldsymbol{e}^{jj'}_{mm'}]$$

and similarly, using equations (15.36) and (15.41a)

$$A_z[T(I)\boldsymbol{e}^{jj'}_{mm'}] = -im'[T(I)\boldsymbol{e}^{jj'}_{mm'}] \tag{15.42}$$

while

$$B_z[T(I)\boldsymbol{e}^{jj'}_{mm'}] = -im[T(I)\boldsymbol{e}^{jj'}_{mm'}]$$

From the set of equations (15.42) one concludes that the set of $(2j+1)(2j'+1)$ vectors $T(I)\boldsymbol{e}^{jj'}_{mm'}$ form the basis of a representation $L^{(j',j)}$ of $\mathscr{L}$ and in fact we use the notation

$$\boldsymbol{f}^{j'j}_{m'm} = T(I)\boldsymbol{e}^{jj'}_{mm'} \tag{15.43}$$

Furthermore, since $I^2 = E$, the identity, we have

$$\boldsymbol{e}^{jj'}_{mm'} = T(I)\boldsymbol{f}^{j'j}_{m'm}$$

Now so long as $j' \neq j$, the vectors $\boldsymbol{e}^{jj'}_{mm'}$ and $\boldsymbol{f}^{j'j}_{mm'}$ must be linearly independent and so, from the above equations, the set of $2(2j+1)(2j'+1)$ vectors $\boldsymbol{e}^{jj'}_{mm'}$ and $\boldsymbol{f}^{j'j}_{mm'}$ with fixed j and j' is invariant under all the operators A_q, B_q and I of the group $\mathscr{L}_s$. Hence they form an irreducible representation which we shall denote by $L_s^{(j,j')}$, although the order of j and j' is irrelevant in this case. Clearly, on restriction to the subgroup $\mathscr{L}$ we have the reduction

$$L_s^{(j,j')} = L^{(j,j')} \dot{+} L^{(j',j)} \tag{15.44}$$

From equation (15.43) we see that the basis vectors $\boldsymbol{e}$ and $\boldsymbol{f}$ do not have definite parity. This may be achieved only by taking the combinations

$$\boldsymbol{e}^{jj'}_{mm'} \pm \boldsymbol{f}^{j'j}_{m'm} \tag{15.45}$$

which have even or odd parity depending on the sign $\pm$. These combinations, although not eigenfunctions of $\mathbf{A}^2$ or $\mathbf{B}^2$, are nevertheless eigenfunctions of the operator $\mathbf{X}^2 - \mathbf{Y}^2$ defined in equation (15.35).

A separate discussion is required for the special case of $j = j'$ since the vectors $\boldsymbol{e}^{jj}_{mm'}$ and $\boldsymbol{f}^{jj}_{mm'}$ are not then necessarily linearly independent. In fact we shall show that the representation generated from $\boldsymbol{e}^{jj}_{mm'}$ is not irreducible if they are linearly independent. This is done by using a *reductio ad absurdum* argument. Suppose that $\boldsymbol{f}^{jj}_{mm'}$ and $\boldsymbol{e}^{jj}_{mm'}$ were independent, then the irreducible representation which contains $\boldsymbol{e}^{jj}_{mm'}$ must also contain the basis vectors $\boldsymbol{f}^{jj}_{mm'}$ and so have dimension $2(2j+1)^2$. But since

$$T(I)(\boldsymbol{e}^{jj}_{mm'} + \boldsymbol{f}^{jj}_{mm'}) = \boldsymbol{f}^{jj}_{m'm} + \boldsymbol{e}^{jj}_{m'm}$$

and as in equation (15.42), both $\boldsymbol{e}$ and $\boldsymbol{f}$ transform identically under A_q and B_q, it follows that the subspace of $(2j+1)^2$ basis vectors $(\boldsymbol{e}^{jj}_{mm'} + \boldsymbol{f}^{jj}_{mm'})$ is invariant under all the group operations. Thus the representation will have reduced, contrary to the hypothesis that it is irreducible. The only escape from this contradiction is that $\boldsymbol{f}^{jj}_{mm'} = c\boldsymbol{e}^{jj}_{mm'}$, for some constant c and since $I^2 = E$ then $c^2 = 1$ and $c = \pm 1$. Thus, for each j, there are two possible $(2j+1)^2$-dimensional irreducible representations of $\mathscr{L}_s$ which we denote by $L^{(j+)}$ and

$L^{(j-)}$ which are both identical with $L^{(j,j)}$ for proper Lorentz transformation and have the respective properties

$$T(I)e^{jj}_{mm'} = e^{jj}_{m'm} \qquad \text{for } L^{(j+)} \qquad (15.46)$$

and

$$T(I)e^{jj}_{mm'} = -e^{jj}_{m'm} \qquad \text{for } L^{(j-)}$$

Notice that the $\pm$ sign on $L^{(j\pm)}$ does *not* mean that all the basis vectors have even or odd parity. The equations (15.46) show that T(I) is not diagonal in the mm'-basis. For example, the four-dimensional representation of the matrices L is the $L^{(\frac{1}{2}-)}$ representation. The basis $\hat{e}_x, \hat{e}_y, \hat{e}_z, \hat{e}_t$ in which it was set up actually has T(I) in diagonal form with three odd-parity vectors and one of even parity. From equation (15.46) the matrix of T(I) in the mm'-basis would be

$$T(I) = \begin{pmatrix} -1 & 0 & 0 & 0 \\ 0 & 0 & -1 & 0 \\ 0 & -1 & 0 & 0 \\ 0 & 0 & 0 & -1 \end{pmatrix}$$

15.4 Translations and the Poincaré group $\mathscr{P}$

The previous two sections have been concerned with the (homogeneous) Lorentz transformations, which leave the origin unmoved. We now consider the inclusion of space–time translations with the Lorentz group which generates the Poincaré group $\mathscr{P}$ or, as it is sometimes called, the inhomogeneous Lorentz group. We begin with a short section on the translations themselves before moving on to the Poincaré group. The inclusion of the improper elements of space and time inversion is left for later sections, as is the discussion of the physical significance of the different representations of the Poincaré group.

15.4.1 Translations in space–time

We define translations in space–time by simply extending the arguments of subsection 15.1.1 to a fourth dimension. The translation operator is written $P(\hat{\varepsilon})$, where $\hat{\varepsilon} = (\varepsilon_x, \varepsilon_y, \varepsilon_z, \varepsilon_t)$ is a four-vector parameter, and is defined by the equation

$$P(\hat{\varepsilon})\hat{e} = \hat{e} + \hat{\varepsilon} \qquad (15.47)$$

Notice that the time translation adds a quantity ε_t to the value of ct, corresponding to a change ε_t/c in t. As usual, the infinitesimal operators P_x, P_y, P_z, P_t are defined by writing, for small $\hat{\varepsilon}$,

$$P(\hat{\varepsilon}) = 1 + \varepsilon_x P_x + \varepsilon_y P_y + \varepsilon_z P_z - \varepsilon_t P_t = 1 - \hat{\varepsilon}.\hat{\mathbf{P}} \qquad (15.48)$$

The choice of a negative sign in this definition of P_t means that it denotes a negative time translation, whereas the space components denote positive translations as in section 15.1. The reason for this apparently perverse definition is to make P_x, P_y, P_z and P_t the components of a four-vector $\hat{\mathbf{P}}$. They then transform like the components of any other four-vector when going from one frame to another, see problem 15.6, and we are able to use the scalar product in equation (15.48). (Had we not introduced this negative sign we would have needed to distinguish between covariant and contravariant vectors, see the note in subsection 15.2.1.) The four-dimensional translation group is an Abelian product group just as in three dimensions so that the irreducible representations are one-dimensional and labelled by four numbers k_x, k_y, k_z and k_t. By defining the four-vector $\hat{\boldsymbol{k}} = (k_x, k_y, k_z, k_t)$ we may write the representation as $T^{(\hat{\boldsymbol{k}})}$, and if we denote the basis vector by $|\hat{\boldsymbol{k}}\rangle$ then the representation is given by

$$T(\hat{\varepsilon})|\hat{\boldsymbol{k}}\rangle = \exp(i\hat{\boldsymbol{k}}.\hat{\varepsilon})|\hat{\boldsymbol{k}}\rangle \tag{15.49}$$

For the three-space translations this is consistent with subsection 15.1.1 and is the defining equation for the parameters $\hat{\boldsymbol{k}}$.

Comparing the preceding two equations shows that in $T^{(\hat{\boldsymbol{k}})}$ the infinitesimal operators have the values $\hat{\mathbf{P}} \equiv -i\hat{\boldsymbol{k}}$. If we consider the explicit form of the infinitesimal operators on a function $\psi(\hat{e})$ of position $\hat{e}$ then we have for small $\hat{\varepsilon}$, following subsection 7.3.5,

$$T(\hat{\varepsilon})\psi(\hat{e}) = \psi(\hat{e}-\hat{\varepsilon}) = \psi(\hat{e}) - \left(\sum_q \varepsilon_q \frac{\partial}{\partial e_q} + \varepsilon_t \frac{\partial}{\partial(ct)}\right)\psi(\hat{e}) \tag{15.50}$$

so that from equation (15.48),

$$P_x \equiv -\frac{\partial}{\partial x}, \quad P_y \equiv -\frac{\partial}{\partial y}, \quad P_z = -\frac{\partial}{\partial z} \text{ and } P_t = \frac{1}{c}\frac{\partial}{\partial t} \tag{15.51}$$

As an example of a typical function transforming like $T^{(\hat{\boldsymbol{k}})}$ we choose

$$\psi(\hat{e}) = \exp(-i\hat{\boldsymbol{k}}.\hat{e}) = \exp(i\boldsymbol{k}.\boldsymbol{r} - ik_t ct) \tag{15.52}$$

where $\boldsymbol{k}$ and k_t denote the three-space part and fourth component of $\hat{\boldsymbol{k}}$, respectively.

In discussing the physical significance of the space–time translations we need only consider the time translation since we have already seen in subsection 15.1.1 how translation invariance in space leads to momentum conservation. Invariance under time translation means that the infinitesimal operator P_t must also represent a conserved quantity, which we call energy. Again this operator is skew-Hermitian and has inappropriate dimension. The actual energy operator is written $H = i\hbar c P_t$. The invariance of the Hamiltonian under time translations means that it does not depend explicitly on the time. For a Hamiltonian which is invariant under translations in both space and time one expects to find states labelled by $\hat{\boldsymbol{k}}$ corresponding to momentum $\hbar\boldsymbol{k}$, as explained in subsection 15.1.1, and energy $i\hbar c(-ik_t) = \hbar c k_t$ which is usually denoted by E. For a system with time translation symmetry only we retain only the label k_t or E. In fact the familiar expression (5.3) for a stationary state simply reflects the fact that under time translations it transforms according to the representation labelled by $k_t = E/\hbar c$. We note that the Schrodinger equation (5.2) is obtained by equating the explicit form $i\hbar\ \partial/\partial t$ for the energy operator, deduced from P_t to some assumed form such as T + V for the energy operator H. Notice that since $\hat{P}$ is a four-vector operator it follows that the energy and momentum operators come together into a four-vector operator $(p_x, p_y, p_z, H/c)$ with eigenvalues $\hbar(k_x, k_y, k_z, k_t)$. In classical mechanics also, one sees that the lack of any explicit time dependence in the Hamiltonian leads to the conservation of energy (see subsection 16.1.2).

In principle, k_t may take either sign which would imply both positive and negative energies. There are difficulties in assigning physical significance to states with negative energies; for example, why should the positive energy states not decay into them? The postulate that all negative energy states are occupied has been made but was never satisfactory. The modern interpretation is to postulate that all free particles have positive energy since this is consistent with observation. Nevertheless the representations corresponding to negative k_t have a role to play when one constructs a quantum field. We discuss this role briefly in chapter 16.

15.4.2 The Poincaré group and its representations

The Poincaré group $\mathscr{P}$ is obtained by including both Lorentz transformations L and translations $P(\hat{\varepsilon})$ and their products. These two kinds of transformation do not commute but they have a simple multiplication law. To find it, consider the two products

$$P(\hat{\varepsilon})L\hat{e} = L\hat{e} + \hat{\varepsilon}$$

and

$$LP(\hat{\varepsilon})\hat{e} = L(\hat{e} + \hat{\varepsilon}) = L\hat{e} + L\hat{\varepsilon}$$

from which one concludes that

$$LP(\hat{\varepsilon}) = P(L\hat{\varepsilon})L \tag{15.53}$$

The most general Poincaré transformation may therefore be written

$$\hat{e}' = P(\hat{\varepsilon})L\hat{e} = L\hat{e} + \hat{\varepsilon} \tag{15.54}$$

with the Lorentz transformation acting first, followed by the translation. The group $\mathscr{P}$ is very similar to the Euclidean group of section 15.1 except that there are now four dimensions and the rotations have been replaced by Lorentz transformations. There are now ten parameters, six from L and four from $P(\hat{\varepsilon})$. We shall use the notation $T(\hat{\varepsilon}, L)$ to denote the transformation induced in representation space by the Poincaré transformation $P(\hat{\varepsilon})L$ and, as usual, the operations $T(\hat{\varepsilon}, L)$ will satisfy the same multiplication rules as the corresponding group operations.

We now construct the irreducible representations of the group $\mathscr{P}$ following closely the four steps described in subsection 15.1.3 for the Euclidean group.

Step (1). We choose the basis vectors $|\hat{\boldsymbol{k}}\rangle$ to belong to irreducible representations of the translation subgroup and thus to satisfy equation (15.49).

Step (2). Next we argue that an irreducible representation containing $|\hat{\boldsymbol{k}}\rangle$ must also contain basis vectors $|\hat{\boldsymbol{k}}'\rangle$, where $\hat{\boldsymbol{k}}' = \mathrm{L}\hat{\boldsymbol{k}}$ for all L. In other words $\hat{\boldsymbol{k}}'$ has the same 'length' as $\hat{\boldsymbol{k}}$ and lies in the same region of space – time in the sense defined in subsections 15.2.1 and 15.2.2. To justify this statement consider

$$\begin{aligned}\mathrm{T}(\hat{\varepsilon})\,\mathrm{T}(\mathrm{L})|\hat{\boldsymbol{k}}\rangle &= \mathrm{T}(\mathrm{L})\,\mathrm{T}(\mathrm{L}^{-1}\hat{\varepsilon})|\hat{\boldsymbol{k}}\rangle\\ &= \mathrm{T}(\mathrm{L})\exp(i\hat{\boldsymbol{k}}\,.\,\mathrm{L}^{-1}\hat{\varepsilon})|\hat{\boldsymbol{k}}\rangle\\ &= \exp(i\mathrm{L}\hat{\boldsymbol{k}}\,.\,\hat{\varepsilon})\mathrm{T}(\mathrm{L})|\hat{\boldsymbol{k}}\rangle \qquad (15.55)\end{aligned}$$

using equations (15.53), (15.49) and (15.22). Thus if $|\hat{\boldsymbol{k}}\rangle$ is a basis vector then $\mathrm{T}(\mathrm{L})|\hat{\boldsymbol{k}}\rangle$, which must also belong to the representation, transforms according to the representation of the translation group labelled by $\hat{\boldsymbol{k}}' = \mathrm{L}\hat{\boldsymbol{k}}$, and the assertion above is proved.

The irreducible representations of $\mathscr{P}$ may therefore be first classified according to the region of four-space in which the four-vector $\hat{\boldsymbol{k}}$ lies and as we saw in subsection 15.2.2 there are six regions. The structure of the representation is quite different for each region so that the remaining two steps must be discussed separately for each region.

Region (6), $\hat{\boldsymbol{k}} = 0$

This case may be quickly disposed of since with $\hat{\boldsymbol{k}} = 0$ all basis vectors must be invariant under translations and the group is effectively restricted from $\mathscr{P}$ to $\mathscr{L}$. The irreducible representations are then simply the $\mathrm{L}^{(j,j')}$ described in subsection 15.2.5.

Regions (2) and (3), time-like $\hat{\boldsymbol{k}}$ (the representations $\mathrm{P}^{(k,s)}$)

Step (3). To construct the irreducible representations in this case we choose, for convenience, the simple time-like vector $\hat{\boldsymbol{k}}_0 = (0, 0, 0, k)$ of length k. To be definite, we take only $k > 0$, the future time-like case, corresponding to region (2). Identical results follow for the past time-like case. Since $\hat{\boldsymbol{k}}_o$ is unchanged by any rotation $\mathrm{R}(\boldsymbol{a})$ it follows from equation (15.55) that the vector $\mathrm{T}(\mathrm{R}(\boldsymbol{a}))|\hat{\boldsymbol{k}}_0\rangle$ transforms like $|\hat{\boldsymbol{k}}_0\rangle$ under translations. Hence the set of all basis vectors which transform like $|\hat{\boldsymbol{k}}_0\rangle$ in a representation forms an invariant space under $\mathscr{R}_3$, so that they may be simultaneously labelled by $\hat{\boldsymbol{k}}_0$ and by an irreducible representation label of the group $\mathscr{R}_3$. We use the symbol $s(= 0, \frac{1}{2}, 1, \frac{3}{2}, \ldots)$ for the $\mathscr{R}_3$ representation label and $m_s = s, s-1, \ldots, -s$ to label the $\mathscr{R}_3$ basis vector (see subsection 7.4.2), so that we henceforth write $|\hat{\boldsymbol{k}}_0 s m_s\rangle$ in place of

$|\hat{\boldsymbol{k}}_0\rangle$. In the notation of subsection 7.4.2 there will then be a set of $(2s+1)$ basis vectors with the property

$$\mathrm{T}(\mathrm{R}(\boldsymbol{a}))|\hat{\boldsymbol{k}}_0 s m_s\rangle = \sum_{m_s'} D^{(s)}_{m_s' m_s}(\boldsymbol{a})|\hat{\boldsymbol{k}}_0 s m_s'\rangle \tag{15.56}$$

as well as the property (15.49).

Step (4). Starting from these $(2s+1)$ basis vectors we now argue that the representation is generated by constructing all vectors of the kind

$$|\hat{\boldsymbol{k}} s m_s\rangle = \mathrm{T}(\mathrm{Q}[\boldsymbol{b}(\hat{\boldsymbol{k}})])|\hat{\boldsymbol{k}}_0 s m_s\rangle \tag{15.57}$$

where $\hat{\boldsymbol{k}}$ is any four-vector in the same region as $\hat{\boldsymbol{k}}_0$ and having the same 'length' and $\boldsymbol{b}(\hat{\boldsymbol{k}})$ describes that unique pure Lorentz transformation which carries $\hat{\boldsymbol{k}}_0$ into $\hat{\boldsymbol{k}}$, i.e.

$$\mathrm{Q}[\boldsymbol{b}(\hat{\boldsymbol{k}})]\hat{\boldsymbol{k}}_0 = \hat{\boldsymbol{k}} \tag{15.58}$$

One sees from equation (15.26) that the three-vector $\boldsymbol{b}(\hat{\boldsymbol{k}})$ has magnitude $\cosh^{-1}(k_t/k)$ and direction $-\boldsymbol{k}$, where $\boldsymbol{k}$ denotes the three-vector part of $\hat{\boldsymbol{k}}$ and k_t its fourth component.

To show that the set (15.57) with fixed $\hat{\boldsymbol{k}}_0$ and s forms the basis of a representation we consider the effect of an arbitrary group operation. In doing this we shall need to use the result (15.27) that an arbitrary Lorentz transformation may be written as a product of a pure Lorentz transformation and a rotation. We have

$$\mathrm{T}(\hat{\varepsilon},\mathrm{L})|\hat{\boldsymbol{k}} s m_s\rangle = \mathrm{T}(\hat{\varepsilon})\mathrm{T}(\mathrm{L})\mathrm{T}(\mathrm{Q}[\boldsymbol{b}(\hat{\boldsymbol{k}})])|\hat{\boldsymbol{k}}_0 s m_s\rangle \quad \text{using equation (15.57)}$$

$$= \mathrm{T}(\hat{\varepsilon})\mathrm{T}(\mathrm{L}')|\hat{\boldsymbol{k}}_0 s m_s\rangle \quad \text{where } \mathrm{L}' = \mathrm{L}\mathrm{Q}[\boldsymbol{b}(\hat{\boldsymbol{k}})]$$

$$= \mathrm{T}(\hat{\varepsilon})\mathrm{T}(\mathrm{Q}')\mathrm{T}(\mathrm{R}')|\hat{\boldsymbol{k}}_0 s m_s\rangle \quad \text{using equation (15.27)}$$

$$= \mathrm{T}(\hat{\varepsilon})\mathrm{T}(\mathrm{Q}')\sum_{m_s'} D^{(s)}_{m_s' m_s}(\mathrm{R}')|\hat{\boldsymbol{k}}_0 s m_s'\rangle \quad \text{using equation (15.56)}$$

$$= \mathrm{T}(\hat{\varepsilon})\sum_{m_s'} D^{(s)}_{m_s' m_s}(\mathrm{R}')|\hat{\boldsymbol{k}}' s m_s'\rangle \quad \text{using equation (15.57) with } \hat{\boldsymbol{k}}' = \mathrm{Q}'\hat{\boldsymbol{k}}_0$$

$$= \exp(i\hat{\boldsymbol{k}}'.\hat{\varepsilon})\sum_{m_s'} D^{(s)}_{m_s' m_s}(\mathrm{R}')|\hat{\boldsymbol{k}}' s m_s'\rangle \quad \text{using equation (15.49).} \tag{15.59}$$

Notice that the vector $\hat{\boldsymbol{k}}'$ is given simply by $\hat{\boldsymbol{k}}' = \mathrm{L}\hat{\boldsymbol{k}}$ because

$$\hat{\boldsymbol{k}}' = \mathrm{Q}'\hat{\boldsymbol{k}}_0 = \mathrm{L}'(\mathrm{R}')^{-1}\hat{\boldsymbol{k}}_0 = \mathrm{L}'\hat{\boldsymbol{k}}_0 = \mathrm{L}\mathrm{Q}[\boldsymbol{b}(\hat{\boldsymbol{k}})]\hat{\boldsymbol{k}}_0 = \mathrm{L}\hat{\boldsymbol{k}}$$

but this result was to be expected from equation (15.55). The parameters of the rotation R′ may be deduced for any given $\hat{\boldsymbol{k}}$ and L from the defining equations

$$\mathrm{L}' = \mathrm{Q}'\mathrm{R}' \tag{15.60}$$

and

$$\mathrm{L}' = \mathrm{L}\mathrm{Q}[\boldsymbol{b}(\hat{\boldsymbol{k}})] \tag{15.61}$$

but we shall not go into any details.

The equation (15.59) shows that the set (15.57) of basis vectors is invariant under the general Poincaré transformation, and so forms the basis for a representation which we might denote by $P^{(\hat{k}_0,s)}$. It may be shown, as for the Euclidean group in subsection 15.1.3, that representations generated from any future time-like vector $\hat{k}$ with the same 'length' as $\hat{k}_0$ are equivalent to $P^{(\hat{k}_0,s)}$. The inequivalent representations are therefore denoted simply by $P^{(k,s)}$ where the index k denotes the 'length' of all the vectors $\hat{k}$ which occur in the basis vectors $|\hat{k}sm_s\rangle$. The proof that the representations $P^{(k,s)}$ are irreducible follows the argument referred to in subsection 15.1.3 for the group $\mathscr{E}_3$. Because of the infinite variety of $\hat{k}$ with fixed length, these representations are infinite-dimensional.

Regions (4) and (5), null $\hat{k}$ (the representations $P^{(0,m)}$)

Following step (3), for convenience we again choose a simple vector $\hat{k}_0$, this time in the future null region, namely $\hat{k}_0 = (0, 0, 1, 1)$. (The past null region may be treated in an identical way.) To deduce the irreducible representations we follow the same general procedure as above, but the group which leaves $\hat{k}_0$ unchanged is no longer the group $\mathscr{R}_3$. Our first task is to find this group and for this purpose we turn to the infinitesimal operators. If $\hat{k}_0$ is to be unchanged then $\Lambda\hat{k}_0 = 0$ in the notation of equation (15.30). Carrying out the matrix multiplications with $\hat{k}_0 = (0, 0, 1, 1)$ and the matrices (15.31) leads to the conditions $a_x = -b_y, \quad a_y = b_x, \quad b_z = 0$. The three independent infinitesimal operators which satisfy these conditions may be taken as

$$X_z, X_x - Y_y \text{ and } X_y + Y_x \tag{15.62}$$

Their commutation relations are, from equations (15.32),

$$[X_z, X_x - Y_y] = X_y + Y_x \qquad [X_z, X_y + Y_x] = -X_x + Y_y \tag{15.63}$$

and

$$[X_x - Y_y, X_y + Y_x] = 0$$

The operator X_z generates the group $\mathscr{R}_2$ of rotations about the z-axis and we now show that the commutation relations (15.63) are precisely those of the Euclidean group $\mathscr{E}_2$ which describes rotations and translations in a plane. From equation (15.15) and since translations commute with each other, we deduce the following commutation relations for the infinitesimal operators P_x, P_y and X_z of $\mathscr{E}_2$,

$$[X_z, P_x] = P_y, \quad [X_z, P_y] = -P_x, \quad [P_x, P_y] = 0 \tag{15.64}$$

These are identical with equations (15.63) if we make the following associations: $X_z \to X_z$, $X_x - Y_y \to P_x$, $X_y + Y_x \to P_y$. Thus the subgroup that we are seeking, which leaves $\hat{k}_0$ invariant, is isomorphic with $\mathscr{E}_2$ so far as infinitesimals are concerned, and hence has the same irreducible representations. Physically, the two groups are quite different although they do have one operator X_z in common.

In subsection 15.1.4 we deduced that the irreducible representations of $\mathscr{E}_2$ could be labelled by $E^{(|k|)}$ and $E^{(0,m)}$. We shall not pursue the consequences of choosing $E^{(|k|)}$ for the $\mathscr{E}_2$ group representation since as we shall see later in subsection 15.8.3 this has, as yet, no physical application. It would be relevant in describing a particle with continuous spin but no such particle has been observed. We therefore move directly to the other alternative $E^{(0,m)}$. The fact that $\hat{\boldsymbol{k}}_0$ is invariant under $\mathscr{E}_2$ means that the set of basis vectors transforming like $\hat{\boldsymbol{k}}_0$ under translation is also invariant under $\mathscr{E}_2$. They may therefore be labelled both by $\hat{\boldsymbol{k}}_0$ and the representation $E^{(0,m)}$ of $\mathscr{E}_2$, so we use the notation $|\hat{\boldsymbol{k}}_0 m\rangle$. From the definition of $E^{(0,m)}$ in subsection 15.1.4 these basis vectors must have the properties

$$\begin{aligned} T(R_z(a))|\hat{\boldsymbol{k}}_0 m\rangle &= \exp(-ima)|\hat{\boldsymbol{k}}_0 m\rangle \\ (X_x - Y_y)|\hat{\boldsymbol{k}}_0 m\rangle &= 0 \\ (X_y + Y_x)|\hat{\boldsymbol{k}}_0 m\rangle &= 0 \end{aligned} \tag{15.65}$$

as well as (15.49). The last two equations express the 'translation invariance' of the vectors of $E^{(0,m)}$ for 'translations' in the $\mathscr{E}_2$ group.

In constructing the representation we shall need two more properties of Lorentz transformations. Firstly that there is a unique Lorentz transformation of the kind $R_{xy}Q_z$ which carries $\hat{\boldsymbol{k}}_0$ into any given future null $\hat{\boldsymbol{k}}$. The role of the boost Q_z is to change the magnitudes of the space and time components of $\hat{\boldsymbol{k}}_0$ without affecting the space direction while the rotation R_{xy} about an axis in the xy-plane simply changes this direction. It is not difficult to see that R_{xy} and Q_z are unique, given $\hat{\boldsymbol{k}}$. The second property says that any Lorentz transformation may be expressed in the form

$$L = R_{xy}Q_z\tilde{L} \tag{15.66}$$

where $\tilde{L}$ belongs to the $\mathscr{E}_2$ subgroup which leaves $\hat{\boldsymbol{k}}_0 = (0, 0, 1, 1)$ invariant. To show this result, which is analogous to equation (15.27), we define $\hat{\boldsymbol{k}} = L\hat{\boldsymbol{k}}_0$ and define $R_{xy}Q_z$ by $\hat{\boldsymbol{k}} = R_{xy}Q_z\hat{\boldsymbol{k}}_0$. Then we see that

$$(R_{xy}Q_z)^{-1}L\hat{\boldsymbol{k}}_0 = (R_{xy}Q_z)^{-1}\hat{\boldsymbol{k}} = \hat{\boldsymbol{k}}_0$$

showing that the product $(R_{xy}Q_z)^{-1}L$ leaves $\hat{\boldsymbol{k}}_0$ invariant and therefore that $\tilde{L}$ in equation (15.66) belongs to the $\mathscr{E}_2$ subgroup.

Following step (4), we now construct the representation of $\mathscr{P}$ corresponding to null $\hat{\boldsymbol{k}}$ by generating the set of basis vectors

$$|\hat{\boldsymbol{k}}m\rangle = T(R_{xy}Q_z)|\hat{\boldsymbol{k}}_0 m\rangle \tag{15.67}$$

with any future null $\hat{\boldsymbol{k}}$. To show that this set provides a representation we consider the effect of a general Poincaré operation

$$\begin{aligned} T(\hat{\varepsilon}, L)|\hat{\boldsymbol{k}}m\rangle &= T(\hat{\varepsilon})T(L)T(R_{xy}Q_z)|\hat{\boldsymbol{k}}_0 m\rangle && \text{from equation (15.67)} \\ &= T(\hat{\varepsilon})T(L')|\hat{\boldsymbol{k}}_0 m\rangle && \text{defining } L' = LR_{xy}Q_z \\ &= T(\hat{\varepsilon})T(R'_{xy}Q'_z)T(\tilde{L}')|\hat{\boldsymbol{k}}_0 m\rangle && \text{using equation (15.66)} \end{aligned}$$

$$= \mathrm{T}(\mathscr{E})\mathrm{T}(\mathrm{R}'_{xy}\mathrm{Q}'_z)\exp(-ima)|\hat{k}_0 m\rangle \quad \text{from equation (15.65), defining } a$$
$$= \mathrm{T}(\mathscr{E})\exp(-ima)|\hat{k}' m\rangle \quad \text{using equation (15.67) with } \hat{k}' = \mathrm{R}'_{xy}\mathrm{Q}'_z\hat{k}_0$$
$$= \exp(i\hat{k}'.\mathscr{E} - ima)|\hat{k}' m\rangle \quad \text{from equation (15.49).} \qquad (15.68)$$

One quickly deduces that $\hat{k}'$ is given simply by $\hat{k}' = \mathrm{L}\hat{k}$ but the value of the $\mathscr{R}_2$ rotation angle a must be deduced in detail from its defining equations. L′ is known from $\hat{k}$ and L and the factorisation (15.66) of L′ then gives L′, an element of $\mathscr{E}_2$. But elements of $\mathscr{E}_2$ are products of a 'translation' with an $\mathscr{R}_2$ rotation. The 'translation' is irrelevant here since $|\hat{k}_0 m\rangle$ is 'translation' invariant, see equation (15.65).

The equation (15.68) shows that the set (15.67) of basis vectors forms a representation, which we denote by $\mathrm{P}^{(0,m)}$. It may be shown, as indicated before, that this representation is irreducible and that the representation generated from an arbitrary future null vector $\hat{k}_0$ is equivalent to the $\mathrm{P}^{(0,m)}$ deduced above for the simple choice $\hat{k}_0 = (0, 0, 1, 1)$. Remember that the index m, which arose from the group $\mathscr{R}_2$ may take the usual values $m = 0, \pm\frac{1}{2}, \pm 1, \ldots,$ etc.

Region (1) space-like $\hat{k}$

The representations of this type may be deduced using the same technique. However we shall not describe them here since, as we shall see in subsection 15.7.1, they would seem to have physical application only for particles with imaginary mass!

15.4.3 Casimir operators

In other continuous groups we have seen the usefulness of the Casimir operator which was introduced in section 7.5. It is constructed from the infinitesimal operators and commutes with them so that in an irreducible representation it is a simple multiple of the unit operator. The multiple relates directly to the labels of the irreducible representation. The two Casimir operators for the Lorentz group $\mathscr{L}$ were given in equation (15.35). We now construct the Casimir operators for the Poincaré group. We have at our disposal the six operators X_q, Y_q of $\mathscr{L}$ and the four infinitesimal translation operators P_q and P_t, where $q = x, y, z$ and P_t denotes the time translation. The commutation relations of the X_q and Y_q are given in equation (15.32), the translations commute among themselves and the commutation relations between translations and Lorentz transformations may be deduced from equation (15.53), see problem 15.7. The results are, in addition to those given in equation (15.15),

$$[\mathrm{P}_t, \mathrm{X}_q] = 0, \quad [\mathrm{P}_q, \mathrm{Y}_{q'}] = -\delta_{q,q'}\mathrm{P}_t, \quad [\mathrm{P}_t, \mathrm{Y}_q] = -\mathrm{P}_q \qquad (15.69)$$

Since $\hat{\mathbf{P}}$ is a four-vector it follows that the operator

$$\hat{\mathbf{P}}.\hat{\mathbf{P}} = -P_x^2 - P_y^2 - P_z^2 + P_t^2$$

is a Lorentz invariant and since it obviously commutes with the translations it is a Poincaré invariant. To deduce its value in a given irreducible representation of $\mathscr{P}$ we note from subsection 15.4.1 that if $|\hat{\boldsymbol{k}}\rangle$ denotes any basis vector transforming like $T^{(\hat{\boldsymbol{k}})}$ under translations then

$$\hat{\mathbf{P}}|\hat{\boldsymbol{k}}\rangle = -i\hat{\boldsymbol{k}}|\hat{\boldsymbol{k}}\rangle \tag{15.70}$$

so that immediately

$$\hat{\mathbf{P}}.\hat{\mathbf{P}}|\hat{\boldsymbol{k}}\rangle = (k_x^2 + k_y^2 + k_z^2 - k_t^2)|\hat{\boldsymbol{k}}\rangle = -k^2|\hat{\boldsymbol{k}}\rangle \tag{15.71}$$

where $k = (\hat{\boldsymbol{k}}.\hat{\boldsymbol{k}})^{\frac{1}{2}}$ is the 'length' of $\hat{\boldsymbol{k}}$. Hence, in the irreducible representation $P^{(k,s)}$ of the group $\mathscr{P}$, the Casimir operator $\hat{\mathbf{P}}.\hat{\mathbf{P}}$ will simply be a multiple $-k^2$ of the unit operator. In the representation $P^{(0,m)}$ the basis vectors all transform like null $\hat{\boldsymbol{k}}$ under translation so that $k = 0$ and $\hat{\mathbf{P}}.\hat{\mathbf{P}}$ has the value zero, although of course $\hat{\boldsymbol{k}} \neq 0$.

It is not possible to form a second Casimir operator by taking only quadratic functions of the infinitesimal operators. This may be seen by noting that, under Lorentz transformations, $\hat{\mathbf{P}}$ transforms according to the representation $L^{(\frac{1}{2},\frac{1}{2})}$, while $\mathbf{X} \pm i\mathbf{Y}$ transform according to $L^{(1,0)}$ and $L^{(0,1)}$, respectively, see subsection 15.2.5. The rule (15.37) for the reduction of product representations tells us that the only quadratic Lorentz invariants are obtained by taking products of any one of these representations with itself, leading to $\hat{\mathbf{P}}.\hat{\mathbf{P}}$ and $\mathbf{X}^2 - \mathbf{Y}^2 \pm 2i\mathbf{X}.\mathbf{Y}$. We already have the first of these and no combination of the others can be made translationally invariant. Another Casimir operator may however be formed by first constructing a translationally invariant four-vector $\hat{\mathbf{W}}$ and then forming the Lorentz invariant scalar product $\hat{\mathbf{W}}.\hat{\mathbf{W}}$. We have already seen in subsection 15.1.5 that the operator $\mathbf{P}.\mathbf{X}$ is invariant under translations and rotations and therefore serves as the t-component of $\hat{\mathbf{W}}$. To find the other components we note that, if $\hat{\mathbf{W}}$ is to be a four-vector operator then its components must satisfy the same commutation relations with $\mathbf{X}$ and $\mathbf{Y}$ as those of $\hat{\mathbf{P}}$. Thus defining $W_t = \mathbf{P}.\mathbf{X}$ we find from equation (15.69), see problem 15.8,

$$W_q = -[W_t, Y_q] = (\mathbf{P} \wedge \mathbf{Y})_q + P_t X_q \tag{15.72}$$

The structure of $\hat{\mathbf{W}}$ could equally well have been found by using the $\mathscr{R}_3$ vector coupling coefficients to produce a resultant $L^{(\frac{1}{2},\frac{1}{2})}$ from the product $L^{(\frac{1}{2},\frac{1}{2})} \times L^{(1,0)}$. The operator $\hat{\mathbf{W}}.\hat{\mathbf{P}}$ would seem to provide a third Casimir operator but one sees from the definition (15.72) that it vanishes identically

$$\hat{\mathbf{W}}.\hat{\mathbf{P}} = 0 \tag{15.73}$$

To find the value of $\hat{\mathbf{W}}.\hat{\mathbf{W}}$ in each of the irreducible representations of the Poincaré group, it is sufficient to choose any basis vector (since Casimir operators are a multiple of the unit operator in any irreducible representation).

Thus for $P^{(k,s)}$ we may choose the basis vector $|\hat{\boldsymbol{k}}_0 sm_s\rangle$ corresponding to $\hat{\boldsymbol{k}}_0 = (0, 0, 0, k)$. Then $P_q|\hat{\boldsymbol{k}}_0 sm_s\rangle = 0$ for $q = x$, y and z, while $P_t|\hat{\boldsymbol{k}}_0 sm_s\rangle = -ik|\hat{\boldsymbol{k}}_0 sm_s\rangle$. Hence from equation (15.72)

$$W_t|\hat{\boldsymbol{k}}_0 sm_s\rangle = 0$$

and $$W_q|\hat{\boldsymbol{k}}_0 sm_s\rangle = -ikX_q|\hat{\boldsymbol{k}}_0 sm_s\rangle$$

so that

$$\hat{\mathbf{W}}.\hat{\mathbf{W}}|\hat{\boldsymbol{k}}_0 sm_s\rangle = k^2\mathbf{X}^2|\hat{\boldsymbol{k}}_0 sm_s\rangle = -k^2 s(s+1)|\hat{\boldsymbol{k}}_0 sm_s\rangle \tag{15.74}$$

We have used the fact that $\mathbf{X}^2$ is just the Casimir operator for the $\mathscr{R}_3$ subgroup whose irreducible representations were labelled by s. The value $s(s+1)$ for the $\mathscr{R}_3$ Casimir operator was deduced in section 7.4 and the negative sign comes from the factor i introduced in section 7.4 when the Hermitian operators J_q were defined as $J_q = iX_q$. The result (15.74) is valid for all vectors belonging to $P^{(k,s)}$.

For the irreducible representations $P^{(0,m)}$ both Casimir operators $\hat{\mathbf{P}}.\hat{\mathbf{P}}$ and $\hat{\mathbf{W}}.\hat{\mathbf{W}}$ have the value zero. The latter result follows by choosing the particular basis vector with $\hat{\boldsymbol{k}}_0 = (0, 0, 1, 1)$ whereupon

$$\begin{aligned}
W_x|\hat{\boldsymbol{k}}_0 m\rangle &= -i(X_x - Y_y)|\hat{\boldsymbol{k}}_0 m\rangle = 0,\\
W_y|\hat{\boldsymbol{k}}_0 m\rangle &= -i(X_y + Y_x)|\hat{\boldsymbol{k}}_0 m\rangle = 0,\\
W_z|\hat{\boldsymbol{k}}_0 m\rangle &= -iX_z|\hat{\boldsymbol{k}}_0 m\rangle = -m|\hat{\boldsymbol{k}}_0 m\rangle\\
W_t|\hat{\boldsymbol{k}}_0 m\rangle &= -iX_z|\hat{\boldsymbol{k}}_0 m\rangle = -m|\hat{\boldsymbol{k}}_0 m\rangle
\end{aligned} \tag{15.75}$$

using equation (15.65) and hence $\hat{\mathbf{W}}.\hat{\mathbf{W}}|\hat{\boldsymbol{k}}_0 m\rangle = 0$.

Since both Casimir operators are zero they cannot serve to distinguish representations $P^{(0,m)}$ with different m. However, in a sense, it is possible to use the ratio of $\hat{\mathbf{W}}$ to $\hat{\mathbf{P}}$ to distinguish between them. For the particular vector $|\hat{\boldsymbol{k}}_0 m\rangle$ the equations (15.75) imply that, since $\hat{\mathbf{P}}|\hat{\boldsymbol{k}}_0 m\rangle = -i\hat{\boldsymbol{k}}|\hat{\boldsymbol{k}}_0 m\rangle$,

$$\hat{\mathbf{W}}|\hat{\boldsymbol{k}}_0 m\rangle = -im\hat{\mathbf{P}}|\hat{\boldsymbol{k}}_0 m\rangle$$

In other words we may write

$$(\hat{\mathbf{W}} + im\hat{\mathbf{P}})|\hat{\boldsymbol{k}}_0 m\rangle = 0 \tag{15.76}$$

However since all basis vectors in the representation are generated by Lorentz transformations (15.67) from $|\hat{\boldsymbol{k}}_0 m\rangle$ and since both $\hat{\mathbf{W}}$ and $\hat{\mathbf{P}}$ are four-vectors, transforming in the same way under Lorentz transformations, it follows that the relation (15.76) is true not only for the special vector $|\hat{\boldsymbol{k}}_0 m\rangle$, but for all $|\hat{\boldsymbol{k}}m\rangle$ in the representation $P^{(0,m)}$ (see problem 15.9). Thus the relation (15.76) may be used, in addition to $\hat{\mathbf{P}}.\hat{\mathbf{P}} = 0$, to characterise the representation $P^{(0,m)}$. It says that the four-vector operators $\hat{\mathbf{W}}$ and $\hat{\mathbf{P}}$ are in the same 'direction' with a proportionality constant $-im$ which depends on the representation. Notice that the relation (15.76) came from a consideration of the *future* null vector $\hat{\boldsymbol{k}}_0 = (0, 0, 1, 1)$ and it is therefore only applicable to the representation referring to future null $\hat{\boldsymbol{k}}$. For the representation relating to past null $\hat{\boldsymbol{k}}$ we must choose $(0, 0, 1, -1)$ in place of $(0, 0, 1, 1)$. This slightly modifies equation (15.76) and leads to the relation

$$(\hat{\mathbf{W}} - im\hat{\mathbf{P}})|\hat{\boldsymbol{k}}m\rangle = 0 \tag{15.77}$$

for all past null $\hat{\boldsymbol{k}}$.

The proportionality that we have established between $\hat{\mathbf{W}}$ and $\hat{\mathbf{P}}$ is not unexpected since, if $\hat{\mathbf{W}}$ and $\hat{\mathbf{P}}$ were ordinary four-vectors rather than operators, the relations $\hat{\boldsymbol{W}}.\hat{\boldsymbol{W}} = \hat{\boldsymbol{P}}.\hat{\boldsymbol{P}} = 0$ together with $\hat{\boldsymbol{W}}.\hat{\boldsymbol{P}} = 0$ imply that $(\hat{\boldsymbol{W}} - \alpha\hat{\boldsymbol{P}}).(\hat{\boldsymbol{W}} - \alpha\hat{\boldsymbol{P}}) = 0$ for all α, so that by taking $\alpha = W_t/P_t$ we conclude that $(\boldsymbol{W} - \alpha\boldsymbol{P}).(\boldsymbol{W} - \alpha\boldsymbol{P}) = 0$ and hence that $\boldsymbol{W} = \alpha\boldsymbol{P}$ and indeed $\hat{\boldsymbol{W}} = \alpha\hat{\boldsymbol{P}}$ for this value of α.

15.4.4 Definition of scalar product

The scalar product for two vectors belonging to an irreducible representation of the Poincaré group may be defined by an extension of the method used in subsection 15.1.6 for the group $\mathscr{E}_3$. There is the same problem of the continuum of basis vectors with two small complications. For the representation $\mathrm{P}^{(k,s)}$ and following equation (15.19), we write an arbitrary vector as

$$|\psi\rangle = \sum_{m_s} \int \psi_{m_s}(\hat{\boldsymbol{k}})|\hat{\boldsymbol{k}}sm_s\rangle k_t^{-1}\,\mathrm{d}\boldsymbol{k} \tag{15.78}$$

Taken together, the sum and integral run over all basis vectors $|\hat{\boldsymbol{k}}sm_s\rangle$ of $\mathrm{P}^{(k,s)}$ and the $\psi_{m_s}(\hat{\boldsymbol{k}})$ are the numbers which determine $|\psi\rangle$. To cover all $\hat{\boldsymbol{k}}$ in four dimensions with fixed 'length' k, one needs a triple integral and there is naturally some freedom in choosing the three integration variables. It is convenient to choose the three components of the space part $\boldsymbol{k}$ of $\hat{\boldsymbol{k}}$. From the relation $k^2 = -|\boldsymbol{k}|^2 + k_t^2$ and the condition of future time-like $\hat{\boldsymbol{k}}$ one sees that $\hat{\boldsymbol{k}}$ is determined by $\boldsymbol{k}$ and that $\boldsymbol{k}$ must range over all three-space. The factor k_t^{-1} has been included in equation (15.78) for convenience because, as we show below, the volume element $k_t^{-1}\mathrm{d}\boldsymbol{k}$ is Lorentz invariant. One might have omitted the factor k_t^{-1}, essentially absorbing it into the coefficients $\psi_{m_s}(\hat{\boldsymbol{k}})$.

The scalar product is now defined, following equation (15.20) as

$$\langle\phi|\psi\rangle = \sum_{m_s} \int \phi_{m_s}^*(\hat{\boldsymbol{k}})\psi_{m_s}(\hat{\boldsymbol{k}})k_t^{-1}\,\mathrm{d}\boldsymbol{k} \tag{15.79}$$

with the same volume element as above. The proof that the representation $\mathrm{P}^{(k,s)}$ given by equation (15.59) is unitary then follows as in subsection 15.1.6 but we shall not write it out. In that subsection we made use of the fact that if $\boldsymbol{k}' = \mathrm{R}\boldsymbol{k}$ then the surface element $\mathrm{d}\Omega_{\boldsymbol{k}}$ could be replaced by $\mathrm{d}\Omega_{\boldsymbol{k}'}$. The analogous problem here is to transform from an integral $\mathrm{d}\boldsymbol{k}$ to an integral $\mathrm{d}\boldsymbol{k}'$, where $\boldsymbol{k}'$ is the space part of $\hat{\boldsymbol{k}}' = \mathrm{L}\hat{\boldsymbol{k}}$. This requires calculation of the Jacobian $\partial(k_x'k_y'k_z')/\partial(k_xk_yk_z)$ but since we may write $\mathrm{L} = \mathrm{QR}$, from equation (15.27), and the Jacobian for a rotation is unity, we need only consider a boost in any direction. If we choose the z-direction then x and y are unchanged so that the

Jacobian is simply $\partial k'_z/\partial k_z$. From the explicit transformation (15.25) for such a boost

$$k'_z = (k_z - \beta k_t)/(1-\beta^2)^{\frac{1}{2}}, \qquad k'_t = (k_t - \beta k_z)/(1-\beta^2)^{\frac{1}{2}} \qquad (15.80)$$

Thus

$$\partial k'_z/\partial k_z = (1 - \beta \partial k_t/\partial k_z)/(1-\beta^2)^{\frac{1}{2}}$$

but since $\quad k_t^2 = k^2 + k_x^2 + k_y^2 + k_z^2 \qquad$ we have $\qquad \partial k_t/\partial k_z = k_z/k_t$

giving

$$\partial k'_z/\partial k_z = (1 - \beta k_z/k_t)/(1-\beta^2)^{\frac{1}{2}}$$
$$= k_t^{-1} k'_t \qquad \text{using equation (15.80)}.$$

Thus the volume element $d\boldsymbol{k}'$ may be replaced by $k_t^{-1} k'_t d\boldsymbol{k}$ or, in other words, $k_t^{-1} d\boldsymbol{k}'$ may be replaced by $k_t^{-1} d\boldsymbol{k}$. Essentially the same scalar product may be used for the representations $P^{(0,\, m)}$, except that the sum over m_s is no longer required and m_s is replaced by m.

As we have seen in subsection 15.4.1 the vector $\hat{\boldsymbol{k}}$ labels a state with definite momentum and energy. Thus if the numbers $\psi_{m_s}(\hat{\boldsymbol{k}})$ are normalised so that $\langle\psi|\psi\rangle = 1$ we may interpret $|\psi_{m_s}(\hat{\boldsymbol{k}})|^2$ as the probability density as a function of $\hat{\boldsymbol{k}}$ and m_s for given k. One sometimes refers to the $\psi_{m_s}(\hat{\boldsymbol{k}})$ as the wave functions in momentum space. We warn that in non-relativistic treatments it is usual to define momentum space wave functions normalised with the k_t^{-1} factor missing from (15.79). This is a matter of convention.

We note that, so far as the basis vectors $|\hat{\boldsymbol{k}} s m_s\rangle$ themselves are concerned, the above definition of scalar product implies that

$$\langle \hat{\boldsymbol{k}}' s m'_s | \hat{\boldsymbol{k}} s m_s \rangle = k_t \delta_{m'_s m_s} \delta(\boldsymbol{k} - \boldsymbol{k}') \qquad (15.81)$$

where $\delta(\boldsymbol{k} - \boldsymbol{k}')$ denotes the three-dimensional delta-function. The function $\psi_{m_s}(\hat{\boldsymbol{k}})$ which describes one of the basis vectors itself, say $|\psi\rangle = |\tilde{\boldsymbol{k}} \tilde{m}_s\rangle$ is given simply, see equation (15.78), by

$$\psi_{m_s}(\hat{\boldsymbol{k}}) = \delta_{m_s \tilde{m}_s} \delta(\boldsymbol{k} - \tilde{\boldsymbol{k}}) k_t \qquad (15.82)$$

15.5 The Poincaré group with space inversions $\mathscr{P}_s$

The addition of the space inversion I to the Poincaré group makes only a slight change to the representations. We now study this extension of the group, following quite closely the methods used in section 15.3. We have already discussed in section 15.3 the fact that I commutes with rotations but not with Lorentz boosts and the multiplication rule

$$\mathrm{IQ}(\boldsymbol{b}) = \mathrm{Q}(-\boldsymbol{b})\mathrm{I} \qquad (15.83)$$

was deduced. The multiplication rule with translations follows directly from the definitions (15.39) and (15.47) of I and P($\hat{\varepsilon}$),

$$\mathrm{IP}(\hat{\varepsilon}) = \mathrm{P}(\mathrm{I}\hat{\varepsilon})\mathrm{I} \tag{15.84}$$

The irreducible representations of $\mathscr{P}_s$ may be readily constructed from those of $\mathscr{P}$. We show that to each representation $\mathrm{P}^{(k,s)}$ of $\mathscr{P}$ there are two representations $\mathrm{P}^{(k,s)\pm}$ of $\mathscr{P}_s$. Recall that $\mathrm{P}^{(k,s)}$ was generated from a special basis vector $|\hat{\boldsymbol{k}}_0 s m_s\rangle$, where $\hat{\boldsymbol{k}}_0 = (0, 0, 0, 1)$, using equation (15.57). Since the inversion I leaves $\hat{\boldsymbol{k}}_0$ invariant and also commutes with $\mathscr{R}_3$ we may choose this special basis vector to have definite parity in addition to the labels $\hat{\boldsymbol{k}}_0$, s and m_s. Thus we write $|\hat{\boldsymbol{k}}_0 s m_s \pm\rangle$, where

$$\mathrm{T}(\mathrm{I})|\hat{\boldsymbol{k}}_0 s m_s \pm\rangle = \pm|\hat{\boldsymbol{k}}_0 s m_s \pm\rangle \tag{15.85}$$

and it is understood that the upper (or lower) signs must be used throughout. From each of these possibilities we can now generate an irreducible representation of $\mathscr{P}_s$ exactly as for the group $\mathscr{P}$ using equation (15.57) and defining

$$|\hat{\boldsymbol{k}} s m_s \pm\rangle = \mathrm{T}(\mathrm{Q}[\boldsymbol{b}(\hat{\boldsymbol{k}})])|\hat{\boldsymbol{k}}_0 s m_s \pm\rangle \tag{15.86}$$

The actual representation matrix for proper elements T($\hat{\varepsilon}$, L) is given as before by equation (15.59), while for the inversion

$$\begin{aligned}
\mathrm{T}(\mathrm{I})|\hat{\boldsymbol{k}} s m_s \pm\rangle &= \mathrm{T}(\mathrm{I})\mathrm{T}(\mathrm{Q}[\boldsymbol{b}(\hat{\boldsymbol{k}})])|\hat{\boldsymbol{k}}_0 s m_s \pm\rangle \\
&= \mathrm{T}(\mathrm{Q}[-\boldsymbol{b}(\hat{\boldsymbol{k}})])\mathrm{T}(\mathrm{I})|\hat{\boldsymbol{k}}_0 s m_s \pm\rangle \quad \text{using equation (15.83)} \\
&= \pm\mathrm{T}(\mathrm{Q}[-\boldsymbol{b}(\hat{\boldsymbol{k}})])|\hat{\boldsymbol{k}}_0 s m_s \pm\rangle \quad \text{using equation (15.85)} \\
&= \pm|\mathrm{I}\hat{\boldsymbol{k}} s m_s \pm\rangle
\end{aligned} \tag{15.87}$$

In the last step we have used the fact that if $\boldsymbol{b}$ denotes the boost parameter required to carry $\hat{\boldsymbol{k}}_0$ into $\hat{\boldsymbol{k}}$ then $-\boldsymbol{b}$ will carry $\hat{\boldsymbol{k}}_0$ into $\mathrm{I}\hat{\boldsymbol{k}}$, see equation (15.26). The important point about equation (15.87) is that T(I), acting on a general basis vector $|\hat{\boldsymbol{k}} s m_s \pm\rangle$, leads to another basis vector of the set (15.86). Notice that T(I) is not a diagonal operator. Not surprisingly, T(I) changes the space direction of $\hat{\boldsymbol{k}}$ and, as we shall see later, in section 15.7, the $\pm$ refers to an internal (or intrinsic) parity of the system.

The arguments used above are not applicable to the representations $\mathrm{P}^{(0,m)}$, since the special vector in this case, $\hat{\boldsymbol{k}}_0 = (0, 0, 1, 1)$, is not invariant under inversions. In fact we shall find that the inversion operator T(I) transforms a basis vector of the representation $\mathrm{P}^{(0,m)}$ into a basis vector of $\mathrm{P}^{(0,-m)}$. It will then follow that the representation space of $\mathrm{P}^{(0,m)}$ cannot remain invariant under the extended group $\mathscr{P}_s$ but that, because T(I)T(I) = 1, the sum of the vector spaces of $\mathrm{P}^{(0,m)}$ and $\mathrm{P}^{(0,-m)}$ is invariant under $\mathscr{P}_s$ and therefore provides a representation of $\mathscr{P}_s$ which must be irreducible. We denote it by $\mathrm{P}^{(0,|m|)}$. To justify these statements we shall need to use the relations

$$\mathrm{P}_q\mathrm{I} = -\mathrm{IP}_q, \qquad \mathrm{P}_t\mathrm{I} = \mathrm{IP}_t \tag{15.88}$$

which follow directly from equation (15.84) and which lead to the results

$$W_q I = I W_q, \quad W_t I = -I W_t, \quad [\hat{W}.\hat{W}, I] = [\hat{P}.\hat{P}, I] = 0 \quad (15.89)$$

Now if $|km\rangle$ belongs to the representation $P^{(0,m)}$ of the group $\mathscr{P}$ so that equation (15.76) holds then we see that the vector defined by $T(I)|\hat{k}m\rangle$ has the following properties

$$\hat{W}.\hat{W}\,T(I)|\hat{k}m\rangle = 0$$

$$\hat{P}.\hat{P}\,T(I)|\hat{k}m\rangle = 0$$

$$(W_q - imP_q)T(I)|\hat{k}m\rangle = T(I)(W_q + imP_q)|\hat{k}m\rangle = 0$$

$$(W_t - imP_t)T(I)|\hat{k}m\rangle = -T(I)(W_t + imP_t)|\hat{k}m\rangle = 0$$

so that $(\hat{W} - im\hat{P})T(I)|\hat{k}m\rangle = 0$ (15.90)

Furthermore,

$$\begin{aligned} P(\hat{\varepsilon})T(I)|\hat{k}m\rangle &= T(I)P(I\hat{\varepsilon})|\hat{k}m\rangle \\ &= \exp(i\hat{k}.I\hat{\varepsilon})T(I)|\hat{k}m\rangle \\ &= \exp(iI\hat{k}.\hat{\varepsilon})T(I)|\hat{k}m\rangle \end{aligned}$$

so that the vector $T(I)|\hat{k}m\rangle$ transforms under translations according to the representation $T^{(I\hat{k})}$ of the translation group. Since by definition, $\hat{k}$ is future null, so is $I\hat{k}$ and thus, comparing equation (15.90) with equation (15.76), we conclude that $T(I)|\hat{k}m\rangle$ belongs to a representation $P^{(0,-m)}$ of $\mathscr{P}$. Thus, unless $m = 0$, the vectors $|\hat{k}m\rangle$ and $T(I)|\hat{k}m\rangle$ are linearly independent. We may thus write $T(I)|\hat{k}_0 m\rangle = |I\hat{k}_0 - m\rangle$ so that the set of $|\hat{k}m\rangle$ with $|\hat{k} - m\rangle$, generated from equation (15.67) for all future null $\hat{k}$, provide the basis for the representation $P^{(0,|m|)}$ of the extended group $\mathscr{P}_s$. It follows generally that

$$T(I)|\hat{k}m\rangle = |I\hat{k} - m\rangle \quad (15.91)$$

and hence $T(I)|\hat{k} - m\rangle = |I\hat{k}m\rangle$. Together with equation (15.68), used within each of the representations $P^{(0,m)}$ and $P^{(0,-m)}$ for group elements $T(\hat{\varepsilon}, L)$, the representation $P^{(0,|m|)}$ of $\mathscr{P}_s$ is thus determined.

The case $m = 0$ is an exception since $T(I)|\hat{k}m\rangle$ and $|\hat{k} - m\rangle$ both transform according to the same representation $P^{(0,0)}$ of $\mathscr{P}$. Then, as with the representations $P^{(k,s)}$, one obtains two representations $P^{(0,0)\pm}$ of $\mathscr{P}_s$ depending on whether $T(I)|\hat{k}_0 0\rangle = \pm|I\hat{k}_0 0\rangle$. We shall not go into any details.

15.6 The Poincaré group with time inversion, $\mathscr{P}_t$

Having discussed the space inversion I let us now consider the time inversion operator I_t defined by $I_t\hat{e} = \hat{e}' = (x, y, z, -ct)$. As in the previous section the addition of this operation to the Poincaré group generates an extended group which we denote by $\mathscr{P}_t$. We see directly from its definition that the products of translations with I_t satisfy the relation

$$P(\hat{\varepsilon})I_t = I_t P(I_t \hat{\varepsilon}) \tag{15.92}$$

Thus, if we denote by $|\hat{\boldsymbol{k}}\rangle$ a basis vector which transforms according to the representation $T^{(\hat{k})}$ of the translation group, we see that

$$\begin{aligned} T(\hat{\varepsilon})T(I_t)|\hat{\boldsymbol{k}}\rangle &= T(I_t)T(I_t\hat{\varepsilon})|\hat{\boldsymbol{k}}\rangle \\ &= \exp(i\hat{\boldsymbol{k}}.I_t\hat{\varepsilon})T(I_t)|\hat{\boldsymbol{k}}\rangle \\ &= \exp(iI_t\hat{\boldsymbol{k}}.\hat{\varepsilon})T(I_t)|\hat{\boldsymbol{k}}\rangle \end{aligned} \tag{15.93}$$

showing that the new vector $T(I_t)|\hat{\boldsymbol{k}}\rangle$ transforms according to $T^{(I_t\hat{k})}$ under translations. In other words, the time component of $\hat{\boldsymbol{k}}$ is reversed. But we have seen in section 15.4.1 that the physical significance of this component k_t of $\hat{\boldsymbol{k}}$ is the energy, $E = \hbar c k_t$. Thus the time inversion operation as given by equation (15.93) interchanges positive and negative energy states. There is however no evidence that this is a symmetry operation or indeed any evidence for the existence of negative energy states. For this reason we shall not pursue the representations based on (15.93).

We shall nevertheless return to the group $\mathscr{P}_t$ in subsection 15.7.4 in discussing time reversal, which is known experimentally to be an almost universally valid symmetry operation. This operation, which corresponds physically to a reversal of the direction of motion, is obtained by seeking a representation of the group element I_t which avoids the difficulties which follow from equation (15.93). In deriving (15.93) we have assumed that $T(I_t)$ is a linear operator in the representation space of the vectors $|\hat{\boldsymbol{k}}\rangle$. If one takes the operators $T(I_t)$ to be 'antilinear' then the appearance of negative energy states is avoided. Because new concepts are involved we defer the discussion of time reversal until subsection 15.7.4.

If we wish to include both the space inversion I and the time inversion I_t defined by $I_t\hat{\boldsymbol{e}} = (x, y, z, -ct)$ then to form a group we must also include the product II_t which changes the sign of all four components, $II_t\hat{\boldsymbol{e}} = -\hat{\boldsymbol{e}}$. Let us denote the group formed in this way by $\mathscr{P}_{st}$. We note that the product II_t commutes with all Lorentz transformations but not with translations.

15.7 Physical interpretation of the irreducible representations of the Poincaré group

We have already discussed the physical significance of many of the symmetry operations in the Poincaré group: translations in three-space in subsection 15.1.1, translations and rotations in three-space (the group $\mathscr{E}_3$) in subsection 15.1.5 and translations in four-space in subsection 15.4.1. We now investigate the additional consequences which result from the full Poincaré group.

It was already clear in subsection 15.1.5 that the group $\mathscr{E}_3$ was relevant only for a free particle or for the external motion of a system of particles and the representation labels corresponded to various properties of the system. Thus $E^{(|\boldsymbol{k}|,m)}$ specified the magnitude $|\boldsymbol{k}|$ of the momentum and the internal angular momentum (or spin) m about the direction of motion. States corresponding to different directions of $\boldsymbol{k}$ were equivalent in the sense that they could be obtained one from another by rotations. The invariant quantities were $|\boldsymbol{k}|$ and m. Since these remarks relate to any free system they must also relate even to elementary particles whose structure we may know nothing about. Thus we are able to characterise different elementary particles by different values of these invariants. By this argument however and using only the group $\mathscr{E}_3$ we should refer to particles with different magnitudes $|\boldsymbol{k}|$ of their momentum as different particles, and likewise for different projections m of their internal angular momenta on to the direction of motion. This would be a rather improbable use of the expression 'different particle' but we can now see that its unreasonable aspects are due to our use of $\mathscr{E}_3$ rather than $\mathscr{P}$ as the symmetry group. The inclusion of transformations between systems moving with uniform relative velocity would remove the improbable features mentioned above and these are precisely the transformations added to $\mathscr{E}_3$ to form the group $\mathscr{P}$. We therefore expect to find some more reasonable fundamental invariants from the study of the Poincaré group $\mathscr{P}$.

15.7.1 Mass

The irreducible representations of the Poincaré group are characterised firstly by the Casimir operator $\hat{\mathbf{P}}\,.\,\hat{\mathbf{P}}$ whose value, from section 15.4.3, is given by $-k^2$ in representations $\mathrm{P}^{(k,s)}$ and by zero in $\mathrm{P}^{(0,m)}$. In the representations corresponding to space-like $\hat{k}$, which we did not describe in detail, $\hat{\mathbf{P}}.\hat{\mathbf{P}}$ would be positive. For reasons which become clear as we proceed we associate the operator $\hat{\mathbf{P}}\,.\,\hat{\mathbf{P}}$ with the square of the mass. Precisely, the operator for the 'square of the mass' is defined, including appropriate dimensional factors, to be $-\hbar^2\hat{\mathbf{P}}\,.\,\hat{\mathbf{P}}/c^2$. Thus if M^2 denotes the value of the 'square of the mass' then in representations $\mathrm{P}^{(k,s)}$ we have $M^2 = \hbar^2 k^2/c^2$, while in $\mathrm{P}^{(0,m)}$ we have $M^2 = 0$ and for space-like $\hat{k}$, $M^2 < 0$. With this interpretation, the mass would be imaginary for space-like $\hat{k}$, would be zero for $\mathrm{P}^{(0,m)}$ and take the value $M = \hbar k/c$ in $\mathrm{P}^{(k,s)}$. (Notice that it is M^2 which has significance, rather than M; a situation rather similar to angular momentum where $\mathbf{J}\,.\,\mathbf{J}$ is the Casimir operator with value $J(J+1)$ but we use the label J.)

Let us now give some justification for using the word 'mass'. Since we have earlier given physical significance, momentum and energy, to the four components of $\hat{\mathbf{P}}$, the very definition $\hat{\mathbf{P}}\,.\,\hat{\mathbf{P}} = \mathrm{P}_t^2 - \sum_q \mathrm{P}_q^2$ implies a relation between the eigenvalues of these operators. In $\mathrm{P}^{(k,s)}$ the relation becomes

$$-c^2M^2/\hbar^2 = -E^2/\hbar^2c^2 + \sum_q p_q^2/\hbar^2$$

i.e.

$$E^2 = M^2c^4 + c^2p^2 \tag{15.94}$$

making use of the definitions of $\boldsymbol{p}$ and E in subsections 15.1.1 and 15.4.1 and with M defined above. (This is the familiar relation between energy and momentum in classical relativity theory, see section 16.1, and the word 'rest-mass' is sometimes used for M.) If the momentum is small, $p \ll Mc$, then

$$E = Mc^2(1 + p^2/M^2c^2)^{\frac{1}{2}} \approx Mc^2 + p^2/2M \tag{15.95}$$

which gives the energy as the sum of the rest-energy Mc^2 and the kinetic energy $p^2/2M = \frac{1}{2}Mv^2$.

So far as the label $\hat{\boldsymbol{k}}$ is concerned, the different vectors $|\hat{\boldsymbol{k}} s m_s\rangle$ in the representation $\mathrm{P}^{(k,s)}$ correspond to different states of motion of a particle (or system) with mass $M = \hbar k/c$. Not only may the momentum $\boldsymbol{p} = \hbar \boldsymbol{k}$ be in any direction, but it may have any magnitude with corresponding energy given by equation (15.94). Thus, even if we restrict to $s = 0$, the single representation $\mathrm{P}^{(k,0)}$ encompasses all possible states of motion of a classical particle of mass M. We shall see presently that the label s relates to the internal angular momentum or spin of the particle.

Before discussing zero mass we briefly consider the representation corresponding to $\hat{\boldsymbol{k}} = 0$ and referred to in subsection 15.4.2 under region (6). This would not only have zero mass but also zero energy and momentum in all states, i.e. in all frames of reference. No such object has been observed and we discuss the possibility no further, noting however that the point $\hat{\boldsymbol{k}} = 0$ must be excluded from the representation $\mathrm{P}^{(0,m)}$.

Let us now turn our attention to the representation $\mathrm{P}^{(0,m)}$ corresponding to zero mass. This seems a rather unlikely description for a particle until we notice that it may nevertheless have finite energy and momentum satisfying, from equation (15.94), the relation

$$E = pc \tag{15.96}$$

Thus, although having zero mass, the object acquires some physical properties and in fact such particles are well known in physics. In the quantum treatment of the electromagnetic field, the interaction takes place through the exchange of photons which need to have zero mass. Also, in β-decay one finds neutral particles emitted which have zero mass and are called neutrinos.

Whereas for a particle with finite mass, there is always a state with $\boldsymbol{p} = 0$, in which the particle is at rest, with $E = Mc^2$, this is not the case for a zero-mass particle. One cannot set $\boldsymbol{p} = 0$ without moving to the limit point $\hat{\boldsymbol{k}} = 0$ which defines a different irreducible representation in which all states of the particle have zero energy and momentum as described above. Classically this implies that zero-mass particles have velocity $v = c$ because as we have seen in subsection 15.2.3, the velocity is then $v = c$ in all frames of reference and no state of rest is possible. (Another classical argument supporting the statement that $v = c$ is that with zero mass a particle can acquire finite energy and momentum only in the limit of $v = c$, see equation (16.10).)

15.7.2 Spin

Having seen how the first Casimir operator $\hat{\mathbf{P}}.\hat{\mathbf{P}}$ is associated with mass and the components of $\hat{\mathbf{P}}$ are associated with momentum and energy we now turn our attention to the second Casimir operator $\hat{\mathbf{W}}.\hat{\mathbf{W}}$ defined in subsection 15.4.3. The interpretation of $\hat{\mathbf{W}}.\hat{\mathbf{W}}$ takes rather different forms for finite and zero mass and we describe them separately.

Finite mass

Consider first the case of finite mass, described by the representations $P^{(k,s)}$. From equation (15.74) we recall that the number s, which may take values $0, \frac{1}{2}, 1, \frac{3}{2}, \ldots$ labels the eigenvalues $-k^2 s(s+1)$ of $\hat{\mathbf{W}}.\hat{\mathbf{W}}$ for given k. In terms of the mass, introduced in equation (15.94) the eigenvalues of $\hat{\mathbf{W}}.\hat{\mathbf{W}}$ are

$$-M^2c^2 s(s+1)/\hbar^2 \tag{15.97}$$

Since $\hat{\mathbf{W}}.\hat{\mathbf{W}}$ is a Casimir operator, all states belonging to the representation $P^{(k,s)}$ are eigenfunctions of $\hat{\mathbf{W}}.\hat{\mathbf{W}}$ with the same eigenvalue. Thus s describes some intrinsic property of the particle, like the mass, which is the same in all frames of reference.

We shall refer to this intrinsic property as the spin. Strictly, $s\hbar$ is called the spin, so that s is the spin in units of $\hbar$. The reason for using this word is clear if we study the operators W_q for a particle in a state of rest, i.e. when $\hat{\boldsymbol{k}} = (0, 0, 0, k)$. Then from equation (15.72)

$$W_q = -i(Mc/\hbar)X_q = -(Mc/\hbar)J_q, \quad W_t = 0$$

and

$$\hat{\mathbf{W}}.\hat{\mathbf{W}} = (M^2c^2/\hbar^2)(X_x^2 + X_y^2 + X_z^2) = -(M^2c^2/\hbar^2)\mathbf{J}^2 \tag{15.98}$$

showing that, for a particle at rest, W_q is proportional to the angular momentum J_q. Of course, a classical point-particle at rest has no angular momentum so that it is appropriate to use the term 'intrinsic spin' to describe the label s. Furthermore, since $\hat{\mathbf{W}}$ is translation invariant it follows that, when operating on a general basis vector $|\hat{\boldsymbol{k}} s m_s\rangle$ of $P^{(k,s)}$, it cannot change $\hat{\boldsymbol{k}}$. Thus $\hat{\mathbf{W}}$ simply transforms among different m_s with fixed $\hat{\boldsymbol{k}}$. Notice that the basis $|\hat{\boldsymbol{k}} s m_s\rangle$ was chosen so that W_z is diagonal on the special vector $|\hat{\boldsymbol{k}}_0 s m_s\rangle$ through the definition of m_s, i.e.

$$W_z|\hat{\boldsymbol{k}}_0 s m_s\rangle = -m_s k|\hat{\boldsymbol{k}}_0 s m_s\rangle \tag{15.99}$$

Since $\hat{\mathbf{W}}$ is a four-vector it follows that, for an arbitrary basis vector $|\hat{\boldsymbol{k}} s m_s\rangle$, some transformed component of $\hat{\mathbf{W}}$ will be diagonal. This may be seen by transforming both sides of equation (15.99) with the boost which carries $\hat{\boldsymbol{k}}_0$ into $\hat{\boldsymbol{k}}$ and using equation (15.57)

$$T(Q[b(\hat{\boldsymbol{k}})])W_z T^{-1}(Q[b(\hat{\boldsymbol{k}})])|\hat{\boldsymbol{k}} s m_s\rangle = -m_s k|\hat{\boldsymbol{k}} s m_s\rangle$$

which gives, from the explicit form (15.26) for the boost of a four-vector, and using the values for $\boldsymbol{b}(\hat{\boldsymbol{k}})$ given after equation (15.58)

$$\{W_z - (k_t + k)^{-1} k_z W_t\} |\hat{\boldsymbol{k}} s m_s\rangle = -m_s k |\hat{\boldsymbol{k}} s m_s\rangle \tag{15.100}$$

In deriving this result we have used the property $\hat{\mathbf{W}}.\hat{\mathbf{P}} = 0$ from subsection 15.4.3 which enables us to replace $\mathbf{W}.\mathbf{P}$ by $W_t P_t$. It is possible to choose a new basis (helicity) in which the component of $\hat{\mathbf{W}}$ in the direction $\boldsymbol{k}$ of motion is always diagonal but this would have led to a more complicated expression than (15.59) for the general transformation.

From equation (15.59) one sees that the effect of a Lorentz transformation T(0, L) on an arbitrary vector $|\hat{\boldsymbol{k}} s m_s\rangle$ is in two parts. There is a matrix sum over m_s' and a change in the vector $\hat{\boldsymbol{k}}$. Thus an infinitesimal Lorentz transformation is described by the sum of a matrix operator acting on the m_s and a differential operator which produces an infinitesimal change in $\hat{\boldsymbol{k}}$ without affecting m_s. This situation is reminiscent of the separation $\mathbf{j} = \mathbf{s} + \mathbf{l}$ described in section 8.4 for the non-relativistic case. However, the basis $|\hat{\boldsymbol{k}} s m_s\rangle$ does not lead to complete separation because the rotation $R' = Q'^{-1}LQ$ entering the matrix in equation (15.59) depends on $\hat{\boldsymbol{k}}$ as well as L. Nevertheless, by a change of basis, it is possible to achieve complete separation writing not only $\mathbf{j} = \mathbf{s} + \mathbf{l}$ for the infinitesimal rotations but also $\mathbf{Y} = \mathbf{Y}_s + \mathbf{Y}_l$ for the boosts where $\mathbf{s}$ and $\mathbf{Y}_s$ are 'spin' operators, given by matrices, which commute with the 'orbital' operators $\mathbf{l}$ and $\mathbf{Y}_l$. Because this separation is closely connected with the Dirac equation we defer its discussion until subsection 15.8.4.

Experimentally, one finds that the electron, proton and neutron all have $s = \frac{1}{2}$ while π-mesons have $s = 0$ and ρ-mesons $s = 1$. Complex systems like atoms and nuclei can have much greater values for s but always an integer or half-integer.

Zero mass

As we have seen in subsection 15.7.1 the representations $P^{(0,m)}$ of the Poincaré group provide a description for particles with zero mass. The discussion of spin given above for the representations $P^{(k,s)}$ is inapplicable for particles with zero mass because it began by examining the behaviour of the particle at rest and zero mass particles always move with the velocity of light. However, using equations (15.72) and (15.76) we see that, for any vector $|\hat{\boldsymbol{k}} m\rangle$ of $P^{(0,m)}$

$$-(\mathbf{X}.\mathbf{P})|\hat{\boldsymbol{k}} m\rangle = -W_t|\hat{\boldsymbol{k}} m\rangle = imP_t|\hat{\boldsymbol{k}} m\rangle = mk_t|\hat{\boldsymbol{k}} m\rangle = m|\boldsymbol{k}||\hat{\boldsymbol{k}} m\rangle \tag{15.101}$$

But in physical terms, $-\mathbf{X}.\mathbf{P}$ is the component of angular momentum in the direction of motion multiplied by the magnitude of momentum. Since a classical point particle would have no such component of angular momentum we again use the word 'spin' to describe the number m, but we must realise that the spin of a zero-mass particle differs greatly from that for finite mass. There is now no $(2s+1)$-fold degeneracy of different spin orientations. In fact, even the state with opposite spin $-m$ would belong to a different irreducible representation of the group $\mathscr{P}$ namely $P^{(0,-m)}$ rather than $P^{(0,m)}$. A particle with positive m is said to have positive 'helicity' or to be right-handed in the usual sense of a screw. We discuss the significance of helicity in the next section in connection with parity. However, there is a simple physical argument which shows how this right- or left-handedness may exist in zero mass particles but not in finite mass particles. The helicity of a particle will be reversed in the frame of an observer travelling faster than the particle, compared with that of an observer moving more slowly. Thus, for a finite mass particle which travels at speed $v < c$ any one-handedness would violate Lorentz invariance. However, for zero mass, the particle must travel at speed $v = c$ so that no observers may travel faster than the particle and the contradiction cannot arise.

Of the known particles with zero mass, the photon is found to have both $m = \pm 1$ while the neutrino and the antineutrino have $m = -\frac{1}{2}$ and $m = \frac{1}{2}$, respectively. (See also the discussion of antiparticles in subsection 16.3.5.)

15.7.3 Parity

The representations discussed so far have related to the proper Poincaré group $\mathscr{P}$ without inversions in space or time. Let us now suppose that the space inversion I is also a symmetry element so that the full symmetry group becomes $\mathscr{P}_s$ whose representations were constructed in section 15.5. Again we study the consequences separately for finite and zero mass.

Finite mass

It was shown in section 15.5 that, when the group $\mathscr{P}$ is extended to $\mathscr{P}_s$ there are two irreducible representations $P^{(k,s)\pm}$ of $\mathscr{P}_s$ for each representation $P^{(k,s)}$ of $\mathscr{P}$. The inversion operator was shown in equation (15.87) to have two effects; it changed the direction of $\boldsymbol{k}$ and it gave a factor ± 1 in $P^{(k,s)\pm}$, respectively. The first of these effects gives the expected reversal in the direction of motion while the second applies even to a particle at rest. Thus one refers to the $\pm$ factor as the 'intrinsic parity' of the particle, even or odd, which, like the spin, is independent of the state of motion and is a characteristic of the particle. It may be imagined to refer to some 'internal' structure of the particle.

In fact it is possible to determine the absolute intrinsic parity of a particle only in rare cases like the π^0. Usually, two or more changes occur in a reaction so that only the relative intrinsic parity may be deduced. Furthermore, because of what are believed to be absolute conservation laws, such as charge conservation, certain classes of transition are forbidden, preventing the determination of even the relative parities between certain sets of particles. The absolute intrinsic parity of the π^0 may be found from a reaction like $p+p \rightarrow p+p+\pi^0$, and a detailed analysis of the results of such experiments shows that the π^0 has odd parity. Since they have a charge it is not possible to devise an experiment to measure the absolute intrinsic parity of the $\pi^\pm$ but because they are part of the isospin triplet ($T = 1$) with the π^0 (see section 10.2), it is natural to assign an odd parity also to the $\pi^{\pm}$. The relative parity of neutron and proton is then found to be positive from the analysis of reactions like $p+p \rightarrow n+p+\pi^+$ and it is convention to choose them both to have positive parity. It is crucial to the argument above that the reactions proceed via the strong nuclear forces which are known to conserve parity.

Zero mass

For a particle with zero mass we recall from section 15.5 that the irreducible representations of the extended group $\mathscr{P}_s$ are made up of two irreducible representations of $\mathscr{P}$, $P^{(0,|m|)} = P^{(0,m)} \dot{+} P^{(0,-m)}$ and the space inversion carries a vector of one into a vector of the other. This is to be expected since the inversion commutes with the spin and thus a change in direction of $\boldsymbol{k}$ must imply a change in helicity. One cannot assign an intrinsic parity here as we did for finite mass because the irreducible representations $P^{(0,|m|)}$ of the group $\mathscr{P}_s$ do not carry such a label $\pm$. Physically, the intrinsic parity cannot be studied in the state of rest since no such state exists for zero mass.

The fact that the photon is found experimentally in both $m = \pm 1$ states suggests that it is described by the representation $P^{(0,1)} \dot{+} P^{(0,-1)}$ of the group $\mathscr{P}_s$ or in other words that it has $\mathscr{P}_s$ as its symmetry group. On the other hand for the neutrino which is found always in the $m = -\frac{1}{2}$ state, the appropriate group is $\mathscr{P}$ excluding the inversion. Thus whereas parity is conserved in electromagnetic interactions, involving the exchange of photons, one finds experimentally that parity is not conserved in processes like β-decay which involve neutrinos. It is true that antineutrinos, with $m = \frac{1}{2}$, exist also but they must be regarded as different particles since they do not occur in the same reactions as neutrinos, see subsection 16.3.7.

15.7.4 Time-reversal

If we run a movie film backwards we shall see all movements reversed; a falling stone will be replaced by a stone projected upwards. The reversed motion is also consistent with physical laws in the sense that a stone actually projected would behave (in a vacuum) just like the backwards run film of a falling stone. This is true because Newton's equation of motion in a uniform gravitational field is unchanged when the time t is replaced by $-t$. However, in the Schrodinger picture of quantum mechanics, the simple time inversion operator $t \rightarrow -t$ also changes the sign of the energy, as we have seen in section 15.6, because the energy operator is given by $i\hbar\,\partial/\partial t$. Thus in quantum mechanics, the time inversion operation has a much more drastic effect than simply reversing the motion. Since the idea of reversing the motion is perfectly sensible in classical mechanics one would expect to find a corresponding operation in quantum mechanics, i.e. one which reverses directions of motion but does not change the sign of the energy. In this section we construct such an operation, called 'time-reversal' and denoted by Υ. It will turn out that Υ is a very unusual operator, being non-linear, so we must digress to explain the meaning of such operators. (A brief mention of this operator has already been made in sections 5.10 and 9.8.)

In all the examples of symmetry in quantum mechanics given so far in this book, the transformations in the wave functions have been unitary and linear. Let us look more closely into the reason for this choice and we shall find that it is not the only possibility: let $|\psi\rangle$ and $|\phi\rangle$ denote two states of a system. One of the postulates of quantum mechanics is that, if a system is in state $|\psi\rangle$ and a measurement is made to determine whether it is in state $|\phi\rangle$, then the probability that it will be found to be in state $|\phi\rangle$ is given by the squared modulus $|\langle\phi|\psi\rangle|^2$ of the scalar product. If we denote by $|\psi'\rangle = \mathrm{T}|\psi\rangle$ and $|\phi'\rangle = \mathrm{T}|\phi\rangle$ the new states following a symmetry transformation T, then since the result of the measurement must be unaltered we have

$$|\langle \mathrm{T}\phi|\mathrm{T}\psi\rangle|^2 = |\langle\phi|\psi\rangle|^2 \tag{15.102}$$

This must follow if the primed system is to have the same physical properties as before. It is clear that this equation is satisfied if T is unitary, i.e. $\langle \mathrm{T}\phi|\mathrm{T}\psi\rangle = \langle\phi|\psi\rangle$ for all $|\psi\rangle$ and $|\phi\rangle$ but, because of the modulus signs, there are other possibilities. It may be deduced from equation (15.102) that, apart from trivial phase changes, the operator may *either* be unitary and linear as we have assumed hitherto in the book, i.e.

$$\langle \mathrm{T}\phi|\mathrm{T}\psi\rangle = \langle\phi|\psi\rangle \tag{15.103}$$

and

$$\mathrm{T}(a|\phi\rangle + b|\psi\rangle) = a\mathrm{T}|\phi\rangle + b\mathrm{T}|\psi\rangle$$

or that T is anti-unitary and antilinear, i.e.

$$\langle \mathrm{T}\phi|\mathrm{T}\psi\rangle = \langle\psi|\phi\rangle = \langle\phi|\psi\rangle^*$$

and

$$\mathrm{T}(a|\phi\rangle + b|\psi\rangle) = a^*\mathrm{T}|\phi\rangle + b^*\mathrm{T}|\psi\rangle \tag{15.104}$$

For continuous groups we are led naturally to the choice (15.103) since we take the unit operator to represent the identity and the unit operator satisfies this equation. Again, when considering time inversion in section 15.6, we chose the more usual possibility (15.103). By taking now the second possibility (15.104) we shall find a transformation which represents time-reversal and does not change the sign of the energy.

Consider the representations of the group $\mathscr{P}_t$ obtained by adding the time inversion operator I_t to $\mathscr{P}$ but where we use an antilinear operator Υ to represent I_t. Thus we retain equation (15.92) for the multiplication of group elements but, using the non-linear Υ in place of $\mathrm{T}(\mathrm{I}_t)$ the equation (15.93) is replaced by

$$\begin{aligned}\mathrm{T}(\boldsymbol{\varepsilon})\Upsilon|\hat{\boldsymbol{k}}\rangle &= \Upsilon\mathrm{T}(\mathrm{I}_t\boldsymbol{\varepsilon})|\hat{\boldsymbol{k}}\rangle = \Upsilon\exp(i\hat{\boldsymbol{k}}\,.\,\mathrm{I}_t\boldsymbol{\varepsilon})|\hat{\boldsymbol{k}}\rangle \\ &= \exp(-i\hat{\boldsymbol{k}}\,.\,\mathrm{I}_t\boldsymbol{\varepsilon})\Upsilon|\hat{\boldsymbol{k}}\rangle = \exp(-i\mathrm{I}_t\hat{\boldsymbol{k}}\,.\,\boldsymbol{\varepsilon})\Upsilon|\hat{\boldsymbol{k}}\rangle \\ &= \exp(i\mathrm{I}\hat{\boldsymbol{k}}\,.\,\boldsymbol{\varepsilon})\Upsilon|\hat{\boldsymbol{k}}\rangle\end{aligned} \tag{15.105}$$

where we have used the second of equations (15.104) and the elementary result $I_t\hat{\boldsymbol{k}} = -I\hat{\boldsymbol{k}}$, where I is the space inversion. Thus, under translations, the vector $\Upsilon|\hat{\boldsymbol{k}}\rangle$ transforms according to $T^{(I\hat{\boldsymbol{k}})}$ and the difficulty with negative energies is avoided. The operator Υ also has the desired effect of reversing the direction of $\boldsymbol{k}$. Although time-reversal is similar to space inversion we cannot assign a 'time-reversal parity' with any physical significance. This stems directly from the antilinear nature of Υ. For suppose that $|\psi\rangle$ was an eigenfunction of Υ with eigenvalue λ, so that $\Upsilon|\psi\rangle = \lambda|\psi\rangle$. The antilinear nature of Υ now implies that for any phase η

$$\begin{aligned}\Upsilon \exp(i\eta)|\psi\rangle &= \exp(-i\eta)\Upsilon|\psi\rangle = \exp(-i\eta)\lambda|\psi\rangle \\ &= [\exp(-2i\eta)\lambda]\exp(i\eta)|\psi\rangle\end{aligned}$$

Hence the function $\exp(i\eta)|\psi\rangle$, which must physically be indistinguishable from $|\psi\rangle$, has eigenvalue $\exp(-2i\eta)\lambda$ for Υ and so the eigenvalue of Υ can have no physical meaning within a phase. In particular, the sign of λ would be meaningless. These remarks apply both to finite and zero mass but to study the irreducible representations of $\mathscr{P}_t$ any further we must treat the two cases separately. In both cases we shall find that the representation spaces do not need to be increased in dimension when the extra element Υ is added to make $\mathscr{P}_t$. To make any progress we must use the multiplication law between time inversion and Lorentz transformations

$$I_t L(\boldsymbol{a}, \boldsymbol{b}) = L(\boldsymbol{a}, -\boldsymbol{b}) I_t \tag{15.106}$$

which follows from the 4×4 matrices. We shall assume as usual that the representation operators satisfy the same law. In words, this says that the time-reversal operator Υ commutes with rotations and changes the direction of the boosts. From the very nature of the physical operation of time-reversal, the square Υ^2 must reproduce the original physical system. Thus $\Upsilon^2|\psi\rangle = \exp(i\alpha)|\psi\rangle$, where α is any phase. Combining this with the anti-unitary condition (15.104) leads to the further restriction (see problem 15.10) that $\Upsilon^2|\psi\rangle = \pm|\psi\rangle$. For a strict, single-valued representation we should take only the plus sign since the group element satisfies $I_t^2 = E$. However, if we allow double-valued representations (like the half-integer representation of $\mathscr{R}_3$) then the minus sign is permitted.

Finite mass

In studying the behaviour of the basis vectors $|\hat{\boldsymbol{k}} s m_s\rangle$ of the representation $P^{(k,s)}$ of $\mathscr{P}$ when the new element Υ is added we follow the technique of section 15.5 and look first at the special vectors $|\hat{\boldsymbol{k}}_0 s m_s\rangle$ with $\hat{\boldsymbol{k}}_0 = (0, 0, 0, 1)$. From equation (15.105) the vector $\Upsilon|\hat{\boldsymbol{k}}_0 s m_s\rangle$ has the same label $\hat{\boldsymbol{k}} = \hat{\boldsymbol{k}}_0$. Because Υ commutes with rotations one might have expected that the vector $\Upsilon|\hat{\boldsymbol{k}}_0 s m_s\rangle$ would have the same value of m_s but this does not take account of the antilinear nature of Υ. Because the rotation operator X_z has an imaginary eigenvalue, $X_z|\hat{\boldsymbol{k}}_0 sm_s\rangle = -im_s|\hat{\boldsymbol{k}}_0 sm_s\rangle$, see for example section 7.3.5, we have

$$X_z \Upsilon|\hat{\boldsymbol{k}}_0 sm_s\rangle = \Upsilon X_z|\hat{\boldsymbol{k}}_0 sm_s\rangle = \Upsilon(-im_s)|\hat{\boldsymbol{k}}_0 sm_s\rangle$$
$$= im_s \Upsilon|\hat{\boldsymbol{k}}_0 sm_s\rangle$$

which shows that, under rotations about the z-axis, the vector $\Upsilon|\hat{\boldsymbol{k}}_0 sm_s\rangle$ transforms like $-m_s$ although it is easily seen that the value of s is unchanged. In fact, for a general rotation

$$\begin{aligned} T(R(\boldsymbol{a}))\Upsilon|\hat{\boldsymbol{k}}_0 sm_s\rangle &= \Upsilon T(R(\boldsymbol{a}))|\hat{\boldsymbol{k}}_0 sm_s\rangle \\ &= \sum_{m_s'} \Upsilon D^{(s)}_{m_s' m_s}(\boldsymbol{a})|\hat{\boldsymbol{k}}_0 sm_s'\rangle \\ &= \sum_{m_s'} D^{(s)*}_{m_s' m_s}(\boldsymbol{a})\Upsilon|\hat{\boldsymbol{k}}_0 sm_s'\rangle \end{aligned} \quad (15.107)$$

Thus the set of vectors $\Upsilon|\hat{\boldsymbol{k}}_0 sm_s\rangle$ with fixed $\hat{\boldsymbol{k}}_0$ and s transform like the complex conjugate of the representation $D^{(s)}$ of $\mathscr{R}_3$. However, the complex conjugate of $D^{(s)}$ is equivalent to $D^{(s)}$, see section 7.7, and with the usual convention $D^{(s)*}_{m_s' m_s}(\boldsymbol{a}) = (-1)^{m_s - m_s'} D^{(s)}_{-m_s', -m_s}(\boldsymbol{a})$. Thus the set of vectors $\Upsilon|\hat{\boldsymbol{k}}_0 sm_s\rangle$ transform precisely like the set $(-1)^{m_s}|\hat{\boldsymbol{k}}_0 s - m_s\rangle$. There are now two possibilities: either $\Upsilon|\hat{\boldsymbol{k}}_0 sm_s\rangle$ is linearly independent of $|\hat{\boldsymbol{k}}_0 s - m_s\rangle$ or we may write $\Upsilon|\hat{\boldsymbol{k}}_0 sm_s\rangle = \gamma(-1)^{m_s}|\hat{\boldsymbol{k}}_0 s - m_s\rangle$ with some constant γ. Because we are looking for an irreducible representation of $\mathscr{P}_t$ the first possibility can be dismissed since it can be shown, following the technique of section 15.3, that the representation of $\mathscr{P}_t$ generated from $|\hat{\boldsymbol{k}}_0 sm_s\rangle$ would not then be irreducible. Returning to the second possibility it is usual to choose the phase factor $\gamma = (-1)^s$ so that, even for half-integers, the factor $(-1)^{s+m_s}$ is real. Having seen that the $(2s+1)$ vectors $|\hat{\boldsymbol{k}}_0 sm_s\rangle$ with fixed $\hat{\boldsymbol{k}}_0$ and s form an invariant space under rotations and time-reversal, we generate the remaining basis vectors of the representation of $\mathscr{P}_t$ by using the boost equation (15.57). It then follows that for the general basis vector of the representation,

$$\begin{aligned} \Upsilon|\hat{\boldsymbol{k}} sm_s\rangle &= \Upsilon T(Q[\boldsymbol{b}(\hat{\boldsymbol{k}})])|\hat{\boldsymbol{k}}_0 sm_s\rangle \\ &= T(Q[-\boldsymbol{b}(\hat{\boldsymbol{k}})])(-1)^{s+m_s}|\hat{\boldsymbol{k}}_0 s - m_s\rangle \\ &= (-1)^{s+m_s}|I\hat{\boldsymbol{k}} s - m_s\rangle \end{aligned} \quad (15.108)$$

showing how Υ changes the sign of both the momentum and the spin. We see from this equation that

$$\Upsilon^2|\hat{\boldsymbol{k}} sm_s\rangle = (-1)^{s+m_s}(-1)^{s-m_s}|\hat{\boldsymbol{k}} sm_s\rangle = (-1)^{2s}|\hat{\boldsymbol{k}} sm_s\rangle \quad (15.109)$$

showing that $\Upsilon^2 = 1$ in a representation with integer spin and $\Upsilon^2 = -1$ for half-integer spin. This conclusion is independent of the choice of the phase factor γ. From equation (15.108) we may immediately deduce the effect of Υ on an arbitrary vector $|\psi\rangle$ as defined in equation (15.78); the new vector

$|\psi'\rangle = \Upsilon|\psi\rangle$ is given by the coefficients $\psi'_{m_s}(\hat{\boldsymbol{k}}) = (-1)^{s-m_s}\psi^*_{-m_s}(-\mathrm{I}\hat{\boldsymbol{k}})$. The time-reversal operator may be written as a product of a unitary operator and an operator K which takes the complex conjugate of the c-numbers, i.e. the expansion coefficients in some basis, but the explicit form of Υ expressed in this way must clearly depend on the basis. If we note from equation (20.40) that the spin rotation $\mathrm{R}^s_y(-\pi)$ transforms m_s into $-m_s$ with a phase change $(-1)^{s+m_s}$ and if we define $\mathrm{T}_k(\mathrm{I})$ as an operator which changes $\hat{\boldsymbol{k}}$ into $\mathrm{I}\hat{\boldsymbol{k}}$, i.e. which changes the sign of the space part of $\hat{\boldsymbol{k}}$, then in the basis $|\hat{\boldsymbol{k}}sm_s\rangle$ the transformation (15.108) shows the equivalence $\Upsilon = \mathrm{K}\mathrm{R}^s_y(-\pi)\mathrm{T}_k(\mathrm{I})$. However, in a coordinate representation it is given by $\Upsilon = \mathrm{K}\mathrm{R}^s_y(-\pi)\mathrm{T}(\mathrm{I}_t)$ where $\mathrm{T}(\mathrm{I}_t)$ replaces t by $-t$. When $s = \frac{1}{2}$, $\mathrm{R}^s_y(-\pi) \equiv 2is_y$.

Zero mass

The multiplication law (15.106) implies that $\Upsilon\mathbf{X} = \mathbf{X}\Upsilon$ and $\Upsilon\mathbf{Y} = -\mathbf{Y}\Upsilon$, while equation (15.92) gives $\Upsilon\mathbf{P} = \mathbf{P}\Upsilon$ and $\Upsilon\mathrm{P}_t = -\mathrm{P}_t\Upsilon$. Thus $\Upsilon\mathbf{W} = -\mathbf{W}\Upsilon$ and $\Upsilon\mathrm{W}_t = \mathrm{W}_t\Upsilon$. Now consider a basis vector belonging to the representation $\mathrm{P}^{(0,m)}$ of $\mathscr{P}$, which is appropriate for zero mass. Then starting from equation (15.76) we have $\Upsilon(\hat{\mathbf{W}} + im\hat{\mathbf{P}})|\hat{\boldsymbol{k}}m\rangle = 0$ so that, making use of the multiplication rules given above and the antilinearity of Υ,

$$(-\mathbf{W} - im\mathbf{P})\,\Upsilon\,|\hat{\boldsymbol{k}}m\rangle = 0$$

and

$$(\mathrm{W}_t + im\mathrm{P}_t)\Upsilon\,|\hat{\boldsymbol{k}}m\rangle = 0$$

or in other words

$$(\hat{\mathbf{W}} + im\hat{\mathbf{P}})\Upsilon|\hat{\boldsymbol{k}}m\rangle = 0 \tag{15.110}$$

Thus we conclude that the vector $\Upsilon|\hat{\boldsymbol{k}}m\rangle$ also belongs to a representation $\mathrm{P}^{(0,m)}$ of $\mathscr{P}$ and, using equation (15.105), that it transforms like $|\mathrm{I}\hat{\boldsymbol{k}}m\rangle$ under the group $\mathscr{P}$. Again we can argue that if $\Upsilon|\hat{\boldsymbol{k}}m\rangle$ and $|\mathrm{I}\hat{\boldsymbol{k}}m\rangle$ are linearly independent then the representation of $\mathscr{P}_t$ generated from them will reduce. Thus for an irreducible representation of $\mathscr{P}_t$ we must have

$$\Upsilon|\hat{\boldsymbol{k}}m\rangle = |\mathrm{I}\hat{\boldsymbol{k}}m\rangle \tag{15.111}$$

where we have chosen the phase factor to be $+1$. Notice that $\Upsilon^2 = +1$ in this case, irrespective of the choice of phase. The interpretation of equation (15.111) is again that both momentum and spin are reversed but, since m is the spin in the direction of motion, its value is unchanged. From the point of view of the representations we conclude that the vector space of $\mathrm{P}^{(0,m)}$ remains invariant when Υ is added to the group $\mathscr{P}$ and therefore provides also the basis for an irreducible representation of $\mathscr{P}_t$.

15.7.5 Some consequences of time-reversal symmetry

(1) Kramer's theorem

As a first example of the consequences of time-reversal we deduce Kramer's theorem, first enunciated in 1930, which says that, in a system governed by a time-reversal invariant Hamiltonian, any states of an odd number of particles with half-integer spin and finite mass must be degenerate in pairs. For a state $|\psi\rangle$ of n particles the time-reversal operator is defined as the product of such operations on each particle. Now consider the operator Υ^2. For each particle it contributes a factor $(-1)^{2s}$ from equation (15.109), irrespective of the state of motion of the particle. Thus if $|\psi\rangle$ is a state of n particles with half-integer spin,

$$\Upsilon^2|\psi\rangle = (-1)^n|\psi\rangle = -|\psi\rangle \qquad \text{for odd } n$$

Now if $|\psi\rangle$ is an eigenfunction of a Υ-invariant Hamiltonian then so is the function $|\phi\rangle = \Upsilon|\psi\rangle$. But $|\phi\rangle$ can be shown to be independent of $|\psi\rangle$, in fact orthogonal to $|\psi\rangle$, since from the equation before (15.104)

$$\langle\psi|\phi\rangle = \langle\psi|\Upsilon\psi\rangle = \langle\Upsilon^2\psi|\Upsilon\psi\rangle = -\langle\psi|\Upsilon\psi\rangle = -\langle\psi|\phi\rangle$$

Thus we conclude that $\langle\psi|\phi\rangle = 0$, that $|\phi\rangle$ and $|\psi\rangle$ are independent and hence that they give a two-fold degeneracy. The addition of Υ to a space symmetry does not always increase the degeneracy, for example in a spherical system this two-fold degeneracy relates to $\pm m$, where m is the z-projection of angular momentum and is just a part of the familiar $(2j+1)$-fold degeneracy.

(2) Reactions

In a collision process, the time-reversal operation will interchange the role of the incoming and outgoing particles. An assumption of time-reversal invariance therefore relates the transition probabilities of inverse processes, a property known as the 'principle of detailed balance'. In an interaction process which may be treated by perturbation theory it is possible to deduce relations between matrix elements within the same process. To illustrate this point we must classify operators Q as even or odd under time-reversal, according as $\Upsilon Q = \pm Q\Upsilon$, respectively. For example we have seen above that **X** and **P** are even while **Y** is odd. Remembering the factor i which enters in passing from these infinitesimal operators to the Hermitian operators representing angular momentum and momentum, we see that **j**, **s** and **p** are odd, as one would expect, while for example **r** and **s**.**l** are even. (Remember however that one cannot classify wave functions as even or odd under time-reversal.) For the matrix elements of even or odd operators, respectively,

$$\langle\phi|Q|\psi\rangle = \langle\Upsilon\phi|\Upsilon Q\Upsilon^{-1}|\Upsilon\psi\rangle^* = \pm\langle\Upsilon\phi|Q|\Upsilon\psi\rangle^* \qquad (15.112)$$

By making measurements which relate matrix elements to those in time reversed states one can deduce whether Q is even or odd, or indeed some mixture.

As a particular example, consider the electric dipole moment of a particle at rest and with half-integer spin and finite mass. This moment is defined through an energy change proportional to the applied electric field $\boldsymbol{E}$, i.e. through a term of the kind $\mathbf{D}.\boldsymbol{E}$ in the interaction Hamiltonian, where $\mathbf{D}$ is the dipole moment operator. In quantum mechanics **D** is a vector operator and for a particle with spin s we shall be concerned with matrix elements $\langle m_s|\mathrm{D}_z|m_s\rangle$ if we take our z-axis in the direction of the field E. Since **D** is a vector operator, the Wigner–Eckart theorem, (see equation (7.54), gives

$$\langle m_s|\,\mathrm{D}_z\,|\,m_s\rangle = (-1)^{s+m_s}\langle -m_s|\,\mathrm{D}_z\,|-m_s\rangle \qquad (15.113)$$

But from equation (15.108), $\Upsilon|m_s\rangle = (-1)^{s+m_s}|-m_s\rangle$ so that, depending on whether D_z is even or odd under time-reversal,

$$\langle m_s|\mathrm{D}_z|m_s\rangle = \pm\langle -m_s|\mathrm{D}_z|-m_s\rangle^* = \pm\langle -m_s|\mathrm{D}_z|-m_s\rangle$$

since D_z must be Hermitian to give a real energy change. On comparing this equation with equation (15.113) we see that the dipole moment must vanish unless D_z is an odd operator. In the accepted time-reversal invariant theory of the electromagnetic interaction D_z is even under time-reversal and this is consistent with the fact that no dipole moment has been observed for any particle. At the present time very accurate measurements are being made on the neutron to see if even a very small dipole moment exists. Any such observation would indicate a breakdown of time-reversal symmetry in the theory. It would also indicate a breakdown of space inversion symmetry because accepted space inversion invariant theory has D_z as an odd parity operator. Thus if the particle has definite parity the diagonal matrix elements of D_z would also vanish for this reason.

In spite of numerous experiments no firm evidence for any breakdown in time-reversal invariance has been found. This contrasts with the space inversion symmetry where, because of the left-handedness of the neutrino, the weak interactions like β-decay show large violations of space inversion symmetry.

The group $\mathscr{P}_{st}$

Since the extension from the group $\mathscr{P}$ to $\mathscr{P}_t$ did not lead to any change in the vector space of an irreducible representation, it follows that the extension from $\mathscr{P}_t$ to $\mathscr{P}_{st}$ which includes both space inversion and time-reversal, will be just like the extension from $\mathscr{P}$ to $\mathscr{P}_s$ described in section 15.5. In other words we may simply include with the results of section 15.5 the transformations deduced in this section for the operator Υ. The transformations for the new product element ΥT(I) follow directly from those for the two factors.

15.8 Single-particle wave functions and the wave equations

Our approach throughout this chapter has been to study the irreducible representations of the Poincaré group. This tells us the transformation properties of the functions which belong to each representation. A belief in Poincaré invariance then led us to identify the representation labels with invariant properties of the particles, like mass and spin. By comparing with the properties of observed particles we associated each particle with an irreducible representation in the same way that in non-relativistic theory we associated each eigenstate of the Schrodinger equation with a representation of the symmetry group of the Hamiltonian. However we have never constructed the wave function explicitly. The philosophy here follows that used in discussing the group $\mathscr{R}_3$, namely that one can deduce the properties of the basis vectors $|jm\rangle$ of the representations $D^{(j)}$ without specifying their detailed form. One thereby achieved the greater generality that the results were applicable to any spherically symmetric system. For example the wave functions $|jm\rangle$ have the same rotational properties whether they refer to one particle or any number of particles. In the case of a single particle, however, one may construct explicitly the angular dependence of the wave functions by introducing the explicit differential form for the rotation operators. The Casimir operator is then a differential operator and its eigenvalue equation provides a wave equation whose solutions are the basis vectors $|jm\rangle$ of the irreducible representations.

In this section we first elaborate the above remarks for $\mathscr{R}_3$ and then use the same idea in the Euclidean and Poincaré groups to deduce the famous equations of Klein–Gordon, Dirac, Weyl and Maxwell. Although for free particles these equations carry no more information than we have already in the irreducible representations they are useful when interactions are introduced, see subsection 15.8.2, and when a theory of quantised fields is constructed, see section 16.3.

15.8.1 The group $\mathscr{R}_3$

Recall from section 7.5 that the $\mathscr{R}_3$ Casimir operator is $\mathbf{J}^2$ and it has eigenvalue $j(j+1)$ in the representation $D^{(j)}$, where $j = 0, \frac{1}{2}, 1, \frac{3}{2}, \ldots$. The explicit differential form of the infinitesimal operators $J_q = -i(\boldsymbol{r} \wedge \nabla)_q$ was given in subsection 7.4.5. Thus the basis vectors $|jm\rangle$ must satisfy the 'wave equation'

$$\{(\boldsymbol{r} \wedge \nabla)^2 + j(j+1)\}\,|jm\rangle = 0 \qquad (15.114)$$

Since rotations leave the length of $\boldsymbol{r}$ unchanged we may regard r as a constant in this study of the basis vectors of $D^{(j)}$. In this case, from equation (7.57), we see that the equation reduces to

$$\{r^2\nabla^2 + j(j+1)\}\,|jm\rangle = 0 \qquad (15.115)$$

Thus the behaviour of the basis vectors $|jm\rangle$ could be found by solving the wave equation (15.115). In fact this is the Schrodinger equation for the free motion of a particle on a sphere of radius r and its solutions, see section 7.5, are the spherical harmonics for integer j, namely $Y^{(j)}_m(\theta, \phi)$.

To construct wave functions with half-integer j we must extend equation (15.115) by introducing a framework with several components as described in section 8.4. If, in particular, we take two components, transforming like $D^{(\frac{1}{2})}$, then the explicit forms for the rotation operators are $\mathbf{J} = \mathbf{l}+\mathbf{s} = -i\boldsymbol{r}\wedge\nabla+\mathbf{s}$ where $\mathbf{s}$ denotes the set of three 2×2 matrices s_q given in equation (8.15). Following the same steps as before leads to the new wave equation

$$\{r^2\nabla^2 - \tfrac{3}{4} + 2i\mathbf{s}.\boldsymbol{r}\wedge\nabla + j(j+1)\}\,|jm\rangle = 0 \qquad (15.116)$$

where we have inserted the value $\frac{3}{4}$ for $\mathbf{s}^2$. The terms which do not involve $\mathbf{s}$ are understood to contain the 2×2 unit matrix and the wave function $|jm\rangle$ has two components

$$|jm\rangle = \begin{pmatrix} \psi_+(\theta,\phi) \\ \psi_-(\theta,\phi) \end{pmatrix}$$

in a notation similar to that of section 8.4. Thus equation (15.116) provides a pair of coupled differential equations for the two functions $\psi_\pm(\theta,\phi)$. This sounds formidable but we have already solved the problem in section 8.4. The two differential operators in equation (15.116) commute with each other so that they may be diagonalised simultaneously and we know that the first leads to spherical harmonics $Y^{(l)}_{m_l}$. Furthermore from the vector coupling in section 8.4 we know that for given j and with $s=\frac{1}{2}$ the only possible values of l are $j\pm\frac{1}{2}$. By using the properties (7.40) of the raising and lowering operators $l_\pm$ one can show (see problem 15.11) that these two solutions are given by

$$|jm\rangle = \begin{pmatrix} \{(l+\frac{1}{2}+m)/(2l+1)\}^{\frac{1}{2}}\,Y^{(l)}_{m-\frac{1}{2}}(\theta,\phi) \\ \{(l+\frac{1}{2}-m)/(2l+1)\}^{\frac{1}{2}}\,Y^{(l)}_{m+\frac{1}{2}}(\theta,\phi) \end{pmatrix} \quad \text{for } l=j+\tfrac{1}{2}$$

and by

$$|jm\rangle = \begin{pmatrix} \{(l+\frac{1}{2}-m)/(2l+1)\}^{\frac{1}{2}}\,Y^{(l)}_{m-\frac{1}{2}}(\theta,\phi) \\ \{(l+\frac{1}{2}+m)/(2l+1)\}^{\frac{1}{2}}\,Y^{(l)}_{m+\frac{1}{2}}(\theta,\phi) \end{pmatrix} \quad \text{for } l=j-\tfrac{1}{2}$$

The numerical coefficients in front of the spherical harmonics are simply vector-coupling coefficients and in fact the solutions above are precisely those given by equation (8.24) for $s=\frac{1}{2}$.

15.8.2 The group $\mathscr{E}_3$

We have seen in section 15.1 that the symmetry group $\mathscr{E}_3$ has irreducible representations $\mathrm{E}^{(|\boldsymbol{k}|,m)}$ with $m=0,\pm\frac{1}{2},\pm 1,\ldots$ and $|\boldsymbol{k}|>0$, and $\mathrm{E}^{(0,s)}\equiv\mathrm{D}^{(s)}$. The Casimir operators are $\mathbf{P}.\mathbf{P}$ and $\mathbf{P}.\mathbf{X}$ with eigenvalues $-|\boldsymbol{k}|^2$ and $-|\boldsymbol{k}|m$, in $\mathrm{E}^{(|\boldsymbol{k}|,m)}$. If we use the explicit differential forms $\mathbf{P}=-\nabla$ and $\mathbf{X}=-\boldsymbol{r}\wedge\nabla$ then $\mathbf{P}.\mathbf{X}$ vanishes so that we can only construct the representation $\mathrm{E}^{(|\boldsymbol{k}|,0)}$ with $m=0$. The corresponding wave equation is then

$$(\nabla^2+|\boldsymbol{k}|^2)|\psi\rangle = 0 \qquad (15.117)$$

which is simply the Schrodinger equation for a free particle with kinetic energy $|\boldsymbol{k}|^2$ in units of $\hbar^2/2M$, and without spin.

To construct a wave equation which is appropriate for $m\neq 0$ we again introduce several components. Then, writing the rotation operator $\mathbf{X} = -i\mathbf{J} = -i(\mathbf{l}+\mathbf{s}) = -\boldsymbol{r}\wedge\nabla - i\mathbf{s}$ as before, the Casimir operator $\mathbf{P}.\mathbf{X}$ is given by $-i\mathbf{P}.\mathbf{s} = i\nabla.\mathbf{s}$. Taking two components, with $\mathbf{s}$ again given by the familiar 2×2 matrices, we shall expect to produce basis vectors with $m = \pm\frac{1}{2}$. This is soon verified by writing down the new wave equation

$$(i\nabla.\mathbf{s}+|\boldsymbol{k}|m)|\psi\rangle = 0$$

which implies that

$$\{(\nabla.\mathbf{s})^2+|\boldsymbol{k}|^2m^2\}|\psi\rangle = 0 \qquad (15.118)$$

but since the spin matrices satisfy $\mathrm{s}_q^2 = \frac{1}{4}$, $\mathrm{s}_x\mathrm{s}_y+\mathrm{s}_y\mathrm{s}_x = 0$, etc., it follows that $(\nabla.\mathbf{s})^2 = \frac{1}{4}\nabla^2$ so that by comparison with equation (15.117) $m^2 = \frac{1}{4}$ and $m = \pm\frac{1}{2}$. Thus, in the two-component framework, we may construct basis vectors belonging to $\mathrm{E}^{(|\boldsymbol{k}|,\frac{1}{2})}$ and $\mathrm{E}^{(|\boldsymbol{k}|,-\frac{1}{2})}$. From the explicit forms (8.15) for the spin matrices one deduces that the appropriate basis vectors (un-normalised) are

$$|m=\tfrac{1}{2}\rangle = \begin{pmatrix}|\boldsymbol{k}|+k_z\\ k_x+ik_y\end{pmatrix}\mathrm{e}^{i\boldsymbol{k}.\boldsymbol{r}} \quad\text{and}\quad |m=-\tfrac{1}{2}\rangle = \begin{pmatrix}-k_x+ik_y\\ |\boldsymbol{k}|+k_z\end{pmatrix}\mathrm{e}^{i\boldsymbol{k}.\boldsymbol{r}} \qquad (15.119)$$

with the usual convention for the two components, i.e. s_z diagonal.

The spin gyromagnetic ratio

We are now in a position to deduce the value $g_s = 2$ which we quoted in section 8.4 for the spin g-factor of the electron. It is often said that this value is a consequence of the Dirac equation but such statements are misleading. It is true that this value of g_s comes naturally from the Dirac equation but it comes equally naturally from the wave equation (15.118) which is non-relativistic. The introduction of a magnetic field to the free motion of a particle with charge $-e$ may be accomplished in classical mechanics by the substitution of $\boldsymbol{p}+e\boldsymbol{A}/c$ for the momentum $\boldsymbol{p}$ in the Hamiltonian, where $\boldsymbol{A}$ is the vector potential of the field. The same thing may be done in quantum mechanics in the approximation where the field itself is not quantised. With this modification and remembering that $\mathbf{p} = -i\hbar\nabla$, the equation (15.118) for $m = \pm\frac{1}{2}$ becomes

$$[\{(\nabla+ie\boldsymbol{A}/c\hbar).\mathbf{s}\}^2+\tfrac{1}{4}|\boldsymbol{k}|^2]|\psi\rangle = 0 \qquad (15.120)$$

which is sometimes called the Pauli equation. For a uniform magnetic field we may take $\boldsymbol{A} = \frac{1}{2}\boldsymbol{B}\wedge\boldsymbol{r}$, where $\boldsymbol{B} = \nabla\wedge\boldsymbol{A}$ denotes the constant strength and direction of the field. Then, using the properties of the spin matrices again and remembering that ∇ does not commute with $\boldsymbol{A}$ this equation (15.120) reduces to

$$[\nabla^2+|\boldsymbol{k}|^2-(e/\hbar c)\{\boldsymbol{B}.(\mathbf{l}+2\mathbf{s})\}]|\psi\rangle = 0 \qquad (15.121)$$

where we have omitted terms of second order in $\boldsymbol{B}$. Comparing this with the

Schrodinger equation (15.117) one sees the appearance of interaction terms between the field $\boldsymbol{B}$ and the orbital and spin angular momenta of the electron. If we multiply equation (15.121) through by the constant $-\hbar^2/2M$, to bring it into the standard form of a Schrodinger equation with the correct dimensions of energy, then the interaction term may be written as $-\boldsymbol{\mu}.\boldsymbol{B}$, where $\boldsymbol{\mu} = -\mu_B(\mathbf{l}+g_s\mathbf{s})$ with the Bohr magneton μ_B defined by $\mu_B = e\hbar/2Mc$ and the spin g-factor given by $g_s = 2$. This result is in agreement with the observed value for g_s, which is very close to 2 and was discussed in section 8.4.

It should be emphasised that we have not proved that every particle with $s = \frac{1}{2}$ has $g_s = 2$ but simply that this value occurs naturally. It is always possible to add an extra term to the Hamiltonian to produce any value of g_s. Indeed, for the proton which also has $s = \frac{1}{2}$, $g_s = 5.58$ in units of the nuclear magneton. This value is said to be 'anomalous' and one supposes that the difference from the natural value of 2 is due to the internal motion of its constituent parts, see section 12.3. A particle like the electron or the muon for which g_s is close to its natural value is regarded as more 'elementary' than those for which it is not. Even the electron has $g_s = 2.0023$ but this small departure may be understood when the electromagnetic field is properly quantised.

15.8.3 The Poincaré group with $s=0$—the Klein–Gordon equation

We now move on to consider the wave equations governing the motion of free particles moving at relativistic speeds. Thus we must seek equations whose solutions belong to irreducible representations of the Poincaré group. First we study the particles with finite mass so that we are interested in the representations $\mathrm{P}^{(k,s)}$. In this subsection we concentrate on the spinless particles, $s = 0$, and in the next we investigate the case $s = \frac{1}{2}$.

The representations $\mathrm{P}^{(k,s)}$ are distinguished by the eigenvalues $-k^2$ and $-k^2 s(s+1)$ of the two Casimir operators $\hat{\mathbf{P}}.\hat{\mathbf{P}}$ and $\hat{\mathbf{W}}.\hat{\mathbf{W}}$, see subsection 15.4.3. Following the procedure in earlier sections we introduce the explicit differential forms $\mathbf{P} = -\boldsymbol{\nabla}$, $\mathrm{P}_t = (1/c)\partial/\partial t$, $\mathbf{X} = -\boldsymbol{r}\wedge\boldsymbol{\nabla}$ and $\mathbf{Y} = ct\boldsymbol{\nabla} + (\boldsymbol{r}/c)\partial/\partial t$ for the infinitesimal operators. Then from the definition (15.72) one sees that the operator $\hat{\mathbf{W}}$ vanishes identically. For non-zero k this implies that $s = 0$, and the Casimir operator $\hat{\mathbf{P}}.\hat{\mathbf{P}}$ leads to the simple Klein–Gordon wave equation

$$(-\boldsymbol{\nabla}^2 + c^{-2}\frac{\partial^2}{\partial t^2} + k^2)|\psi\rangle = 0 \tag{15.122}$$

If we introduce the notation $\Box^2 = -\boldsymbol{\nabla}^2 + c^{-2}\,\partial^2/\partial t^2$ the form

$$(\Box^2 + k^2)|\psi\rangle = 0$$

of this equation is very similar to the Schrodinger equation (15.117). But whereas in the Schrodinger equation the constant $|\boldsymbol{k}|^2$ has physical significance as energy $E = \hbar^2|\boldsymbol{k}|^2/2M$, the constant k^2 in the Klein–Gordon equation is related to the mass $M = \hbar k/c$. The plane-wave solutions of equation (15.122) are

$$|\psi\rangle = \exp[i(\boldsymbol{k}\,.\,\boldsymbol{r} - k_t ct)] \tag{15.123}$$

and we have discussed them already in subsection 15.4.1. Recall also from subsection 15.4.2 that the representations $\mathrm{P}^{(k,s)}$ have been chosen to have future time-like $\hat{\boldsymbol{k}}$, i.e. $k_t > 0$, so that the energy $E = \hbar c k_t$ is always positive. Thus we are imposing a restriction on the solutions of equation (15.122) which clearly has solutions with either sign for k_t.

As in classical mechanics, the inclusion of an electromagnetic field in the relativistic Hamiltonian may be accomplished by replacing the energy-momentum four-vector $\hat{\boldsymbol{p}} = (\boldsymbol{p}, E/c)$ by $\hat{\boldsymbol{p}} + e\hat{\boldsymbol{A}}/c$, for a particle with charge $-e$, where $\hat{\boldsymbol{A}}$ is the four-vector $\hat{\boldsymbol{A}} = (\boldsymbol{A}, \phi)$ describing the field with ϕ the usual scalar potential (see subsection 16.1.3). The Klein–Gordon equation (15.122) is thus modified with $\partial/\partial t - ie\phi/\hbar$ replacing $\partial/\partial t$ and $\nabla + ie\boldsymbol{A}/c\hbar$ replacing ∇.

15.8.4 The Poincaré group with $s = \frac{1}{2}$—the Dirac equation

To construct a wave equation which is appropriate for $s \neq 0$ we must again introduce several components. In group-theoretical language this is equivalent to the construction of product representations. For example in discussing the representations $\mathrm{E}^{(|\boldsymbol{k}|, \pm\frac{1}{2})}$ of $\mathscr{E}_3$ in subsection 15.8.2 we were effectively constructing the product representation $\mathrm{E}^{(|\boldsymbol{k}|,0)} \times \mathrm{E}^{(0,\frac{1}{2})} \equiv \mathrm{E}^{(|\boldsymbol{k}|,0)} \times \mathrm{D}^{(\frac{1}{2})}$ so that the infinitesimal operators were sums of the differential operators relating to $\mathrm{E}^{(|\boldsymbol{k}|,0)}$ and the matrix (spin) operators relating to $\mathrm{D}^{(\frac{1}{2})}$. We found that the product reduced to the sum $\mathrm{E}^{(|\boldsymbol{k}|,\frac{1}{2})} \dotplus \mathrm{E}^{(|\boldsymbol{k}|,-\frac{1}{2})}$. The same technique will now be followed to describe the representations $\mathrm{P}^{(k,\frac{1}{2})}$ of the Poincaré group and to deduce the Dirac equation.

A natural choice for the product representation in the $s = \frac{1}{2}$ case will be $\mathrm{P}^{(k,0)} \times \mathrm{L}^{(\frac{1}{2},0)}$ where the second factor is the translation-invariant representation corresponding to $\hat{\boldsymbol{k}} = 0$ and referred to under the subheading region (6) in subsection 15.4.2. Being translation-invariant it is a representation of the Lorentz group $\mathscr{L}$, see subsection 15.2.5. (The choice of $\mathrm{L}^{(0,\frac{1}{2})}$ instead of $\mathrm{L}^{(\frac{1}{2},0)}$ would be an equally natural choice but leads to precisely the same results.) The basis vectors in this product representation are labelled by $|\hat{\boldsymbol{k}}n\rangle$, where $\hat{\boldsymbol{k}}$ refers to $\mathrm{P}^{(k,0)}$ and $n = \pm\frac{1}{2}$ distinguishes the two components of $\mathrm{L}^{(\frac{1}{2},0)}$. The Poincaré transformations in this basis are thus given simply by

$$\mathrm{T}(\hat{\varepsilon}, \mathrm{L})|\hat{\boldsymbol{k}}n\rangle = \exp(i\hat{\boldsymbol{k}}'.\hat{\varepsilon}) \sum_{n'} L^{(\frac{1}{2},0)}_{n'n}(\mathrm{L})|\hat{\boldsymbol{k}}'n'\rangle \tag{15.124}$$

where $\hat{\boldsymbol{k}}' = \mathrm{L}\hat{\boldsymbol{k}}$. The matrix elements of the representation $\mathrm{L}^{(\frac{1}{2},0)}$ can be deduced from the matrix of $\mathrm{D}^{(\frac{1}{2})}$ by noting that in $\mathrm{L}^{(\frac{1}{2},0)}$ the infinitesimal operators take the form $\mathbf{X} = \mathbf{A} + \mathbf{B} = -i\mathbf{s}$ and $\mathbf{Y} = -i(\mathbf{A} - \mathbf{B}) = -\mathbf{s}$ in the notation of subsection 15.2.4 and where $\mathbf{s}$ is the usual spin matrix. However, we shall not need such details here. The essential feature of equation (15.124) is the simple factorisation in which the matrix is independent of $\hat{k}$. This contrasts with the basis $|\hat{k}\frac{1}{2}m_s\rangle$ used for the representation $P^{(k,\frac{1}{2})}$ in subsection 15.4.2, where the corresponding equation (15.59) may appear to factorise but the rotation R′ depends on $\hat{k}$ through equations (15.60) and (15.61). In fact we may transform from the basis $|\hat{k}n\rangle$ to the basis $|\hat{k}\frac{1}{2}m_s\rangle$ and this verifies that the product representation $P^{(k,0)} \times L^{(\frac{1}{2},0)}$ is equivalent to $P^{(k,\frac{1}{2})}$. The transformation is

$$|\hat{k}\tfrac{1}{2}m_s\rangle = \sum_n L^{(\frac{1}{2},0)}_{nm_s}(Q)|\hat{k}n\rangle \tag{15.125}$$

where the boost Q was defined in equation (15.58). To verify this result we use equations (15.124) and (15.125) to see that

$$\begin{aligned} T(\hat{\varepsilon}, L)|\hat{k}\tfrac{1}{2}m_s\rangle &= \exp(i\hat{k}'.\hat{\varepsilon})\sum_n [L^{(\frac{1}{2},0)}(L)L^{(\frac{1}{2},0)}(Q)]_{nm_s}|\hat{k}'n\rangle \\ &= \exp(i\hat{k}'.\hat{\varepsilon})\sum_{m_s'}[L^{(\frac{1}{2},0)^{-1}}(Q')L^{(\frac{1}{2},0)}(L)L^{(\frac{1}{2},0)}(Q)]_{m_s'm_s}|\hat{k}'\tfrac{1}{2}m_s'\rangle \end{aligned}$$

using also the inverse of equation (15.125). But because $L^{(\frac{1}{2},0)}$ is a group representation the matrix here is simply $L^{(\frac{1}{2},0)}(Q'^{-1}LQ)$ and from equation (15.60) this is just $L^{(\frac{1}{2},0)}(R') = D^{(\frac{1}{2})}(R')$. Thus the states constructed in equation (15.125) have the correct transformation property (15.59).

The basis $|\hat{k}n\rangle$ thus provides a simple two-component description for a particle with spin $s = \frac{1}{2}$. The wave equation would be simply the Klein–Gordon equation

$$(\Box^2 + k^2)|\psi\rangle = 0 \tag{15.126}$$

where $|\psi\rangle$ is now a two-component wave function. The role of this equation is to provide the plane-wave factor (15.123) appropriate to the factor $P^{(k,0)}$ in the product representation. Note that the wave equation (15.126) contains no spin operators which says that no constraint is being put on the 'direction' of $|\psi\rangle$ in the two-component space.

As far as the second Casimir operator $\hat{W}.\hat{W}$ is concerned it is easily shown (see problem 15.12) that in the product representation $P^{(k,0)} \times L^{(\frac{1}{2},0)}$ one has the equivalence $\hat{W}.\hat{W} = \frac{3}{4}\hat{P}.\hat{P}$ which is to be expected for the representation $P^{(k,\frac{1}{2})}$ from equation (15.74). However, in the presence of an electromagnetic field the substitution of $\hat{p} + e\hat{A}/c$ for $\hat{p}$ in $\hat{W}.\hat{W}$ gives rise to a new term in the Klein–Gordon equation which couples the electron spin to the field.

The two-component description given above for a particle with spin $s = \frac{1}{2}$ is unsatisfactory for two reasons. Firstly the transformation (15.124) is not unitary (recall from subsection 15.2.5 that the representation $L^{(\frac{1}{2},0)}$ of the Lorentz group was not unitary). The unitary representation could only be recovered by returning, through the transformation (15.125) to the original basis $|\hat{k}\frac{1}{2}m_s\rangle$ for the representation $P^{(k,\frac{1}{2})}$ and thus losing the factorisation. The second reason is that the two-component space does not remain invariant when the space inversion is introduced (recall from section 15.3 that the space inversion carries vectors of $L^{(\frac{1}{2},0)}$ into vectors of $L^{(0,\frac{1}{2})}$ and these two representations of $\mathscr{L}$ may be added to form a single four-dimensional irreducible representation $L^{(\frac{1}{2},0)} \dotplus L^{(0,\frac{1}{2})}$ of the Lorentz group with space inversions $\mathscr{L}_s$) and is therefore unsuitable for a description of particles with definite parity. We now show that a four-component description based on the product representation $P^{(k,0)} \times (L^{(\frac{1}{2},0)} \dotplus L^{(0,\frac{1}{2})})$ overcomes both these difficulties and the restriction in the number of spin states from four to the value two, which is appropriate for the representation $P^{(k,\frac{1}{2})}$, is achieved by solving what is known as the Dirac wave equation.

Following a procedure very similar to that above we introduce basis vectors $|\hat{\boldsymbol{k}}\alpha\rangle$ for the product representation $P^{(k,0)} \times (L^{(\frac{1}{2},0)} \dotplus L^{(0,\frac{1}{2})})$, where $\alpha = 1, 2, 3, 4$ runs over the four components of the second factor. The Poincaré transformations are then given by

$$T(\hat{\varepsilon}, L)|\hat{\boldsymbol{k}}\alpha\rangle = \exp(i\hat{\boldsymbol{k}}'.\hat{\varepsilon}) \sum_{\beta=1}^{4} M_{\beta\alpha}(L)|\hat{\boldsymbol{k}}'\beta\rangle \tag{15.127}$$

where $M_{\beta\alpha}$ denotes the matrix elements of the 4×4 matrix

$$M = \begin{pmatrix} L^{(\frac{1}{2},0)} & 0 \\ 0 & L^{(0,\frac{1}{2})} \end{pmatrix} \tag{15.128}$$

in partitioned form with $L^{(\frac{1}{2},0)}$, etc., denoting 2×2 matrices. Now the four-component space is clearly too big for describing the representation $P^{(k,\frac{1}{2})}$; in fact $P^{(k,0)} \times (L^{(\frac{1}{2},0)} \dotplus L^{(0,\frac{1}{2})}) = 2P^{(k,\frac{1}{2})}$. The previous two-component description, based on the $L^{(\frac{1}{2},0)}$ piece, was one way of selecting a single $P^{(k,\frac{1}{2})}$ representation but there are other ways which involve the mixing of $L^{(\frac{1}{2},0)}$ and $L^{(0,\frac{1}{2})}$. To discuss them we must first define some operators which couple these two two-dimensional subspaces. From the rule (15.37) for reducing product representations in the group $\mathscr{L}$ such operators must transform according to $L^{(\frac{1}{2},\frac{1}{2})}$ and thus form a four-vector which we denote by $\hat{\gamma}$. It is soon verified (see problem 15.13) that such a set is given by the four 4×4 matrices

$$\gamma_t = \begin{pmatrix} 0 & 1 \\ 1 & 0 \end{pmatrix}, \quad \gamma_q = 2\begin{pmatrix} 0 & s_q \\ s_q & 0 \end{pmatrix} \quad \text{with } q = x, y \text{ or } z \tag{15.129}$$

in partitioned form where 1 denotes the 2×2 unit matrix and s_q are the 2×2 spin matrices. We may now construct the Poincaré invariant operator $\hat{\gamma}.\hat{\mathbf{P}}$ and diagonalise it. To find its eigenvalues we note that

$$(\hat{\gamma}.\hat{\mathbf{P}})^2 = \sum_{i,j} g_{ii}\gamma_i P_i g_{jj}\gamma_j P_j = \sum_i \gamma_i^2 P_i^2 + \sum_{i \neq j} g_{ii}g_{jj} P_i P_j(\gamma_i\gamma_j + \gamma_j\gamma_i)$$

while, from the definitions (15.129) and the properties of the spin matrices, the $\hat{\gamma}$-matrices satisfy the anticommutation relations

$$\gamma_i\gamma_j + \gamma_j\gamma_i = 2g_{ij} \tag{15.130}$$

Thus we have the equivalence $(\hat{\gamma}.\hat{\mathbf{P}})^2 = \hat{\mathbf{P}}.\hat{\mathbf{P}}$ so that, within the product representation $\mathrm{P}^{(k,0)} \times (\mathrm{L}^{(\frac{1}{2},0)} \dot{+} \mathrm{L}^{(0,\frac{1}{2})})$, the operator $(\hat{\gamma}.\hat{\mathbf{P}})^2$ is just $-k^2$ times the unit operator. Hence the possible eigenvalues of $\hat{\gamma}.\hat{\mathbf{P}}$ are $\pm ik$ and if we classify the basis vectors of the product representation according to which of these two eigenvalues they have, the representation space will have broken into two invariant subspaces each of which forms the basis of a representation $\mathrm{P}^{(k,\frac{1}{2})}$. Thus by restricting our wave functions to one of these subspaces we have constructed a basis for $\mathrm{P}^{(k,\frac{1}{2})}$. It is unimportant which of the two we choose and if we choose $-ik$ the restriction is imposed by demanding that the four-component wave-function $|\psi\rangle$ should satisfy the condition

$$[\hat{\gamma}.\hat{\mathbf{P}} + ik]\,|\psi\rangle = 0 \tag{15.131}$$

which is called the Dirac equation. This acquires a more familiar form if we write $k = cM/\hbar$ in terms of the mass M. (see subsection 15.7.1) and introduce the differential form $\hat{\mathbf{P}} = (-\nabla, (1/c)\,\partial/\partial t)$. Then

$$\left[i\hbar\gamma_t\frac{\partial}{\partial t} + i\hbar c\gamma.\nabla - Mc^2\right]|\psi\rangle = 0$$

or, multiplying through by γ_t and using $\gamma_t^2 = 1$,

$$\left[i\hbar\frac{\partial}{\partial t} + i\hbar c\gamma_t\gamma.\nabla - Mc^2\gamma_t\right]|\psi\rangle = 0 \tag{15.132}$$

For our continuing discussion of the Dirac equation we prefer to use the form (15.131).

To appreciate the form of the solutions of the Dirac equation and to show that for given $\hat{\boldsymbol{k}}$ there are just two solutions rather than four we first note that, for a particle at rest, $\mathbf{P}|\psi = 0$ and $\mathrm{P}_t|\psi\rangle = -ik|\psi\rangle$, so that equation (15.131) becomes

$$(\gamma_t - 1)\,|\psi\rangle = 0 \tag{15.133}$$

and from the explicit form (15.129) for γ_t it is easily seen that the solutions are any linear combinations of the two solutions

$$|\hat{\boldsymbol{k}}_0\tfrac{1}{2}\tfrac{1}{2}\rangle = 2^{-\frac{1}{2}}\begin{pmatrix}1\\0\\1\\0\end{pmatrix}|\hat{\boldsymbol{k}}_0\rangle \quad\text{and}\quad |\hat{\boldsymbol{k}}_0\tfrac{1}{2}-\tfrac{1}{2}\rangle = 2^{-\frac{1}{2}}\begin{pmatrix}0\\1\\0\\1\end{pmatrix}|\hat{\boldsymbol{k}}_0\rangle \tag{15.134}$$

where $|\hat{\boldsymbol{k}}_0\rangle$ denotes the plane wave (15.123) with $\boldsymbol{k} = 0$. For general $\hat{\boldsymbol{k}}$ the matrix equation corresponding to (15.133) is obtained simply from equation (15.131) and (15.129) by using $\mathbf{P}|\psi\rangle = -i\boldsymbol{k}|\psi\rangle$. The solutions are then expressed as linear combinations of

$$|\hat{\boldsymbol{k}}\tfrac{1}{2}\tfrac{1}{2}\rangle = \tfrac{1}{2}\{k(k+k_t)\}^{-\frac{1}{2}}\begin{pmatrix} k+k_t+k_z \\ k_x+ik_y \\ k+k_t-k_z \\ -k_x-ik_y \end{pmatrix}|\hat{\boldsymbol{k}}\rangle$$

$$|\hat{\boldsymbol{k}}\tfrac{1}{2}-\tfrac{1}{2}\rangle = \tfrac{1}{2}\{k(k+k_t)\}^{-\frac{1}{2}}\begin{pmatrix} k_x-ik_y \\ k+k_t-k_z \\ -k_x+ik_y \\ k+k_t+k_z \end{pmatrix}|\hat{\boldsymbol{k}}\rangle \tag{15.135}$$

this particular pair having been chosen so that they reduce to (15.134) in the non-relativistic limit $\boldsymbol{k} \to 0$. The normalisation factor will be explained later. Recalling the structure $L^{(\frac{1}{2},0)} \dotplus L^{(0,\frac{1}{2})}$ of the four components it is clear that in this limit the states $|\hat{\boldsymbol{k}}_0\tfrac{1}{2}\pm\tfrac{1}{2}\rangle$ correspond to the two spin states $m_s = \pm\tfrac{1}{2}$ of a particle at rest. It may also be shown (see problem 15.14) that the general wave function (15.135) may be obtained from the solutions (15.134) for a particle at rest by the operation of a boost $Q[\boldsymbol{b}(\hat{\boldsymbol{k}})]$, as in equation (15.57) for the vectors of $P^{(k,\frac{1}{2})}$. Finally we stress that, although we are working in a four-component space, there are only two independent states for a particle with fixed $\hat{\boldsymbol{k}}$ given by equation (15.135) and that any state of the particle is expressible as a linear combination of these two. This is consistent with the conclusions reached from studying the Poincaré representations where there were two states $m_s = \pm\tfrac{1}{2}$ for each $\hat{\boldsymbol{k}}$.

The basis which one uses in the four-component space is clearly a matter of choice and our choice was determined by equation (15.128), i.e. the first two rows transform like $L^{(\frac{1}{2},0)}$. In this basis we saw that, even in the non-relativistic limit, there was mixing of components, see equation (15.134). When discussing phenomena near this limit it would clearly simplify the algebra if one chose a new basis in which the states (15.134) are given by the column vectors (1, 0, 0, 0) and (0, 1, 0, 0). In the new basis one refers to the first two components as 'large' and the last two as 'small' because of their behaviour in this non-relativistic limit, when $|\boldsymbol{k}|/k$ is small. We shall not use this new basis.

The solutions (15.135) could also have been obtained directly by constructing a state of definite parity from the state (15.125) and the corresponding state generated from $L^{(0,\frac{1}{2})}$. If we denote by $|\hat{\boldsymbol{k}}n\rangle'$ the two states transforming like the product $P^{(k,0)} \times L^{(0,\frac{1}{2})}$ then we find, as in (15.125), that the two solutions (15.135) may be written as

$$|\hat{\boldsymbol{k}}\tfrac{1}{2}m_s\rangle = \sum_n \{L^{(\frac{1}{2},0)}_{nm_s}(Q)|\hat{\boldsymbol{k}}n\rangle + L^{(0,\frac{1}{2})}_{nm_s}(Q)|\hat{\boldsymbol{k}}n\rangle'\}/2^{\frac{1}{2}} \tag{15.135a}$$

as may be verified by using the explicit form

$$L^{(\frac{1}{2},0)}(Q) = \{(k+k_t)+2\boldsymbol{k}.\mathbf{s}\}/\{2k(k+k_t)\}^{\frac{1}{2}}$$

together with $L^{(0,\frac{1}{2})}[Q(\hat{\boldsymbol{k}})] = L^{(\frac{1}{2},0)}[Q(I\hat{\boldsymbol{k}})]$ which follow from equation (15.58) and subsection 15.2.5.

We now show how to define a scalar product in the four-component space which is invariant with respect to Poincare transformations. In other words we construct a scalar product with respect to which the Poincaré transformations are unitary. Such a scalar product is then suitable for use in calculating values of physical observables. We write an arbitrary solution as

$$|\psi\rangle = \sum_{\alpha} \int \psi_\alpha(\hat{\boldsymbol{k}})|\hat{\boldsymbol{k}}\alpha\rangle k_t^{-1}\,d\boldsymbol{k} \tag{15.136}$$

which is very like equation (15.78). However, the scalar product is now defined as

$$\langle\phi|\psi\rangle = \sum_{\alpha,\beta} \int \phi_\beta^*(\hat{\boldsymbol{k}})(\gamma_t)_{\beta\alpha}\psi_\alpha(\hat{\boldsymbol{k}})k_t^{-1}\,d\boldsymbol{k} \tag{15.137}$$

which differs from the corresponding equation (15.79) by the presence of the matrix γ_t. The reason for including this matrix is to make the scalar product invariant under the transformations (15.127). As we have remarked before, the matrix M in that transformation is not unitary so that, had we omitted the matrix γ_t, the scalar product would not have been invariant. To show the invariance of the definition (15.137) one must show the matrix equality $M^\dagger\gamma_t M = \gamma_t$ which from equations (15.128) and (15.129) reduces to $(L^{(0,\frac{1}{2})})^\dagger = (L^{(\frac{1}{2},0)})^{-1}$. But this relation follows directly from the matrices of $L^{(0,\frac{1}{2})}$ and $L^{(\frac{1}{2},0)}$ for pure rotations and for pure boosts and thus for all Lorentz transformations. The set of four functions

$$\bar{\psi}_\alpha(\hat{\boldsymbol{k}}) = \sum_\beta \psi_\beta^*(\hat{\boldsymbol{k}})(\gamma_t)_{\beta\alpha} \tag{15.138}$$

is sometimes called the adjoint of the set $\psi_\alpha(\hat{\boldsymbol{k}})$ and it is clear that the expression (15.137) is simpler with this notation. An alternative, but precisely equivalent, form for the scalar product is obtained from equation (15.137) by using the Dirac equation (15.131),

$$\langle\phi|\psi\rangle = \sum_\alpha \int \phi_\alpha^*(\hat{\boldsymbol{k}})\psi_\alpha(\hat{\boldsymbol{k}})kk_t^{-2}\,d\boldsymbol{k} \tag{15.139}$$

If we choose for $|\psi\rangle$ a particular plane wave solution $|\tilde{\boldsymbol{k}}\,\frac{1}{2}\frac{1}{2}\rangle$ given by (15.135) then the appropriate coefficients $\psi_\alpha(\hat{\boldsymbol{k}})$ are given by

$$\begin{aligned}
\psi_1(\hat{\boldsymbol{k}}) &= (k+k_t+k_z)k_t\delta(\boldsymbol{k}-\tilde{\boldsymbol{k}})\tfrac{1}{2}\{k(k+k_t)\}^{-\frac{1}{2}}\\
\psi_2(\hat{\boldsymbol{k}}) &= (k_x+ik_y)k_t\delta(\boldsymbol{k}-\tilde{\boldsymbol{k}})\tfrac{1}{2}\{k(k+k_t)\}^{-\frac{1}{2}}\\
\psi_3(\hat{\boldsymbol{k}}) &= (k+k_t-k_z)k_t\delta(\boldsymbol{k}-\tilde{\boldsymbol{k}})\tfrac{1}{2}\{k(k+k_t)\}^{-\frac{1}{2}}\\
\psi_4(\hat{\boldsymbol{k}}) &= (-k_x-ik_y)k_t\delta(\boldsymbol{k}-\tilde{\boldsymbol{k}})\tfrac{1}{2}\{k(k+k_t)\}^{-\frac{1}{2}}
\end{aligned}$$

with corresponding expressions for the second solution $|\hat{\boldsymbol{k}}\frac{1}{2}-\frac{1}{2}\rangle$. It is soon verified that these two solutions are orthogonal with our definition of scalar product and their normalisation is given by

$$\langle \hat{\boldsymbol{k}}'\tfrac{1}{2}m_s|\hat{\boldsymbol{k}}\tfrac{1}{2}m_s'\rangle = k_t\,\delta(\boldsymbol{k}'-\boldsymbol{k})\,\delta_{m_s m_s'} \tag{15.140}$$

So far as space inversion and parity is concerned the same results as in section 15.5 may be arrived at in the four-component description by writing the inversion operator T(I) as the product of three factors

$$\mathrm{T(I)} = \mathrm{T}_{\mathrm{intr}}(\mathrm{I})\mathrm{T}_k(\mathrm{I})\mathrm{T}_s(\mathrm{I})$$

where the last two factors refer to the two factors in the product representation $\mathrm{P}^{(k,0)} \times (\mathrm{L}^{(\frac{1}{2},0)} \dot{+} \mathrm{L}^{(0,\frac{1}{2})})$ and the first factor is the intrinsic parity. Now, as we have seen before, $\mathrm{T}_k(\mathrm{I})$ will simply change the direction of the space part of $\hat{\boldsymbol{k}}$ while from section 15.3 the matrix form of $\mathrm{T}_s(\mathrm{I})$ is simply γ_t. Thus for a particle with intrinsic parity $\pi = \pm 1$ we have

$$\mathrm{T(I)}|\hat{\boldsymbol{k}}\alpha\rangle = \pi\sum_{\beta}(\gamma_t)_{\beta\alpha}|\mathrm{I}\hat{\boldsymbol{k}}\beta\rangle \tag{15.141}$$

It is soon verified, see problem 15.15, that T(I) commutes with $\hat{\gamma}.\hat{\mathbf{P}}$ so that the space inversion carries one solution of the Dirac equation into another solution of the same equation.

The inclusion of an electromagnetic field is achieved as in subsection 15.8.3 by replacing $\hat{\mathfrak{p}}$ by $\hat{\mathfrak{p}}+e\hat{A}/c$ where as usual $\hat{\mathfrak{p}} = i\hbar\hat{\mathbf{P}}$.

We conclude this section on the Dirac equation by emphasising that, in the four-component framework, the transformations separate into orbital and spin factors and consequently the infinitesimal operators are sums $\mathbf{X} = \mathbf{X}_l + \mathbf{X}_s$, $\mathbf{Y} = \mathbf{Y}_l + \mathbf{Y}_s$ of differential operators and 4×4 matrix operators. From the matrix M given in equation (15.128) and the explicit form for the infinitesimal operators in the Lorentz group (see subsection 15.2.4) we have, for the matrix operators,

$$(\mathrm{X}_s)_x = \mathrm{A}_x + \mathrm{B}_x = -i\begin{pmatrix} \mathrm{S}_x & 0 \\ 0 & \mathrm{S}_x \end{pmatrix} = \tfrac{1}{2}\gamma_y\gamma_z, \quad \text{etc.} \tag{15.142}$$

and

$$(\mathrm{Y}_s)_x = -\mathrm{i}(\mathrm{A}_x - \mathrm{B}_x) = -\begin{pmatrix} \mathrm{S}_x & 0 \\ 0 & -\mathrm{S}_x \end{pmatrix} = -\tfrac{1}{2}\gamma_t\gamma_x, \quad \text{etc.}$$

For the differential part we need an operator to represent the infinitesimal change from $|\hat{\boldsymbol{k}}\rangle$ to $|\mathrm{L}\hat{\boldsymbol{k}}\rangle$ when the Lorentz transformation L is close to the identity. For this part of the operator we may ignore the component labels α. Thus for a general state $|\psi\rangle$, using equation (15.136), the transformed state is given by

$$|\psi'\rangle = \int \psi(\hat{\boldsymbol{k}})|\mathrm{L}\hat{\boldsymbol{k}}\rangle k_t^{-1}\,\mathrm{d}\boldsymbol{k} = \int \psi(\mathrm{L}^{-1}\hat{\boldsymbol{k}})|\hat{\boldsymbol{k}}\rangle k_t^{-1}\,\mathrm{d}\boldsymbol{k}$$

where we have changed variables for the integration and made use of the invariance of the volume element, see subsection 15.4.4. Thus the function $\psi(\hat{k})$ describing the state $|\psi\rangle$ is carried into $\psi(\mathrm{L}^{-1}\hat{k})$. If we now write $\mathrm{L} = 1+\Lambda$, as in subsection 15.2.4, for infinitesimal Λ, and develop a Taylor expansion for $\psi(\mathrm{L}^{-1}\hat{k})$ as we did for rotations in subsection 7.3.5 then we deduce the explicit differential forms.

$$(X_l)_x = -\left(k_y\frac{\partial}{\partial k_z} - k_z\frac{\partial}{\partial k_y}\right), \qquad \text{etc.}$$

$$(Y_l)_x = \left(k_x\frac{\partial}{\partial k_t} + k_t\frac{\partial}{\partial k_x}\right), \qquad \text{etc.}$$

The first of these is just the familiar form for the rotation operator (7.21) when expressed in the momentum representation, while the second gives the corresponding expression for the infinitesimal boosts.

15.8.5 Particles with zero mass and spin $|m| = \frac{1}{2}$ – the Weyl equation

The object here is to construct a factorised form for the representation $\mathrm{P}^{(0,m)}$ of the Poincaré group, see subsections 15.4.2 and 15.4.3, when $|m| = \frac{1}{2}$. We naturally consider the product of the representation $\mathrm{P}^{(0,0)}$ with $\mathrm{L}^{(\frac{1}{2},0)}$ or $\mathrm{L}^{(0,\frac{1}{2})}$, where we stress that $\mathrm{P}^{(0,0)}$ does not denote the identity representation but $\mathrm{P}^{(k,0)}$ with $k = 0$; in other words $k = 0$ but $\hat{k} \neq 0$. To be definite, we consider the product $\mathrm{P}^{(0,0)} \times \mathrm{L}^{(0,\frac{1}{2})}$ which we shall find to be appropriate for the case $m = -\frac{1}{2}$ corresponding to the neutrino. Since $\mathrm{P}^{(0,m)}$ has only one basis vector for each $\hat{k}$ while $\mathrm{P}^{(0,0)} \times \mathrm{L}^{(0,\frac{1}{2})}$ has two, it is clear that these two representations cannot be equivalent but we shall aim to construct the former from vectors of the latter. If we use the notation $|\hat{k}m\rangle$, as in subsection 15.4.2 for vectors of $\mathrm{P}^{(0,m)}$, and $|\hat{k}\alpha\rangle_0$ with $\alpha = \pm\frac{1}{2}$ for basis vectors of $\mathrm{P}^{(0,0)} \times \mathrm{L}^{(0,\frac{1}{2})}$ then we show that

$$|\hat{k}-\tfrac{1}{2}\rangle = \sum_\alpha L^{(0,\frac{1}{2})}_{\alpha-\frac{1}{2}}(\mathrm{R}_{xy}\mathrm{Q}_z)|\hat{k}\alpha\rangle_0 \qquad (15.143)$$

where, as in subsection 15.4.2, the Lorentz transformation $\mathrm{R}_{xy}\mathrm{Q}_z$ carries the vector (0, 0, 1, 1) into $\hat{k}$. This equation is analogous to equation (15.125) and generalises immediately for any (negative) m. For $m = +\frac{1}{2}$ we must use $\mathrm{L}^{(\frac{1}{2},0)}$ instead for reasons which are explained below. The justification for equation (15.143) follows that given for equation (15.125), with

$$\mathrm{T}(\mathcal{E},\mathrm{L})|\hat{k}-\tfrac{1}{2}\rangle = \exp(i\hat{k}'.\mathcal{E})L^{(0,\frac{1}{2})}_{-\frac{1}{2}-\frac{1}{2}}[(\mathrm{R}'_{xy}\mathrm{Q}'_z)^{-1}\mathrm{L}\mathrm{R}_{xy}\mathrm{Q}_z]|\hat{k}'-\tfrac{1}{2}\rangle \qquad (15.144)$$

The absence of any sum on the right arises from the fact that the group operation $(\mathrm{R}'_{xy}\mathrm{Q}'_z)^{-1}\mathrm{L}\mathrm{R}_{xy}\mathrm{Q}_z$ is an element of the subgroup $\mathscr{E}_2$, see subsection 15.4.2, whose infinitesimal operators were given in equation (15.62) by X_z, $\mathrm{X}_x - \mathrm{Y}_y$ and $\mathrm{X}_y + \mathrm{Y}_x$. But in $\mathrm{L}^{(0,\frac{1}{2})}$, $\mathbf{X} = -i\mathbf{Y}$ so that $\mathrm{X}_x - \mathrm{Y}_y = \mathrm{X}_x - i\mathrm{X}_y$

and $X_y + Y_x = i(X_x - iX_y)$ which are both lowering operators for m and give no contribution for $m = -\frac{1}{2}$. This leaves the single $\mathscr{R}_2$ operator X_z which leads to the simple exponential transformation (15.68) for $|\hat{\boldsymbol{k}} - \frac{1}{2}\rangle$.

We now show how it is possible to arrive at this same result (15.143) by imposing a wave equation constraint on the two-component space. We recall from section 15.4 that $P^{(0,m)}$ is characterised by equation (15.76), $(\hat{\mathrm{W}} + im\hat{\mathrm{P}})|\psi\rangle = 0$ in addition to $\hat{\mathbf{W}}.\hat{\mathbf{W}} = \hat{\mathbf{P}}.\hat{\mathbf{P}} = 0$. It is clear that the product representation $P^{(0,0)} \times L^{(0,\frac{1}{2})}$ satisfies the latter pair of equations but the constraint $(\hat{\mathbf{W}} + im\hat{\mathbf{P}})|\psi\rangle = 0$ leads to a 2×2 matrix equation which must be satisfied. To find the matrix form for $\hat{\mathbf{W}}$ we can start from the definition (15.72) of $\hat{\mathbf{W}}$ and use the second two rows and columns of equation (15.142) for the matrix forms of $\mathbf{X}$ and $\mathbf{Y}$. (Remember that the differential operator part of $\hat{\mathbf{W}}$ vanishes identically, see subsection 15.8.3). In this way the condition (15.76) becomes

$$\{mP_t - \mathbf{P}.\mathbf{s}\}|\psi\rangle = 0 \tag{15.145}$$

and

$$\{m\mathbf{P} - P_t\mathbf{s} - i\mathbf{P} \wedge \mathbf{s}\}|\psi\rangle = 0 \tag{15.145a}$$

This is really a set of four equations since (15.76) is a four-vector equation. However, if the time-component equation (15.145) is satisfied then it follows that for $m = -\frac{1}{2}$ the other three equations (15.145a) are also satisfied, as may be seen by multiplying equation (15.145) by $\mathbf{s}$. Thus the vital condition to be satisfied in the case $m = -\frac{1}{2}$ is equation (15.145) and this is known as the Weyl equation. Inserting the differential operator forms for $\hat{\mathbf{P}}$ it takes the more familiar form

$$\left\{\frac{\partial}{\partial t} - 2c\boldsymbol{\nabla}.\mathbf{s}\right\}|\psi\rangle = 0 \tag{15.146}$$

To find a solution for the case $m = +\frac{1}{2}$ which, see subsection 16.3.7, corresponds to the antineutrino one must use the representation $L^{(\frac{1}{2},0)}$ but the method is otherwise unchanged.

We now return to the form (15.145) to study a plane-wave solution inserting the values $-i\hat{\boldsymbol{k}}$ for $\hat{\mathbf{P}}$. With the explicit matrices for $\mathbf{s}$ it is simple to solve the matrix equation (15.145) and obtain a solution which is unique, apart from normalisation,

$$|\hat{\boldsymbol{k}} - \tfrac{1}{2}\rangle = \{2(k_t + k_z)\}^{-\frac{1}{2}} \begin{pmatrix} -k_x + ik_y \\ k_t + k_z \end{pmatrix} |\hat{\boldsymbol{k}}\rangle \tag{15.147}$$

This is consistent with the properties of the representation $P^{(0,-\frac{1}{2})}$ in which, for given $\hat{\boldsymbol{k}}$, there is only one basis vector. Here we have only one acceptable vector $|\hat{\boldsymbol{k}} - \frac{1}{2}\rangle$ but it is expressed in a two-component framework. In fact, equation (15.145) may be written as $(\boldsymbol{k}.\mathbf{s})|\psi\rangle = m|\boldsymbol{k}||\psi\rangle$ which says that $|\psi\rangle$ is the eigenstate of the component of spin in the $\boldsymbol{k}$-direction, with eigenvalue m. The expression (15.147) is seen to be identical with (15.143) if one inserts the explicit form for the $L^{(0,\frac{1}{2})}$ matrix, see subsection 15.2.5.

It is possible to arrive at this same result by starting from the four-component Dirac framework in the limit $k \to 0$ and imposing the additional constraint $(\hat{\mathbf{W}} + im\hat{\mathbf{P}})|\psi\rangle = 0$ with $m = -\frac{1}{2}$. Considering again just the time component of this equation and using the expressions (15.142) for **X** this constraint reduces to

$$(1 + \gamma_5)|\psi\rangle = 0 \tag{15.148}$$

where for convenience we have introduced the symbol γ_5 to denote the matrix $\gamma_5 = i\gamma_t\gamma_x\gamma_y\gamma_z$. Since one quickly verifies that the explicit form of this 4×4 matrix is $\gamma_5 = \begin{pmatrix} 1 & 0 \\ 0 & -1 \end{pmatrix}$, where ± 1 are 2×2 unit matrices, it is clear that the effect of the constraint (15.148) is simply to restrict $|\psi\rangle$ to those vectors with zero in their first and second components. In other words, it takes us back to the simpler product representation $P^{(0,0)} \times L^{(0,\frac{1}{2})}$ used above.

For the scalar product we may make use of the discussions for the Dirac equation, since the solutions (15.147) of the Weyl equation are a subset of the Dirac solutions for $k \to 0$. The form (15.137) for $\langle\phi|\psi\rangle$ would be unsuitable since it would always vanish, but a slight modification of the equivalent form (15.139) by the removal of the invariant constant k leads to a non-vanishing definition for $\langle\phi|\psi\rangle$. In fact, one might have removed this constant from both the earlier forms for $\langle\phi|\psi\rangle$. Notice that the sum in (15.139) now extends only over $\alpha = 3$ and 4 since all first and second components vanish. The normalisation constant in equation (15.147) was chosen to give

$$\langle \hat{\boldsymbol{k}}' m | \hat{\boldsymbol{k}} m \rangle = k_t \delta(\boldsymbol{k}' - \boldsymbol{k})$$

Note the similarity between the solution (15.147) and the solution (15.119) for the Euclidean group, remembering that, for zero mass, $k_t = |\boldsymbol{k}|$. This similarity is, of course, to be expected in view of the interpretation given in subsection 15.7.2 that zero mass particles spin about their direction of motion. To illustrate this, take $k_x = k_y = 0$ and $k_z > 0$ so that $k_t = k_z$, giving $|\hat{\boldsymbol{k}} - \frac{1}{2}\rangle = \binom{0}{1}|\hat{\boldsymbol{k}}\rangle$ and hence the spin about the direction of motion is negative. If, on the other hand, one takes $k_x = k_y = 0$ with $k_z < 0$ so that $k_t = -k_z$ then $|\hat{\boldsymbol{k}} - \frac{1}{2}\rangle \propto \binom{1}{0}|\hat{\boldsymbol{k}}\rangle$, making the spin about the z-axis to be positive, but since the particle is now moving in the negative direction it still has negative spin about its direction of motion.

15.8.6 Particles with zero mass and spin $|m| = 1$—the Maxwell equations

For this case we follow the previous section very closely with $m = 1$ in place of $m = \frac{1}{2}$, using the product representation $P^{(0,0)} \times L^{(1,0)}$. This gives us a three-component space and we must impose the constraint $(\hat{\mathbf{W}} + im\hat{\mathbf{P}})|\psi\rangle = 0$ with $m = 1$. In constructing the 3×3 matrices for $\hat{\mathbf{W}}$ we must now use the matrices for **X** and **Y** in the $L^{(1,0)}$ representation. However since in $L^{(1,0)}$ we have $\mathbf{B} = 0$ in the notation of subsection 15.2.4 it follows from equation (15.33) that $\mathbf{Y} = i\mathbf{X}$. But so far as $\mathbf{X}$ is concerned, $L^{(1,0)}$ is simply the representation $D^{(1)}$ of $\mathscr{R}_3$. Thus the matrices of $\mathbf{X}$ are as given in equation (7.24) and this also determines the matrices of $\mathbf{Y}$ and $\hat{\mathbf{W}}$. One has the choice of two familiar bases for $D^{(1)}$ and we prefer the Cartesian basis, as used in equation (7.24). The alternative would have been the m-basis as used, for example, in equation (8.15). As in the previous section there is some redundancy in the four equations $(\hat{\mathbf{W}} + i\hat{\mathbf{P}})|\psi\rangle = 0$ and after a little elementary algebra one finds that they take a concise form in a vector notation, with the three-component wave function written as a vector $|\boldsymbol{\psi}\rangle$,

$$iP_t|\psi\rangle = -\mathbf{P} \wedge |\psi\rangle \tag{15.149}$$

and

$$\mathbf{P}\,.\,|\psi\rangle = 0 \tag{15.150}$$

If we work in configuration space, introducing the differential forms for $\hat{\mathbf{P}}$, these equations become

$$\text{curl}\,|\psi\rangle = \frac{i}{c}\frac{\partial}{\partial t}|\psi\rangle$$

$$\text{div}\,|\psi\rangle = 0$$

If we use a plane wave basis so that for definite $\hat{\boldsymbol{k}}$ the solution has the form $|\psi\rangle = \begin{pmatrix} a \\ b \\ c \end{pmatrix}|\hat{\boldsymbol{k}}\rangle$ then the equations (15.149) and (15.150) provide a matrix equation for the coefficients a, b and c by writing, as before, $\hat{\mathbf{P}} \equiv -i\hat{\boldsymbol{k}}$. If for simplicity we choose $\boldsymbol{k}$ along the positive z-direction, so that $k_t = k_z$ then one finds that the three-component structure of $|\psi\rangle$ is given by $\begin{pmatrix} a \\ b \\ c \end{pmatrix} = \begin{pmatrix} 1 \\ i \\ 0 \end{pmatrix}$. Since this vector is clearly orthogonal to the direction $\boldsymbol{k}$ of motion one refers to the solution as 'transverse'. This is, of course, a general property following directly from equation (15.150). As we should expect for $m = 1$, it represents a state of positive helicity with spin $= 1$ about the direction of motion.

Only a trivial change of sign is needed to adapt the above to the case $m = -1$. In nature, the photons, which are the field particles responsible for electromagnetic interactions, have zero- mass and $m = \pm 1$. Their motion is therefore governed by the Maxwell equations given above (see also subsection 16.3.7).

Bibliography

For more details on special relativity and references to original papers see

Muirhead, H. (1973). *The Special Theory of Relativity* (Macmillan, London)

A rigorous discussion of the Lorentz and Poincare groups runs into deep water but for further reading we suggest Boerner (1963), see bibliography to chapter 4, and the article by T. D. Newton in

Kahan, T. (1965). *Theory of Groups in Classical and Quantum Physics* (Oliver and Boyd, Edinburgh)

and the references which they contain. The original papers of E. P. Wigner are conveniently collected as reprints in

Dyson, F. J. (1966). *Symmetry Groups in Nuclear and Particle Physics* (Benjamin, New York)

An account of the use of the Poincaré group including a careful discussion of phases is given by

Halpern, F. R. (1968). *Special Relativity and Quantum Mechanics* (Prentice Hall, Englewood Cliffs, N. J.)

The role of the wave equations is also discussed in

Omnes, R. (1969). *Introduction to Particle Physics* (Wiley-Interscience, London)

A convenient summary of the properties of the Lorentz and Poincaré groups and their representations is given in

Lomont, J. S. (1959). *Applications of Finite Groups* (Academic Press, New York)

Problems

15.1 Writing $\mathrm{P}(\boldsymbol{\rho}) = 1 + \xi \mathrm{P}_x + \eta \mathrm{P}_y + \zeta \mathrm{P}_z$ and $\mathrm{R}(\boldsymbol{a}) = 1 + \sum_q a_q \mathrm{X}_q$ for small $\boldsymbol{\rho}$ and $\boldsymbol{a}$, use equation (15.5) together with equation (7.22) to deduce the commutation relations (15.15). (Keep terms to first order in $\boldsymbol{a}$ and ρ.)

15.2 From the matrix definition (15.23) of the Lorentz transformations, show that they form a group.

15.3 From equation (15.26) show that the boost matrix element Q_{yt} is given by $-u_y \sinh b$.

15.4 Show that, if $ct > z$, it is not possible to find a proper Lorentz transformation which carries $(0, 0, z, ct)$ into $(0, 0, z, -ct)$.

15.5 Write down the matrices of A_z and B_z in the representation $\mathrm{L}^{(\frac{1}{2}\frac{1}{2})}$ using the basis $\boldsymbol{e}^{\frac{1}{2}\frac{1}{2}}_{mm'}$. Hence deduce the matrices of X_z and Y_z and show that they agree with equation (15.30) with a suitable change of basis.

15.6 If the translation $\mathrm{P}(\hat{\boldsymbol{\varepsilon}})$ of equation (15.48) is expressed in terms of the components $\bar{\varepsilon}_i$ of $\hat{\boldsymbol{\varepsilon}}$ with respect to a new basis $\hat{\boldsymbol{e}}'_i = \mathrm{L}\hat{\boldsymbol{e}}_i$, show that the corresponding infinitesimal operators $\bar{\mathrm{P}}_i$ are related to the P_i in the original basis by the usual transformation $\bar{\mathrm{P}}_{-i} = \sum_j (\mathrm{L}^{-1})_{ij} \mathrm{P}_j$. In other words, the P_i transform like the components of a four-vector. (Use equation (15.23) and the relation for $\bar{\varepsilon}_i$ given just before it.)

15.7 Use equation (15.53) for infinitesimal $\boldsymbol{a}$, $\boldsymbol{b}$ and $\mathcal{E}$, together with equation (15.48) and the matrix (15.30) of $\Lambda = \mathrm{L} - 1$, to deduce the commutation relations (15.69).

15.8 Use the commutation relations (15.32) and (15.69) to justify equation (15.72).

15.9 The components P_i of the four-vector $\hat{\mathbf{P}}$ satisfy the relation $\mathrm{T(L)P}_i\mathrm{T}^{-1}(\mathrm{L}) = \sum_j (\mathrm{L}^{-1})_{ij}\mathrm{P}_j$ with a similar relation for $\hat{\mathbf{W}}$. Hence show that equation (15.76) implies that $(\hat{\mathbf{W}} + im\hat{\mathbf{P}})|\hat{\boldsymbol{k}}m\rangle = 0$, where $|\hat{\boldsymbol{k}}m\rangle = \mathrm{T(L)}|\hat{\boldsymbol{k}}_0 m\rangle$.

15.10 Given that $\Upsilon^2|\psi\rangle = \exp(i\alpha)|\psi\rangle$, Show that $\exp(i\alpha) = \pm 1$. (Consider the operation of Υ^2 on the state $|\psi\rangle + |\phi\rangle$, where $|\phi\rangle = \Upsilon|\psi\rangle$, and use the antiunitary nature of Υ.)

15.11 Show that the 2×2 matrix form for the operator $2(\mathbf{s}.\mathbf{l})$ is $\begin{pmatrix} l_0 & l_- \\ l_+ & -l_0 \end{pmatrix}$ and hence verify that the eigenvectors $|jm\rangle$ of equation (15.116) are as given.

15.12 Use equation (15.33) to show that, in the $\mathrm{L}^{(\frac{1}{2}0)}$ representation, $\mathbf{X} = i\mathbf{Y} = -i\mathbf{s}$ and hence from equation (15.72) that $\mathbf{W}_t^2 = \frac{1}{4}\mathbf{P}^2$, $\mathbf{W}^2 = \frac{1}{2}\mathbf{P}^2 + \frac{3}{4}\mathbf{P}_t^2$ so that $(\hat{\mathbf{W}}.\hat{\mathbf{W}}) = \frac{3}{4}(\hat{\mathbf{P}}.\hat{\mathbf{P}})$.

15.13 Show that the matrix γ_t defined in equation (15.129) commutes with the X_q and hence that it is the time component of a representation $\mathrm{L}^{(\frac{1}{2}\frac{1}{2})}$. Use equation (15.69) to generate from γ_t the other three components γ_q.

15.14 Use the 4×4 matrices of $\mathbf{Y}$ in the basis of $\mathrm{L}^{(\frac{1}{2}0)} + \mathrm{L}^{(0\frac{1}{2})}$ to show that the finite boost $\mathrm{Q}(\boldsymbol{b}) = \exp(\boldsymbol{b}.\mathbf{Y})$ takes the form $\cosh\frac{1}{2}b + 2b^{-1}(\boldsymbol{b}.\mathbf{Y})\sinh\frac{1}{2}b$. Hence deduce the solutions (15.135) from equation (15.134), taking $\boldsymbol{b}(\hat{\boldsymbol{k}})$ as given just after equation (15.58).

15.15 Show that $\gamma_t\gamma_q\gamma_t^{-1} = -\gamma_q$ and hence that the inversion operator T(I) defined just before equation (15.141) commutes with $(\hat{\gamma}.\hat{\mathbf{P}})$.

16

Particles, Fields and Antiparticles

The concepts of momentum, energy, mass and spin were introduced in the previous chapter entirely from the transformation properties of the Poincaré group. We worked in the algebraic framework of state vectors, which is appropriate in quantum mechanics, and we associated different elementary particles with different irreducible representations of the group. In introducing these concepts we did not make use of any fundamental equation, like the Schrodinger equation, which dominated the discussion of symmetry in the first twelve chapters. In fact in section 15.8 we were able to deduce the forms of the wave equations necessary to reproduce the transformation properties previously described. These comments only relate to free particles, however, and when it comes to interactions it is necessary to have some dynamical foundation. The foundation which seems to have universal validity is known as Lagrangian theory or equivalently as Hamiltonian theory and rests on Hamilton's principle. This principle in its simplest form is applicable to the motion of particles in non-relativistic classical mechanics. It extends naturally to relativistic classical mechanics of particles. In the description of electromagnetic phenomena it extends to incorporate the concept of interaction with a field and the behaviour of the field itself. Finally it is generalised into a quantum mechanical framework in which the concepts of particles and fields are unified and one finds the need to introduce 'antiparticles'. This brings us to the point in quantum field theory where many problems remain unsolved. Necessarily therefore this chapter will be somewhat more tentative than those which have gone before.

16.1 Classical mechanics of particles

16.1.1 Lagrange formalism

The motion of particles in classical mechanics is governed by the principle of least action, or Hamilton's principle. This asserts that to every mechanical system one may associate a Lagrangian function $L(q_i, \dot{q}_i, t)$ which depends on the coordinates q_i, their time derivatives $\dot{q}_i$ and the time. The motion of the system is then given by those functions $q_i(t)$ which lead to the integral

$$S = \int_{t_1}^{t_2} L\,\mathrm{d}t \tag{16.1}$$

being a minimum for any two times t_1 and t_2. This is a variational principle. To ensure a minimum (or at least an extremum), the change in S due to a small change in the functional form of any of the $q_i(t)$ must be zero and we write this condition as $\delta S = 0$. The quantity S is called the 'action'. Using the variational calculus it may be shown that the condition $\delta S = 0$ leads to the Lagrange equations

$$\frac{\mathrm{d}}{\mathrm{d}t}\left(\frac{\partial L}{\partial \dot{q}_i}\right) - \frac{\partial L}{\partial q_i} = 0 \tag{16.2}$$

Given the form of L, these are a set of differential equations for the coordinates $q_i(t)$ as functions of time. There are as many equations as coordinates and, given the initial conditions, a unique solution for the $q_i(t)$ may be found. Hence the motion of the system is determined directly from the Lagrangian. One system differs from another by the form of L as a function of q_i, $\dot{q}_i$ and t.

16.1.2 Hamiltonian formalism

The Lagrangian formalism refers to coordinates and velocities but it is sometimes more convenient to work in terms of coordinates and momenta. This is particularly so in connection with symmetry and the link between classical and quantum mechanics. There is in fact an alternative, but precisely equivalent, formalism due to Hamilton which uses momenta rather than velocities. One first defines the generalised momenta

$$p_i = \frac{\partial L}{\partial \dot{q}_i} \tag{16.3}$$

Using the Lagrange equation (16.2) the differential $\mathrm{d}L$ may then be written

$$\mathrm{d}L = \sum_i \frac{\partial L}{\partial q_i}\mathrm{d}q_i + \sum_i \frac{\partial L}{\partial \dot{q}_i}\mathrm{d}\dot{q}_i + \frac{\partial L}{\partial t}\mathrm{d}t$$

$$= \sum_i \dot{p}_i \mathrm{d}q_i + \sum_i p_i \mathrm{d}\dot{q}_i + \frac{\partial L}{\partial t}\mathrm{d}t$$

but $$\mathrm{d}\left(\sum_i p_i\dot{q}_i\right) = \sum_i \dot{q}_i \mathrm{d}p_i + \sum_i p_i \mathrm{d}\dot{q}_i$$

so that the difference

$$\mathrm{d}\left(\sum_i p_i\dot{q}_i - L\right) = \sum_i \dot{q}_i \mathrm{d}p_i - \sum_i \dot{p}_i \mathrm{d}q_i - \frac{\partial L}{\partial t}\mathrm{d}t \tag{16.4}$$

does not contain differentials $\mathrm{d}\dot{q}_i$ of the velocities. Hence the quantity $\sum_i p_i\dot{q}_i - L$ does not contain the velocities explicitly and we call it the Hamiltonian

$$H(p_i, q_i, t) = \sum_i p_i\dot{q}_i - L \tag{16.5}$$

From equation (16.4) we have

$$\frac{\partial H}{\partial p_i} = \dot{q}_i, \qquad \frac{\partial H}{\partial q_i} = -\dot{p}_i \tag{16.6}$$

These are the Hamilton equations. Whereas the Lagrange equations will involve the second time-derivatives of q_i (since $\partial L/\partial \dot{q}_i$ will generally contain $\dot{q}_i$), the Hamilton equations involve only first time-derivatives of p_i and q_i. However there are now twice as many equations. Naturally, the two techniques lead to precisely the same solution.

From the point of view of symmetry one sees that if L (or H) is independent of a certain coordinate q_i so that $\partial L/\partial q_i = 0$, then the corresponding generalised momentum p_i is constant, since from either equations (16.2) or (16.6) we have $\dot{p}_i = 0$. Notice also that, from equation (16.4),

$$\frac{\mathrm{d}H}{\mathrm{d}t} = \sum_i \dot{q}_i\dot{p}_i - \sum_i \dot{p}_i\dot{q}_i - \frac{\partial L}{\partial t} = -\frac{\partial L}{\partial t} \tag{16.7}$$

Thus if L (or H) is independent of time (explicitly) then H is constant. As one might expect, this constant which is associated with homogeneity in time, may be identified with the energy of the system in the same way that the space homogeneity $\partial L/\partial q_i = 0$ leads to constancy of the momenta p_i.

We have already seen a simple example of the use of the Lagrange equations in describing molecular vibrations in section 6.2.

16.1.3 Examples from relativistic mechanics

Consider first a free particle of mass M. We postulate that S should be a Poincaré invariant, which is just the statement that the motion does not depend on the position, orientation or uniform velocity of the system in space. Since the integral (16.1) applies to all intervals this invariance must apply to the integrand. In the notation of section 15.2 the coordinates of a particle are denoted by

$$\hat{e} = (x, y, z, ct)$$

and

$$\mathrm{d}\hat{e} = (\mathrm{d}x, \mathrm{d}y, \mathrm{d}z, c\mathrm{d}t) = (v_x, v_y, v_z, c)\mathrm{d}t$$

so that

$$|\mathrm{d}\hat{e}| = (\mathrm{d}\hat{e}\,.\,\mathrm{d}\hat{e})^{\frac{1}{2}} = (c^2 - v^2)^{\frac{1}{2}}\mathrm{d}t$$

where v is the velocity. From its manner of construction, $|\mathrm{d}\hat{e}|$ is an invariant so that at leas' 'rom the invariance point of view the expression $(c^2 - v^2)^{\frac{1}{2}}$ would be a suitable form for L. The quantity $|\mathrm{d}\hat{e}|$ is the 'interval' between neighbouring points $\hat{e}$ and $\hat{e} + \mathrm{d}\hat{e}$ on the path of the particle in four-dimensional space. It is like the small distance $\mathrm{d}s = (\mathrm{d}x^2 + \mathrm{d}y^2)^{\frac{1}{2}}$ along a curve in two-dimensional space. In fact we see that the choice

$$L = -Mc(c^2 - v^2)^{\frac{1}{2}} \tag{16.8}$$

leads precisely to the usual equations of motion for a particle of mass M. In this formalism, the mass would be defined as the constant M appearing in the expression (16.8) for L. From the Lagrange equation (16.2) the absence of x, y or z in L leads directly to the constancy of $\partial L/\partial \dot{x}$, etc. giving

$$p_x = Mv_x(1 - v^2/c^2)^{-\frac{1}{2}} = \text{constant}, \quad \text{etc.} \tag{16.9}$$

and for the energy

$$E = H = \sum_i p_i \dot{q}_i - L = Mv^2(1 - v^2/c^2)^{-\frac{1}{2}} + Mc^2(1 - v^2/c^2)^{\frac{1}{2}}$$

$$= Mc^2(1 - v^2/c^2)^{-\frac{1}{2}} = Mc^2(1 + p^2/M^2c^2)^{\frac{1}{2}} \tag{16.10}$$

From equations (16.9) and (16.10) we deduce the familiar energy-momentum formula

$$E^2 - p^2c^2 = M^2c^4$$

as in the quantum case, see equation (15.94). For small v/c, equation (16.10) reduces to the familiar expression

$$E = Mc^2 + \tfrac{1}{2}Mv^2 \tag{16.11}$$

containing the rest-energy Mc^2 and the kinetic energy.

As a second simple example we introduce an electromagnetic field which we assume to be described by a four-vector potential $\hat{A} = (A_x, A_y, A_z, \phi)$. To describe the motion of a particle with charge e in this field we must modify the Lagrangian (16.8) to include $\hat{A}$ but to remain invariant. The most obvious invariant to include is the scalar product

$$\hat{\boldsymbol{A}}.\mathrm{d}\hat{\boldsymbol{e}} = (-\boldsymbol{A}.\boldsymbol{v} + c\phi)\,\mathrm{d}t$$

The conventional equations describing the motion of a charged particle in an electromagnetic field are obtained by including just this term, with a suitable constant $-e/c$ so that

$$L = -Mc(c^2 - v^2)^{\frac{1}{2}} + (e/c)(\boldsymbol{A}.\boldsymbol{v}) - e\phi \tag{16.12}$$

The generalised momenta are now given by

$$p_x = \frac{\partial L}{\partial \dot{x}} = Mv_x(1 - v^2/c^2)^{-\frac{1}{2}} + (e/c)A_x \tag{16.13}$$

and the Hamiltonian by

$$\begin{aligned} H &= Mc^2(1 - v^2/c^2)^{-\frac{1}{2}} + e\phi \\ &= Mc^2\{1 + (\boldsymbol{p} - e\boldsymbol{A}/c)^2/M^2c^2\}^{\frac{1}{2}} + e\phi \end{aligned} \tag{16.14}$$

Application of the Lagrange equation (16.2) to the Lagrangian (16.12) now leads, after some algebraic manipulation, to the familiar equations of motion for a charge in a field. In the non-relativistic limit $v \ll c$ one finds

$$m\ddot{\boldsymbol{v}} = -(e/c)\frac{\partial}{\partial t}\boldsymbol{A} - e\,\mathrm{grad}\,\phi + (e/c)\boldsymbol{v} \wedge \mathrm{curl}\,\boldsymbol{A} \tag{16.15}$$

which is often written in the form

$$m\ddot{\boldsymbol{v}} = e\boldsymbol{E} + (e/c)\boldsymbol{v} \wedge \boldsymbol{B} \tag{16.16}$$

by defining

$$\boldsymbol{E} = -\frac{\partial}{\partial t}\boldsymbol{A}/c - \mathrm{grad}\,\phi, \qquad \boldsymbol{B} = \mathrm{curl}\,\boldsymbol{A} \tag{16.17}$$

The vectors $\boldsymbol{E}$ and $\boldsymbol{B}$ are called the electric and magnetic field intensities. Since it is equated to (mass) × (acceleration), the right-hand side of equation (16.16) is called the Lorentz force.

The differential operator $\Box = (\partial/\partial x, \partial/\partial y, \partial/\partial z, -\partial/\partial ct)$ is a four-vector, see subsection 15.4, so that the sixteen products $\Box_i A_j$ transform like the product representation $\mathrm{L}^{(\frac{1}{2},\frac{1}{2})} \times \mathrm{L}^{(\frac{1}{2},\frac{1}{2})}$ of the Lorentz group. Being first derivatives of the components of $\hat{A}$, it is clear that $\boldsymbol{E}$ and $\boldsymbol{B}$ are contained in these sixteen products and using the reduction (15.37) of the product representation one can identify $\boldsymbol{E} \pm i\boldsymbol{B}$ with the representations $\mathrm{L}^{(1,0)}$ and $\mathrm{L}^{(0,1)}$, respectively, see problem 16.1.

An electromagnetic field has meaning only by the way in which it influences the motion of a charged particle, through equation (16.16). Thus any two fields $\hat{A}$ which lead to the same $\boldsymbol{E}$ and $\boldsymbol{B}$ are physically the same field. From equation

(16.17) one sees that this leaves $\hat{A}$ undetermined to the extent that if $f(\boldsymbol{r}, t)$ is any scalar function then the vector potential $\hat{A}' = (\boldsymbol{A}', \phi')$, where

$$\boldsymbol{A}' = \boldsymbol{A} + \operatorname{grad} f, \qquad \phi' = \phi - \frac{1}{c}\frac{\partial f}{\partial t}$$

will describe the same physical situation as $\hat{A}$. The freedom to choose f is referred to as the choice of gauge.

16.2 Classical mechanics of fields

The concept of a field is introduced to describe interaction at a distance. Thus if we have one charge e fixed at the origin and another charge e which is free to move we may say that the first charge produces a field of force with strength e^2/r^2 and directed away from the origin and the second charge moves in this field. In this case the field is static but more generally a field may also depend on time. Furthermore a field of force, such as the example above, has a direction at every point. In fact in this example the direction is always given simply by the vector $\boldsymbol{r}$ but more general fields may be imagined. As is well known the force field in this example may be described by a potential energy field $V(r) = e^2/r$ with the force given in both magnitude and direction as $\boldsymbol{F} = -\operatorname{grad} V(r)$. Notice that the field $V(r)$ does not have a direction and is an example of a scalar field while $\boldsymbol{F}$ is an example of a vector field. The small displacements $\boldsymbol{q}$ which we used in studying molecular vibrations in chapter 6 are another example of a vector field, except that it is not a function of a continuous variable $\boldsymbol{r}$ but associates a vector displacement only with the discrete set of equilibrium positions of the vibrating atoms. We now define more precisely the concepts of scalar, vector and more general fields.

16.2.1 The transformation of fields

If under a rotation R a field $\phi(\boldsymbol{r}, t)$ is transformed into

$$\phi'(\boldsymbol{r}, t) = \phi(\mathrm{R}^{-1}\boldsymbol{r}, t)$$

then ϕ is said to be a scalar field, with respect to rotations. If, on the other hand, the field has $2s+1$ components $\phi_m(\boldsymbol{r}, t)$ with $m = s, s-1, \ldots, -s$ such that the m-component of the rotated field is given by

$$\phi'_m(\boldsymbol{r}, t) = \sum_{\bar{m}} D^{(s)}_{m\bar{m}}(\mathrm{R})\phi_{\bar{m}}(\mathrm{R}^{-1}\boldsymbol{r}, t) \tag{16.18}$$

then the field is said to be a tensor field of degree s. This is the same transformation that we deduced in equation (8.20) for the components of a wave function with spin s. The most familiar example is the vector field with $s = 1$ so that at each point in space the three components define a direction for the field. It is of course possible to construct fields which are mixtures of different s. A field with fixed s is irreducible with respect to rotations and transforms like the irreducible representation $D^{(s)}$.

In a four-dimensional framework, fields may be classified by their behaviour under Poincaré transformations. In the notation of subsection 15.4.2 we would call $\phi(\hat{e})$ a scalar field if the Poincaré transformation produces a new field

$$\phi'(\hat{e}) = \phi(\mathrm{L}^{-1}(\hat{e} - \hat{\varepsilon}))$$

and tensor fields would be classified by the representation $\mathrm{L}^{(j,j')}$ to which they belong, in a natural extension of equation (16.18),

$$\phi'_{mm'}(\hat{e}) = \sum_{\bar{m}\bar{m}'} L^{(j,j')}_{mm',\bar{m}\bar{m}'}(\mathrm{L})\phi_{\bar{m}\bar{m}'}(\mathrm{L}^{-1}(\hat{e} - \hat{\varepsilon})) \qquad (16.19)$$

16.2.2 The Lagrange equation for fields

In the second example of subsection 16.1.3 we included a field as part of the Lagrangian but it was assumed that the field was given externally to the problem. We were concerned only with the motion of a particle in the given field. We now consider the way in which fields may behave on their own, i.e. in free space. The more general problem, in which the fields interact with particles whose motion in turn affects the fields, is clearly more complicated and we discuss it only very briefly. The equations governing the behaviour of a field may be deduced from the variational principle (16.1) with a suitably chosen Lagrangian. The Lagrangian will now depend on the field components $\phi_{mm'}(\hat{e})$ rather than the coordinates q_i and will be written as an integral over all space.

For a scalar field,

$$L = \int \mathrm{d}V\, \mathscr{L}(\phi, \nabla\phi, \dot{\phi}) \qquad (16.20)$$

where $\mathscr{L}$, which is a function of ϕ and its space and time derivatives $\nabla\phi$ and $\dot{\phi}(=\partial\phi/\partial t)$ is called the Lagrangian density. Application of the variational principle $\delta S = 0$ now leads to a generalisation of the Lagrange equation

$$\frac{\partial}{\partial t}\left(\frac{\partial \mathscr{L}}{\partial \dot{\phi}}\right) + \nabla\cdot\frac{\partial \mathscr{L}}{\partial \nabla\phi} - \frac{\partial \mathscr{L}}{\partial \phi} = 0 \qquad (16.21)$$

which is called the field equation.

Just as equation (16.2) gave the equations of motion for a particle, so equation (16.21) is the equation describing the field. If, as is generally the case, we choose $\mathscr{L}$ to be a quadratic function of ϕ, $\nabla\phi$ and $\dot{\phi}$ then equation (16.21) is a linear partial differential equation of, at most, second order for the fields $\phi(\boldsymbol{r}, t)$. Thus the ordinary differential equations of section 16.1 for the particle coordinates $q_i(t)$ are replaced by a partial differential equation for the field $\phi(\boldsymbol{r}, t)$. The extension of the field equations to tensor fields is straightforward.

The symmetry of fields

In constructing the Lagrangians for particles in subsection 16.1.3 we made use of the Poincaré invariance of the integrand $L\mathrm{d}t$ in the action integral. The same principle applied to field Lagrangians, like that in equation (16.20), will lead to the invariance of the Lagrangian density $\mathscr{L}$ because the volume element $\mathrm{d}V\mathrm{d}t$ is an invariant. (The determinant of the Lorentz transformation has the numerical value 1.) In other words $\mathscr{L}$ must satisfy an equation which may be written formally as $\mathscr{L}[\phi(\hat{e})] = \mathscr{L}[\phi'(\mathrm{L}\hat{e}+\hat{\varepsilon})]$, where for brevity we have omitted derivatives. A scalar field as defined in subsection 16.2.1 will satisfy this requirement but for tensor fields and for the derivatives $\nabla\phi$ and $\dot{\phi}$, the Lagrangian density must contain sums over components to form a scalar.

Conservation laws for fields

Just as in subsection 16.1.2 we defined the Hamiltonian and found it to be a constant of the motion, so for fields we shall be able to define the Hamiltonian density

$$\mathscr{H} = \dot{\phi}(\partial\mathscr{L}/\partial\dot{\phi}) - \mathscr{L}$$

Then, from the invariance of $\mathscr{L}$ under time translations we are able to show that $H = \int \mathscr{H}\,\mathrm{d}V$ is constant. In very similar fashion, if the Lagrangian density is translation invariant in space, then the vector $\boldsymbol{P}$ with components $P_q = \int \mathscr{P}_q \mathrm{d}V$ is constant where

$$\mathscr{P}_x = \frac{\partial\phi}{\partial x}\frac{\partial\mathscr{L}}{\partial\dot{\phi}}, \quad \text{etc.}$$

The proof of these results is outlined in problem 16.2. It is natural to call $\mathscr{P}_q$ the components of the momentum density of the field because they are the constant quantities arising from translation invariance. The conservation of angular momentum follows in a similar way from the rotational invariance of $\mathscr{L}$.

16.2.3 The electromagnetic field

As an example, consider an electromagnetic field which, as we have seen in subsection 16.1.3, is described by the four-vector potential $\hat{A}$ or, equivalently, by the field intensities $\boldsymbol{E}$ and $\boldsymbol{B}$. The Lagrangian density must be invariant and one obvious choice would be $\hat{A}\,.\,\hat{A}$. However, this would lead to a trivial field equation and furthermore we have seen in subsection 16.1.3 that it is the derivatives $\boldsymbol{E}$ and $\boldsymbol{B}$ of $\hat{A}$ which have physical significance. From the fact that $\boldsymbol{E} \pm i\boldsymbol{B}$ transform like $\mathrm{L}^{(1,0)}$ and $\mathrm{L}^{(0,1)}$, respectively, it follows that $E^2 - B^2$ and $\boldsymbol{E}\,.\,\boldsymbol{B}$ are both Lorentz invariant. Since the latter is not invariant under space inversion we might prefer the former as our Lagrangian density and this is found to agree with experiment. Conventionally, we write

$$\mathscr{L} = \frac{(\boldsymbol{E}^2 - \boldsymbol{B}^2)}{8\pi} \tag{16.22}$$

We cannot immediately apply equation (16.21) since that referred to a scalar field. However if ϕ were replaced by the four-vector $\hat{A}$ in (16.20) the field-equation (16.21) would be found to apply separately to each of the four components of $\hat{A}$. Noting the definitions (16.17) of $\boldsymbol{E}$ and $\boldsymbol{B}$ we see that the expression (16.22) for $\mathscr{L}$ is a quadratic in the first derivatives of $\hat{A}$. After some vector algebra the four field equations reduce to

$$\text{curl } \boldsymbol{B} = \frac{1}{c}\frac{\partial \boldsymbol{E}}{\partial t}$$

and

$$\text{div } \boldsymbol{E} = 0 \tag{16.23}$$

These are just the Maxwell equations which describe the behaviour of a field in the absence of charged particles. The other two Maxwell equations were contained in the definitions (16.17) and follow directly from them,

$$\text{div } \boldsymbol{B} = 0 \quad \text{and} \quad \text{curl } \boldsymbol{E} = -\frac{1}{c}\frac{\partial \boldsymbol{B}}{\partial t} \tag{16.24}$$

We discussed in subsection 16.1.3 the behaviour of a particle in a field which was regarded as fixed, in the sense that it was not influenced by the particle. Above we have described the behaviour of the field in the absence of charges. In general we must allow for the effect of the charged particles on the field and this is done formally by taking a Lagrangian density which is a sum of the field term (16.22) and a term like (16.12) integrated over all charged particles present. One then deduces field equations which are generalised from equation (16.23) by the inclusion of terms arising from the presence of $\hat{A}$ in (16.12) and which represent the charge and current density due to the charged particles. Thus the motion of the particles, through equation (16.16), and the motion of the field are coupled.

16.3 Quantum fields

Classically, a field is introduced to describe the interaction between particles. For example, a charged particle will produce a field and another charged particle will interact with the field thus effectively producing an interaction between the two particles. It is well known that, at small distances, one must use quantum mechanics for describing the motion of particles and this implies some imprecision, as given by the uncertainty principle. There is therefore some inconsistency if one describes the motion of a particle in a field by using a quantum mechanical treatment for the particle and a precise classical description for the field. We therefore seek a quantum treatment of the field. The technique is to replace the field by a field operator and to consider matrix elements of this operator as is the usual practice in quantum mechanics. The form which the operator takes is a combination of what are called creation and annihilation operators of field particles. Thus in addition to the particles which are interacting via the field we introduce the new field particles. For example, the photon is the field particle of the electromagnetic field and the π-meson the principal field particle of the strong nuclear forces. The introduction of operators which create and annihilate particles is not simply a mathematical device. Such processes are commonplace both with the zero mass photons in the emission of light and for finite mass particles such as the π-meson in the high-energy collision of protons $p+p \rightarrow p+p+\pi^0$. The creation of mass does not violate the Poincaré invariance of the system, see problem 16.4. In a complete theory one should also describe the interacting particles themselves by a field so that, in the example above, one would have a mechanism which allowed the creation of more protons as well as π-mesons and again such processes are observed.

16.3.1 Second quantisation

This subsection introduces the algebraic framework used to describe the creation and annihilation of particles. We have already noted in subsection 8.6.2 that the wave functions of a collection of identical particles are found to be either totally symmetric or totally antisymmetric under exchange of particles. One observes that particles with integer spin (called 'bosons') are symmetric, while those with half-integer spin (called 'fermions') are antisymmetric. This feature is also discussed in section 5.9 and the connection between the spin value and the symmetry (or statistics) is explained in subsection 16.3.4. Because of this complete symmetry or antisymmetry of the wave functions and the symmetry of all physical operators, the numbering of particles has no physical significance and serves only as a device for ensuring the relevant symmetry. It is therefore not too surprising that one can construct a technique in which the particle numbers do not appear at all and the symmetry is achieved by insisting on certain multiplication rules for the operators which create and annihilate particles.

To be definite, and for simplicity, let us consider the case of bosons with zero spin. The modifications necessary for the case of fermions is given at the end of the section and the extension to non-zero spin is straightforward. For particles of fixed mass $M = \hbar k/c$ the complete set of single-particle states is denoted by $|\hat{\boldsymbol{k}}\rangle$ where the length k of the four-vector $\hat{\boldsymbol{k}}$ is fixed. A symmetric state of n particles may be denoted by $|\hat{\boldsymbol{k}}_1\, \hat{\boldsymbol{k}}_2, \ldots, \hat{\boldsymbol{k}}_n\rangle$, where the set of n labels $\hat{\boldsymbol{k}}_i$ describe the n states occupied by the particles (the labels need not all be different). The state with no particles present is called the 'vacuum' and denoted by $|0\rangle$. It is normalised $\langle 0|0\rangle = 1$. (There should be no confusion between the notation $|0\rangle$ for the vacuum and $|\hat{\boldsymbol{k}}\rangle$ for the single particle states since, as remarked in subsection 15.7.1, $\hat{\boldsymbol{k}} = 0$ is not acceptable for a particle.) The vector space (called a 'Fock space') in which we are working is not now confined to a fixed n but includes all possible n. The number of particles must thus be regarded as an operator N which will not generally be diagonal and n is the eigenvalue of N in a state of n particles. To exploit this larger vector space we must clearly introduce operators which couple parts of the space with different n. The simplest of these is an operator, denoted by $a^\dagger(\hat{\boldsymbol{k}})$ with the property

$$a^\dagger(\hat{\boldsymbol{k}})|0\rangle = |\hat{\boldsymbol{k}}\rangle \tag{16.25}$$

and called the creation operator for a particle in state $|\hat{\boldsymbol{k}}\rangle$. On a more general state of n particles the definition is

$$a^\dagger(\hat{\boldsymbol{k}})|\hat{\boldsymbol{k}}_1\hat{\boldsymbol{k}}_2, \ldots, \hat{\boldsymbol{k}}_n\rangle = C|\hat{\boldsymbol{k}}\hat{\boldsymbol{k}}_1\hat{\boldsymbol{k}}_2, \ldots, \hat{\boldsymbol{k}}_n\rangle \tag{16.26}$$

and we shall not concern ourselves with the normalisation factor C. Because of the assumed symmetry of the wave function it follows from equation (16.26) that the commutator

$$[a^\dagger(\hat{\boldsymbol{k}}), a^\dagger(\hat{\boldsymbol{k}}')] = 0 \tag{16.27}$$

The Hermitian adjoint $a(\hat{\boldsymbol{k}})$ of $a^\dagger(\hat{\boldsymbol{k}})$ must reduce the number of particles by one and is called the annihilation (or destruction) operator. It therefore gives zero when operating on the vacuum, $a(\hat{\boldsymbol{k}})|0\rangle = 0$. By taking the adjoint of equation (16.27) we have

$$[a(\hat{\boldsymbol{k}}), a(\hat{\boldsymbol{k}}')] = 0 \tag{16.28}$$

For the commutator between creation and annihilation operators it is quickly seen that

$$\langle 0|[a(\hat{\boldsymbol{k}}), a^\dagger(\hat{\boldsymbol{k}}')]|0\rangle = \langle 0|a(\hat{\boldsymbol{k}})a^\dagger(\hat{\boldsymbol{k}}')|0\rangle = \langle \hat{\boldsymbol{k}}|\hat{\boldsymbol{k}}'\rangle$$

so that in the vacuum state we may write

$$[a(\hat{\boldsymbol{k}}), a^\dagger(\hat{\boldsymbol{k}}')] = \langle \hat{\boldsymbol{k}}|\hat{\boldsymbol{k}}'\rangle \tag{16.29}$$

With the help of equation (16.26) it can be shown that this commutation relation is valid not only in the vacuum but generally. With the normalisation (15.81), it takes the form

$$[a(\hat{\boldsymbol{k}}), a^\dagger(\hat{\boldsymbol{k}}')] = k_t\delta(\boldsymbol{k} - \boldsymbol{k}') \tag{16.29a}$$

Physical operators may now be expressed in terms of these creation and annihilation operators. For example, an operator which does not change the number of particles must contain an equal number of a and $a^\dagger$ factors. In particular, the number operator is given (see problem 16.5) by

$$N = \int a^\dagger(\hat{\boldsymbol{k}})a(\hat{\boldsymbol{k}})k_t^{-1}\,d\boldsymbol{k} \tag{16.30}$$

As in subsection 15.4.4 the range of integration extends over all $\hat{k}$ with fixed length (mass) and positive k_t so that $k_t = (k^2 + |\boldsymbol{k}|^2)^{\frac{1}{2}}$.

From the symmetry point of view the Poincaré transformations will not change the number of particles so that, if we assume the vacuum to be unique, it must be invariant. Thus one would expect that the creation operators $a^\dagger(\hat{k})$ transform like the single-particle states, according to equation (15.59), and this may soon be justified using equation (16.26). For the zero-spin case being considered here,

$$T(\hat{\varepsilon}, L)a^\dagger(\hat{k})T^{-1}(\hat{\varepsilon}, L) = \exp(iL\hat{k}.\hat{\varepsilon})a^\dagger(L\hat{k}) \tag{16.31}$$

In the case of fermions, for which the wave functions must be antisymmetric rather than symmetric, the results of this subsection are modified simply by the appearance of the anticommutator $[A, B]_+ = AB + BA$ in place of the commutator $[A, B] = AB - BA$. The need for this modification may be seen in the step from equation (16.26) to (16.27).

16.3.2 Field operators

We now seek a linear combination of the operators $a^\dagger(\hat{k})$ which represents the creation of a particle at a point $\hat{e}$ in space–time rather than in a state $|\hat{k}\rangle$. This new operator is denoted by $\phi^\dagger(\hat{e})$ and is called a 'field operator'. From this description the transformed operator must be the operator at the transformed point $L\hat{e}$ so that we shall require

$$T(\hat{\varepsilon}, L)\phi^\dagger(\hat{e})T^{-1}(\hat{\varepsilon}, L) = \phi^\dagger(L\hat{e} + \hat{\varepsilon}) \tag{16.32}$$

Using the property (16.31) one quickly verifies that the necessary linear combination of the $a^\dagger(\hat{k})$ is given by

$$\phi^\dagger(\hat{e}) = \int \exp(i\hat{k}.\hat{e})a^\dagger(\hat{k})k_t^{-1}\,d\boldsymbol{k}(2\pi)^{-\frac{3}{2}}2^{-\frac{1}{2}} \tag{16.33}$$

with the conventional normalisation. The verification is straightforward,

$$\begin{aligned} T(\hat{\varepsilon}, L)\phi^\dagger(\hat{e})T^{-1}(\hat{\varepsilon}, L) &= \int \exp[i(\hat{k}.\hat{e} + L\hat{k}.\hat{\varepsilon})]a^\dagger(L\hat{k})k_t^{-1}d\boldsymbol{k}(2\pi)^{-\frac{3}{2}}2^{-\frac{1}{2}} \\ &= \int \exp[iL\hat{k}.(L\hat{e} + \hat{\varepsilon})]a^\dagger(L\hat{k})k_t^{-1}d\boldsymbol{k}(2\pi)^{-\frac{3}{2}}2^{-\frac{1}{2}} \\ &= \int \exp[i\hat{k}.(L\hat{e} + \hat{\varepsilon})]a^\dagger(\hat{k})k_t^{-1}d\boldsymbol{k}(2\pi)^{-\frac{3}{2}}2^{-\frac{1}{2}} \\ &= \phi^\dagger(L\hat{e} + \hat{\varepsilon}) \end{aligned}$$

where we have changed integration variables $L\hat{k} \to \hat{k}$ and used the invariance (see subsection 15.4.4) of the volume element $k_t^{-1}\,d\hat{k}$. Bearing in mind the discussions in subsection 16.2.1 we shall say that the operators $\phi^\dagger(\hat{e})$ describe a scalar field. (The reason why we have $L\hat{e}$ appearing in equation (16.32) and

$L^{-1}\hat{e}$ in subsection 16.2.1 is that $\phi^{\dagger}(\hat{e})$ is an operator whereas $\phi(\hat{e})$ in subsection 16.2.1 denoted the value of a classical field at $\hat{e}$.)

In the case of non-zero spin one may similarly construct field operators $\phi_{\alpha}(\hat{e})$ with several components α which transform according to

$$T(\hat{\varepsilon}, L)\phi_{\alpha}(\hat{e})T^{-1}(\hat{\varepsilon}, L) = \sum_{\beta} M^{-1}_{\alpha\beta}(L)\phi_{\beta}(L\hat{e}+\hat{\varepsilon}) \tag{16.34}$$

where M is a representation of the Lorentz group. This equation implies a factorisation between the transformation of the indices α and the transformation of the fields (i.e. the fact that M does not depend on $\hat{e}$) which is the same feature that was discussed in subsection 15.8.4 in connection with the Dirac equation. Thus again for a finite-mass particle with spin $s = \frac{1}{2}$, four components are required in a field of the type (16.34). We shall discuss the non-zero spin case briefly in subsection 16.3.7.

16.3.3 The physical role of field operators

Before continuing with the discussion of some of the consequences of symmetry in quantum fields we briefly illustrate the way in which the field operators are used in the physical theory.

The first point to clarify is that whereas it is more usual in quantum mechanics for the operators which represent physical observables to be time independent and the time development of the system to be contained in the wave function, it is also possible to employ a time-independent wave function and to have the time development of the system described by an explicit time dependence in the operators. One refers to these two approaches as the Schrodinger and the Heisenberg pictures, respectively. In relativistic quantum mechanics the Heisenberg picture has the advantage that the relativistic invariance may more readily be described when the operators depend on the four coordinates x, y, z and t. The lack of time dependence in the wave function is no disadvantage since this acts as the 'initial conditions' on the problem. Mathematically, in the Schrodinger picture the Hamiltonian $H(\boldsymbol{p}, \boldsymbol{r})$ is a function of coordinates $\boldsymbol{r}$ and momenta $\boldsymbol{p}$ with the equation of motion

$$H(\boldsymbol{p}, \boldsymbol{r})\,\psi(\boldsymbol{r}, t) = i\hbar\frac{\partial}{\partial t}\psi(\boldsymbol{r}, t) \tag{16.35}$$

The Heisenberg picture is obtained, formally, by introducing the transformation $S = \exp(iHt/\hbar)$ so that, given any initial state $\psi(\boldsymbol{r}, 0)$, the solution at subsequent time t is given by

$$\psi(\boldsymbol{r}, t) = S^{-1}\psi(\boldsymbol{r}, 0) \tag{16.36}$$

The expectation value $\langle \psi(\boldsymbol{r}, t)|\,Q\,|\psi(\boldsymbol{r}, t)\rangle$ of an operator $Q(\boldsymbol{p}, \boldsymbol{r})$ in the Schrodinger picture may then be reproduced in the Heisenberg picture by taking the expectation value of the transformed operator $Q' = SQS^{-1}$ in the initial state since

$$\langle \psi(\boldsymbol{r},0)|\,Q'\,|\psi(\boldsymbol{r},0)\rangle = \langle \psi(\boldsymbol{r},t)|\,S^{-1}(SQS^{-1})S\,|\psi(\boldsymbol{r},t)\rangle$$
$$= \langle \psi(\boldsymbol{r},t)|\,Q\,|\psi(\boldsymbol{r},t)\rangle$$

using the fact that S is unitary for Hermitian H. Thus, in the Heisenberg picture if the time-dependent operators Q′ are known, we may deduce any required expectation value, given the initial state $\psi(\boldsymbol{r}, 0)$. Instead of having to find the wave function $\psi(\boldsymbol{r}, t)$, the problem in the Heisenberg picture is to find the $Q'(\boldsymbol{p}, \boldsymbol{r}, t)$. But the 'equation of motion' for Q′ follows immediately from its definition since if we assume Q to be time independent then $dQ'/dt = iHQ'/\hbar - iQ'H/\hbar$, so that

$$[H, Q'] = -i\hbar\frac{d}{dt}Q' \tag{16.37}$$

which is the Heisenberg equivalent of the Schrodinger equation (16.35). The transformation S is in fact a finite translation by an amount t in the time direction, with $-iH/\hbar c$ the infinitesimal operator, see subsection 15.4.1.

Let us now consider the simplest kind of field, a Hermitian (real) field $\Phi = \phi + \phi^\dagger$, where $\phi^\dagger$ was defined in equation (16.33) in terms of the particle operators $a^\dagger(\hat{k})$ for particles with mass $M = \hbar k/c$ and zero spin. (In fact $\phi + \phi^\dagger$ is the only combination of these two fields, apart from phase, which satisfies the causality requirement discussed in the next section.) We also take the particles to be bosons so that the commutation relation (16.29a) holds. We must regard the time-dependent field operators Φ as operators, like Q′, in the Heisenberg sense. Picking up the Lagrangian formalism of subsection 16.2.2 for classical fields, we now construct a simple Poincaré invariant Lagrangian density operator

$$\mathscr{L} = \tfrac{1}{2}(\Box\Phi\,.\,\Box\Phi - k^2\Phi^2)\hbar c \tag{16.38}$$

from the field operator Φ and its first derivatives □Φ. Since Φ is a scalar field, the second term satisfies the Poincaré invariance condition on $\mathscr{L}$ and by taking the scalar product of derivatives we have ensured that the first term is invariant also. The reason for having both terms in $\mathscr{L}$ with the factor k^2 will be explained below. Following the procedure in subsection 16.2.2 for constructing a Hamiltonian from the Lagrangian we see that

$$\mathscr{H} = \tfrac{1}{2}(\dot{\Phi}^2 c^{-2} + \nabla\Phi . \nabla\Phi + k^2\Phi^2)\hbar c \tag{16.39}$$

and the momentum density is given by its components

$$\mathscr{P}_q = \dot{\Phi}\ \nabla_q \Phi \hbar c^{-1}$$

From the definition (16.33) of the field operator $\phi^\dagger$ some algebra leads to the following expressions for H and **P** in terms of the creation and annihilation operators for the field particles of mass $M = \hbar k/c$,

$$\mathrm{H} = \tfrac{1}{2}\hbar c \int k_t[\mathrm{a}^\dagger(\hat{\boldsymbol{k}})\mathrm{a}(\hat{\boldsymbol{k}}) + \mathrm{a}(\hat{\boldsymbol{k}})\mathrm{a}^\dagger(\hat{\boldsymbol{k}})]k_t^{-1}\mathrm{d}\boldsymbol{k}$$

$$\mathbf{P} = \tfrac{1}{2}\hbar \int \boldsymbol{k}[\mathrm{a}^\dagger(\hat{\boldsymbol{k}})\mathrm{a}(\hat{\boldsymbol{k}}) + \mathrm{a}(\hat{\boldsymbol{k}})\mathrm{a}^\dagger(\hat{\boldsymbol{k}})]k_t^{-1}\mathrm{d}\boldsymbol{k}$$

Most field theories suffer from divergence problems and the simple example above is no exception. In fact the vacuum expectation value $\langle 0|\mathrm{H}|0\rangle$ is infinite. This may be seen by writing $\mathrm{a}(\hat{\boldsymbol{k}})\mathrm{a}^\dagger(\hat{\boldsymbol{k}}') = \mathrm{a}^\dagger(\hat{\boldsymbol{k}}')\,\mathrm{a}^\dagger(\hat{\boldsymbol{k}}) + k_t\delta(\boldsymbol{k}-\boldsymbol{k}')$ from equation (16.29a) and using the property $\mathrm{a}(\hat{\boldsymbol{k}})0\rangle = 0$, leaving an infinity from the δ-function. However if one assigns physical significance only to the difference between the values of H and its value in the vacuum then we obtain finite results for the operators

$$\begin{aligned} \tilde{\mathrm{H}} &= \mathrm{H} - \langle 0|\mathrm{H}|0\rangle = \hbar c \int k_t \mathrm{a}^\dagger(\hat{\boldsymbol{k}})\mathrm{a}(\hat{\boldsymbol{k}})k_t^{-1}\mathrm{d}\boldsymbol{k}, \\ \tilde{\mathbf{P}} &= \mathbf{P} - \langle 0|\mathbf{P}|0\rangle = \hbar \int \boldsymbol{k}\mathrm{a}^\dagger(\hat{\boldsymbol{k}})\mathrm{a}(\hat{\boldsymbol{k}})k_t^{-1}\mathrm{d}\boldsymbol{k} \end{aligned} \tag{16.40}$$

Comparing the expression (16.40) with the number operator (16.30) one sees that $\tilde{\mathrm{H}}$ may be interpreted as a sum over the possible states $\boldsymbol{k}$ of the number of particles in that state multiplied by the energy $\hbar c k_t$ of the particle in that state. A similar interpretation is valid for the momentum operators $\tilde{\mathbf{P}}$. Thus, starting from the field description we have arrived at a particle description.

Since Φ contains both $\mathrm{a}^\dagger$ and a operators one would have expected H to contain terms like $\mathrm{a}^\dagger\mathrm{a}^\dagger$. In fact there is cancellation between such terms arising from the two pieces of the Lagrangian. This explains our choice of the factor k^2 in $\mathscr{L}$, since only the absence of terms like $\mathrm{a}^\dagger\mathrm{a}^\dagger$ enabled us to interpret H as the Hamiltonian for a system of non-interacting particles and this was our object. Naturally a theory of non-interacting particles such as we have given above is rather empty but by adding other terms to the Lagrangian, as we did in the classical problems in subsection 16.1.3, one may introduce interactions between fields and thus between particles.

The conservation of **P** and H may be shown to follow from the invariance of $\mathscr{L}$ with respect to space and time translations as was the case for classical fields, see subsection 16.2.2.

The field described above is appropriate for the neutral π^0 mesons. Because some of the arguments may appear to be circular we briefly summarise the philosophy and content of the discussion of quantum fields so far. In section 15.4 we classified all possible particles according to irreducible representations of the Poincaré group. Using the creation and annihilation operators we next constructed a scalar field operator $\phi^\dagger(\hat{\boldsymbol{e}})$ with the transformation property (16.32), using the operators for zero-spin particles. From these we constructed a Lagrangian and hence a Hamiltonian whose eigenstates corresponded to definite numbers of particles. In doing this we did not make use of the variational principle described in subsection 16.1.1 or the field equations which, as shown in subsection 16.2.2, result from this principle. However, if we were to apply the field equation (16.21) to the Lagrangian density operator (16.38) we obtain the differential equation

$$(\Box^2 + k^2)\Phi(\hat{e}) = 0$$

This is the familiar Klein – Gordon equation which we met in subsection 15.8.3 in connection with the wave functions for particles. Here it enters in a different role as a condition on the field operators. From the expression (16.33) for $\phi^\dagger(\hat{e})$ one sees that $\Phi(\hat{e})$ does indeed satisfy this field equation and hence satisfies the variational principle. (Note the similarity here with our discussion of wave equations for particles in section 15.8). When interactions are included the field equations play a more significant role.

16.3.4 Causality and the spin-statistics theorem

In classical relativity theory, no particle or signal may travel with a speed greater than c. Thus one would expect also that quantum mechanical measurements at two space – time points $\hat{e}$ and $\hat{e}'$ would not interfere with each other if the difference $\hat{e}' - \hat{e}$ is space-like, in other words if $|\boldsymbol{r} - \boldsymbol{r}'| > c|t' - t|$. This property is called 'microscopic causality'. The mathematical statement of non-interference in quantum mechanics is that the operators shall commute so that we shall expect

$$[\mathrm{Q}(\hat{e}), \mathrm{Q}(\hat{e}')] = 0 \qquad (16.41)$$

if $\hat{e}' - \hat{e}$ is space-like and $\mathrm{Q}(\hat{e})$ is the operator for some observable at $\hat{e}$. The operators $\mathrm{Q}(\hat{e})$ are usually given, like $\mathscr{H}$ and $\mathscr{P}_q$ in equation (16.39) by quadratic expressions in the fields and their derivatives. Hence it follows that the causality condition (16.41) will be satisfied if the field operators either commute *or* anticommute for space-like separations. Let us first see whether the field $\Phi = \phi + \phi^\dagger$ discussed in the previous section satisfies the condition. From the property (16.27) and the definition (16.33) it is clear that $[\phi^\dagger(\hat{e}), \phi^\dagger(\hat{e}')] = [\phi(\hat{e}), \phi(\hat{e}')] = 0$ so that

$$[\Phi(\hat{e}), \Phi(\hat{e}')] = [\phi(\hat{e}), \phi^\dagger(\hat{e}')] + [\phi^\dagger(\hat{e}), \phi(\hat{e}')]$$

$$= \tfrac{1}{2}\iint k_t^{-1} k_t'^{-1}\,\mathrm{d}\boldsymbol{k}\,\mathrm{d}\boldsymbol{k}'\{\exp[i(\hat{\boldsymbol{k}}'.\hat{e}' - \hat{\boldsymbol{k}}.\hat{e})]$$

$$- \exp[i(\hat{\boldsymbol{k}}.\hat{e} - \hat{\boldsymbol{k}}'.\hat{e}')]\}\, k_t\,\delta(\boldsymbol{k} - \boldsymbol{k}')(2\pi)^{-3}$$

$$= i\int k_t^{-1}\,\mathrm{d}\boldsymbol{k}\,\sin\{\hat{\boldsymbol{k}}.(\hat{e}' - \hat{e})\}(2\pi)^{-3} \qquad (16.42)$$

The integral clearly depends only on the difference $\hat{e}' - \hat{e}$ and furthermore it depends only on the 'length' $[c^2(t'-t)^2 - |\boldsymbol{r}'-\boldsymbol{r}|^2]^{\frac{1}{2}}$ of $\hat{\boldsymbol{e}}' - \hat{\boldsymbol{e}}$. To see this we note that any other difference with the same 'length' may be written as $\mathrm{L}(\hat{\boldsymbol{e}}'-\hat{\boldsymbol{e}})$, where L is a Lorentz transformation, but since $\hat{\boldsymbol{k}}.\mathrm{L}(\hat{\boldsymbol{e}}'-\hat{\boldsymbol{e}}) = \mathrm{L}^{-1}\hat{\boldsymbol{k}}.(\hat{\boldsymbol{e}}'-\hat{\boldsymbol{e}})$ and the volume element $k_t^{-1}\mathrm{d}\boldsymbol{k}$ is invariant (see subsection 15.4.4) the integral (16.42) is unchanged when $\hat{\boldsymbol{e}}'-\hat{\boldsymbol{e}}$ is replaced by $\mathrm{L}(\hat{\boldsymbol{e}}'-\hat{\boldsymbol{e}})$. Hence if (16.42) were to vanish for one space-like difference $\hat{\boldsymbol{e}}'-\hat{\boldsymbol{e}}$ it would vanish for all space-like differences. The simplest case to study would be $t' = t$ for which we have simply

$$[\Phi(\hat{\boldsymbol{e}}), \Phi(\hat{\boldsymbol{e}}')] = -i\int k_t^{-1}\,\mathrm{d}\boldsymbol{k}\sin\{\boldsymbol{k}.(\boldsymbol{r}'-\boldsymbol{r})\}(2\pi)^{-3} \qquad (16.43)$$

which clearly vanishes because the sine function is odd and the integral extends over all three-space of $\boldsymbol{k}$.

Thus we conclude that the field Φ built from zero-spin particles with symmetric many-particle states, and therefore with commutation relations (16.27)–(16.29) between creation and annihilation operators, satisfies the causality condition. Had we chosen to construct Φ from zero-spin particles with antisymmetric many-particle states, i.e. with anticommutation relations in place of (16.27)–(16.29) then a repetition of the argument above leads to a cosine in equation (16.43) in place of the sine function. The integral will not then vanish and causality is not satisfied. Thus, if we accept the causality condition, we conclude that zero-spin particles cannot obey Fermi statistics, i.e. have antisymmetric wave functions. The arguments above can be generalised to the case of any integer spin with precisely the same conclusion. For half-integer spins a change of sign occurs in the algebra and one concludes that Bose statistics, i.e. symmetric states, would violate causality. One refers to these results as the 'spin-statistics theorem'.

16.3.5 Antiparticles

We first remark that the Hermitian field $\Phi = \phi + \phi^\dagger$ discussed above is the only combination (apart from phase) of ϕ and $\phi^\dagger$ which satisfies causality. A more general, non-Hermitian field may be constructed only by introducing a new field operator $\chi^\dagger$ defined just like $\phi^\dagger$ in equation (16.33) except that in place of $\mathrm{a}^\dagger(\hat{k})$ we have $\mathrm{b}^\dagger(\hat{k})$ which creates a particle with the same Poincaré behaviour as before, i.e. same mass and spin, but which differs in some other, internal, property as yet unspecified, e.g. charge or hypercharge. It then follows as before that the non-Hermitian field Φ defined by

$$\Phi = \phi + \chi^\dagger, \qquad \Phi^\dagger = \phi^\dagger + \chi \qquad (16.44)$$

satisfies causality, assuming that the new particle operators $\mathrm{b}^\dagger$ and b satisfy the same commutation relations (16.27)–(16.29) as the $\mathrm{a}^\dagger$ and a and that all the new operators commute with all the old. (For half-integer spin particles the anticommutation relations apply instead.) The new particles are called the 'antiparticles' of the old ones..

A simple Lagrangian like (16.38) may again be constructed, with terms like $\Phi^\dagger\Phi$ replacing Φ^2 to ensure that $\mathscr{L}$ is Hermitian. The expressions for H and **P** then come out to be the same as before except that there are additional terms with the b-operators in place of the a-operators. There is also a new conserved quantity

$$Q = i\int dV(\dot{\Phi}^\dagger\Phi - \Phi^\dagger\dot{\Phi})$$

which, when expressed in terms of a- and b-operators, becomes

$$Q = \int [a^\dagger(\hat{k})a(\hat{k}) - b^\dagger(\hat{k})b(\hat{k})]k_t^{-1}dk$$

and thus measures the difference between the number of particles and the number of antiparticles. In a single-particle state $|\hat{k}\rangle$ the value of Q is $\langle\hat{k}|Q|\hat{k}\rangle = 1$, while for a single antiparticle $\langle Q\rangle = -1$. The operator Q clearly distinguishes particle and antiparticle and in the case that the field particles and antiparticles are the π^+ and π^- mesons, respectively, this operator will serve to represent the electric charge of the field. On the other hand if the field is used for the neutral K^0 and $\overline{K}^0$ mesons, which differ in having hypercharges of ± 1 respectively, then Q will represent the hypercharge. For the pure $K^\pm$ field, which has both charge and hypercharge, Q will be able to represent both charges simultaneously. (When several different particles are present, the operator expressions for Q become more elaborate than that given above, with additional terms arising from the other particles.) In this situation the expressions for the electric charge and for the hypercharge will naturally become different from each other. There are indeed charges other than these two like the baryon number and the lepton number (see section 11.3).

Notice that the field Φ has simple properties with respect to Q, with $\Phi^\dagger$ increasing the value of Q by one unit and Φ decreasing it by one unit. As a result we may retain charge conservation even when interaction terms are included in the Lagrangian. This can be achieved by adding to $\mathscr{L}$ the product of Φ with a corresponding term of another field which has the opposite effect on Q. The conservation of charge relates to an intrinsic property of the particle but we may nevertheless associate charge conservation with a transformation of the field (as momentum conservation is associated with translations) by introducing the transformation $\Phi \to U\Phi U^{-1}$, where $U = \exp(i\varepsilon Q)$. Then since Φ decreases the value of Q by unity, we have $[Q, \Phi] = -\Phi$ and hence the transformation is given by $\Phi \to \exp(-i\varepsilon)\Phi$, a constant phase change. This is called a gauge transformation (see also subsection 16.1.3). Thus Q is the infinitesimal operator for U, as **P** is for translations. In fact it is a general property that the invariance of the Lagrangian with respect to transformations of this kind leads to a conserved charge. Furthermore there is an associated 'conserved current' which, in the example above, is defined as the four-vector

$$\mathbf{j} = i\{(\nabla\Phi^\dagger)\Phi - \Phi^\dagger(\nabla\Phi)\}, \qquad \mathrm{j}_t = -i\{\dot{\Phi}^\dagger\Phi - \Phi^\dagger\dot{\Phi}\}$$

It is trivial to verify, using the Klein–Gordon equation, that $\nabla.\mathbf{j}+\partial \mathrm{j}_t/\partial t = 0$ which is the property which gives rise to the name conserved current. Integrating this equation over all three-space, using Gauss's theorem $\int \nabla.\mathbf{j}\mathrm{d}V = \int \mathbf{j}.\mathrm{d}\boldsymbol{S}$ and assuming $\mathbf{j}$ to drop off more rapidly than r^{-2} at large r so that the surface integral vanishes we have $(\partial/\partial t)\int \mathrm{j}_t \mathrm{d}V = 0$. This is the conservation of charge since, comparing with the expressions above, $\mathrm{Q} = -\int \mathrm{j}_t \mathrm{d}V$.

Perhaps the best known antiparticle is the positron, a positively charged particle with the mass of the electron and therefore regarded as the anti-electron. In high-energy collisions the antiproton, negatively charged, has been observed. The fields for these particles are similar to the one described above except that they have a spin of $\frac{1}{2}\hbar$. We discuss non-zero spin fields briefly in subsection 16.3.7.

16.3.6 Charge conjugation and the PCT theorem

We continue this very brief discussion of quantum fields by introducing the PCT theorem. This concerns the product of the three operations space inversion P, which in this book (see sections 15.3 and 15.5) we have denoted by I, the time-reversal operation T, which (see subsection 15.7.4) we have denoted by Υ, and a new operation C known as 'charge conjugation' which transforms a particle into an antiparticle and vice versa. The reason for considering the product PCT is that, under very general conditions, it may be shown that PCT is a symmetry operation. For electromagnetic and the strong nuclear interactions this is not of great interest because experiment shows that the three operations P, C and T are each symmetry operations. However for the weak nuclear interactions neither P nor C are symmetry operations separately but the evidence suggests that the product PC and also T are symmetry operations, which is consistent with the PCT theorem. (There may be some experimental evidence for a tiny violation of PC symmetry in weak interactions but this could still be consistent with PCT symmetry.)

Let us then consider the effect of these transformations on the field Φ introduced in subsection 16.3.5. We shall restrict our discussion to this zero-spin case although the arguments may be extended to any spin. For consistency with previous chapters the operators representing P and T will be denoted by T(I) and Υ, respectively. From the work of section 15.5 the behaviour of the particle operators under space inversion is $\mathrm{T(I)a}^\dagger(\hat{k})\mathrm{T}^{-1}(\mathrm{I}) = \pm \mathrm{a}^\dagger(\mathrm{I}\hat{k})$, where the $\pm$ denotes the intrinsic parity of the particle. Also, from equation (15.108) for zero spin, time-reversal gives $\Upsilon \mathrm{a}^\dagger(\hat{k})\Upsilon^{-1} = \mathrm{a}^\dagger(\mathrm{I}\hat{k})$. We now define the unitary charge–conjugation operator C by the relations $\mathrm{C}^2 = 1$ and $\mathrm{Ca}^\dagger(\hat{k})\mathrm{C}^{-1} = \mathrm{b}^\dagger(\hat{k})$, where $\mathrm{b}^\dagger$ refers to the antiparticle. It then follows directly that

$$\mathrm{T(I)C\Upsilon\Phi^{\dagger}}(\hat{e})(\mathrm{T(I)C\Upsilon})^{-1} = \pm\Phi(-\hat{e}) \tag{16.45}$$

using the anti-unitary property of Υ. Thus the effect of PCT (or T(I)CΥ in our notation) on the field is to take the Hermitian adjoint and to replace $\hat{e}$ by $-\hat{e}$. The phase $\pm$ in equation (16.45) is not significant because of the arbitrariness in choosing the phase for Υ, see subsection 15.7.4. The transformation $\hat{e} \to -\hat{e}$ which reflects both space and time is sometimes called 'strong reflection' and because of the Hermitian property of the simple Lagrangian density $\mathscr{L}$, constructed for the field Φ, as in equation (16.38), it follows that the PCT transformation induces the change $\mathscr{L}(\hat{e}) \to \mathscr{L}(-\hat{e})$. When the Hamiltonian density $\mathscr{H}(\hat{e})$ is constructed from $\mathscr{L}(\hat{e})$, as in equation (16.39), the same change occurs, $\mathscr{H}(\hat{e}) \to \mathscr{H}(-\hat{e})$ and finally the Hamiltonian operator $\mathrm{H} = \int \mathscr{H}(\hat{e})\mathrm{d}V$ formed by integrating over all three-space satisfies $\mathrm{H}(t) \to \mathrm{H}(-t)$. But since H must be time independent this means that H is unchanged by the PCT operation, which completes the argument that PCT is a symmetry operation. The power of this result lies in the fact that the arguments outlined above are equally applicable when the Lagrangian contains complicated interaction terms and is dependent only on the Lagrangian being Hermitian and invariant under the proper Poincaré transformations. (There is also the implicit assumption of point particles, without structure, and our use of differential equations which implies a continuity in space, without any granularity.)

A more formal proof of the PCT theorem may be constructed by arguing that invariance of the field theory with respect to proper Poincaré transformations implies invariance with respect to proper *complex* Poincaré transformations and that this complex group contains the strong reflection $\hat{e} \to -\hat{e}$.

To illustrate the PCT symmetry we give two examples where there is no symmetry with respect to P or C separately but where the product PC is conserved. In subsection 15.7.3 it was argued that the neutrino did not possess definite parity. In fact the parity operation produced a right-handed spinning particle which is not found in nature. However the operation CP will take the left-handed neutrino into the right-handed antineutrino which is found to exist. One finds here that, although P is not conserved, the product CP is conserved as also is T.

The K^0 meson with finite mass, zero spin and definite strangeness -1 has as its antiparticle the $\overline{K^0}$ meson with strangeness $+1$. These particles are produced via the strong nuclear interaction which conserves strangeness. However they decay via the weak interaction which does not conserve strangeness, which does not conserve C or P separately but which to a high degree conserves the product CP. The K^0 is observed to decay in two ways either to two π-mesons with a lifetime of about $(10)^{-10}$ sec or to three π-mesons with a lifetime of about $(10)^{-7}$ sec. These results may be understood as follows. Since the K^0 particle has definite parity we may write

$CP|K^0\rangle = |\overline{K}^0\rangle$ so that it is necessary to take linear combinations

$$|K^0_S\rangle = 2^{-\frac{1}{2}}(|K^0\rangle + |\overline{K}^0\rangle)$$

$$|K^0_L\rangle = 2^{-\frac{1}{2}}(|K^0\rangle - |\overline{K}^0\rangle)$$

to produce states with definite CP, i.e.

$$CP|K^0_S\rangle = |K^0_S\rangle$$

$$CP|K^0_L\rangle = -|K^0_L\rangle$$

One can then write $|K^0\rangle$ as the sum of two components $|K^0\rangle = 2^{-\frac{1}{2}}(|K^0_S\rangle + |K^0_L\rangle)$. Now the lowest state of the two-π system, with no relative angular momentum, has definite CP $= +1$ so that in a CP-conserving process only the component $|K^0_S\rangle$ may decay in this way. The other component $|K^0_L\rangle$ must decay by a more complex mode involving three π-mesons combined to give CP $= -1$. Not unnaturally, the two-π mode of decay has the shorter decay time and the suffices S and L on K^0 refer to short and long decay times. Experimentally this implies the following, rather amusing situation. Consider the collisions of π^- mesons on protons which can produce a beam of K^0 particles, $\pi^- + p = K^0 + \Lambda$. After travelling a short distance the K^0_S component has decayed leaving K^0_L which is a mixture of K^0 and its antiparticle $\overline{K}^0$. In other words a beam which originally contained only K^0 particles gradually acquires a $\overline{K}^0$ component through the decay of K^0_S. The presence of $\overline{K}^0$ in the beam has been demonstrated by observing the reaction

$$\overline{K}^0 + p = \pi^+ + \Lambda \tag{16.46}$$

which could not be produced by K^0 particles because of strangeness conservation. In other words this reaction (16.46) is not produced by the original beam but is produced once the K^0_S component in the beam has decayed.

Finally, we should remark that recent experiments show evidence for a very small degree of CP violation in the K^0 decay and it has been suggested that there may be some 'superweak' interactions which violate both CP and T but still conserve CPT. Their strength would need to be no greater than $(10)^{-8}$ that of the weak interactions. One seems therefore to have very few absolute symmetries but rather a hierarchy of interactions with the strength dropping sharply as each symmetry is violated.

16.3.7 Field for particles with non-zero spin

In discussing fields in the present chapter we have so far restricted our attention to the case of zero spin. The technique extends naturally to the more general case and we carry out this extension for three interesting cases $s = \frac{1}{2}$ with finite mass (the Dirac field) and for zero mass with $|m| = \frac{1}{2}$ (the Weyl, neutrino, field) and $|m| = 1$ (electromagnetic field).

The Dirac field

Recall from subsection 15.8.4 that, although there are only two independent particle states $m_s = \pm\frac{1}{2}$ for each $\hat{\boldsymbol{k}}$, it was necessary to introduce a four-component space in order to achieve a factorisation between the transformation of $\hat{\boldsymbol{k}}$ and the transformation of the components. The four-component space was effectively reduced to two by the imposition of the Dirac equation (15.132). We shall follow the same approach here by constructing a four-component field. In place of the simple transformation law (16.32) for the scalar field we shall now require the four components $\Phi_\alpha(\hat{e})$ of the field operators to satisfy equation (16.34) which may be written

$$\mathrm{T}(\hat{\varepsilon}, \mathrm{L})\boldsymbol{\Phi}(\hat{e})\,\mathrm{T}^{-1}(\hat{\varepsilon}, \mathrm{L}) = \mathrm{M}^{-1}(\mathrm{L})\boldsymbol{\Phi}(\mathrm{L}\hat{e}+\hat{\varepsilon}) \tag{16.47}$$

where M is the 4×4 matrix introduced in equation (15.128) and $\boldsymbol{\Phi}$ now denotes a column vector. This requirement is consistent with the transformation properties (16.19) of the classical fields since the expectation values $\langle\psi|\Phi_\alpha(\hat{e})|\psi\rangle$ are associated with the classical field $\phi_\alpha(\hat{e})$. Remember that $\mathrm{T}(\hat{\varepsilon}, \mathrm{L})$ is a unitary operator acting on the state vectors $|\psi\rangle$, although M is not a unitary matrix but satisfies $\mathrm{M}^\dagger\gamma_t\mathrm{M} = \gamma_t$, as was shown in subsection 15.8.4. Thus, taking the Hermitian adjoint of equation (16.47) we have

$$\mathrm{T}(\hat{\varepsilon}, \mathrm{L})\boldsymbol{\Phi}^\dagger(\hat{e})\mathrm{T}^{-1}(\hat{\varepsilon}, \mathrm{L}) = \boldsymbol{\Phi}^\dagger(\mathrm{L}\hat{e}+\hat{\varepsilon})(\mathrm{M}^{-1})^\dagger = \boldsymbol{\Phi}^\dagger(\mathrm{L}\hat{e}+\hat{\varepsilon})\gamma_t\mathrm{M}\gamma_t$$

It is convenient to introduce the notation $\overline{\boldsymbol{\Phi}}(\hat{e})$ by writing $\overline{\boldsymbol{\Phi}}(\hat{e}) = \boldsymbol{\Phi}^\dagger(\hat{e})\,\gamma_t$ so that

$$\mathrm{T}(\hat{\varepsilon}, \mathrm{L})\overline{\boldsymbol{\Phi}}(\hat{e})\mathrm{T}^{-1}(\hat{\varepsilon}, \mathrm{L}) = \overline{\boldsymbol{\Phi}}(\mathrm{L}\hat{e}+\hat{\varepsilon})\mathrm{M}(\mathrm{L}) \tag{16.48}$$

showing that the row-vector $\overline{\boldsymbol{\Phi}}$ transforms by post-multiplication with the matrix M(L).

We now construct the four-component field operator $\boldsymbol{\Phi}$ in a fashion similar to equation (16.44) with equation (16.33) but making use of creation operators $\mathrm{a}^\dagger(\hat{\boldsymbol{k}}m_s)$ for particles with spin $s=\frac{1}{2}$ and the corresponding antiparticle operators $\mathrm{b}^\dagger(\hat{\boldsymbol{k}}m_s)$. We write

$$\Phi_\alpha(\hat{e}) = k^{\frac{1}{2}}(2\pi)^{-\frac{3}{2}}\int k_t^{-1}\,\mathrm{d}\boldsymbol{k}\sum_{m_s}\{u_{\alpha m_s}(\hat{\boldsymbol{k}})\mathrm{a}(\hat{\boldsymbol{k}}m_s)\exp(-i\hat{\boldsymbol{k}}.\hat{\boldsymbol{e}})$$
$$+v_{\alpha m_s}(\hat{\boldsymbol{k}})\mathrm{b}^\dagger(\hat{\boldsymbol{k}}m_s)\exp(i\hat{\boldsymbol{k}}.\hat{\boldsymbol{e}})\} \tag{16.49}$$

where the normalisation factor is conventional and the coefficients u and v are determined to ensure the transformation property (16.47) and causality. Regarding the u and v as 4×2 matrices, it is argued below that they are given by

$$\mathrm{u}(\hat{\boldsymbol{k}}) = \begin{pmatrix}\mathrm{L}^{(\frac{1}{2},0)}(\mathrm{Q})\\ \mathrm{L}^{(0,\frac{1}{2})}(\mathrm{Q})\end{pmatrix},\ \mathrm{v}(\hat{\boldsymbol{k}}) = \begin{pmatrix}-\mathrm{L}^{(\frac{1}{2},0)}(\mathrm{Q})\\ \mathrm{L}^{(0,\frac{1}{2})}(\mathrm{Q})\end{pmatrix}\times\begin{pmatrix}0 & 1\\ -1 & 0\end{pmatrix} \tag{16.50}$$

where the boost Q in the 2×2 matrices L carries the vector (0 0 0 1) into $\hat{\boldsymbol{k}}$, see equation (15.125). (In fact, the two columns of $\mathrm{u}(\hat{\boldsymbol{k}})$ are the column vectors in the two single-particle states $|\hat{\boldsymbol{k}}\pm\rangle$ given in equation (15.135a).)

To show that $\mathbf{\Phi}$ has the required transformation properties we must start from the known transformation (15.59) of the particle (and antiparticle) states

$$\mathrm{T}(\hat{\varepsilon}, \mathrm{L})\mathrm{a}^{\dagger}(\hat{\boldsymbol{k}}m_s)\mathrm{T}^{-1}(\hat{\varepsilon}, \mathrm{L}) = \exp(i\hat{\boldsymbol{k}}'.\hat{\varepsilon})\sum_{m_s'} D^{(\frac{1}{2})}_{m_s'm_s}(\mathrm{R}')\mathrm{a}^{\dagger}(\hat{\boldsymbol{k}}'m_s')$$

where $\hat{\boldsymbol{k}}' = \mathrm{L}\hat{\boldsymbol{k}}$ and $\mathrm{R}' = \mathrm{Q}'^{-1}\mathrm{L}\mathrm{Q}$ from equation (15.60) with Q' the boost for $\hat{\boldsymbol{k}}'$. Taking the Hermitian adjoint of this equation gives

$$\mathrm{T}(\hat{\varepsilon}, \mathrm{L})\mathrm{a}(\hat{\boldsymbol{k}}m_s)\mathrm{T}^{-1}(\hat{\varepsilon}, \mathrm{L}) = \exp(-i\hat{\boldsymbol{k}}'.\hat{\varepsilon})\sum_{m_s'} D^{(\frac{1}{2})}_{m_s m_s'}(\mathrm{R}'^{-1})\mathrm{a}(\hat{\boldsymbol{k}}'\mathrm{m}_s')$$

using the unitarity of the D-matrix. Since, for rotations, $\mathrm{D}^{(\frac{1}{2})} = \mathrm{L}^{(\frac{1}{2},0)} = \mathrm{L}^{(0,\frac{1}{2})}$, we may write, as a matrix product,

$$\mathrm{D}^{(\frac{1}{2})}(\mathrm{R}'^{-1}) = \mathrm{L}^{(\frac{1}{2},0)}(\mathrm{Q}^{-1})\mathrm{L}^{(\frac{1}{2},0)}(\mathrm{L}^{-1})\mathrm{L}^{(\frac{1}{2},0)}(\mathrm{Q}') \tag{16.51}$$

$$= \mathrm{L}^{(0,\frac{1}{2})}(\mathrm{Q}^{-1})\mathrm{L}^{(0,\frac{1}{2})}(\mathrm{L}^{-1})\mathrm{L}^{(0,\frac{1}{2})}(\mathrm{Q}') \tag{16.51a}$$

From equation (16.49) we now have

$$\begin{aligned}\mathrm{T}(\hat{\varepsilon}, \mathrm{L})\Phi_\alpha(\hat{e})\mathrm{T}^{-1}(\hat{\varepsilon}, \mathrm{L}) = k^{\frac{1}{2}}(2\pi)^{-\frac{3}{2}}\int k_t^{-1}\mathrm{d}\boldsymbol{k}\sum_{m_s'}\{&\exp(-i\hat{\boldsymbol{k}}'.\hat{\varepsilon} - i\hat{\boldsymbol{k}}.\hat{e})\\ &\times[u(\hat{\boldsymbol{k}})\mathrm{D}^{\frac{1}{2}}(\mathrm{R}'^{-1})]_{\alpha m_s'}\mathrm{a}(\hat{\boldsymbol{k}}'m_s') + \exp(i\hat{\boldsymbol{k}}'.\hat{\varepsilon} + i\hat{\boldsymbol{k}}.\hat{e})\\ &\times[v(\hat{\boldsymbol{k}})\mathrm{D}^{(\frac{1}{2})*}(\mathrm{R}'^{-1})]_{\alpha m_s'}\mathrm{b}^{\dagger}(\hat{\boldsymbol{k}}'m_s')\}\end{aligned} \tag{16.52}$$

where we have again used the unitarity of D to write $D^{(\frac{1}{2})}_{m_s'm_s}(\mathrm{R}') = D^{(\frac{1}{2})*}_{m_s m_s'}(\mathrm{R}'^{-1})$. The matrix products uD and vD* simplify considerably on using (16.50) and the pair of equations (16.51),

$$\mathrm{u}(\hat{\boldsymbol{k}})\mathrm{D}^{(\frac{1}{2})}(\mathrm{R}'^{-1}) = \begin{pmatrix}\mathrm{L}^{(\frac{1}{2},0)}(\mathrm{L}^{-1}) & \mathrm{L}^{(\frac{1}{2},0)}(\mathrm{Q}')\\ \mathrm{L}^{(0,\frac{1}{2})}(\mathrm{L}^{-1}) & \mathrm{L}^{(0,\frac{1}{2})}(\mathrm{Q}')\end{pmatrix} = \mathrm{M}^{-1}\mathrm{u}(\hat{\boldsymbol{k}}')$$

$$\mathrm{v}(\hat{\boldsymbol{k}})\mathrm{D}^{(\frac{1}{2})*}(\mathrm{R}'^{-1}) = \mathrm{v}(\hat{\boldsymbol{k}})\begin{pmatrix}0 & -1\\ 1 & 0\end{pmatrix}\mathrm{D}^{(\frac{1}{2})}(\mathrm{R}'^{-1})\begin{pmatrix}0 & 1\\ -1 & 0\end{pmatrix}$$

$$= \begin{pmatrix}-\mathrm{L}^{(\frac{1}{2},0)}(\mathrm{L}^{-1}) & \mathrm{L}^{(\frac{1}{2},0)}(\mathrm{Q}')\\ \mathrm{L}^{(0,\frac{1}{2})}(\mathrm{L}^{-1}) & \mathrm{L}^{(0,\frac{1}{2})}(\mathrm{Q}')\end{pmatrix}\begin{pmatrix}0 & 1\\ -1 & 0\end{pmatrix} = \mathrm{M}^{-1}\mathrm{v}(\hat{\boldsymbol{k}}') \tag{16.53}$$

where the form (15.128) has been used for M. The role of the matrix $\begin{pmatrix}0 & 1\\ -1 & 0\end{pmatrix} = i\sigma_y$ is to transform D* into D since these representations are equivalent, see section 7.7. The desired result (16.47) now follows immediately on putting the expressions (16.53) into (16.52) and making a change of integration variable from $\boldsymbol{k}$ to $\boldsymbol{k}'$. Note that this derivation would still be valid had we not included the negative sign in the first two rows of v in equation (16.50). However, this choice is crucial in ensuring causality, as may be seen by calculating the anticommutator of $\mathbf{\Phi}^{\mathrm{T}}(\hat{\boldsymbol{e}})$ and $\mathbf{\Phi}(\hat{\boldsymbol{e}}')$ following subsection 16.3.4.

An interesting consequence of the structure of the Dirac field is that the intrinsic parity of particle and antiparticle must be opposite. This differs from the zero-spin case where the two parities were the same. Let us return briefly to that case before discussing the Dirac field. Let T(I) denote the unitary transformation induced by the space inversion I. Then if π denotes the intrinsic parity of the particle we have, from equation (15.87),

$$\mathrm{T(I)a}^{\dagger}(\hat{\boldsymbol{k}})\mathrm{T}^{-1}(\mathrm{I}) = \pi \mathrm{a}^{\dagger}(\mathrm{I}\hat{\boldsymbol{k}})$$

with

$$\mathrm{T(I)a}(\hat{\boldsymbol{k}})\mathrm{T}^{-1}(\mathrm{I}) = \pi \mathrm{a}(\mathrm{I}\hat{\boldsymbol{k}})$$

Let us denote the intrinsic parity of the antiparticle by π' so that

$$\mathrm{T(I)b}^{\dagger}(\hat{\boldsymbol{k}})\mathrm{T}^{-1}(\mathrm{I}) = \pi' \mathrm{b}^{\dagger}(\mathrm{I}\hat{\boldsymbol{k}})$$

Now if we require the field Φ to have definite parity so that

$$\mathrm{T(I)}\Phi(\hat{\boldsymbol{e}})\mathrm{T}^{-1}(\mathrm{I}) = \pm\Phi(\mathrm{I}\hat{\boldsymbol{e}}) \tag{16.54}$$

then from the definition (16.44) of Φ it follows quickly, using the properties of a and $\mathrm{b}^{\dagger}$ above, that equation (16.54) will be satisfied only if $\pi = \pi'$ and then

$$\mathrm{T(I)}\Phi(\hat{\boldsymbol{e}})\mathrm{T}^{-1}(\mathrm{I}) = \pi\Phi(\mathrm{I}\hat{\boldsymbol{e}}) \tag{16.55}$$

showing that the parity of the particle determines the parity of the field. For the π-mesons the parity is $\pi = -1$ so that the field is odd and since it is also scalar it is called pseudo-scalar. (We apologise for the double use of the symbol π in this sentence!)

Turning to the Dirac field we must start from the inversion transformation in the particle states,

$$\mathrm{T(I)a}^{\dagger}(\hat{\boldsymbol{k}}m_s)\mathrm{T}^{-1}(\mathrm{I}) = \pi \mathrm{a}^{\dagger}(\mathrm{I}\hat{\boldsymbol{k}}m_s) \tag{16.56}$$

and let us write

$$\mathrm{T(I)b}^{\dagger}(\hat{\boldsymbol{k}}m_s)\mathrm{T}^{-1}(\mathrm{I}) = \pi' \mathrm{b}^{\dagger}(\mathrm{I}\hat{\boldsymbol{k}}m_s) \tag{16.57}$$

Now, recalling from subsection 15.8.4 that in the four-component space the inversion operator is represented by the matrix γ_t, we shall require a field with definite parity to satisfy

$$\mathrm{T(I)}\mathbf{\Phi}(\hat{\boldsymbol{e}})\mathrm{T}^{-1}(\mathrm{I}) = \pm\gamma_t\mathbf{\Phi}(\mathrm{I}\hat{\boldsymbol{e}}) \tag{16.58}$$

where again $\mathbf{\Phi}(\hat{\boldsymbol{e}})$ denotes a column vector. But, using the results (16.56) and (16.57) in (16.49), we have

$$\mathrm{T(I)}\Phi_\alpha(\hat{\boldsymbol{e}})\mathrm{T}^{-1}(\mathrm{I}) = k^{\frac{1}{2}}(2\pi)^{-\frac{3}{2}}\int k_t^{-1}\,\mathrm{d}\boldsymbol{k}\sum_{m_s}\{u_{\alpha m_s}(\hat{\boldsymbol{k}})\pi \mathrm{a}(\mathrm{I}\hat{\boldsymbol{k}}m_s)\exp(-i\hat{\boldsymbol{k}}.\hat{\boldsymbol{e}}) + v_{\alpha m_s}(\hat{\boldsymbol{k}})\pi' \mathrm{b}^{\dagger}(\mathrm{I}\hat{\boldsymbol{k}}m_s)\exp(i\hat{\boldsymbol{k}}.\hat{\boldsymbol{e}})\} \tag{16.59}$$

To relate this expression to $\mathbf{\Phi}(\mathrm{I}\hat{e})$ we need to change the notation for the integration variable, writing $\mathrm{I}\hat{\boldsymbol{k}} \to \hat{\boldsymbol{k}}$. We must also use the property $\mathrm{u}(\mathrm{I}\hat{\boldsymbol{k}}) = \gamma_t \mathrm{u}(\hat{\boldsymbol{k}})$ which may be seen directly from the explicit form (15.135a) for $\mathrm{u}(\hat{\boldsymbol{k}})$, and the consequent property $\mathrm{v}(\mathrm{I}\hat{\boldsymbol{k}}) = -\gamma_t \mathrm{v}(\hat{\boldsymbol{k}})$. Because of this sign change it follows that the expression (16.59) reduces to the form (16.58) only when $\pi' = -\pi$ and then

$$\mathrm{T}(\mathrm{I})\mathbf{\Phi}(\hat{e})\mathrm{T}^{-1}(\mathrm{I}) = \pi\gamma_t\mathbf{\Phi}(\mathrm{I}\hat{e}) \tag{16.60}$$

Experimentally, the study of the electron – positron system confirms this result that for $s = \frac{1}{2}$, the antiparticle has a parity opposite to that of the particle.

The Dirac equation (15.131) referred to the one-particle states and contained operators $\hat{\mathbf{P}}$ which described infinitesimal translations in the state vectors. We now see that the field operators $\mathbf{\Phi}(\hat{e})$ satisfy a Dirac equation

$$(\hat{\gamma}.\square + ik)\mathbf{\Phi}(\hat{e}) = 0 \tag{16.61}$$

where $\square = (-\nabla, \partial/\partial ct)$ is a differential operator acting on the position variables $\hat{e}$. This result follows directly from the definition (16.49) by operating with $\square$ on the exponentials and using equation (16.60). The Dirac equation (16.61) is again the field equation which arises from the Lagrangian. In this case the appropriate Lagrangian density which gives rise to the particle picture, as in subsection 16.3.3, and also leads to this field equation is

$$\mathscr{L} = \mathbf{\Phi}(\hat{e})(\hat{\gamma}.\square + ik)\mathbf{\Phi}(\hat{e})$$

The neutrino field

In subsection 15.8.5 we showed that the single-particle state for the neutrino, zero mass and $m = -\frac{1}{2}$, could be expressed in two-component form using the representation $\mathrm{L}^{(0,\frac{1}{2})}$ together with the Weyl equation. Thus we shall seek a two-component field operator $\mathbf{\Phi}(\hat{e})$ similar to that given in equation (16.49). We shall expect it to transform according to

$$\mathrm{T}(\hat{\varepsilon}, \mathrm{L})\mathbf{\Phi}(\hat{e})\mathrm{T}^{-1}(\hat{\varepsilon}, \mathrm{L}) = (\mathrm{L}^{(0,\frac{1}{2})})^{-1}\mathbf{\Phi}(\mathrm{L}\hat{e} + \hat{\varepsilon}) \tag{16.62}$$

The field will be constructed from the neutrino operators $\mathrm{a}^{\dagger}(\hat{\boldsymbol{k}}-)$ and the antineutrino operators $\mathrm{b}^{\dagger}(\hat{\boldsymbol{k}}+)$. The negative sign in the operator $\mathrm{a}^{\dagger}$ serves to remind us that the neutrino has $m = -\frac{1}{2}$ and so transforms according to $\mathrm{P}^{(0,-\frac{1}{2})}$ as given in equation (15.68) or equivalently in equation (15.144). We have assigned the antineutrino a positive helicity but this will be seen to be necessary if the field is to satisfy the invariance and causality conditions. We shall write

$$\Phi_\alpha(\hat{e}) = (2\pi)^{-\frac{3}{2}} \int k_t^{-1}\,\mathrm{d}\boldsymbol{k}\, w_\alpha(\hat{\boldsymbol{k}})\{\mathrm{a}(\hat{\boldsymbol{k}}-)\exp(-i\hat{\boldsymbol{k}}.\hat{e}) + \mathrm{b}^{\dagger}(\hat{\boldsymbol{k}}+)\exp(i\hat{\boldsymbol{k}}.\hat{e})\} \tag{16.63}$$

and show that the coefficients w, which in this case form a 2×1 matrix, are given by the second column of the matrix $\mathrm{L}^{(0,\frac{1}{2})}(\mathrm{R}_{xy}\mathrm{Q}_z)$, where the Lorentz transformation $R_{xy}Q_z$ was defined in subsection 15.4.2 as that which carries the vector (0, 0, 1, 1) into $\hat{\boldsymbol{k}}$. To justify this expression we use the particle transformation (15.144) in equation (16.63) giving

$$\mathrm{T}(\hat{\varepsilon}, \mathrm{L})\Phi_\alpha(\hat{e})\mathrm{T}^{-1}(\hat{\varepsilon}, \mathrm{L}) = (2\pi)^{-\frac{3}{2}}\int k_t^{-1}\mathrm{d}\boldsymbol{k}w_\alpha(\hat{\boldsymbol{k}})\{\exp(-i\hat{\boldsymbol{k}}'.\hat{\varepsilon} - i\hat{\boldsymbol{k}}.\hat{e})$$
$$\times \mathrm{L}^{(0,\frac{1}{2})}_{-\frac{1}{2}-\frac{1}{2}}[(\mathrm{R}'_{xy}\mathrm{Q}'_z)^{-1}\mathrm{L}\mathrm{R}_{xy}\mathrm{Q}_z]^* a(\hat{\boldsymbol{k}}'-) + \exp(i\hat{\boldsymbol{k}}'.\hat{\varepsilon} + i\hat{\boldsymbol{k}}.\hat{e})$$
$$\times \mathrm{L}^{(\frac{1}{2},0)}_{\frac{1}{2}\frac{1}{2}}[(\mathrm{R}'_{xy}\mathrm{Q}'_z)^{-1}\mathrm{L}\mathrm{R}_{xy}\mathrm{Q}_z]b^\dagger(\hat{\boldsymbol{k}}'+)\} \tag{16.64}$$

Writing $w(\hat{\boldsymbol{k}}) = \mathrm{L}^{(0,\frac{1}{2})}(\mathrm{R}_{xy}\mathrm{Q}_z)\binom{0}{1}$ as the second column of $\mathrm{L}^{(0,\frac{1}{2})}$ and using the unitarity of the particle transformation (15.144) we see that

$$w(\hat{\boldsymbol{k}})\mathrm{L}^{(0,\frac{1}{2})}_{-\frac{1}{2}-\frac{1}{2}}[(\mathrm{R}'_{xy}\mathrm{Q}'_z)^{-1}\mathrm{L}\mathrm{R}_{xy}\mathrm{Q}_z]^*$$
$$= \{\mathrm{L}^{(0,\frac{1}{2})}(\mathrm{R}_{xy}\mathrm{Q}_z)\mathrm{L}^{(0,\frac{1}{2})}[(\mathrm{R}_{xy}\mathrm{Q}_z)^{-1}\mathrm{L}^{-1}\mathrm{R}'_{xy}\mathrm{Q}'_z]\}\begin{pmatrix}0\\1\end{pmatrix}$$
$$= \mathrm{L}^{(0,\frac{1}{2})}(\mathrm{L}^{-1})w(\hat{\boldsymbol{k}}')$$

where we have also used the fact that $\mathrm{L}^{(0,\frac{1}{2})}_{\frac{1}{2}-\frac{1}{2}}[(\mathrm{R}'_{xy}\mathrm{Q}'_z)^{-1}\mathrm{L}\mathrm{R}_{xy}\mathrm{Q}_z] = 0$, see the discussion after equation (15.144). A similar result

$$w(\hat{\boldsymbol{k}})\mathrm{L}^{(\frac{1}{2},0)}_{\frac{1}{2}\frac{1}{2}}[(\mathrm{R}'_{xy}\mathrm{Q}'_z)^{-1}\mathrm{L}\mathrm{R}_{xy}\mathrm{Q}_z] = \mathrm{L}^{(0,\frac{1}{2})}(\mathrm{L}^{-1})w(\hat{\boldsymbol{k}}')$$

holds for the second term in equation (16.64) using the equivalence of $\mathrm{L}^{(\frac{1}{2},0)}$ and $\mathrm{L}^{(0,\frac{1}{2})*}$, see subsection 15.2.5. Putting these two results into equation (16.64) and making the change $\hat{\boldsymbol{k}}' \to \hat{\boldsymbol{k}}$ in the integration variable leads to the desired result (16.62).

As in previous examples one sees that the field $\boldsymbol{\Phi}(\hat{e})$ satisfies the appropriate field equation which, in this case, is the Weyl equation (15.146)

$$\left(\mathbf{s}.\nabla - \frac{1}{2c}\frac{\partial}{\partial t}\right)\boldsymbol{\Phi}(\hat{e}) = 0$$

The Lagrangian density for the free neutrino field is

$$\mathscr{L} = \boldsymbol{\Phi}^\dagger(\hat{e})\left(\mathbf{s}.\nabla - \frac{1}{2c}\frac{\partial}{\partial t}\right)\boldsymbol{\Phi}(\hat{e})$$

Note that $\boldsymbol{\Phi}^\dagger$ transforms according to $\mathrm{L}^{(\frac{1}{2},0)}$ and the Weyl operator is a component of a four-vector $\hat{\mathbf{W}} + im\hat{\mathbf{P}}$. It is rather surprising that one does not need to include the other components to ensure the invariance of $\mathscr{L}$ but this is due to the special relations between these components as pointed out after equation (15.145).

Although the neutrino has no electric charge we can define an operator Q as in subsection 16.3.5 which measures the difference between the numbers of neutrinos and antineutrinos. It is called the 'lepton charge' and if a similar charge is assigned to electrons and muons then one finds experimentally that this lepton charge is conserved, like the electric charge. This is illustrated in the β-decay of a neutron, $n \to p + e + \bar{\nu}$ into a proton, electron and antineutrino $\bar{\nu}$, since one assigns a zero lepton charge to the heavier particles n and p. Confirmation of these ideas is found in many experiments; for example the process $\bar{\nu} + n \to p + e$ does not take place whereas $\bar{\nu} + p \to n + \bar{e}$, with $\bar{e}$ denoting the anti-electron (or positron), is observed. We might briefly remark that the heavier particles like n and p belong to a class of particles called 'baryons' with a baryon charge of $+1$ and that this baryon charge provides a further conserved charge.

We have seen in subsection 15.7.3 that space inversion changes the helicity, i.e. changes the sign of m. Thus the neutrino field cannot have definite parity like the Dirac field. The space inversion would carry the neutrino ($m = -\frac{1}{2}$) into a neutrino with $m = \frac{1}{2}$ but such particles do not occur in nature and are therefore not contained in the field. However if we introduce the charge conjugation operator C as in subsection 16.3.6 then the existence of antineutrinos with $m = \frac{1}{2}$ suggests that the field may transform simply under the combined operation of charge conjugation and space inversion which we denote by CP. Defining this unitary operator by the relations

$$\mathrm{CPa}^{\dagger}(\hat{\boldsymbol{k}}-)(\mathrm{CP})^{-1} = \eta(\hat{\boldsymbol{k}})\mathrm{b}^{\dagger}(\mathrm{I}\hat{\boldsymbol{k}}+), \quad (\mathrm{CP})^2 = 1$$

where $\eta(\hat{\boldsymbol{k}})$ is a phase factor, we are able to show, by using the properties of $\mathrm{w}(\hat{\boldsymbol{k}})$, that CP transforms the components of $\boldsymbol{\Phi}(\hat{\boldsymbol{e}})$ into those of $\boldsymbol{\Phi}^{\dagger}(\mathrm{I}\hat{\boldsymbol{e}})$. In fact

$$\mathrm{CP}\Phi_{\alpha}(\hat{\boldsymbol{e}})(\mathrm{CP})^{-1} = \sum_{\beta} (i\sigma_y)_{\alpha\beta}\, \Phi_{\beta}^{\dagger}(\mathrm{I}\hat{\boldsymbol{e}})$$

where $\sigma_y = 2\mathrm{s}_y$ is the 2×2 spin matrix. One can therefore construct a Lagrangian containing the neutrino field and which is invariant under CP but not separately under C or P. (It is perhaps worth remarking that charge conservation and the invariance under charge conjugation are two quite distinct properties.)

The electromagnetic field

The electromagnetic field is a familiar classical concept with consequences over macroscopic distances. This contrasts with the nuclear fields whose interactions drop off exponentially with distance with dimensions of order 10^{-13} cm. Nevertheless, for a consistent theory and indeed to agree with accurate experiments, the electromagnetic field must be constructed in quantised form. We shall see below that if we construct field operators appropriate to particles with zero mass and $m = \pm 1$, the Poincaré representations $\mathrm{P}^{(0, \pm 1)}$, then such a field has the familiar properties of the electromagnetic field. The particles are called photons. As in the passage from quantum to classical mechanics for particles one can recover the classical field interpretation. The method is very similar to that of the previous discussion of the neutrino field with the trivial change from $|m| = \frac{1}{2}$ to $|m| = 1$ and two significant changes. In the first place the photon exists in both helicity states $m = \pm 1$ so that the field may be constructed with definite parity and the electromagnetic interactions may conserve parity. The second change is that the photon has no charge of any kind and thus has no distinct antiparticle. Taking these two changes together and noting that, in a sense, both helicity states were present in the neutrino field, one for particle and one for antiparticle, we have as a natural extension of equation (16.63) to the case $|m| = 1$,

$$\Phi_\alpha(\hat{e}) = (2\pi)^{-\frac{3}{2}} \int k_t^{-1}\,\mathrm{d}\boldsymbol{k}\, w_\alpha(\hat{\boldsymbol{k}})\{\mathrm{a}(\hat{\boldsymbol{k}}-)\exp(-i\hat{\boldsymbol{k}}\,.\,\hat{\boldsymbol{e}}) + \mathrm{a}^\dagger(\hat{\boldsymbol{k}}+)\exp(i\hat{\boldsymbol{k}}.\hat{\boldsymbol{e}})\} \qquad (16.65)$$

where $\mathrm{a}^\dagger(\hat{\boldsymbol{k}}\pm)$ creates photons with helicity ± 1 and the fields and the coefficients $\mathrm{w}(\hat{\boldsymbol{k}})$ are now three-vectors. As before we can ensure that the fields satisfy the transformation properties

$$\mathrm{T}(\hat{\varepsilon}, \mathrm{L})\boldsymbol{\Phi}(\hat{e})\,\mathrm{T}^{-1}(\hat{\varepsilon}, \mathrm{L}) = (\mathrm{L}^{(0,\,1)})^{-1}\boldsymbol{\Phi}(\mathrm{L}\hat{e} + \hat{\varepsilon})$$
$$\mathrm{T}(\hat{\varepsilon}, \mathrm{L})\boldsymbol{\Phi}^\dagger(\hat{e})\mathrm{T}^{-1}(\hat{\varepsilon}, \mathrm{L}) = \boldsymbol{\Phi}^\dagger(\mathrm{L}\hat{e} + \hat{\varepsilon})\mathrm{L}^{(1,\,0)} \qquad (16.66)$$

by choosing $w(\hat{\boldsymbol{k}})$ to be the three-vector appearing in the third column of $\mathrm{L}^{(0,\,1)}(\mathrm{R}_{xy}\mathrm{Q}_z)$ corresponding to $m = -1$. The justification for this choice follows that given for the neutrino so closely that we shall not give it. We do, however, need to understand the structure of the vector $w(\hat{\boldsymbol{k}})$ which is given by

$$w(\hat{\boldsymbol{k}}) = \mathrm{L}^{(0,\,1)}(\mathrm{R}_{xy}\mathrm{Q}_z)\begin{pmatrix}0\\0\\1\end{pmatrix} = \mathrm{L}^{(0,\,1)}(\mathrm{R}_{xy})\mathrm{L}^{(0,\,1)}(\mathrm{Q}_z)\begin{pmatrix}0\\0\\1\end{pmatrix}$$
$$= k_t\mathrm{D}^{(1)}(\mathrm{R}_{xy})\begin{pmatrix}0\\0\\1\end{pmatrix} \qquad (16.67)$$

where we have used, for rotations, $\mathrm{L}^{(0,\,1)}(\mathrm{R}_{xy}) = \mathrm{D}^{(1)}(\mathrm{R}_{xy})$, while for the boost in $\mathrm{L}^{(0,\,1)}(\mathrm{Q}_z)$,

$$\mathrm{Q}_z = \exp(b\mathrm{Y}_z) = \exp(ib\mathrm{X}_z) = \exp(bs_z)$$

making $\mathrm{L}^{(0,\,1)}(\mathrm{Q}_z)$ diagonal with $L^{(0,1)}_{-1\,-1}(\mathrm{Q}_z) = \exp(-b) = k_t$. The relation between b and k_t comes about because $\mathrm{Q}_z(0\,0\,1\,1) = (0\,0\,k_t\,k_t)$ so that from equation (15.24), $\cosh b - \sinh b = k_t$. Now recall from subsection 7.4.5 that the vector $\begin{pmatrix}0\\0\\1\end{pmatrix}$ in the m-basis is given by $(\boldsymbol{e}_x - i\boldsymbol{e}_y)/2^{\frac{1}{2}}$ in the Cartesian basis so that equation (16.67) tells us that $w(\hat{\boldsymbol{k}})$ is a vector of length k_t, of the kind $\begin{pmatrix}0\\0\\1\end{pmatrix}$

but rotated by R_{xy}. Since R_{xy} carries the z-axis into the direction $\boldsymbol{k}$, the vector $w(\hat{\boldsymbol{k}})$ may therefore be written

$$w(\hat{\boldsymbol{k}}) = k_t[\boldsymbol{e}_1(\hat{\boldsymbol{k}}) - i\boldsymbol{e}_2(\hat{\boldsymbol{k}})]/2^{\frac{1}{2}} \tag{16.68}$$

where $\boldsymbol{e}_1$ and $\boldsymbol{e}_2$ are a pair of orthogonal unit vectors in the plane perpendicular to $\boldsymbol{k}$. The position of $\boldsymbol{e}_1$ in this plane is unimportant since any rotation in this plane changes only the phase of $w(\hat{\boldsymbol{k}})$. However, by choosing $\boldsymbol{e}_2$ to be the axis of the rotation R_{xy}, these unit vectors acquire the simple properties $\boldsymbol{e}_2(I\hat{\boldsymbol{k}}) = \boldsymbol{e}_2(\hat{\boldsymbol{k}})$ and $\boldsymbol{e}_1(I\hat{\boldsymbol{k}}) = -\boldsymbol{e}_1(\hat{\boldsymbol{k}})$, since $I\hat{\boldsymbol{k}}$ is arrived at by an extra rotation of π in R_{xy}. Hence from (16.68), $w(I\hat{\boldsymbol{k}}) = -w^*(\hat{\boldsymbol{k}})$.

From equation (15.91) the behaviour of the particle operators under space inversion is given by

$$T(I)a^\dagger(\hat{\boldsymbol{k}}+)T^{-1}(I) = -a^\dagger(I\hat{\boldsymbol{k}}-) \tag{16.69}$$

where the choice of negative sign is only a convention, since the relative phase of the two helicity states is free. (The positive sign was used in equation (15.91).) However, once this choice is made, the positive sign between $a(\hat{\boldsymbol{k}}-)$ and $a^\dagger(\hat{\boldsymbol{k}}+)$ in (16.65) acquires significance. Using (16.69) we see that the field satisfies the equation

$$T(I)\boldsymbol{\Phi}(\hat{e})T^{-1}(I) = \boldsymbol{\Phi}^\dagger(I\hat{e})$$

We may therefore form linear combinations of $\boldsymbol{\Phi}$ and $\boldsymbol{\Phi}^\dagger$ which have even and odd parity, respectively:

$$\mathbf{B}(\hat{e}) = [\boldsymbol{\Phi}(\hat{e}) + \boldsymbol{\Phi}^\dagger(\hat{e})]/2^{\frac{1}{2}} \quad \text{and} \quad \mathbf{E}(\hat{e}) = -i[\boldsymbol{\Phi}(\hat{e}) - \boldsymbol{\Phi}^\dagger(\hat{e})]/2^{\frac{1}{2}}$$

The numerical factors are conventional and the factor i makes $\mathbf{E}$ Hermitian as well as $\mathbf{B}$. By using the symbols $\mathbf{E}$ and $\mathbf{B}$ we are anticipating their association with the familiar magnetic and electric fields of classical theory, see subsection 16.2.3. To construct the quantised field corresponding to the classical vector potential $\hat{\mathbf{A}}$ it is convenient to introduce the particle operators

$$\begin{aligned} a_1^\dagger(\hat{\boldsymbol{k}}) &= [a^\dagger(\hat{\boldsymbol{k}}+) - a^\dagger(\hat{\boldsymbol{k}}-)]/2^{\frac{1}{2}} \\ a_2^\dagger(\hat{\boldsymbol{k}}) &= -i[a^\dagger(\hat{\boldsymbol{k}}+) + a^\dagger(\hat{\boldsymbol{k}}-)]/2^{\frac{1}{2}} \end{aligned} \tag{16.70}$$

which are linear combinations of the two helicity states $\pm$ and describe states of plane polarisation. In terms of these new operators and using the form (16.68) for w, the expressions (16.65) lead to

$$\begin{aligned} \mathbf{E}(\hat{e}) = (2\pi)^{-\frac{3}{2}}2^{-\frac{1}{2}}i\int \mathrm{d}\boldsymbol{k}\{&[\boldsymbol{e}_1(\hat{\boldsymbol{k}})a_1(\hat{\boldsymbol{k}}) + \boldsymbol{e}_2(\hat{\boldsymbol{k}})a_2(\hat{\boldsymbol{k}})]\exp(-i\hat{\boldsymbol{k}}.\hat{e}) \\ &-[\boldsymbol{e}_1(\hat{\boldsymbol{k}})a_1^\dagger(\hat{\boldsymbol{k}}) + \boldsymbol{e}_2(\hat{\boldsymbol{k}})a_2^\dagger(\hat{\boldsymbol{k}})]\exp(i\hat{\boldsymbol{k}}.\hat{e})\} \\ \mathbf{B}(\hat{e}) = (2\pi)^{-\frac{3}{2}}2^{-\frac{1}{2}}i\int \mathrm{d}\boldsymbol{k}\{&[\boldsymbol{e}_2(\hat{\boldsymbol{k}})a_1(\hat{\boldsymbol{k}}) - \boldsymbol{e}_1(\hat{\boldsymbol{k}})a_2(\hat{\boldsymbol{k}})]\exp(-i\hat{\boldsymbol{k}}.\hat{e}) \\ &-[\boldsymbol{e}_2(\hat{\boldsymbol{k}})a_1^\dagger(\hat{\boldsymbol{k}}) - \boldsymbol{e}_1(\hat{\boldsymbol{k}})a_2^\dagger(\hat{\boldsymbol{k}})]\exp(i\hat{\boldsymbol{k}}.\hat{e})\} \end{aligned} \tag{16.71}$$

From the form of the expressions (16.71) we see that both **E** and **B** may be expressed in terms of a single vector field

$$\mathbf{A}(\hat{e}) = (2\pi)^{-\frac{3}{2}}2^{-\frac{1}{2}}\int k_t^{-1}\,\mathrm{d}\boldsymbol{k} \sum_{\lambda=1,2} \boldsymbol{e}(\hat{k},\lambda)\{\mathrm{a}(\hat{k},\lambda)\exp(-i\hat{k}.\hat{e}) + \mathrm{a}^{\dagger}(\hat{k},\lambda)\exp(i\hat{k}.\hat{e})\} \tag{16.72}$$

by writing

$$\mathrm{E}(\hat{e}) = -\frac{1}{c}\frac{\partial}{\partial t}\mathbf{A}(\hat{e}), \qquad \mathbf{B}(\hat{e}) = \mathrm{curl}\,\mathbf{A}(\hat{e}) \tag{16.73}$$

and using the trivial properties $\boldsymbol{e}_z \wedge \boldsymbol{e}_1 = \boldsymbol{e}_2$, $\boldsymbol{e}_z \wedge \boldsymbol{e}_2 = -\boldsymbol{e}_1$ for a right-handed set of orthonormal vectors.

It is quickly verified that, as in the other examples, the field satisfies the appropriate wave equations deduced in subsection 15.8.6. In fact it is $\mathbf{\Phi}^{\dagger}(\hat{e})$, transforming like $\mathrm{L}^{(1,0)}$, which satisfies the equations given there while $\mathbf{\Phi}(\hat{e})$ needs a change of sign in (15.149). Thus

$$\mathrm{curl}\,\mathbf{\Phi}(\hat{e}) = -\frac{i}{c}\frac{\partial}{\partial t}\mathbf{\Phi}(\hat{e}), \qquad \mathrm{curl}\,\mathbf{\Phi}^{\dagger}(\hat{e}) = \frac{i}{c}\frac{\partial}{\partial t}\mathbf{\Phi}^{\dagger}(\hat{e})$$

$$\mathrm{div}\,\mathbf{\Phi}(\hat{e}) = 0, \qquad \mathrm{div}\,\mathbf{\Phi}^{\dagger}(\hat{e}) = 0$$

and these equations lead to the more familiar form of Maxwell's equations when they are expressed in terms of **E** and **B**,

$$\mathrm{curl}\,\mathbf{B} = \frac{1}{c}\frac{\partial}{\partial t}\mathbf{E}, \qquad \mathrm{curl}\,\mathbf{E} = -\frac{1}{c}\frac{\partial}{\partial t}\mathbf{B}$$

$$\mathrm{div}\,\mathbf{B} = \mathrm{div}\,\mathbf{E} = 0 \tag{16.74}$$

One therefore identifies this field, constructed from the zero-mass particles with $|m| = 1$ (the photons), with the familiar electromagnetic field of $\boldsymbol{E}$ and $\boldsymbol{B}$ which it approaches in the classical limit. As one would expect, the way in which **E** and **B** are obtained from the single field **A** is the same as in the classical theory, see subsection 16.1.3. Recall, however, that in the classical problem we used a four-vector potential $\hat{A} = (\boldsymbol{A}, \Phi)$ to describe the Lorentz invariance of the theory, whereas in equation (16.72) we have only a three-vector. However in subsection 16.1.3 we showed that any two potentials $\hat{A}$ which led to the same $\boldsymbol{E}$ and $\boldsymbol{B}$ were physically equivalent. There was therefore freedom in the choice of $\hat{A}$ and one possibility, called the 'radiation (or Coulomb) gauge' is to set $\phi = 0$. The simple choice of $\mathbf{A}(\hat{e})$ in equation (16.72) corresponds to this gauge.

We have constructed the field $\mathbf{A}(\hat{e})$ by a somewhat circuitous path, starting from the product representations $\mathrm{P}^{(0,0)} \times \mathrm{L}^{(1,0)}$ and $\mathrm{P}^{(0,0)} \times \mathrm{L}^{(0,1)}$. This had the advantage of similarity with the neutrino field. However it would have been possible to arrive more directly at $\mathbf{E}(\hat{e})$ by using the product representation $\mathrm{P}^{(0,0)} \times \mathrm{L}^{(\frac{1}{2},\frac{1}{2})}$ which also contains $\mathrm{P}^{(0,\pm 1)}$.

Finally we note that, since the fields **E** and **B** were constructed to have even and odd parity, respectively, it follows from equation (16.72) that **A** must have odd parity,

$$T(I)\mathbf{A}(\hat{e})T^{-1}(I) = -\mathbf{A}(I\hat{e})$$

For this reason the photon is said to have odd intrinsic parity. By taking the opposite relative sign of $a(\hat{\boldsymbol{k}}-)$ and $\overset{+}{a}(\hat{\boldsymbol{k}}+)$ in $\Phi_\alpha(\hat{e})$ in equation (16.65) we could have constructed a field with positive parity but this would not have been consistent with experiment for the electromagnetic field.

Bibliography

For further reading in classical mechanics and fields we suggest

Landau, L. D. and Lifshitz, E. M. (1972). *A Shorter Course of Theoretical Physics*, vol. 1, Mechanics and electrodynamics (Pergamon Press, London)

A more complete introduction to relativistic quantum fields may be found in one of the following:

Bjorken, J. D. and Drell, S. D. (1965). *Relativistic Quantum Fields* (McGraw-Hill, New York)

Schweber, S. (1961). *An Introduction to Relativistic Quantum Field Theory* (Harper and Row, New York)

For a more mathematical treatment of field theory we suggest

Streater, R. F. and Wightman, A. S. (1964). *PCT, Spin and Statistics and all that* (Benjamin, New York)

For details of the experimental data on which the new concepts like charge conjugation are based, one should refer to the following particle physics references: Perkins (1972) of chapter 11 and Dyson (1966) of chapter 15.

Problems

16.1 Show that the fields $\boldsymbol{E} \pm i\boldsymbol{B}$ defined in equation (16.17) transform according to the representations $L^{(10)}$ and $L^{(01)}$, respectively, of the Lorentz group. (Use the matrices (15.30) of **X** and **Y** and for $L^{(10)}$ to show that $(\mathbf{X} - i\mathbf{Y})(\boldsymbol{E} + i\boldsymbol{B}) = 0$.

16.2 If the Lagrangian density is invariant under time translation $\left(\dfrac{d\mathscr{L}}{dt} = 0\right)$ show that $H = \int \mathscr{H}\, dV$ is constant. (Use the field equation (16.21) and Gauss's theorem, assuming the fields vanish at infinity.)

16.3 In the same way, show that the field momentum $\boldsymbol{P}$ defined in subsection 16.2.2 is constant when $\mathscr{L}$ is invariant under space translations.

16.4 Two particles with rest mass M and equal and opposite momenta $\pm \boldsymbol{p}$ collide and come to rest with the production, also at rest, of a third particle. Show that its rest mass is given by $2\left\{\left(M^2+\frac{p^2}{c^2}\right)^{\frac{1}{2}}-M\right\}$.

16.5 Show that the number operator defined by equation (16.30) has the properties $\mathrm{N}|0\rangle = 0$, $\mathrm{N}|\hat{k}\rangle = |\hat{k}\rangle$ and generally $\mathrm{N}|\hat{k}_1\hat{k}_2 \ldots \hat{k}_n\rangle = n|\hat{k}_1\hat{k}_2 \ldots \hat{k}_n\rangle$.

17

The Symmetric Group $\mathscr{S}_n$

The symmetric group $\mathscr{S}_n$, which is composed of all permutations of n objects, plays a curious role in the theory of symmetry. It is possible to obtain a very good understanding of symmetry without any knowledge of the properties of $\mathscr{S}_n$ but, on the other hand, this group is to be found in the background of many physical problems. It is connected with the point groups of chapter 9 through a result, called Cayley's theorem, that every point group is isomorphic with a group of permutations, though not necessarily with the group $\mathscr{S}_n$ of all permutations. For example, we have seen the isomorphism between D_3 and $\mathscr{S}_3$ in chapter 2. The symmetric group is also connected with the rotation and unitary groups because the construction of the irreducible representations of those groups may be accomplished by building products of elementary factors and studying the behaviour of the products under permutations of the factors. We elaborate this point in chapter 18. In applications to physical problems the Bose or Fermi statistics ensure that the overall wave function is either totally symmetric or totally antisymmetric, see section 5.9, but when this wave function is built up from separate wave functions describing the position coordinates, the spin coordinates and other degrees of freedom the behaviour of the separate factors under permutation can be much more elaborate. In fact, we have already made use of the symmetric group $\mathscr{S}_3$ in describing the structure of atoms in subsection 8.6.4 and the structure of nuclei and elementary particles in chapter 12. We were able to do this without much discussion because of the simplicity for small n and in particular because of the isomorphism with the group D_3 which we studied in some detail early in the book. For higher values of n, the way in which the group is applied to physical problems is exactly the same as for small n so we give no more applications in this chapter. Our aim here is to describe generally the properties of the group $\mathscr{S}_n$ and its representations.

One simplifying feature of the group $\mathscr{S}_n$ is that, in contrast to the point groups, its properties may be described for general n instead of having to consider each group separately. We shall often refer to the n objects being permuted as particles, since this is the most usual situation in applications. The first three sections describe some properties of the permutations themselves. Sections 17.4–17.9 are concerned with the irreducible representations and characters of $\mathscr{S}_n$ and a convenient method of labelling both irreducible representations and basis vectors by Young diagrams and tableaux is introduced. A rule for writing down the general representation matrix is deferred until section 17.13. Following a discussion of the familiar direct product in section 17.10 we introduce in section 17.11 the concept of an outer product which will also have relevance in chapter 18. The emphasis throughout this chapter is on explanation and understanding rather than rigour. For this reason we do not prove all results generally for all n. Neither do we deduce general formula for such things as the characters, although we do describe how they may be deduced for any particular n.

17.1 Cycles

A cycle is a rather special type of permutation, defined as follows. Suppose that the integers $p_1, p_2, \ldots, p_l$ are placed in order, at equal intervals of $2\pi/l$ around the circumference of a circle. In the notation of subsection 2.2(10), a rotation of $2\pi/l$ will induce the permutation

$$\begin{pmatrix} p_1 p_2 p_3 \cdots p_{l-1} \, p_l \\ p_2 p_3 p_4 \cdots p_l \quad p_1 \end{pmatrix}$$

Such a permutation is called a 'cycle' of length l and is denoted by $(p_1 p_2 p_3 \ldots p_l)$.

An arbitary permutation $\mathrm{P} = \begin{pmatrix} 1 \; 2 \; \ldots n \\ p_1 \, p_2 \cdots p_n \end{pmatrix}$ may be broken up into a product of cycles. Thus, for example, we may write the particular permutation

$$\begin{pmatrix} 1\,2\,3\,4\,5 \;\; 6\,7\,8\,9\,10 \\ 3\,7\,5\,4\,8\,10\,2\,1\,6 \;\; 9 \end{pmatrix} \equiv \begin{pmatrix} 1\,3\,5\,8 \\ 3\,5\,8\,1 \end{pmatrix} \begin{pmatrix} 2\,7 \\ 7\,2 \end{pmatrix} \begin{pmatrix} 6\,9\,10 \\ 10\,6 \;\; 9 \end{pmatrix}$$

$$\equiv (1\,3\,5\,8)\,(6\,10\,9)(2\,7)(4),$$

showing that it breaks into a product of four cycles of lengths 4, 3, 2 and 1. In the arbitrary permutation P, the number 1 is replaced by p_1, while the number p_1 itself occurs somewhere in the first row of P and is replaced by the number below it, say q_1. Continuing in the same way q_1 will be replaced by some number r_1. We therefore have a sequence $1, p_1, q_1, r_1, \ldots$, which will continue until the number 1 appears again, producing a cycle denoted by $(1\ p_1\ q_1\ r_1 \ldots)$. It is possible that this cycle contains all the numbers 1 to n but generally it does not. In the latter case, choose a number not in the cycle and it will generate, in the same way, a new cycle containing no common element with the first. Hence the permutation P is expressible, uniquely, as a product of cycles. Since there are no numbers common to any two cycles, the permutations represented by each cycle clearly commute. Notice that if a number is unmoved by the permutation P, then it will contribute a cycle of length $l = 1$ containing just that single number. The sum of the lengths l_i of the cycles in a permutation P must be equal to n. Thus the breakdown into cycles associates a partition $n = \sum_i l_i$ of n into integers l_i. To be definite, we always order the cycles by decreasing length so that $l_i \geqq l_{i+1}$ and we use the notation $[l_1\ l_2 \ldots l_n]$. In the example given above for $n = 10$, the associated partition is $[4321]$.

A cycle of length $l = 2$ is called a 'transposition' since it simply transposes two numbers. It is denoted by P_{ij}. In particular, $P_{i\,i+1}$ is called an 'adjacent transposition'.

Any cycle, and therefore any permutation, may be written as a product of transpositions since, as is quickly verified,

$$(123\ldots k) \equiv \begin{pmatrix} 123\ldots k-1\,k \\ 234\ldots k \quad\;\; 1 \end{pmatrix} = P_{12}P_{23}P_{34}\ldots P_{k-1\,k} \tag{17.1}$$

and any transposition may be written as a product of adjacent transpositions using, successively, relations like $P_{1k} = P_{12}P_{2k}P_{12}$.

17.2 The parity of a permutation

It is possible to assign a 'parity' of $+1$ or -1 to a permutation according to the following definition: (1) a cycle of odd length has even parity $+1$; (2) a cycle of even length has odd parity -1; (3) the parity of a permutation is equal to the product of the parities of each of its cycles. This association of even parity with odd length is not deliberately perverse but is in fact natural, implying that a cycle of length one, which causes no permutation, has even parity.

There are two other precisely equivalent definitions of the parity of a permutation. In the first we write each cycle as a product of transpositions and note that a cycle of odd length involves an even number of transpositions and vice versa. Thus a permutation with even parity involves an even number of transpositions and vice versa. In the second equivalent definition we make use of the function

$$\Phi_A = \begin{vmatrix} \phi_1(x_1) & \phi_2(x_1) & \dots & \phi_n(x_1) \\ \phi_1(x_2) & & & \\ \vdots & & & \\ \phi_1(x_n) & \phi_2(x_n) & \dots & \phi_n(x_n) \end{vmatrix} \tag{17.2}$$

which is the determinant formed from n different functions ϕ_q of n different variables $x_1, x_2, \ldots, x_n$. Any permutation of variables will produce a determinant with the rows of Φ_A interchanged in some way. From the theory of determinants this simply introduces a factor ± 1 depending on whether the number of interchanges is even or odd. But this is precisely the parity, giving

$$\mathrm{P}\Phi_A = \pi(\mathrm{P})\Phi_A \tag{17.3}$$

where we have introduced the notation $\pi(\mathrm{P})$ for the parity of P. Of course $\pi(\mathrm{P})$ may only take values ± 1. Thus $\pi(\mathrm{P})$ is defined as the result of P operating on Φ_A.

17.3 Classes

For the rotation groups it was shown in section 2.7 that if two rotations R and R′ are in the same class then the group must contain a rotation which carries the axis of R into the axis of R′. The analogous result for permutations is that if two permutations P and P′ are in the same class of $\mathscr{S}_n$ then there must be a permutation Q which, when carried out on both rows of P, produces P′. To prove this statement we first define the permutations

$$\mathrm{P} = \begin{pmatrix} 1 & 2 & \dots & n \\ p_1 & p_2 & \dots & p_n \end{pmatrix} \tag{17.4}$$

and

$$\mathrm{Q} = \begin{pmatrix} 1 & 2 & \dots & n \\ q_1 & q_2 & \dots & q_n \end{pmatrix} \equiv \begin{pmatrix} p_1 & p_2 & \dots & p_n \\ r_1 & r_2 & \dots & r_n \end{pmatrix} \tag{17.5}$$

where the last equality defines the r_i given the p_i and q_i. Hence

$$\begin{aligned} \mathrm{QPQ}^{-1} &= \begin{pmatrix} p_1 & p_2 & \dots & p_n \\ r_1 & r_2 & \dots & r_n \end{pmatrix} \begin{pmatrix} 1 & 2 & \dots & n \\ p_1 & p_2 & \dots & p_n \end{pmatrix} \begin{pmatrix} q_1 & q_2 & \dots & q_n \\ 1 & 2 & \dots & n \end{pmatrix} \\ &= \begin{pmatrix} q_1 & q_2 & \dots & q_n \\ r_1 & r_2 & \dots & r_n \end{pmatrix} = \mathrm{P}' \end{aligned} \tag{17.6}$$

but the permutation P′ is nothing more than the permutation P of (17.4) with both rows permuted by Q of (17.5), i.e. the numbers $1\,2 \ldots n$ are replaced by $q_1\, q_2 \ldots q_n$ and the numbers $p_1\, p_2 \ldots p_n$ are replaced by $r_1\, r_2 \ldots r_n$.

In terms of cycles this result implies that all elements of $\mathscr{S}_n$ associated with the same partition $[l_1 l_2 \ldots]$ are in the same class and conversely that all elements in the same class have the same structure in terms of cycle length and are thus associated with the same partition. For example, in the group $\mathscr{S}_5$ the two permutations

$$P = \begin{pmatrix} 12345 \\ 31254 \end{pmatrix} \equiv (1\,3\,2)\,(4\,5) \tag{17.7}$$

and

$$P' = \begin{pmatrix} 12345 \\ 21453 \end{pmatrix} = (1\,2)\,(3\,4\,5) = (3\,4\,5)\,(1\,2) \tag{17.8}$$

are in the same class. To find a Q such that $P' = QPQ^{-1}$ one needs simply to permute the cycle labels of (17.7) into those of (17.8), giving

$$Q = \begin{pmatrix} 12345 \\ 35412 \end{pmatrix}$$

It is quickly verified that

$$\begin{aligned} QPQ^{-1} &= \begin{pmatrix} 12345 \\ 35412 \end{pmatrix} \begin{pmatrix} 12345 \\ 31254 \end{pmatrix} \begin{pmatrix} 35412 \\ 12345 \end{pmatrix} = \begin{pmatrix} 35412 \\ 43521 \end{pmatrix} \\ &\equiv \begin{pmatrix} 12345 \\ 21453 \end{pmatrix} = P' \end{aligned}$$

Of course, Q is not unique, but that is always so if it is defined only by the relation $P' = QPQ^{-1}$, because Q may be post-mutiplied by any permutation which commutes with P, without disturbing the relation.

As an illustration we see that the six elements of $\mathscr{S}_3$ fall into three classes

$$\begin{aligned} \mathscr{C}_1 &= \text{E (the identity)} \\ \mathscr{C}_2 &= (1\,2\,3), (1\,3\,2) \\ \mathscr{C}_3 &= (1\,2), (1\,3), (2\,3) \end{aligned}$$

associated with the three partitions [1 1 1], [3] and [2 1], respectively. It is usual to omit the cycles of length one, as in class $\mathscr{C}_3$ above. No ambiguity arises here, the convention being simply that the numbers not written down are unmoved. In this example the ordering of classes $\mathscr{C}_1$, $\mathscr{C}_2$ and $\mathscr{C}_3$ was made to agree with that of examples 2.7.2 and 2.7.3. More systematically, one would order the classes by the length of their longest cycle, starting with the shortest. Classes whose longest cycles have the same length would be ordered by their next longest cycles and so on.

17.4 The identity and alternating representations—symmetric and antisymmetric functions

The remainder of this chapter is devoted mainly to a description of the irreducible representations of $\mathscr{S}_n$, culminating in the construction of the actual matrices T(P) in section 17.13. In this section we restrict our attention to two simple one-dimensional representations which occur for any n. Firstly there is, as for any group, the one-dimensional identity representation which associates $+1$ with every group element. A function Φ_S which transforms according to this representation is therefore unchanged by any permutation and is usually called a totally symmetric function. Thus for all P,

$$\mathrm{P}\Phi_S = \Phi_S \tag{17.9}$$

For any n there is also another one-dimensional representation called the 'alternating representation' which associates the parity $\pi(\mathrm{P}) = \pm 1$ with each element P. That this is in fact a representation follows from the result that the parity of the product of permutations is the product of the parities. To prove this result we consider the effect of a product R = QP on the function Φ_A of equation (17.2)

$$\mathrm{R}\Phi_A = \mathrm{QP}\Phi_A = \mathrm{Q}\pi(\mathrm{P})\Phi_A = \pi(\mathrm{Q})\,\pi(\mathrm{P})\Phi_A$$

which gives the desired result, $\pi(\mathrm{R}) = \pi(\mathrm{Q})\,\pi(\mathrm{P})$. In fact the function Φ_A is a convenient basis function for the alternating representation

$$\mathrm{P}\Phi_A = \pi(\mathrm{P})\Phi_A \tag{17.10}$$

A function like Φ_A which transforms according to the alternating representation is called totally antisymmetric. In particular it has the property

$$\mathrm{P}_{ij}\Phi_A = -\Phi_A \tag{17.11}$$

for all transpositions P_{ij}.

In section 4.19 we constructed a projection operator, which had the property of producing a function of particular symmetry type when operating on an arbitrary function. For the two one-dimensional representations described above, the projection operators are

$$\mathrm{S} = \frac{1}{n!}\sum_{\mathrm{P}} \mathrm{P}$$

and

$$\mathrm{A} = \frac{1}{n!}\sum_{\mathrm{P}} \pi(\mathrm{P})\mathrm{P} \tag{17.12}$$

although for most purposes the numerical factor $1/n!$ is irrelevant. These two operators are called the symmetriser and the antisymmetriser, respectively. According to the general theory of section 4.19 the functions $f_S = \mathrm{S}f$ and $f_A = \mathrm{A}f$ will be totally symmetric and totally antisymmetric respectively, no matter what the function f. It is always possible however, for certain f, that the functions f_S and f_A may vanish identically.

Consider for example $n = 2$ with $f = x_1$. Then

$$\mathrm{S}f = \tfrac{1}{2}(\mathrm{E} + \mathrm{P}_{12})x_1 = \tfrac{1}{2}(x_1 + x_2) = f_S$$

$$\mathrm{A}f = \tfrac{1}{2}(\mathrm{E} - \mathrm{P}_{12})x_1 = \tfrac{1}{2}(x_1 - x_2) = f_A$$

Notice here that $\mathrm{E} = \mathrm{S} + \mathrm{A}$ so that $f = f_S + f_A$ showing that any function of two variables may be expressed as a sum of symmetric and antisymmetric parts.

As a second example take $n = 3$ and again project from $f = x_1$. Then

$$\mathrm{S}f = \tfrac{1}{6}\left[\mathrm{E} + \mathrm{P}_{12} + \mathrm{P}_{13} + \mathrm{P}_{23} + \begin{pmatrix}123\\231\end{pmatrix} + \begin{pmatrix}123\\312\end{pmatrix}\right]x_1$$

$$= \tfrac{1}{6}(x_1 + x_2 + x_3 + x_1 + x_2 + x_3)$$

$$= \tfrac{1}{3}(x_1 + x_2 + x_3) = f_S$$

$$\mathrm{A}f = \tfrac{1}{6}\left[\mathrm{E} - \mathrm{P}_{12} - \mathrm{P}_{13} - \mathrm{P}_{23} + \begin{pmatrix}123\\231\end{pmatrix} + \begin{pmatrix}123\\312\end{pmatrix}\right]x_1$$

$$= \tfrac{1}{6}(x_1 - x_2 - x_3 - x_1 + x_2 + x_3) = 0$$

This means that the function $f = x_1$ is too simple to produce a totally antisymmetric function; it does not contain a totally antisymmetric part to be projected out. One also sees that for $n > 2$ we cannot write $\mathrm{E} = \mathrm{S} + \mathrm{A}$, implying that for $n > 2$ it is necessary to introduce other symmetry operators in addition to S and A in order to allow expansion of an arbitrary function. In other words for $n > 2$ the identity and alternating representations do not exhaust the possible irreducible representations.

17.5 The character table for irreducible representations

For any n, the classes are labelled by the partitions of n, as shown in section 17.3. Hence the general result of section 4.13, that the number of irreducible representations is equal to the number of classes, tells us that the number of irreducible representations of the group $\mathscr{S}_n$ is given by the number of partitions $[n_1 n_2 \ldots]$ of n. Thus for $n = 2$ there are two irreducible representations corresponding to the partitions [2] and [11] while for $n = 3$ there are three corresponding to [3], [21] and [111] and for $n = 4$ there are five.

The character table for $\mathscr{S}_3$ has already been deduced in section 4.10. Actually we deduced the character table for the group D_3 but we noted in section 2.3 an isomorphism between D_3 and $\mathscr{S}_3$. The methods described in section 4.15 may also be used to deduce character tables for other small n, see problem 17.2. There is, however, a general procedure which we now describe which leads to the character tables and also gives some insight into the properties of the basis vectors of the irreducible representations. We shall see that not only is the number of irreducible representations equal to the number of partitions, but also that each irreducible representation may be labelled by a partition in a natural way.

Consider a number n of particles which may be put into a number n of single-particle states ϕ_i so that $\phi_i(k)$ signifies that particle k is in state i. To each partition $[n_1 n_2 \ldots]$ of n we associate the product function

$$\Phi([n_1 n_2 \ldots]) = \phi_1(1)\phi_1(2)\ldots\phi_1(n_1)\phi_2(n_1+1)\phi_2(n_1+2)\ldots$$
$$\ldots\phi_2(n_1+n_2)\phi_3(n_1+n_2+1)\ldots \tag{17.13}$$

in which the first n_1 particles are in the state ϕ_1, the next n_2 particles are in state ϕ_2 and so on. For each partition we now generate the set of $n!/(n_1!\,n_2!\ldots)$ independent product functions $\mathrm{P}\Phi([n_1 n_2 \ldots])$, where P is any permutation of the particles. (Although there are $n!$ permutations P, this number must be divided by $n_1!\,n_2!\ldots$ to allow for those permutations which leave (17.13) unchanged.) This set of states defines, for each partition, a vector space $L([n_1 n_2 \ldots])$ which is invariant under permutations and therefore provides a representation of the group $\mathscr{S}_n$. In general these representations are not irreducible but their characters are relatively easy to calculate. The characters of the irreducible representations may then be deduced by a process of subtraction, starting from the simple partition $[n]$. In this case the function (17.13) is invariant under all permutations so that the corresponding representation is the identity representation.

To calculate the character for a permutation Q in the representation generated by the vector space $L([n_1 n_2 \ldots])$ we must sum the diagonal matrix elements of Q in this space. However, the result of operating with Q on a general basis vector $\mathrm{P}\Phi([n_1 n_2 \ldots])$ is simply another basis vector because QP is just another permutation. Thus every column of the matrix of Q will contain one entry of $+1$ and zero in every other position. The only contribution to the character will occur when this entry $+1$ occurs on the diagonal of the matrix. In other words there is a contribution of $+1$ for every basis vector which is unchanged by Q and hence the character for the permutation Q is given by the number of basis vectors of the kind $\mathrm{P}\Phi([n_1 n_2 \ldots])$ which are unchanged by Q. It is of course only necessary to choose one permutation Q from each class. For the identity element E the character is simply the dimension $n!/n_1!\,n_2!\ldots$ of the space $L([n_1 n_2 \ldots])$. If Q is a single transposition P_{12} the character is given by the number of basis vectors for which the particles 1 and 2 are in the same state, i.e. either they are both in state ϕ_1 or both in state ϕ_2, etc. This number is deduced by counting the number of ways of arranging the remaining $(n-2)$ particles, namely

$$\frac{(n-2)!}{(n_1-2)!\,n_2!\,n_3!\ldots}+\frac{(n-2)!}{n_1!\,(n_2-2)!\,n_3!\ldots}+\ldots \tag{17.14}$$

If Q is a single cycle of length l then a similar argument leads to the expression

$$\frac{(n-l)!}{(n_1-l)!\,n_2!\,n_3!\ldots}+\frac{(n-l)!}{n_1!\,(n_2-l)!\,n_3!\ldots}+\ldots \tag{17.15}$$

for the character of Q. When Q is a product of cycles one must allow for all possible distributions of the cycles between the states allowing any number of complete cycles to lie in any state. It is possible to deduce a cumbersome general formula but we shall not give it here. However, we can see from the above argument that the character will vanish unless the numbers n_i in the partition are large enough to contain the cycles l_i of Q in some order. This explains the triangular blocks of zeros in the tables below.

Application of these results for the characters of Q in the spaces $L([n_1 n_2\ldots])$ for $n \leqq 4$ leads to table 17.1. We use the notation $\psi^{[n_1 n_2\ldots]}$ for the character, while the classes of the group $\mathcal{S}_n$ are denoted by $(l_1 l_2 \ldots)$, where l_i are the lengths of the cycles of any permutation in that class. Having

Table 17.1

$\mathcal{S}_2$	(11)	(2)
$\psi^{[2]}$	1	1
$\psi^{[11]}$	2	0
$\chi^{[2]}$	1	1
$\chi^{[11]}$	1	-1

$\mathcal{S}_3$	(111)	(21)	(3)
$\psi^{[3]}$	1	1	1
$\psi^{[21]}$	3	1	0
$\psi^{[111]}$	6	0	0
$\chi^{[3]}$	1	1	1
$\chi^{[21]}$	2	0	-1
$\chi^{[111]}$	1	-1	1

$\mathcal{S}_4$	(1111)	(211)	(22)	(31)	(4)
$\psi^{[4]}$	1	1	1	1	1
$\psi^{[31]}$	4	2	0	1	0
$\psi^{[22]}$	6	2	2	0	0
$\psi^{[211]}$	12	2	0	0	0
$\psi^{[1111]}$	24	0	0	0	0
$\chi^{[4]}$	1	1	1	1	1
$\chi^{[31]}$	3	1	-1	0	-1
$\chi^{[22]}$	2	0	2	-1	0
$\chi^{[211]}$	3	-1	-1	0	1
$\chi^{[1111]}$	1	-1	1	1	-1

calculated the characters $\psi^{[n_1 n_2\ldots]}$ in this way, the characters χ of the irreducible representations may be deduced as follows. In the first place $\psi^{[n]}$ is clearly irreducible, being one-dimensional, so we call it $\chi^{[n]}$. Now proceed to the second row, considering $\psi^{[n-1,1]}$. Using the techniques described in section 4.11 we can show that $\chi^{[n]}$ appears once in the reduction of $\psi^{[n-1,1]}$ and the remaining character is irreducible by the criterion (4.29). This remainder is denoted by $\chi^{[n-1,1]}$. In this way we may proceed down the table and at each stage it is found that $\psi^{[n_1 n_2\ldots]}$ reduces into a sum of irreducible characters deduced earlier and that the remainder is also irreducible. The number of times that each of the earlier characters appears and the verification that the remainder is irreducible may be obtained with the techniques of section 4.11, see also problem 17.3. The remainder is denoted by $\chi^{[n_1 n_2 \ldots]}$ so that we obtain an irreducible character corresponding to each partition. The results of this analysis are shown in table 17.1 for $n \leqq 4$. It is interesting to note that $\psi^{[111\ldots]}$ is the character of the regular representation, see section 4.13, which contains every irreducible representation a number of times equal to its dimension. In terms of the basis functions (17.13), the progression down the table corresponds to the introduction of a greater variety of functions ϕ_q and hence there is greater scope for antisymmetry. Finally in the last row there are as many functions ϕ_q as particles and every symmetry type may be constructed, including the totally antisymmetric (alternating) representation $\chi^{[111\ldots]}$ already described in section 17.4.

17.6 Young diagrams

Although we did not give a general proof, it was shown in the preceding section that the irreducible representations of $\mathscr{S}_n$ were labelled by a partition $[n_1 n_2 \ldots]$ of the number n. For many purposes it is convenient to use a more visual notation for a partition as follows. To each partition we construct a diagram of n small squares of which n_1 are in the first row, n_2 are in the second row, and so on, with the left-hand ends of all rows being in the same vertical line. Such a diagram is named after the mathematician A. Young. As an illustration, the five partitions of $n = 4$ are given by the Young diagrams below:

[4] [31] [22] [211] [1111]

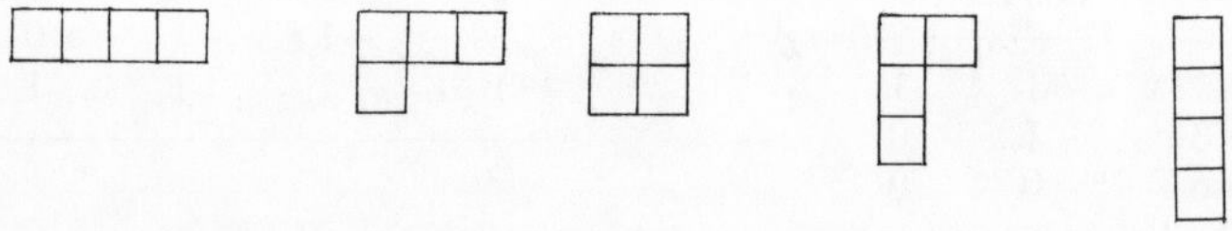

From the results of the previous section we may now label each irreducible representation of $\mathscr{S}_n$ by a Young diagram containing n squares. Although at first sight this notation may seem clumsy it will be seen in section 17.8 to lead to a way of describing not only the irreducible representations of $\mathscr{S}_n$ but also the properties of the basis vectors of the representations.

17.7 The restriction from $\mathscr{S}_n$ to $\mathscr{S}_{n-1}$

Consider the symmetric group $\mathscr{S}_{n-1}$ which permutes the objects 1, 2, . . ., $n-1$, leaving object n unmoved. It is clearly a subgroup of $\mathscr{S}_n$. Hence an irreducible representation of $\mathscr{S}_n$ will also be a representation of $\mathscr{S}_{n-1}$ though generally not irreducible with respect to $\mathscr{S}_{n-1}$. We may therefore ask which irreducible representations of $\mathscr{S}_{n-1}$ will occur in the reduction of an irreducible representation of $\mathscr{S}_n$ and the answer comes immediately from the character table.

Let $T^{(\alpha_n)}$ denote the irreducible representation of $\mathscr{S}_n$ corresponding to a partition α_n of n. The reduction with respect to $\mathscr{S}_{n-1}$ is then written

$$T^{(\alpha_n)} = \dot{\sum_{\alpha_{n-1}}} m(\alpha_{n-1})\, T^{(\alpha_{n-1})} \tag{17.16}$$

where $T^{(\alpha_{n-1})}$ is an irreducible representation of $\mathscr{S}_{n-1}$ and the sum runs over all partitions α_{n-1} of $n-1$.

The character of $T^{(\alpha_n)}$ for those elements which lie in $\mathscr{S}_{n-1}$ is obtained from the character table of $\mathscr{S}_n$ by selecting only those classes with at least one cycle of length unity. Then with the help of the full character table for $\mathscr{S}_{n-1}$ the formula (4.28) enables us to deduce the coefficients $m(\alpha_{n-1})$.

For an example, consider $n = 4$. The only classes of $\mathscr{S}_4$ which contain elements of $\mathscr{S}_3$ will be (1111), (211) and (31) and they contain, respectively, the elements of the classes (111), (21) and (3) of $\mathscr{S}_3$. We give, in table 17.2 the characters for $T^{(\alpha_4)}$ and $T^{(\alpha_3)}$ taken from table 17.1. The results of the reduction are also given on the right, where it is seen that the $m(\alpha_3)$ are either zero or one.

Table 17.2

	(111)	(21)	(3)	
$\chi^{[3]}$	1	1	1	
$\chi^{[21]}$	2	0	-1	
$\chi^{[111]}$	1	-1	1	
$\chi^{[4]}$	1	1	1	$\chi^{[3]}$
$\chi^{[31]}$	3	1	0	$\chi^{[3]} + \chi^{[21]}$
$\chi^{[22]}$	2	0	-1	$\chi^{[21]}$
$\chi^{[211]}$	3	-1	0	$\chi^{[21]} + \chi^{[111]}$
$\chi^{[1111]}$	1	-1	1	$\chi^{[111]}$

It may be shown generally that the coefficients $m(\alpha_{n-1})$ in equation (17.16) are always either zero or one and a very simple rule may be given to deduce which $m(\alpha_{n-1})$ are equal to one. In the language of Young diagrams it says simply that the Young diagrams α_{n-1} for which $m(\alpha_{n-1}) = 1$ are obtained from the Young diagram α_n by the removal of one square. For example the removal of one square from the Young diagram 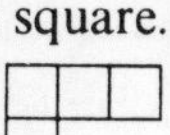 can lead to the diagrams and 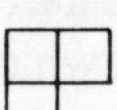 but not to 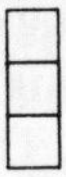.

17.8 The basis vectors of the irreducible representations

The problem of labelling the basis vectors of the irreducible representation $T^{(\alpha_n)}$ of $\mathscr{S}_n$ may be solved by studying their behaviour under the chain of subgroups $\mathscr{S}_n \to \mathscr{S}_{n-1} \to \mathscr{S}_{n-2} \ldots \to \mathscr{S}_2$. At each stage we use the reduction (17.16) described in the preceding section. The chain of subgroups is obtained by first removing object n, then object $(n-1)$, and so on, until finally only objects 2 and 1 remain in $\mathscr{S}_2$. Each basis vector of $T^{(\alpha_n)}$ is assigned a sequence of labels $\alpha_n, \alpha_{n-1}, \ldots, \alpha_2$ describing its behaviour under this succession of subgroups. The argument is conveniently divided into four steps.

(1) It is trivial that all basis vectors of the irreducible representation $T^{(\alpha_n)}$ of $\mathscr{S}_n$ may be assigned, as a first label, the same symbol α_n.

(2) In the reduction of $T^{(\alpha_n)}$, on restricting to the subgroup $\mathscr{S}_{n-1}$, the basis vectors may be chosen to belong to one or another of the irreducible representations $T^{(\alpha_{n-1})}$ of $\mathscr{S}_{n-1}$ which occur in (17.16). As a second label the basis functions may therefore carry the appropriate symbol α_{n-1}. Since no representation $T^{(\alpha_{n-1})}$ occurs more than once, the number of basis vectors carrying the symbol α_{n-1} will be equal to the dimension of the representation $T^{(\alpha_{n-1})}$.

(3) Proceeding from $\mathscr{S}_{n-1}$ to $\mathscr{S}_{n-2}$, each irreducible representation $T^{(\alpha_{n-1})}$ will reduce to a sum of irreducible representations $T^{(\alpha_{n-2})}$ of $\mathscr{S}_{n-2}$. The set of basis vectors with the same pair of labels $\alpha_n \alpha_{n-1}$ may now be chosen to belong to one or another of the $T^{(\alpha_{n-2})}$. Thus the basis vectors acquire a further label α_{n-2} to include with α_n and α_{n-1}. Again the number of basis vectors carrying the sequence of labels $\alpha_n \alpha_{n-1} \alpha_{n-2}$ will be equal to the dimension of the irreducible representation $T^{(\alpha_{n-2})}$.

(4) Clearly this process may be continued until eventually the basis vectors carry the sequence of labels $\alpha_n \alpha_{n-1} \alpha_{n-2} \ldots \alpha_2$. Again, the number of basis vectors with a given sequence will be equal to the dimension of the last irreducible representation in the chain. But this is now $T^{(\alpha_2)}$ and the group $\mathscr{S}_2$ has only one-dimensional irreducible representations. Hence the labelling by the sequence $\alpha_n \alpha_{n-1} \alpha_{n-2} \ldots \alpha_2$ is *complete* in the sense that no two basis vectors of $T^{(\alpha_n)}$ will have the same sequence and that, to every sequence, there corresponds a basis vector of $T^{(\alpha_n)}$. It must of course be remembered that in any such sequence the Young diagram α_{n-1} must be obtainable from α_n by the removal of one square, that α_{n-2} must be obtainable from α_{n-1} by the removal of one square, and so on.

The sequence $\alpha_n \alpha_{n-1} \alpha_{n-2} \ldots \alpha_2$ may seem to be a very complicated label since each α_r represents a Young diagram of r squares. It is possible however to denote the set by a single Young diagram α_n in which the numbers 1 to n have been entered into the squares. The resulting picture is called a Young tableau.

The procedure for entering the numbers is to put the number n into that square which, when removed from α_n, gives the Young diagram α_{n-1}. The number $n-1$ is put into that square of α_{n-1} which, when removed, produces the Young diagram α_{n-2}, and so on. By the manner of construction it is clear that the numbers in the squares of a Young tableau must decrease to the left and upwards.

Because of the completeness of this labelling system it follows immediately that the dimension of the irreducible representation $T^{(\alpha_n)}$ is equal to the number of different tableaux obtainable from the Young diagram α_n. This provides a simple way of deducing, see Littlewood (1950) in the bibliography, the dimension of any irreducible representation of $\mathscr{S}_n$, although the dimension also appears in the character table as the character of the identity element.

Table 17.3 gives the Young tableaux for each irreducible representation of $\mathscr{S}_2, \mathscr{S}_3, \mathscr{S}_4$. For example, the representation [31] of $\mathscr{S}_4$ gives rise to three

Table *17.3* Young tableaux for $n = 2, 3$ and 4

Partition	Young tableau	Partition	Young tableau
$\mathscr{S}_2$ [2]	$\boxed{1\;2}$	$\mathscr{S}_4$ [4]	$\boxed{1\;2\;3\;4}$
[11]	$\begin{array}{c}\boxed{1}\\\boxed{2}\end{array}$	[31]	$\begin{array}{c}\boxed{1\;2\;3}\\\boxed{4}\end{array}$ $\begin{array}{c}\boxed{1\;2\;4}\\\boxed{3}\end{array}$ $\begin{array}{c}\boxed{1\;3\;4}\\\boxed{2}\end{array}$
$\mathscr{S}_3$ [3]	$\boxed{1\;2\;3}$	[22]	$\begin{array}{c}\boxed{1\;2}\\\boxed{3\;4}\end{array}$ $\begin{array}{c}\boxed{1\;3}\\\boxed{2\;4}\end{array}$
[21]	$\begin{array}{c}\boxed{1\;2}\\\boxed{3}\end{array}$ $\begin{array}{c}\boxed{1\;3}\\\boxed{2}\end{array}$	[211]	$\begin{array}{c}\boxed{1\;2}\\\boxed{3}\\\boxed{4}\end{array}$ $\begin{array}{c}\boxed{1\;3}\\\boxed{2}\\\boxed{4}\end{array}$ $\begin{array}{c}\boxed{1\;4}\\\boxed{2}\\\boxed{3}\end{array}$
[111]	$\begin{array}{c}\boxed{1}\\\boxed{2}\\\boxed{3}\end{array}$	[1111]	$\begin{array}{c}\boxed{1}\\\boxed{2}\\\boxed{3}\\\boxed{4}\end{array}$

tableaux corresponding to three basis vectors. This agrees with the dimension given in the character table 17.1. The equivalence between the clumsy notation $\alpha_4\,\alpha_3\,\alpha_2$ used earlier and the Young tableau is illustrated by the example

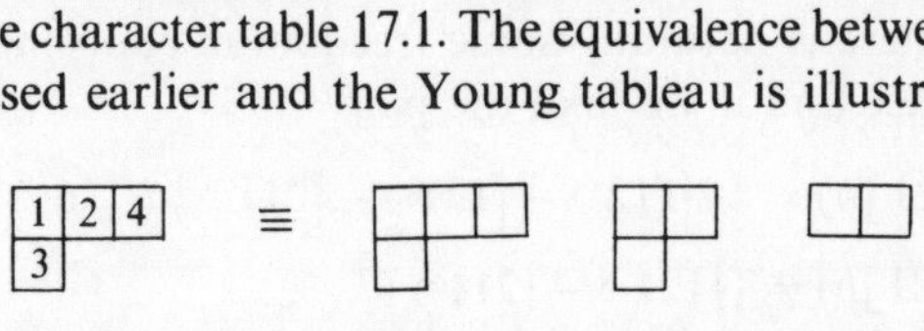

$$\begin{array}{c}\boxed{1\;2\;4}\\\boxed{3}\end{array} \equiv \quad \equiv [31]\;[21]\;[2]$$

An even more convenient notation, for printing, was introduced by Yamanouchi. He defined a Yamanouchi symbol $(r_n r_{n-1} \ldots r_1)$ in place of the Young tableau with r_k denoting the row in which the number k appears. The

Yamanouchi symbol in the example given above would be (1 2 1 1). That this notation is sufficient to specify the tableau is soon clear if one starts at r_1 and moves left, remembering that the numbers in the tableau must increase to the right and downwards. Incidentally, it must always happen that $r_1 = 1$, $r_2 = 1$ or 2, etc. One advantage of the Yamanouchi notation is that by removing r_n one obtains the Yamanouchi symbol specifying the behaviour of the basis vector of $T^{(\alpha_n)}$ under the group $\mathscr{S}_{n-1}$ and the successive removal of r_{n-1}, $r_{n-2}, \ldots, r_3$ specifies the behaviour of the basis vector under the chain of subgroups $\mathscr{S}_{n-2}, \mathscr{S}_{n-3}, \ldots, \mathscr{S}_2$.

17.9 Examples of basis vectors and representation matrices

The labelling system introduced in the previous section for the basis vectors of an irreducible representation is beautifully systematic but rather formal. We now construct some concrete examples of basis vectors for small n, starting from the function (17.13). This will also lead to the actual matrices of the irreducible representations. An elegant general prescription for writing down these matrices is given later, in section 17.13.

For any n, the one-dimensional representations $[n]$ and $[111\ldots]$ clearly correspond to the totally symmetric and totally antisymmetric representations described in section 17.4. Starting from small n the first representation which is not of this kind corresponds to the partition $[21]$ of $n = 3$ and the appropriate function (17.13) is

$$\Phi([21]) = \phi_1(1)\ \phi_1(2)\ \phi_2(3) \tag{17.17}$$

and we abbreviate the notation by writing $\Phi([21]) = |112\rangle$ where, in general, $|ijk\rangle$ is an abbreviation for $\phi_i(1)\ \phi_j(2)\ \phi_k(3)$. In the notation of section 17.5 the space $L([21])$ generated by permutations on $\Phi([21])$ will be three-dimensional with basis vectors $|112\rangle$, $|121\rangle$ and $|211\rangle$. The character table 17.1 in section 17.5 shows that it reduces into a sum of the two irreducible representations $T^{[3]}$ and $T^{[21]}$. The totally symmetric vector is clearly

$$\theta([3]) = \{|112\rangle + |121\rangle + |211\rangle\}/\sqrt{3} \tag{17.18}$$

with the $\sqrt{3}$ included for normalisation and the orthogonal complement, the two-dimensional space of vectors orthogonal to (17.18), must provide the representation $T^{[21]}$. There is naturally some freedom in choosing a pair of basis vectors in this space and if we take the pair

$$\theta([21]a) = \{2|112\rangle - |121\rangle - |211\rangle\}/\sqrt{6} \tag{17.19}$$
$$\theta([21]b) = \{|121\rangle - |211\rangle\}/\sqrt{2}$$

it is seen that they are not only orthogonal to (17.18) and to each other but also belong to irreducible representations of the subgroup $\mathscr{S}_2$ on particles 1 and 2. The first, $\theta([21]a)$, is symmetric under P_{12} while $\theta([21]b)$ is antisymmetric.

Thus, in terms of tableaux they correspond to $\begin{array}{|c|c|}\hline 1 & 2 \\ \hline 3 \\ \cline{1-1}\end{array}$ and $\begin{array}{|c|c|}\hline 1 & 3 \\ \hline 2 \\ \cline{1-1}\end{array}$, respectively.

The matrix of P_{12} in this basis of $T^{[21]}$ is immediately given by

$$\begin{pmatrix} 1 & 0 \\ 0 & -1 \end{pmatrix}$$

and from (17.19) the matrix of P_{23} is soon found by carrying out the permutation, for example

$$P_{23}\ \theta([21]a) = \{2|121\rangle - |112\rangle - |211\rangle\}/\sqrt{6}$$

$$= -\tfrac{1}{2}\theta([21]a) + \sqrt{\tfrac{3}{4}}\,\theta([21]b)$$

leading to the matrix

$$P_{23} = \begin{pmatrix} -\frac{1}{2} & \sqrt{\frac{3}{4}} \\ \sqrt{\frac{3}{4}} & \frac{1}{2} \end{pmatrix}$$

It was shown in section 17.1 that any permutation could be expressed as a product of adjacent transpositions so that, having found matrices for P_{12} and P_{23}, all other matrices in the representation $T^{[21]}$ will follow from the known rules for multiplying group elements. Thus, for example, $P_{13} = P_{12}P_{23}P_{12}$ so that the matrix of P_{13} is given by the product of matrices

$$P_{13} = \begin{pmatrix} 1 & 0 \\ 0 & -1 \end{pmatrix}\begin{pmatrix} -\frac{1}{2} & \sqrt{\frac{3}{4}} \\ \sqrt{\frac{3}{4}} & \frac{1}{2} \end{pmatrix}\begin{pmatrix} 1 & 0 \\ 0 & -1 \end{pmatrix} = \begin{pmatrix} -\frac{1}{2} & -\sqrt{\frac{3}{4}} \\ -\sqrt{\frac{3}{4}} & \frac{1}{2} \end{pmatrix}$$

A similar exercise for $n = 4$ is suggested in problem 17.5. In section 17.13 we give a simple prescription for writing down the matrices of adjacent transpositions in any irreducible representation but the derivation of the prescription is not simple.

We note that, as a result of the isomorphism between $\mathscr{S}_3$ and the point group D_3, see section 2.3, the matrices given above are the same as those given in table 4.1 with a re-ordering of basis vectors.

17.10 The direct product of two representations

Given any two representations $T^{(\alpha_1)}$ and $T^{(\alpha_2)}$ we can form the (direct) product representation $T^{(\alpha_1)} \times T^{(\alpha_2)}$ whose dimension is the product of the dimensions of $T^{(\alpha_1)}$ and $T^{(\alpha_2)}$. This concept was described generally in section 4.17 and may of course be used in the group $\mathscr{S}_n$. The reduction of the product representation into a sum of irreducible representations was studied by using the character table, see the formula (4.45). Thus, for example, table 17.1 of section 17.5 tells us that $T^{[21]} \times T^{[21]} = T^{[3]} \dotplus T^{[21]} \dotplus T^{[111]}$.

There are two important particular examples of such products which are worth describing here. Consider first the product $T^{(\alpha)} \times T^{[111\ldots]}$ of any irreducible representation with the totally antisymmetric representation. Since

$T^{[111\ldots]}$ is one-dimensional the product has the same dimension as $T^{(\alpha)}$. Furthermore if $\chi_p^{(\alpha)}$ denotes the character of $T^{(\alpha)}$ for a permutation in a class $\mathscr{C}_p$ then the character of the product representation is simply $\pi_p\chi_p^{(\alpha)}$, where π_p denotes the parity of elements in the class $\mathscr{C}_p$. Here we have used the result (17.10) that π_p is the character of $T^{[111\ldots]}$. Now if $T^{(\alpha)}$ is irreducible it follows immediately from the criterion (4.29) that the product representation is also irreducible using $\pi_p^2 = 1$. Hence we may write

$$T^{(\alpha)}\times T^{[111\ldots]} = T^{(\tilde{\alpha})} \quad \text{with} \quad \chi_p^{(\tilde{\alpha})} = \pi_p\chi_p^{(\alpha)} \tag{17.20}$$

where $\tilde{\alpha}$ labels another irreducible representation of $\mathscr{S}_n$. For example if $\alpha \equiv [n]$ then $\tilde{\alpha} = [111\ldots]$ so that, in the language of Young diagrams, the two representations $T^{(\alpha)}$ and $T^{(\tilde{\alpha})}$ are related by an interchange of the role of rows and columns. Inspection of table 17.1 shows the same result for the example, $\alpha \equiv [31]$ with $\tilde{\alpha} \equiv [211]$. In fact it may be shown generally that the Young diagram for α and $\tilde{\alpha}$ are obtained from each other by interchanging the roles of rows and columns or, in other words, by a reflection in the downward diagonal at 45° from the top left-hand corner of the diagram. We say that the representation $T^{(\tilde{\alpha})}$ is the 'adjoint' of $T^{(\alpha)}$ and, naturally, some representations like $T^{[21]}$ and $T^{[22]}$ are 'self-adjoint'. In a self-adjoint representation the character must vanish for a class with odd parity, as is verified from table 17.1.

Consider next the reduction

$$T^{(\alpha)}\times T^{(\beta)} = \dot{\sum_{\gamma}} m_\gamma T^{(\gamma)} \tag{17.21}$$

of the product of two irreducible representations and let us determine two rather special coefficients m_γ, namely $m_{[n]}$ and $m_{[111\ldots]}$. From the general formula (4.45) we have

$$m_{[n]} = (n!)^{-1}\sum_p c_p\chi_p^{(\alpha)}\chi_p^{(\beta)} \tag{17.22}$$

$$m_{[111\ldots]} = (n!)^{-1}\sum_p c_p\pi_p\chi_p^{(\alpha)}\chi_p^{(\beta)} = (n!)^{-1}\sum_p c_p\chi_p^{(\tilde{\alpha})}\chi_p^{(\beta)}$$

having inserted the known characters 1 and π_p for $T^{[n]}$ and $T^{[111\ldots]}$ and used equation (17.20). Finally, using the orthogonality formula (4.25b) for characters and the known property that the characters of $\mathscr{S}_n$ are real, we have from equations (17.22)

$$m_{[n]} = \delta_{\alpha,\beta}, \qquad m_{[111\ldots]} = \delta_{\tilde{\alpha},\beta} \tag{17.23}$$

The meaning of these results is that the totally symmetric representation can be produced only if the two irreducible factors are the same, or at least equivalent in the sense defined in section 4.6. In the same way, total antisymmetry may be obtained only in the product of a representation with its adjoint. We have made use of the latter result in constructing antisymmetric wave functions in atomic and nuclear problems, see subsection 8.6.4 and chapter 12. For example, in the atomic structure problems of chapter 8, an orbital state with symmetry α must be combined with a spin state of symmetry $\tilde{\alpha}$. Furthermore, since an electron with spin $s = \frac{1}{2}$ has only two spin states, the Young diagrams $\tilde{\alpha}$ may have, at most, two rows. Thus the Young diagrams α for the orbital part must have, at most, two columns. The precise relation between the total spin S and the Young diagram $\tilde{\alpha}$ is discussed in section 18.10. The result is that $S = \frac{1}{2}(\tilde{n}_1 - \tilde{n}_2)$, where $\tilde{n}_1$ and $\tilde{n}_2$ are the lengths of the two rows of $\tilde{\alpha}$.

To actually produce such totally symmetric or antisymmetric functions from the products it is of course necessary to sum over products of different basis vectors of the two factors with appropriate Clebsch–Gordan coefficients following the general arguments of section 4.17. These coefficients are easily deduced, see problem 17.6.

17.11 The outer product of two irreducible representations

In this section and the next we study a new kind of product of two representations called the outer product. Starting from a representation $T^{(\alpha)}$ of $\mathscr{S}_n$ and a representation $T^{(\alpha')}$ of $\mathscr{S}_{n'}$ we generate a representation T of $\mathscr{S}_{n+n'}$. From the physical point of view this process is useful in building up wave functions for $(n+n')$ particles, given those of the smaller systems of n and n' particles, but we shall not give examples. From the mathematical point of view there is an interesting connection between this outer product for the symmetric groups and the usual inner product for the unitary groups. This connection is described in chapter 18.

Consider products of the type

$$f_i(1, 2, \ldots, n)\; g_j(n+1, n+2, \ldots, n+n') \tag{17.24}$$

where the f_i transform according to some irreducible representation $T^{(\alpha)}$ of the group $\mathscr{S}_n$ on particles 1 to n and the g_j transform according to some representation $T^{(\alpha')}$ of $\mathscr{S}_{n'}$ on particles $n+1$ to $n+n'$. The set of products (17.24), where i runs through the s_α basis vectors of the representation $T^{(\alpha)}$ and j runs through the $s_{\alpha'}$ basis vectors of $T^{(\alpha')}$, will not form an invariant space under $\mathscr{S}_{n+n'}$ but if one enlarges the space to allow all permutations between the particles in f and those in g then this larger space will be invariant. Allowing for the number $(n+n')!/n!n'!$ of ways of selecting n particles from $(n+n')$, the dimension of the larger space is given by

$$s_\alpha s_{\alpha'}(n+n')!/n!n'! \tag{17.25}$$

Hence this large space will provide a representation T of $\mathscr{S}_{n+n'}$ but not, in general, an irreducible one. The representation T of $\mathscr{S}_{n+n'}$ is called the 'outer product' of the representations $T^{(\alpha)}$ of $\mathscr{S}_n$ and $T^{(\alpha')}$ of $\mathscr{S}_{n'}$ and we use the notation $T = T^{(\alpha)} \otimes T^{(\alpha')}$. We are therefore faced with an interesting problem: given the irreducible representation labels α and α' which are partitions of n and n', respectively, can we deduce the possible irreducible representations of $\mathscr{S}_{n+n'}$ which appear in the reduction of T? Let us first consider a few simple examples.

If $n = n' = 1$, then the dimension of T is two, with the two basis vectors $f(1)g(2)$ and $f(2)g(1)$. It is clear that by taking the symmetric and antisymmetric combinations, this two-dimensional representation reduces with respect to the group $\mathscr{S}_2$. In terms of Young diagrams we would write

$$\square \otimes \square = \begin{array}{|c|c|}\hline \ & \ \\ \hline\end{array} + \begin{array}{|c|}\hline \ \\ \hline \ \\ \hline\end{array}$$

For the product $\begin{array}{|c|c|}\hline \ & \ \\ \hline\end{array} \otimes \square$ with $n = 2, n' = 1$ there are three basis vectors and, if we write the symmetric two-particle function $f(1, 2)$ of equation (17.24) as $\phi(1)\phi(2)$, then they may be taken as $\phi(1)\phi(2)g(3)$, $\phi(1)\phi(3)g(2)$ and $\phi(2)\phi(3)g(1)$. This set is identical with the set generated from the function $\Phi([21])$ of equation (17.13) and we have seen in table 17.1 of section 17.5 and in section 17.9 how this three-dimensional space breaks up into a single symmetric vector and a pair of mixed symmetry $[21]$. Thus

$$\begin{array}{|c|c|}\hline \ & \ \\ \hline\end{array} \otimes \square = \begin{array}{|c|c|c|}\hline \ & \ & \ \\ \hline\end{array} + \begin{array}{|c|c|}\hline \ & \ \\ \hline \ \\ \cline{1-1}\end{array} \tag{17.26}$$

This result may also be deduced in a way which leads to a simple generalisation. Expand the product $\phi(1)\phi(2)g(3)$ into components corresponding to the tableaux of the Young diagrams of $n = 3$. Since it is symmetric in 1 and 2 it can only involve the two tableaux $\begin{array}{|c|c|c|}\hline 1 & 2 & 3 \\ \hline\end{array}$ and $\begin{array}{|c|c|}\hline 1 & 2 \\ \hline 3 \\ \cline{1-1}\end{array}$ in which 1 and 2 are in the same row. If now we generate all possible functions $P\phi(1)\phi(2)g(3)$ as P runs through $\mathscr{S}_3$ the only new component which can be produced will be the remaining basis function $\begin{array}{|c|c|}\hline 1 & 3 \\ \hline 2 \\ \cline{1-1}\end{array}$ of the representation $[21]$. Thus we have equation (17.26) which says that the outer product contains all irreducible representations of $\mathscr{S}_3$ which may be formed by adding one square to the original diagram $\begin{array}{|c|c|}\hline \ & \ \\ \hline\end{array}$.

This argument may be extended to the more general reduction

$$T^{(\alpha)} \otimes \square = \dot{\sum_{\alpha'}} T^{(\alpha')} \tag{17.27}$$

where the sum runs over those tableaux α' which are obtainable by adding one square to the tableau α. It is even possible to deduce a rule for obtaining the coefficients $m(\beta; \alpha, \alpha')$ for the most general case

$$T = T^{(\alpha)} \otimes T^{(\alpha')} = \dot{\sum_{\beta}} m(\beta; \alpha, \alpha') T^{(\beta)} \tag{17.28}$$

where β is a partition of $n + n'$. The rule is stated below without proof:

(1) Place a letter a in each square of the first row of the diagram α', a letter b in each square of the second row and so on.

(2) Add the squares of α', complete with their letters, to the Young diagram α subject to the conditions (i) that the a's are added before the b's which in turn

are added before the c's and so on, (ii) that a Young diagram is obtained at every stage, (iii) that no two identical letters appear in the same column, (iv) that if the added letters are finally read off from the completed diagram beginning with the first row and reading from right to left, then at no stage must the number of b's exceed the number of a's or the number of c's exceed the number of b's, etc.

(3) The final Young diagrams β which result from this process when all letters have been added will appear in the sum (17.28) with non-zero coefficients. If, by the given procedure, a particular diagram β may be built in a number p of different ways then for that β, the coefficient $m(\beta; \alpha, \alpha') = p$ in equation (17.28).

Consider two examples,

(i)

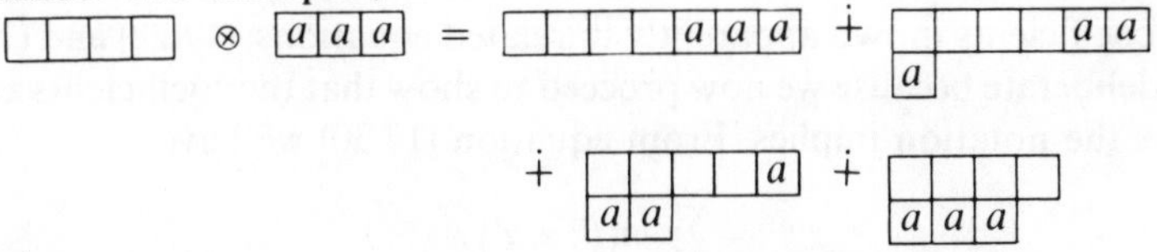

so that

$$T^{[4]} \otimes T^{[3]} = T^{[7]} \dotplus T^{[61]} \dotplus T^{[52]} \dotplus T^{[43]}$$

(ii)

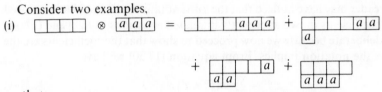

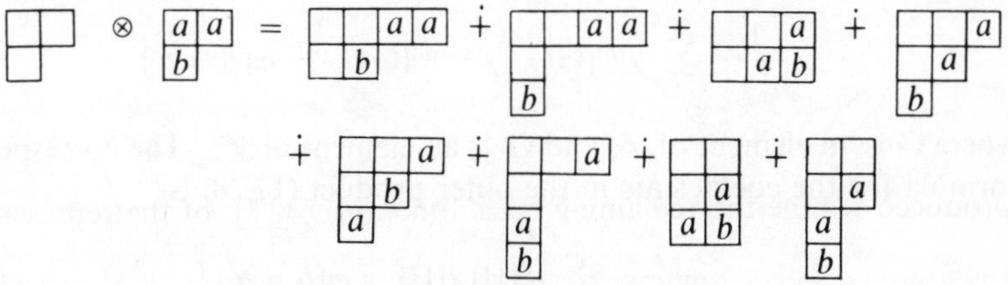

so that

$$T^{[21]} \otimes T^{[21]} = T^{[42]} \dotplus T^{[411]} \dotplus T^{[33]} \dotplus 2T^{[321]} \dotplus T^{[3111]} \dotplus T^{[222]} \dotplus T^{[2211]} \quad (17.29)$$

In example (ii) we see that the partition [321] arises twice in the process, meaning that the representation $T^{[321]}$ appears with $m = 2$ in the reduction (17.28). It is worth making a dimension check on such reductions using equation (17.25). The dimensions in the two cases are $1 \times 1 \times 7!/4!3! = 35$ in example (i) and $2 \times 2 \times 6!/3!3! = 80$ in example (ii). These numbers are soon verified to be equal to the sums of the dimensions of the representations $T^{(\beta)}$ obtained in the reductions, including the factors $m(\beta; \alpha, \alpha')$.

17.12 Restriction to a subgroup and the outer product

In section 17.7 we studied the reduction of irreducible representations of $\mathscr{S}_n$ following the restriction to the subgroup $\mathscr{S}_{n-1}$. More generally, the product group $\mathscr{S}_n \times \mathscr{S}_{n'}$ is a subgroup of $\mathscr{S}_{n+n'}$ (e.g. in section 17.11, $\mathscr{S}_n$ could refer to particles numbered 1, 2, . . ., n and $\mathscr{S}_{n'}$ refer to particles $n+1$, $n+2$, . . ., $n+n'$.) Consequently an irreducible representation $\mathrm{T}^{(\beta)}$ of $\mathscr{S}_{n+n'}$ will generally reduce as a representation of the subgroup $\mathscr{S}_n \times \mathscr{S}_{n'}$,

$$\mathrm{T}^{(\beta)} = \sum_{\alpha, \alpha'} m(\beta;\ \alpha,\ \alpha')\mathrm{T}^{(\alpha \times \alpha')} \tag{17.30}$$

where the two Young diagram labels α and α' are necessary to specify an irreducible representation of the product group $\mathscr{S}_n \times \mathscr{S}_{n'}$. The coefficients $m(\beta; \alpha, \alpha')$ in this reduction may be deduced in the usual way with the help of character tables and using the result (4.66) for the characters of a product group.

The reader may have noticed that the same notation $m(\beta; \alpha, \alpha')$ has been used for the coefficients in two apparently unrelated equations, (17.28) and (17.30). This is deliberate because we now proceed to show that the coefficients are the same, as the notation implies. From equation (17.30) we have

$$\chi^{(\beta)} = \sum_{\alpha, \alpha'} m(\beta; \alpha, \alpha')\chi^{(\alpha \times \alpha')}$$

and using the orthogonality of the irreducible characters of $\mathscr{S}_n \times \mathscr{S}_{n'}$ the coefficients are given by

$$\frac{1}{n!\,n'!} \sum_{\mathrm{G,G'}} \chi^{(\beta)}(\mathrm{GG'})\chi^{(\alpha \times \alpha')}(\mathrm{GG'}) = m(\beta; \alpha, \alpha') \tag{17.31}$$

where G is an element of $\mathscr{S}_n$ and G′ is an element of $\mathscr{S}_{n'}$. The corresponding formula for the coefficients in the outer product (17.28) is

$$\frac{1}{(n+n')!} \sum_{\mathrm{H}} \chi^{\beta}(\mathrm{H})\chi(\mathrm{H}) = m(\beta; \alpha, \alpha') \tag{17.32}$$

where H is an element of $\mathscr{S}_{n+n'}$ and χ is the character of the outer product representation $\mathrm{T} = \mathrm{T}^{(\alpha)} \otimes \mathrm{T}^{(\alpha')}$. Remembering the type of function (17.24) from which T was generated it is seen that any class of $\mathscr{S}_{n+n'}$ whose elements do not belong to a subgroup $\mathscr{S}_n \times \mathscr{S}_{n'}$ must have zero character in T, i.e. $\chi(\mathrm{H}) = 0$ for elements H in such classes. For the remaining elements it can be shown that the character is given by

$$N_{\mathrm{H}}\chi(\mathrm{H}) = \frac{(n+n')!}{n!\,n'!}\tilde{N}_{\mathrm{GG'}}\chi^{(\alpha \times \alpha')}(\mathrm{GG'}) \tag{17.33}$$

where GG′ is an element of $\mathscr{S}_n \times \mathscr{S}_{n'}$ belonging to the same class as H, where N_{H} denotes the number of elements in this class of $\mathscr{S}_{n+n'}$ and $\tilde{N}_{\mathrm{GG'}}$ denotes the number of elements in the corresponding class of $\mathscr{S}_n \times \mathscr{S}_{n'}$. Finally, inserting this result (17.33) into equation (17.32) and remembering that all elements in the same class give the same contribution in the sums (17.31) and (17.32) we see the equivalence of these two equations and hence the justification for using the same notation $m(\beta;\ \alpha,\ \alpha')$ in equations (17.28) and (17.30).

For the particular case $n' = 1$, the reduction (17.30) is none other than the reduction $\mathscr{S}_{n+1} \to \mathscr{S}_n$ described in section 17.7. It was seen there that the coefficients m were all unity which provides another way of deducing equation (17.27).

As an example of the reduction (17.30) consider the group $\mathscr{S}_4$ and its subgroup $\mathscr{S}_2 \times \mathscr{S}_2$ for which the character table is reproduced in table 17.4:

Table 17.4

		(11)(11)	(11)(2)	(2)(11)	(2)(2)	
$\mathscr{S}_2 \times \mathscr{S}_2$	$[2]\times[2]$	1	1	1	1	
	$[2]\times[11]$	1	−1	1	−1	
	$[11]\times[2]$	1	1	−1	−1	
	$[11]\times[11]$	1	−1	−1	1	
$\mathscr{S}_4$	[4]	1	1	1	1	$=[2]\times[2]$
	[31]	3	1	1	−1	$=[2]\times[2]\dotplus[2]\times[11]\dotplus[11]\times[2]$
	[22]	2	0	0	2	$=[2]\times[2]\dotplus[11]\times[11]$
	[211]	3	−1	−1	−1	$=[2]\times[11]\dotplus[11]\times[2]\dotplus[11]\times[11]$
	[1111]	1	−1	−1	1	$=[11]\times[11]$

The classes for the product group are just the possible products of the classes (11) and (2) for each $\mathscr{S}_2$ group. Likewise the irreducible representations, all one-dimensional, are the possible products of the representations [2] and [11] of each $\mathscr{S}_2$ group. For the irreducible representations of $\mathscr{S}_4$ the appropriate characters are read off from the character table for $\mathscr{S}_4$, given in table 17.1 of section 17.5, by identifying the classes (11)(2) and (2)(11) as belonging to the class (211) of $\mathscr{S}_4$, while the product (2)(2) belongs to the class (22). The reductions given to the right of the table are deducible by inspection, although of course one may use the orthogonality formula (4.28) if in doubt.

From this example we may deduce the corresponding reduction (17.28) for the outer product

$$[2] \otimes [2] = [4] \dotplus [31] \dotplus [22] \tag{17.34}$$

by quoting the appropriate coefficients $m(\beta; [2][2])$ given in table 17.4. One soon verifies the dimension check on equation (17.34), namely $1 \times 1 \times 4!/2!2! = 1 + 3 + 2$.

17.13 The standard matrices of the irreducible representations

In section 17.8 we described a labelling system for the basis vectors of irreducible representations of $\mathscr{S}_n$ based on a chain of subgroups and using the Young tableaux. Some explicit examples of such vectors were given in section

17.9 and the corresponding representation matrices were deduced. In this section we first give a completely general prescription, see Rutherford (1948) in the bibliography, for writing down such matrices and after some examples the prescription is later justified. Because of equivalence, these matrices are not unique but they are the ones most commonly used so that we call them standard matrices. They have the advantage of being orthogonal. Once the matrices are known, the projection operators of section 4.19 (called Young operators in the case of $\mathscr{S}_n$) may be used to construct a set of basis vectors from any given function. In a way, this is the reverse of the procedure followed in section 17.9, where in simple cases the basis vectors were constructed first and the matrices deduced from them.

Consider an irreducible representation $T^{(\alpha_n)}$ of $\mathscr{S}_n$. The partition α_n of n defines the Young diagram and from section 17.8 the basis vectors are labelled by the possible tableaux $\alpha_n \alpha_{n-1} \ldots \alpha_2$. (As an example, the nine tableaux corresponding to the partition [42] are drawn in table 17.5.) It was shown in section 17.1 that any permutation may be written in terms of adjacent transpositions $P_{i-1,i}$. If we call $P_{i-1,i}$ the last transposition in the subgroup $\mathscr{S}_i$ it follows that a general description of the matrix of the last transposition $P_{n-1,n}$ in $\mathscr{S}_n$ will enable us to deduce matrices for all the adjacent transpositions and hence for all permutations. Here we rely on the fact that the tableau label $\alpha_n \alpha_{n-1} \ldots \alpha_2$ in $\mathscr{S}_n$ is at the same time a tableau label for the chain of subgroups $\mathscr{S}_{n-1}, \mathscr{S}_{n-2}, \ldots, \mathscr{S}_2$ by removing successively α_n, $\alpha_{n-1}, \ldots, \alpha_3$.

Since $P_{n-1,n}$ is the identity so far as objects $1, 2, \ldots, n-2$ are concerned the only non-zero matrix elements of $P_{n-1,n}$ will occur between those basis vectors for which the tableaux of numbers $1, 2 \ldots, n-2$ are identical. We must therefore enquire which different tableaux, for a given partition $[n_1 n_2 \ldots]$, contain the same tableau of the numbers $1, 2, \ldots, n-2$. We introduce a notation y to denote a tableau for the partition $[n_1 n_2 \ldots]$ with $\tilde{y}$ denoting the tableau obtained by removing the numbers n and $n-1$ from y. It is trivial that the possible tableaux y may be divided into four types which we denote by: (a) in which the numbers n and $n-1$ lie in the same row; (b) in which the numbers n and $n-1$ lie in the same column; (c_1) in which the numbers n and $n-1$ are neither in the same row nor the same column and in which n lies in a row lower than $n-1$; (c_2) which is like (c_1) except that n lies in a row higher than $n-1$. Thus in table 17.5 the first, eighth and ninth rows are of type (a), the second, third and fourth are of type (c_1) and the fifth, sixth and seventh are of type (c_2).

One sees immediately that the tableau $\tilde{y}$ appearing in any tableau y of the type (a) or (b) cannot appear in any other tableau of the partition $[n_1 n_2 \ldots]$. The tableau $\tilde{y}$ appearing in a tableau of type (c_1) will however also appear in the corresponding tableau of type (c_2) in which n and $n-1$ have been interchanged. Hence the only non-zero matrix elements of $P_{n-1,n}$ are on the diagonal in positions labelled by tableaux of type (a) or (b) and in the form of 2×2 matrices coupling pairs of tableaux of types (c_1) and (c_2).

As an example, the non-zero elements of the matrix P_{56} for the partition

Table 17.5 The matrix of P_{56} in the irreducible representation $T^{[42]}$ of $\mathscr{S}_6$

	1 2 3 4 / 5 6	1 2 3 5 / 4 6	1 2 4 5 / 3 6	1 3 4 5 / 2 6	1 2 3 6 / 4 5	1 2 4 6 / 3 5	1 3 4 6 / 2 5	1 2 5 6 / 3 4	1 3 5 6 / 2 4
1 2 3 4 / 5 6	1								
1 2 3 5 / 4 6		$-\frac{1}{3}$			$\sqrt{\frac{8}{9}}$				
1 2 4 5 / 3 6			$-\frac{1}{3}$			$\sqrt{\frac{8}{9}}$			
1 3 4 5 / 2 6				$-\frac{1}{3}$			$\sqrt{\frac{8}{9}}$		
1 2 3 6 / 4 5		$\sqrt{\frac{8}{9}}$			$\frac{1}{3}$				
1 2 4 6 / 3 5			$\sqrt{\frac{8}{9}}$			$\frac{1}{3}$			
1 3 4 6 / 2 5				$\sqrt{\frac{8}{9}}$			$\frac{1}{3}$		
1 2 5 6 / 3 4								1	
1 3 5 6 / 2 4									1

[42] are shown in table 17.5. The derivation of the numerical values is described later. Notice how the first row is labelled by the tableau $\begin{array}{|c|c|c|c|}\hline 1&2&3&4\\ \hline 5&6 \\ \cline{1-2}\end{array}$ which is of type (a). The tableau $\tilde{y}$ for this row is $\begin{array}{|c|c|c|c|}\hline 1&2&3&4\\ \hline\end{array}$ which does not occur again, implying that the only non-zero element in the first row must be on the diagonal. Notice how the second row is of type (c_1) and has for its partner of type (c_2) the fifth row, these two and none others having the tableau $\begin{array}{|c|c|c|}\hline 1&2&3\\ \hline 4 \\ \cline{1-1}\end{array}$ in common. There are therefore non-zero matrix elements coupling the second row and fifth column and the fifth row and second column but, apart from the diagonal positions, all other matrix elements in the second and fifth rows are zero. The rules for deducing the few non-zero matrix elements are as follows:

(1) The diagonal matrix element for a tableau of type (a) is $+1$.
(2) The diagonal matrix element for a tableau of type (b) is -1.
(3) The diagonal matrix elements for tableaux of types (c_1) and (c_2) are given by $\mp l^{-1}$, respectively, where l is called the 'axial distance' from $(n-1)$ to n in the tableau of type c_1 and is defined as the smallest number of steps required to reach n from $(n-1)$, moving in horizontal and vertical steps from one square to the next. A movement of one square to the left or downwards counts as a positive step. In fact, the results (1) and (2) above are special cases of (3).
(4) The off-diagonal matrix elements coupling a pair of tableaux of types (c_1) and (c_2) are given by $+(1-l^{-2})^{\frac{1}{2}}$, thus ensuring that the matrix is orthogonal.

These rules may be used, as explained above, to deduce not only the matrix of P_{56}, as given in table 17.5, but also the matrices for all other adjacent transpositions. Thus, for example, the matrix of P_{34} in the representation $T^{[42]}$ is as follows:

$$\begin{pmatrix} 1 &&&&&&&& \\ & -\frac{1}{3} & \sqrt{\frac{8}{9}} &&&&&& \\ & \sqrt{\frac{8}{9}} & \frac{1}{3} &&&&&& \\ &&& 1 &&&&& \\ &&&& -\frac{1}{3} & \sqrt{\frac{8}{9}} &&& \\ &&&& \sqrt{\frac{8}{9}} & \frac{1}{3} &&& \\ &&&&&& 1 && \\ &&&&&&& 1 & \\ &&&&&&&& -1 \end{pmatrix}$$

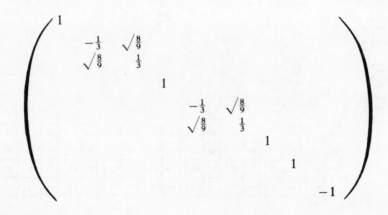

As a further example, the matrices of the transpositions P_{12} and P_{23} in the representation [21] of $\mathscr{S}_3$ which were given in section 17.9 may be verified by the rules above.

We close this section by justifying the rules given above. Denoting the matrix of $P_{n-1,n}$ by $T(P_{n-1,n})$ we have $T^2 = 1$ because $P^2_{n-1,n} = E$ the identity. We are also free to demand that T be a unitary matrix $TT^\dagger = 1$ because of the result in section 4.6 that any representation of a finite group is equivalent to a unitary representation. These two conditions on T show that the diagonal elements for tableaux of types (a) and (b) must be ± 1, while the 2×2 submatrix corresponding to a pair of tableaux of types (c_1) and (c_2) must have the form

$$\begin{pmatrix} -a & \sqrt{(1-a^2)} \\ \sqrt{(1-a^2)} & a \end{pmatrix} \tag{17.35}$$

with some real a. The choice of the positive square root simply defines the relative phase of the basis vectors. It remains to show that $a = l^{-1}$, where l is the axial distance from $(n-1)$ to n in the tableau of type (c_1) and we do this by the method of induction. In other words we show that if the rules are valid for $(n-2)$ and $(n-1)$ then they are valid for n so that knowing the validity in the special cases $n = 2$ and 3 enables us to deduce the validity for all n. The proof makes use of the identity

$$P_{n-1,n}P_{n-2,n-1}P_{n-1,n} = P_{n-2,n-1}P_{n-1,n}P_{n-2,n-1} \tag{17.36}$$

which is soon verified. Suppose that the pair of tableaux of types (c_1) and (c_2) occur in rows r and s of the representation T and let us construct the matrix element in row r and column s, of the two equivalent expressions in equation (17.36). We note that $P_{n-2,n-1}$ must have a zero matrix element in this position since the Young diagrams obtained by removing the number n from these two tableaux have different shape and $P_{n-2,n-1}$ belongs to the subgroup $\mathscr{S}_{n-1}$. The diagonal matrix elements of $P_{n-2,n-1}$ are now assumed to follow the rules set out above so that

$$T_{rr}(P_{n-2,n-1}) = -l_1^{-1}, \qquad T_{ss}(P_{n-2,n-1}) = -l_2^{-1}$$

where l_1 is the axial distance from $n-2$ to $n-1$ in the tableau of row r and l_2 is the axial distance from $n-2$ to $n-1$ in the tableau of row s. Using (17.35) for $T(P_{n-1,n})$ the identity (17.36) gives

$$al_1^{-1}\sqrt{(1-a^2)} - \sqrt{(1-a^2)}l_2^{-1}a = l_1^{-1}\sqrt{(1-a^2)}l_2^{-1}$$

by considering row r and column s and this simplifies to $a = (l_2 - l_1)^{-1}$. However, since the tableaux of rows r and s differ only through the exchange of n and $n-1$ it follows that l_2 is also the axial distance from $n-2$ to n in the tableau of row r. Hence the difference $(l_2 - l_1)$ must be the axial distance from $n-1$ to n in the tableau of row r, in other words $a = l^{-1}$. Thus having assumed the rules to be valid for $P_{n-2,n-1}$ we have shown that they are then valid for $P_{n-1,n}$ and hence the inductive proof is complete. The rules (1) and (2) may be regarded as special cases with axial distances of ∓ 1, respectively.

17.14 The class operator $\sum_{i<j} T(P_{ij})$

It can be shown (see appendix 3.3) that in any irreducible representation $T^{(\alpha)}$ the sum $\sum_\gamma T^{(\alpha)}(G_\gamma)$ of the representation operators over all group elements G_γ in a chosen class $\mathscr{C}$ is a multiple of the unit matrix and that this multiple λ is related to the character in that class by the formula $\lambda_\alpha = n_\mathscr{C}\chi^{(\alpha)}_\mathscr{C}/s_\alpha$, where $n_\mathscr{C}$ is the number of elements in the class and s_α is the dimension of the representation. In the symmetric group $\mathscr{S}_n$ the transpositions P_{ij} form a class (211 . . .), in the notation of section 17.3, so that as a particular case the sum $\sum_{i<j} T^{(\alpha)}(P_{ij})$ of operators in an irreducible representation $T^{(\alpha)}$ will be some multiple λ_α of the unit operator and λ_α may be deduced from the character table. This operator provides a convenient measure of the symmetry of the representation. For example in the totally symmetric representation it has the value $\frac{1}{2}n(n-1)$ and is the negative of this in the totally antisymmetric representation. In a self-adjoint representation it vanishes for the reason given in section 17.10. We may regard this class operator as measuring the difference between the number of symmetric and antisymmetric pairs remembering of course that individual operators $T(P_{ij})$ are not generally diagonal. There is a simple formula for the numbers λ_α which enables them to be deduced quickly from the Young diagram for $T^{(\alpha)}$. If n_p denotes the length of the pth row and m_q denotes the length of the qth column then it may be shown, see problem 17.7, that

$$\lambda_\alpha = \tfrac{1}{2}\sum_p n_p(n_p-1) - \tfrac{1}{2}\sum_q m_q(m_q-1) \tag{17.37}$$

Bibliography

A very complete account of the symmetric group, its representations and projection operators is given by

Rutherford, D. E. (1948). *Substitutional Analysis* (Edinburgh University Press)

The Clebsch – Gordan coefficients for this group are discussed in some detail by

Hamermesh, M. (1962). *Group Theory and its Application to Physical Problems* (Addison Wesley, Reading, Mass.)

The relation between the group $\mathscr{S}_n$ and the continuous groups U_N and $\mathscr{R}_N$ is described and useful characters and formulae are given by

Littlewood, D. E. (1950). *The Theory of Group Characters* (Oxford University Press)

Problems

17.1 Write the permutation $\left(\begin{smallmatrix}1&2&3&4&5&6\\2&4&6&1&5&3\end{smallmatrix}\right)$ as a product of cycles and hence show that it belongs to the class [321] and has odd parity.

17.2 Construct the character table for the group $\mathscr{S}_4$ using the methods of section 4.15 and check your result with table 17.1 of section 17.5.

17.3 Construct the table 17.1 of values of $\psi^{[n_1 n_2 \cdots]}$ and $\chi^{[n_1 n_2 \cdots]}$ for the case $n = 4$.

17.4 Find the dimension of the representation [32] of $\mathscr{S}_5$ by listing the possible Young tableaux.

17.5 Use the methods of section 17.9 to construct representation matrices for the permutations P_{12}, P_{23} and P_{34} in the representation $T^{[31]}$ of $\mathscr{S}_4$ and compare your results with those given by the rules of section 17.13.

17.6 Show that if f_i and g_i denote sets of functions transforming according to an orthogonal matrix representation $T^{(\alpha)}_{ij}$ of $\mathscr{S}_n$ then the sum $F_s = \sum_i f_i g_i$ is totally symmetric. If h_i denotes a set transforming according to the adjoint representation $T^{[11\cdots]} \times T^{(\alpha)}$ then show that $F_a = \sum_i f_i h_i$ is totally antisymmetric.

17.7 Deduce the value (17.37) for the class operator $Q = \sum_{i<j} T(P_{ij})$ in a representation $T^{[n_1 n_2 \cdots]}$ by using the following steps: (a) Let f be the basis vector whose Young tableau y has numbers 1 to n_1 in the first row, $n_1 + 1$ to $n_1 + n_2$ in the second row, etc, and construct the function $g = Af$, where A is the product of the antisymmetrisers for the columns of y. (b) Write $Q = Q_r + Q_c + Q_m$, where Q_r contains pairs ij in the same row of y, Q_c contains pairs in the same column and Q_m the remaining pairs. (c) Show that $Q_c g = -\frac{1}{2}\sum_q m_q(m_q - 1)g$. (d) Show that $(Q_r + Q_m)Af = A(Q_r + Q_m)f$. (e) Show that $Q_r f = \frac{1}{2}\sum_p m_p(m_p - 1)f$. (f) Show that $AQ_m f = 0$.

18

The Unitary Group U_N

The unitary groups SU_2 and SU_3 have been studied in some detail in chapters 10 and 11 and their irreducible representations were found by constructing diagrams in one and two dimensions, respectively, as in figures 11.1 and 11.5 of section 11.6. This method clearly becomes difficult for larger N, as we found in chapter 12 in the brief encounter with SU_4 and SU_6. In the present chapter we introduce a simple method for describing the irreducible representations of U_N for general N which makes use of some properties of the symmetric group $\mathscr{S}_n$ obtained in the preceding chapter. In fact these two very different groups are related in an intimate way which we shall demonstrate in this chapter. The relation is seen most clearly in the physical situation where it is of most interest, namely in the classification of the product wave functions for n particles, where each single particle may be in one of N different states. Thus one may consider both the permutations of the particles and the unitary transformations in the N-dimensional vector space of states of each single particle. Although we shall be deducing properties of the group U_N quite generally we shall use the language of particles and states.

From the physical point of view we have seen in chapters 10, 11 and 12 how the groups SU_2, SU_3, SU_4 and SU_6 have significance as approximate symmetry groups of the nuclear and elementary particle Hamiltonians. The discussion of U_N in this chapter for general N helps to unify those earlier treatments. We shall also see how the groups U_{2l+1} and U_{2j+1} may be used to classify the complicated many-electron wave functions which may be built from n electrons in valence orbits with angular momentum l or j. In this latter problem the unitary groups are being used more as a mathematical device than as a symmetry group of the Hamiltonian.

We first describe the irreducible representations of U_N and then make use of a chain $U_N \rightarrow U_{N-1} \rightarrow \ldots U_1$ of subgroups to label the basis vectors of these representations. In section 18.7 the general results are related to the simple cases of SU_2, SU_3 and SU_4 discussed in earlier chapters. The infinitesimal operators for U_N are described in section 18.8. Some applications of U_N in the study of many-particle wave functions are discussed in section 18.10. Sections 18.11 and 18.12 are concerned with the characters of the irreducible representations of U_N and the last section discusses the connection between SU_2 and $\mathscr{R}_3$.

18.1 The irreducible representations of U_N

In chapter 7 we used the commutation relations of the infinitesimal operators to construct the irreducible representations of the group $\mathscr{R}_3$ and the same technique was used in chapter 11 for SU_3. In this chapter for the group U_N of unitary transformations in N dimensions we adopt a different approach. Starting from the N basis vectors in the original N-dimensional space in which U_N is defined, we construct the product spaces with n factors. In this way new representations are built up from the original $N \times N$ unitary matrices and by suitably symmetrising the product spaces a complete set of irreducible representations of U_N will be constructed.

Let $\phi_1, \phi_2, \ldots, \phi_N$ denote a set of basis vectors in the original N-dimensional space so that the group U_N is defined by the set of unitary transformations

$$\phi_j' = \mathrm{U}\phi_j = \sum_{i=1}^{N} U_{ij}\phi_i \tag{18.1}$$

where U_{ij} is an arbitrary $N \times N$ unitary matrix. We now construct the product space defined by the set of N^n products of the kind

$$\Phi = \phi_i(1)\,\phi_j(2)\,\phi_k(3)\ldots\phi_p(n) \tag{18.2}$$

Each factor carries two labels, a suffix i, j, etc., within the range from 1 to N which describes its properties under the unitary transformation (18.1) and a second label $1, 2, \ldots, n$ which distinguishes the factors and allows the freedom to form antisymmetric products. (Without this second label a product of the kind $\phi_i(1)\,\phi_j(2) - \phi_j(1)\phi_i(2)$ would vanish.) The order of the products is irrelevant; for example $\phi_i(1)\,\phi_j(2)$ means the same as $\phi_j(2)\,\phi_i(1)$, and we usually write them in increasing order $1, 2, \ldots, n$ of the second label. Notice that whereas the second label must be different in each factor the suffices on different factors may be the same. We shall refer to the second label 1, 2, . . ., n as the 'particle' label and the suffix as the 'state' label. (This language is taken from the physical problem of constructing a product wave function for n electrons, each of which may be in one of N degenerate single-particle states. For example $N = 2$ would relate to the possible spin states of n electrons each with spin $s = \frac{1}{2}$, while $N = 2l + 1$ would relate to the possible orbital states of n electrons in a valence orbit with angular momentum l and projections $m_l = l, l-1, \ldots, -l$.)

The transformation induced in the product space (18.2) by the unitary transformation (18.1) on *all* particles is denoted by T(U) and given by

$$\mathrm{T(U)}\Phi = \phi_i'(1)\phi_j'(2)\phi_k'(3) \ldots \phi_p'(n)$$

$$= \sum_{i'j'k'\ldots p'} U_{i'i}U_{j'j}U_{k'k} \ldots U_{p'p}\phi_{i'}(1)\phi_{j'}(2)\phi_{k'}(3) \ldots \phi_{p'}(n) \quad (18.3)$$

Hence the N^n-dimensional space L of the products Φ is invariant under T(U) and provides a representation T of U_N given by the direct product $\mathrm{U} \times \mathrm{U} \times \mathrm{U} \times \ldots \times \mathrm{U}$ of the $N \times N$ matrices U with n factors. However, the representation T is not irreducible and we now show how to reduce L into a number of invariant subspaces by making use of permutations in the particle labels. Clearly the space L is also invariant under the group $\mathscr{S}_n$ of all permutations of the particle labels and these permutations commute with the unitary transformations T(U) since, for example,

$$\mathrm{T(U)\,P_{12}}\Phi = \mathrm{T(U)}\phi_j(1)\phi_i(2)\phi_k(3) \ldots \phi_p(n)$$

$$= \sum_{i'j'k'\ldots p'} U_{j'j}U_{i'i}U_{k'k} \ldots U_{p'p}\phi_{j'}(1)\phi_{i'}(2)\phi_{k'}(3) \ldots \phi_{p'}(n)$$

while

$$\mathrm{P_{12}T(U)}\Phi = \sum_{i'j'k'\ldots p'} U_{i'i}U_{j'j}U_{k'k} \ldots U_{p'p}\phi_{j'}(1)\phi_{i'}(2)\phi_{k'}(3) \ldots \phi_{p'}(n)$$

and the right-hand sides of these equations are identical. Hence T(U) will commute with the projection operators $\mathrm{P}^{(\alpha)}$ for $\mathscr{S}_n$, where $(\alpha) \equiv [n_1 n_2 \ldots]$ is an irreducible representation label for $\mathscr{S}_n$. Thus if we reduce L into subspaces $L^{(\alpha)}$ corresponding to each projection

$$L = \sum_{(\alpha)} L^{(\alpha)}$$

then it follows that each subspace $L^{(\alpha)}$ is invariant under T(U) because

$$\mathrm{T(U)\,P}^{(\alpha)}\Phi = \mathrm{P}^{(\alpha)}\,\mathrm{T(U)}\Phi = \mathrm{P}^{(\alpha)}\Phi'$$

showing that T(U) operating on any member of $L^{(\alpha)}$ produces a vector also lying within $L^{(\alpha)}$. Furthermore, each space $L^{(\alpha)}$ is clearly invariant under the group $\mathscr{S}_n$ so that, since the permutations commute with the unitary transformations, the space $L^{(\alpha)}$ is invariant under the product group $\mathscr{S}_n \times U_N$. Thus we may introduce a notation $\Phi^{(\alpha)}_{tx}$ for the basis vectors of $L^{(\alpha)}$ where, for a unitary transformation,

$$\mathrm{T(U)}\,\Phi^{(\alpha)}_{tx} = \sum_{x'} U^{(\alpha)}_{x'x}\,\Phi^{(\alpha)}_{tx'} \tag{18.4}$$

and for a permutation P,

$$\mathrm{P}\Phi^{(\alpha)}_{tx} = \sum_{t'} T^{(\alpha)}_{t't}(\mathrm{P})\Phi^{(\alpha)}_{t'x} \tag{18.5}$$

Here the index t is the usual row label for the irreducible representation $\mathrm{T}^{(\alpha)}$ of $\mathscr{S}_n$ described in chapter 17, while x is a new index introduced to provide a basis for all vectors of $L^{(\alpha)}$ with the same t. Thus $\mathrm{U}^{(\alpha)}$ is a representation of U_N and it is this which interests us in the present chapter. Now the representation $\mathrm{T}^{(\alpha)}(\mathrm{P})$ of $\mathscr{S}_n$ is necessarily irreducible by its method of construction through the projection operator $\mathrm{P}^{(\alpha)}$. It is a remarkable fact that the representation $\mathrm{U}^{(\alpha)}$ of U_N generated in this way is also irreducible but we shall not give the proof. The set of representations $\mathrm{U}^{(\alpha)}$ for all partitions of all integers n is not actually a complete set but with a small extension described in section 18.9 they become complete. The set of basis vectors $\Phi^{(\alpha)}_{tx}$ of $L^{(\alpha)}$ for fixed α is conveniently pictured in the rectangular array shown below

$$\begin{matrix} \Phi^{(\alpha)}_{11} & \Phi^{(\alpha)}_{12} & \Phi^{(\alpha)}_{13} & \cdots & \Phi^{(\alpha)}_{1d_\alpha} \\ \Phi^{(\alpha)}_{21} & \Phi^{(\alpha)}_{22} & & \cdots & \Phi^{(\alpha)}_{2d_\alpha} \\ \Phi^{(\alpha)}_{31} & & & & \vdots \\ \vdots & & & & \\ \Phi^{(\alpha)}_{s_\alpha 1} & \Phi^{(\alpha)}_{s_\alpha 2} & & \cdots\cdots & \Phi^{(\alpha)}_{s_\alpha d_\alpha} \end{matrix} \tag{18.6}$$

The vectors in each column transform according to the (same) irreducible representation $\mathrm{T}^{(\alpha)}$ of $\mathscr{S}_n$, while each row gives the (same) representation $\mathrm{U}^{(\alpha)}$ of U_N. We use the same notation s_α as in chapter 17 for the dimension of $\mathrm{T}^{(\alpha)}$ and d_α is introduced for the dimension of $\mathrm{U}^{(\alpha)}$. To summarise the results so far; the separability of the labels is a consequence of the invariance of $L^{(\alpha)}$ under the product group $\mathscr{S}_n \times U_N$, the irreducibility of $\mathrm{T}^{(\alpha)}$ was imposed by using the appropriate projection operator and the claim that the representation $\mathrm{U}^{(\alpha)}$ of U_N is irreducible has yet to be proved. For the representation T of $\mathscr{S}_n \times U_N$ generated in L we may write

$$\mathrm{T} = \dot{\sum_{\alpha}} \mathrm{T}^{(\alpha)} \times \mathrm{U}^{(\alpha)} \tag{18.7}$$

and by equating the dimension on both sides of this equation we get the relation

$$N^n = \sum_{\alpha} s_\alpha d_\alpha \tag{18.8}$$

between the dimensions s_α and d_α of $T^{(\alpha)}$ and $U^{(\alpha)}$, respectively. It is important to realise that the partition α serves a double purpose of labelling irreducible representations of both the finite group $\mathscr{S}_n$ and the continuous group U_N. For fixed N we may choose any positive integer n, corresponding to a different number of factors in the products (18.2). Thus, as expected for a continuous group, we have an infinite number of irreducible representations. There is, however, one limitation on the possible partitions $[n_1 n_2 \ldots]$. Remember from chapter 17 that a partition into p parts implies total antisymmetry between sets of p particles out of n. However if $p > N$ this is impossible because there are only N different single-particle states. Hence the irreducible representations $U^{(\alpha)}$ of U_N are labelled by the partitions $[n_1 n_2 \ldots]$ of any integer n into not more than N parts. In other words they may be labelled by the Young diagrams with not more than N rows.

18.2 Some examples

To illustrate the rather abstract statements in the preceding section let us consider some small values of N and n.

(1) $N = 2, n = 2$ There are $N^n = 4$ product functions

$$|11\rangle, \quad |12\rangle, \quad |21\rangle \text{ and } |22\rangle$$

using the notation $\phi_i(1)\phi_j(2)\phi_k(3) \ldots \phi_p(n) \equiv |ijk \ldots p\rangle$. The irreducible representations of $\mathscr{S}_2$ are labelled by the two possible partitions [2] and [11] and the corresponding subspaces are defined by the following basis vectors,

$$L^{[2]}: \quad |11\rangle, \qquad (|12\rangle + |21\rangle)/\sqrt{2}, \qquad |22\rangle$$

$$L^{[11]}: \qquad (|12\rangle - |21\rangle)/\sqrt{2}$$

Thus, for example, the partition [2] is seen to label a three-dimensional representation of U_2 and, from section 17.5, a one-dimensional representation of $\mathscr{S}_2$.

(2) $N = 3, \ n = 2$ Using the same notation as above, the $3^2 = 9$-dimensional space L reduces into

$$L^{[2]}: \quad |11\rangle, |22\rangle, |33\rangle, \quad (|12\rangle + |21\rangle)/\sqrt{2}, \quad (|13\rangle + |31\rangle)/\sqrt{2}, \quad (|23\rangle + |32\rangle)/\sqrt{2}$$

$$L^{[11]}: \quad (|12\rangle - |21\rangle)/\sqrt{2}, \quad (|13\rangle - |31\rangle)/\sqrt{2}, \quad (|23\rangle - |32\rangle)/\sqrt{2}$$

showing that the partitions [2] and [11] now label six-dimensional and three-dimensional representations of U_3.

(3) $N = 2, n = 3$ The $2^3 = 8$ product functions are given by

$$|111\rangle, |112\rangle, |121\rangle, |211\rangle, |122\rangle, |212\rangle, |221\rangle \text{ and } |222\rangle$$

The subspace $L^{[3]}$ is simply the set of totally symmetric combinations of these and is easily constructed,

$$L^{[3]}:\quad |111\rangle, \qquad (|112\rangle + |121\rangle + |211\rangle)/\sqrt{3},$$
$$|222\rangle, \qquad (|221\rangle + |212\rangle + |122\rangle)/\sqrt{3}$$

The representation of $\mathscr{S}_3$ labelled by the partition [21] is two-dimensional, so the corresponding array (18.6) has two rows. From the example considered in section 17.9 or from the projection operator we find the array of basis vectors may be taken as

$$L^{[21]}:\quad (2|112\rangle - |121\rangle - |211\rangle)/\sqrt{6}, \qquad (2|221\rangle - |212\rangle - |122\rangle)/\sqrt{6}$$
$$(|121\rangle - |211\rangle)/\sqrt{2}, \qquad (|212\rangle - |122\rangle)/\sqrt{2}$$

In each column we have chosen the vectors to transform according to the standard representation $\mathrm{T}^{[21]}$ described in section 17.9. We do not yet have a standard for the representation $\mathrm{U}^{[21]}$ but the two vectors in the first row are distinguished by the number of 'particles' in each 'state'. They are clearly orthogonal but any orthogonal pair formed from them by linear combination would serve equally well. The setting up of a standard basis for the representations $\mathrm{U}^{(\alpha)}$ is discussed in section 18.4. The fact that the same representation of U_N is generated by each row is demonstrated by showing that the matrices of the general unitary transformation T(U) are the same in these two spaces, making use of the result

$$\langle i'j'k'|\mathrm{T(U)}|ijk\rangle = U_{i'i}U_{j'j}U_{k'k}$$

from equation (18.3). This completes the reduction of the eight-dimensional space L and notice that there is no space $L^{[111]}$ because $N = 2$. Any attempt to project such a space would give zero.

(4) $N = 3$, $n = 3$ We leave this example as an exercise. The space L now has $3^3 = 27$ dimensions and is seen to reduce into $L^{[3]}$ with a dimension of ten, a sixteen-dimensional space $L^{[21]}$ described by an array with two rows and eight columns and a one-dimensional space $L^{[111]}$.

18.3 The chain of subgroups $U_N \to U_{N-1} \to U_{N-2} \to \ldots \to U_2 \to U_1$

It is always convenient to identify a chain of subgroups since this helps in the labelling of the basis vectors of representations. For example, the use of the subgroup $\mathscr{R}_2$ of $\mathscr{R}_3$ enabled us in chapter 7 to label the basis vectors of the representation $\mathrm{D}^{(j)}$ of $\mathscr{R}_3$ by the number m. Again, in chapter 11 we labelled the basis vectors of the SU_3 representations $(\lambda\mu)$ by the numbers T, M_T and Y relating to the subgroups SU_2, $\mathscr{R}_2$ and U_1 of SU_3. This device was also used for the symmetric group $\mathscr{S}_n$ in section 17.8 using the chain $\mathscr{S}_n \to \mathscr{S}_{n-1} \to \ldots \to \mathscr{S}_2$.

For the unitary groups we use the chain of subgroups $U_N \to U_{N-1} \to \ldots \to U_2 \to U_1$ obtained by successively restricting the transformations to matrices with one less dimension. We need only consider the first step in this reduction and it simplifies the discussion if we consider the restriction $U_N \to U_{N-1} \times U_1$ which retains the simple U_1 transformations in the one excluded dimension. The U_1 group consists of 1×1 matrices $\exp(-i\theta)$ and, as for the group $\mathscr{R}_2$ in section 7.3, has one-dimensional irreducible representations $\exp(-im\theta)$ labelled by the integer m. To be definite, let us take ϕ_N as the basis vector of this excluded dimension in the notation of section 18.1 so that U_{N-1} refers to the basis vectors $\phi_1, \phi_2, \ldots, \phi_{N-1}$. Thus a product of the kind Φ in equation (18.2) will transform according to the representation $\exp(-ir\theta)$ of U_1 if it contains the vector ϕ_N exactly r times, i.e. if r of the n particles are in the state ϕ_N. The problem is to study the reduction of the representation $\mathrm{U}^{(\alpha_n)}$ of U_N following restriction to the subgroup $U_{N-1} \times U_1$. It is convenient to include the suffix n on α_n to indicate that α_n is a partition of n or, in other words, a Young diagram with n squares. Let us first state the result and then justify it.

$$\mathrm{U}^{(\alpha_n)} = \dot{\sum_{r=0}^{n}} \sum_{\alpha_{n-r}}{}' \mathrm{V}^{(\alpha_{n-r})} \times \exp(-ir\theta) \tag{18.9}$$

where $\mathrm{V}^{(\alpha_{n-r})}$ denotes an irreducible representation of U_{N-1} and the prime on the summation means that only those Young diagrams α_{n-r} occur which may be obtained from α_n by the removal of r squares, no two of which come from the same column. Before giving the derivation we illustrate the result with the examples from section 18.2 for the restriction $U_3 \to U_2 \times U_1$ and $n = 2$,

$$\mathrm{U}^{[2]} = \mathrm{V}^{[2]} \dot{+} \exp(-i\theta)\mathrm{V}^{[1]} \dot{+} \exp(-2i\theta)\mathrm{V}^{[0]}$$

$$\mathrm{U}^{[11]} = \mathrm{V}^{[11]} \dot{+} \exp(-i\theta)\mathrm{V}^{[1]}$$

Noting that the value of r corresponds to the number of particles occupying the state ϕ_3 it is easy to identify which of the basis vectors given under example (2) of section 18.2 corresponds to each $\mathrm{V}^{(\alpha_{2-r})}$,

$$\mathrm{U}^{[2]} \begin{cases} r = 0\ \mathrm{V}^{[2]}: & |11\rangle, \quad |22\rangle, \quad (|12\rangle + |21\rangle)/\sqrt{2} \\ r = 1\ \mathrm{V}^{[1]}: & (|13\rangle + |31\rangle)/\sqrt{2}, \quad (|23\rangle + |32\rangle)/\sqrt{2} \\ r = 2\ \mathrm{V}^{[0]}: & |33\rangle \end{cases}$$

$$\mathrm{U}^{[11]} \begin{cases} r = 0\ \mathrm{V}^{[11]}: & (|12\rangle - |21\rangle)/\sqrt{2} \\ r = 1\ \mathrm{V}^{[1]}: & (|13\rangle - |31\rangle)/\sqrt{2}, \quad (|23\rangle - |32\rangle)/\sqrt{2} \end{cases}$$

The vectors given here for $V^{[2]}$ and $V^{[11]}$ are precisely those given in example (1) of section 18.2. The two pairs of vectors given for the $V^{[1]}$ representation are different but transform in the same way under the group U_2 on states ϕ_1 and ϕ_2. In fact they transform like the defining 2×2 matrices of U_2 corresponding to $n = 1$ and the vectors $|1\rangle$ and $|2\rangle$. The remaining vector $|33\rangle$ is clearly invariant under U_2.

To prove the reduction formula (18.9), or 'branching law' as it is sometimes called, we make use of the result given in section 17.11 for the outer product of irreducible representations of $\mathscr{S}_n$. First we reduce the space L of all products (18.2) into subspaces $L = \sum_{r=0}^{n} L_r$ corresponding to behaviour under the subgroup U_1. In other words, L_r is defined by those products which contain r particles in the state ϕ_N and $n-r$ in the remaining states ϕ_1 to ϕ_{N-1}. To analyse the structure of L_r we may regard it as built up from products

$$\phi_i(1)\phi_j(2)\ldots\phi_p(n-r)\phi_N(n-r+1)\ldots\phi_N(n) \tag{18.10}$$

by (a) taking all possible choices of $i, j, \ldots, p$ from $1, 2, \ldots, N-1$ and (b) carrying out all permutations which mix particle numbers 1 to $n-r$ and $(n-r+1)$ to n. This product has a similar structure to the form (17.24) used in discussing outer products. The step (a) is identical with the original reduction of L described in section 18.1 except that n and N are replaced by $n-r$ and $N-1$. Thus, so far as particles 1 to $n-r$ are concerned, we can generate all Young diagrams α_{n-r} with $n-r$ squares and no more than $N-1$ rows. These diagrams α_{n-r} will describe the behaviour both under U_{N-1} and under $\mathscr{S}_{n-r}$. To find the behaviour of the products (18.10) under $\mathscr{S}_n$ we need to form the outer product of α_{n-r} of $\mathscr{S}_{n-r}$ with the totally symmetric representation $[r]$ of $\mathscr{S}_r$ which relates to the last r particles in (18.10). But this can be done as a special case of the rule (17.28) with the result that for given α_{n-r} the possible Young diagrams α_n relating to $\mathscr{S}_n$ are obtained by adding r squares to the diagram α_{n-r} in such a way that no two added squares lie in the same column. Reversing this analysis we may now deduce the result (18.9) that, given α_n and r, the possible representations of U_{N-1} correspond to those Young diagrams α_{n-r} which may be obtained by the removal of r squares, no two of which lie in the same column.

18.4 A labelling system for the basis vectors

In section 17.8 we used the chain of subgroups $\mathscr{S}_{n-1} \to \mathscr{S}_{n-2} \ldots \to \mathscr{S}_2$ of $\mathscr{S}_n$ to provide a unique labelling system for the basis vectors of the irreducible representations $T^{(\alpha_n)}$ of $\mathscr{S}_n$. Exactly similar arguments may be used to obtain a unique labelling system for the basis vectors of the representations $U^{(\alpha_n)}$ of U_N by using the chain of subgroups $U_{N-1} \to U_{N-2} \to \ldots \to U_1$ described in the preceding section. The result is that the basis vectors of $U^{(\alpha_n)}$ are labelled by the sequence

$$\alpha_n, \alpha_{n-r_N}, \alpha_{n-r_N-r_{N-1}}, \ldots, \alpha_{n-r_N-r_{N-1}-\cdots-r_2} \tag{18.11}$$

of Young diagrams where α_{n-r_N} defines the representation of the subgroup U_{N-1} to which that vector belongs, $\alpha_{n-r_N-r_{N-1}}$ refers likewise to the subgroup U_{N-2} and so on. The justification that this labelling system is unique, i.e. that no two basis vectors of $U^{(\alpha_n)}$ have the same set of labels, follows so closely the arguments in section 17.8 that we do not repeat them. As an illustration, the six basis vectors of the representation $U^{[2]}$ of U_3 which were discussed in the previous section would be assigned the sequences of partitions shown in the second column of table 18.1.

Table 18.1

$\|11\rangle$	[2], [2], [2]	$\boxed{1\,\|\,1}$
$(\|12\rangle + \|21\rangle)/\sqrt{2}$	[2], [2], [1]	$\boxed{1\,\|\,2}$
$\|22\rangle$	[2], [2], [0]	$\boxed{2\,\|\,2}$
$(\|13\rangle + \|31\rangle)/\sqrt{2}$	[2], [1], [1]	$\boxed{1\,\|\,3}$
$(\|23\rangle + \|32\rangle)/\sqrt{2}$	[2], [1], [0]	$\boxed{2\,\|\,3}$
$\|33\rangle$	[2], [0], [0]	$\boxed{3\,\|\,3}$

As in section 17.8, the sequence of Young diagrams, or partitions, is a clumsy notation and a more concise labelling is achieved by drawing, for each basis vector, the single Young diagram α_n with the 'state labels' 1 to N entered in the squares in the following way. The number N is placed in those squares of α_n which are absent in α_{n-r_N}, the number $N-1$ is placed in those squares of α_{n-r_N} which are absent in $\alpha_{n-r_N-r_{N-1}}$ and so on. This labelling is illustrated in the third column of table 18.1. As a further example, the eight basis vectors of the [21] representation of U_3 would be labelled by

$$\begin{array}{|c|c|}\hline 1&1\\\hline 2\\\cline{1-1}\end{array}\quad \begin{array}{|c|c|}\hline 1&2\\\hline 2\\\cline{1-1}\end{array}\quad \begin{array}{|c|c|}\hline 1&1\\\hline 3\\\cline{1-1}\end{array}\quad \begin{array}{|c|c|}\hline 1&2\\\hline 3\\\cline{1-1}\end{array}\quad \begin{array}{|c|c|}\hline 2&2\\\hline 3\\\cline{1-1}\end{array}\quad \begin{array}{|c|c|}\hline 1&3\\\hline 2\\\cline{1-1}\end{array}\quad \begin{array}{|c|c|}\hline 1&3\\\hline 3\\\cline{1-1}\end{array}\quad \begin{array}{|c|c|}\hline 2&3\\\hline 3\\\cline{1-1}\end{array} \tag{18.12}$$

in which, for example, the first corresponds to the chain of partitions [21] → [21] → [2], the sixth to the chain [21] → [11] → [1] and the eighth to the chain [21] → [1] → [0].

It must be stressed that this device of writing state labels into the Young diagrams for U_N is quite distinct from the device of writing in particle labels which was used in section 17.8 for $\mathscr{S}_n$.

18.5 The direct product of representations of U_N

Given any two representations $U^{(\alpha_n)}$ and $U^{(\alpha'_{n'})}$ of U_N we may form the direct product as defined generally in section 4.17. This provides a larger representation of dimension equal to the product of the dimensions of the two original representations. We are interested in the reduction of this product representation into its irreducible constituents and once again the result is simple to state.

$$U^{(\alpha_n)} \times U^{(\alpha'_{n'})} = \dot{\sum_{\beta}} m(\beta; \alpha_n, \alpha'_{n'})\, U^{(\beta)} \tag{18.13}$$

where the sum runs over the Young diagrams β of $n+n'$ squares and the coefficients $m(\beta; \alpha_n, \alpha'_{n'})$ are given by the same rules which were stated in section 17.11 for the reduction of the outer product of representations of $\mathscr{S}_n$ and $\mathscr{S}_{n'}$. Diagrams β with more than N rows are disregarded since no such representations of U_N can exist, see section 18.1. In fact, this is the only way in which the number N enters equation (18.13). Before justifying this result we again give some examples.

For the particular case $n = 2$, $n' = 1$ and $\alpha_n = [2]$ the coefficients $m(\beta; \alpha_n, \alpha'_{n'})$ were given in equation (17.26) and the reduction (18.13) is then

$$U^{[2]} \times U^{[1]} = U^{[3]} \dot{+} U^{[21]} \tag{18.14}$$

For the reasons given above, the second term must be omitted when $N = 1$. Of course, for $N = 1$ there is no reduction because the irreducible representations are all one-dimensional $\exp(-in\theta)$ and labelled by the integer n. For $N = 2$ the left-hand side of equation (18.14) has dimension $3 \times 2 = 6$ and on the right the two terms have dimensions 4 and 2, respectively, see examples (1) and (3) of section 18.2. For $N = 3$, the examples (2) and (4) of section 18.2 show that the left-hand side now has dimension $6 \times 3 = 18$, while the right has terms with dimension 10 and 8, respectively.

As a more complicated example consider the product $U^{[21]} \times U^{[21]}$ for which the outer product reduction was given in equation (17.29). Without repeating that equation here, we note that for $N = 2$ the product representation has a dimension of 4 and reduces into a sum of $U^{[42]}$ and $U^{[33]}$ with dimensions 3 and 1, respectively, while for $N = 3$ the product representation has dimension 64 and reduces into the sum of $U^{[42]}$, $U^{[411]}$, $U^{[33]}$ (twice) and $U^{[222]}$ with dimensions of 27, 10, 10, 2×8 and 1.

To justify the result (18.13) we make use of the property, deduced in section 17.12, that the coefficients $m(\beta; \alpha_n, \alpha'_{n'})$ relate also to the reduction (17.30) of a representation $T^{(\beta)}$ of $\mathscr{S}_{n \times n'}$ following restriction to the subgroup $\mathscr{S}_n \times \mathscr{S}_{n'}$.

Consider the space L of products of the kind (18.2) for $n+n'$ particles. As explained in section 18.1 this space reduces

$$\mathrm{T} = \dot{\sum_{\beta}} \mathrm{T}^{(\beta)} \times \mathrm{U}^{(\beta)}$$

into irreducible representations of the product group $\mathscr{S}_{n+n'} \times U_N$ labelled by partitions β of $n+n'$. Restriction to the subgroup $\mathscr{S}_n \times \mathscr{S}_{n'} \times U_N$ leads to the further reduction

$$\mathrm{T} = \dot{\sum_{\beta,\alpha_n,\alpha'_{n'}}} m(\beta; \alpha_n, \alpha'_{n'})\, \mathrm{T}^{(\alpha_n)} \times \mathrm{T}^{(\alpha'_{n'})} \times \mathrm{U}^{(\beta)} \tag{18.15}$$

using equation (17.30). However, by considering the first n and the last n' particles separately, applying equation (18.7) to each part, we also have the reduction

$$\mathrm{T} = \dot{\sum_{\alpha_n,\alpha_{n'}}} \mathrm{T}^{(\alpha_n)} \times \mathrm{U}^{(\alpha_n)} \times \mathrm{T}^{(\alpha'_{n'})} \times \mathrm{U}^{(\alpha'_{n'})} \tag{18.16}$$

Finally, comparing this with the preceding equation gives the desired result

$$\mathrm{U}^{(\alpha_n)} \times U^{(\alpha'_{n'})} = \dot{\sum_{\beta}} m(\beta; \alpha_n, \alpha'_{n'})\ \mathrm{U}^{(\beta)}$$

for the reduction of product representations of U_N.

18.6 The restriction from U_N to its subgroup SU_N

The irreducible representations $\mathrm{U}^{(\alpha)}$ of U_N were constructed in section 18.1 from products like (18.2), where α denotes a partition of n, the number of factors in the product. In this section we study the subgroup consisting of the $N \times N$ unitary matrices with determinant equal to unity. It is denoted by SU_N and called the 'special unitary group' or 'unimodular unitary group'. The relation between U_N and SU_N may best be seen by writing $U_N = U_1 \times SU_N$ as a direct product where U_1 is the group of $N \times N$ matrices of the form $\exp(-i\psi)$ multiplied by the unit matrix and ψ is real. (This group U_1 is not the same as the groups U_1 used in section 18.3 to transform just one of the N dimensions, although the groups are isomorphic.)

If A and B are square matrices then it is an elementary property that $\det \mathrm{AB} = (\det \mathrm{A})(\det \mathrm{B})$. Hence the unitary condition $\mathrm{UU}^{\dagger} = 1$ on the matrix U implies that $|\det \mathrm{U}|^2 = 1$. For any unitary matrix U we may therefore write $\mathrm{U} = \exp(-i\psi)\, \overline{\mathrm{U}}$ where $\det \overline{\mathrm{U}} = +1$. It is soon verified that the set of all unitary $N \times N$ matrices $\overline{\mathrm{U}}$ with $\det \overline{\mathrm{U}} = +1$ satisfies the postulates of a group so that the group U_N has been factorised into a U_1 group of the factor $\exp(-i\psi)$ and the group of the $\overline{\mathrm{U}}$ which we call SU_N.

From the general theory of representations of product groups in section

4.21 we know that the irreducible representations $U^{(\alpha)}$ of U_N must take the form of a direct product of irreducible representations of U_1 and SU_N. The representations of U_1 are, of course, one-dimensional with the form $\exp(-im\psi)$, where m is any integer. Since the representation $U^{(\alpha)}$ was constructed from n factors in section 18.1 it follows that the direct product form for $U^{(\alpha)}$ is

$$U^{(\alpha)} = \exp(-in\psi) \times U^{(\tilde{\alpha})} \tag{18.17}$$

where n is the number of squares in the Young tableau α. Hence, the irreducible representation $U^{(\tilde{\alpha})}$ of SU_N has the same dimension as $U^{(\alpha)}$. In other words, $U^{(\alpha)}$ does not reduce on restriction from U_N to the subgroup SU_N. We may therefore use the same partition notation $(\tilde{\alpha}) = (\alpha) = [n_1 n_2 \ldots]$ to label the irreducible representations of SU_N. However, whereas for U_N it is obvious that two representations with different n are inequivalent that is not the case for SU_N as we now demonstrate.

Consider the representation $[11\ldots1]$ of U_N, where $n = N$. It must be one-dimensional since there is only one totally antisymmetric combination which can be formed from the products (18.2), namely

$$\Psi = \sum_{\mathrm{P}} \pi(\mathrm{P})\mathrm{P}\phi_1(1)\phi_2(2)\ldots\phi_N(N) \tag{18.18}$$

where the sum runs over all permutations of the particle labels and $\pi(\mathrm{P})$ denotes the parity of the permutation P. Using equation (18.3) the effect of a unitary transformation on Ψ is given by

$$\mathrm{T}(\mathrm{U})\Psi = \sum_{ij\ldots p} U_{i1}U_{j2}\ldots U_{pN}\sum_{\mathrm{P}}\pi(\mathrm{P})\mathrm{P}\phi_i(1)\phi_j(2)\ldots\phi_p(N) \tag{18.19}$$

Because of the presence of the antisymmetrising operator, the only combinations of suffices $ij\ldots p$ to give a non-zero result are those in which no suffix is repeated so that $ij\ldots p$ is a rearrangement of $12\ldots N$. Using the notation $\begin{pmatrix} ij & \ldots & p \\ 12 & \ldots & N\end{pmatrix}$ for the permutation which carries the particle labels $ij\ldots p$ into $12\ldots N$ the equation (18.19) may be written

$$\mathrm{T}(\mathrm{U})\Psi = \sum_{ij\ldots p} U_{i1}U_{j2}\ldots U_{pN}\sum_{\mathrm{P}}\pi(\mathrm{P})\mathrm{P}\begin{pmatrix} ij\ldots p \\ 12\ldots N\end{pmatrix}\phi_i(i)\phi_j(j)\ldots\phi_p(p)$$

We stress that the permutation $\begin{pmatrix} ij & \ldots & p \\ 12 & \ldots & N\end{pmatrix}$ operates only on the particle labels, as does P. However, since the order of factors is not significant we may rearrange them so that $\phi_1(1)$ comes first, $\phi_2(2)$ second and so on. Thus we have

$$\begin{aligned}\mathrm{T}(\mathrm{U})\Psi &= \sum_{ij\ldots p} U_{i1}U_{j2}\ldots U_{pN}\sum_{\mathrm{P}}\pi(\mathrm{P})\mathrm{P}\begin{pmatrix} ij\ldots p \\ 12\ldots N\end{pmatrix}\phi_1(1)\phi_2(2)\ldots\phi_N(N)\\ &= \sum_{ij\ldots p} U_{i1}U_{j2}\ldots U_{pN}\pi\begin{pmatrix} 12\ldots N \\ ij\ldots p\end{pmatrix}\sum_{\mathrm{P}'}\pi(\mathrm{P}')\mathrm{P}'\phi_1(1)\phi_2(2)\ldots\phi_N(N)\end{aligned}$$

where we have defined P′ as the product of permutations $\mathrm{P}' = \mathrm{P}\binom{i\,j\,\cdots\,p}{1\,2\,\ldots\,N}$ and used the result of section 17.4 that the parity of a product is the product of the parities. We have also used the fact that as P runs over the group $\mathscr{S}_N$ so does P′, see section 2.9. Finally we note that the sum over P′ is just Ψ, while the sum over $ij \ldots p$ gives the determinant of the matrix U so that

$$\mathrm{T(U)}\Psi = (\det \mathrm{U})\Psi \tag{18.20}$$

The significance of the result (18.20) is that Ψ is invariant for transformations of SU_N and so we have an equivalence between the representation labelled by the partition $[11\ldots1]$ of $n = N$ and the identity representation given trivially by $n = 0$. In terms of Young diagrams this implies equivalence between the single complete column of N rows and the trivial diagram with no squares. Further equivalences now follow using the results of section 18.5 for multiplying representations. If $\mathrm{U}^{(\alpha)}$ is any irreducible representation then from the rules quoted for equation (18.13)

$$\mathrm{U}^{(\alpha)} \times \mathrm{U}^{[11\ldots1]} = \mathrm{U}^{(\beta)}$$

where the Young diagram for β is obtained by adding a complete column to the left of the Young diagram for α. But since $\mathrm{U}^{[11\ldots1]}$ is equivalent to the identity, this means that $\mathrm{U}^{(\alpha)} \equiv \mathrm{U}^{(\beta)}$. Hence the addition, or subtraction, of one (or any number of) complete columns gives an equivalent representation. It is usual to denote the inequivalent irreducible representations by the Young diagram with least squares, obtained by subtracting all complete columns of length N. Thus for SU_N we need only the Young diagrams with $N-1$ rows. It may be shown that no further equivalences exist.

The reduction of product representations in SU_N follows from the rule (18.13) for U_N, making use of the equivalences given above. For example, in the group SU_2, the representations have only one row in their Young diagrams and applying (18.13) for the product $\mathrm{U}^{[3]} \times \mathrm{U}^{[2]}$ of SU_2 gives

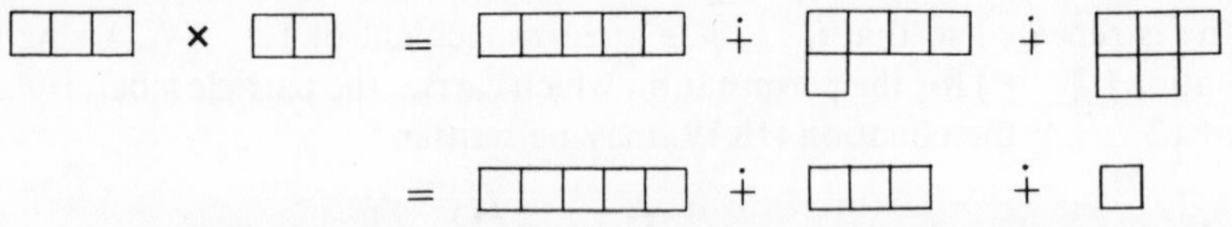

In the more familiar notation $\mathrm{D}^{(j)}$ which was used for the representation of SU_2 in chapters 7 and 10, this is an example of equation (7.44)

$$\mathrm{D}^{(\frac{3}{2})} \times \mathrm{D}^{(1)} = \mathrm{D}^{(\frac{5}{2})} \dotplus \mathrm{D}^{(\frac{3}{2})} \dotplus \mathrm{D}^{(\frac{1}{2})}$$

using the identification of $\mathrm{U}^{[n]}$ with $\mathrm{D}^{(\frac{1}{2}n)}$ which we discuss in the next section.

18.7 The special cases of SU_2, SU_3 and SU_4

We now make contact between the preceding discussion of SU_N and the particular descriptions of SU_2, SU_3 and SU_4 given in chapters 10–12. In the case of SU_2 the irreducible representations are labelled by Young diagrams with one row of length n, in other words by a single integer n. However in chapter 10 we used the notation $D^{(j)}$ with $j = 0, \frac{1}{2}, 1, \frac{3}{2}, \ldots$, for the group SU_2 because it is homomorphic with $\mathcal{R}_3$ (see also section 18.13). We can soon see that the relation $j = \frac{1}{2}n$ unites the two treatments. This relation may be deduced in various ways, one of which is to note that in $D^{(j)}$ the number j refers to the greatest value of the infinitesimal operator J_z which has the matrix $\begin{pmatrix} \frac{1}{2} & 0 \\ 0 & -\frac{1}{2} \end{pmatrix}$ in the original two-dimensional space. Thus, on a product Φ of the type (18.2) this infinitesimal operator is diagonal and its value is made up of contributions $+\frac{1}{2}$ from every particle in state ϕ_1 and $-\frac{1}{2}$ from every particle in state ϕ_2. Thus the greatest value is obtained by putting as many as possible of the n particles into state ϕ_1 and for the totally symmetric functions corresponding to the single-row Young diagram $[n]$ this number is clearly n, so that $j = \frac{1}{2}n$. Thus the integer nature of n leads to the familiar integer or half-integer nature of j.

A similar argument enables us to show the identity between the labels $(\lambda\mu)$ used in chapter 11 for the irreducible representations of SU_3 and the Young diagram $[n_1 n_2]$ with two rows where $n_1 = \lambda + \mu$, $n_2 = \mu$. Remember from chapter 11 that $\frac{1}{3}(\lambda + 2\mu)$ is the greatest value of the infinitesimal operator Y which has the matrix $\frac{1}{3}\begin{pmatrix} 1 & 0 & 0 \\ 0 & 1 & 0 \\ 0 & 0 & -2 \end{pmatrix}$ in the original three-dimensional space and, for this value of Y, the number $\frac{1}{2}\lambda$ is the greatest value of the infinitesimal operator T_z, which has the matrix $\frac{1}{2}\begin{pmatrix} 1 & 0 & 0 \\ 0 & -1 & 0 \\ 0 & 0 & 0 \end{pmatrix}$. In the product Φ, the greatest Y is therefore obtained by putting as few particles into state ϕ_3 as possible. However, to produce a function with only a two-rowed Young diagram $[n_1 n_2]$ it is necessary only to occupy two different states. Thus all particles may be put into states ϕ_1 and ϕ_2 giving $\lambda + 2\mu = n_1 + n_2$. For such functions the maximum value of T_z is obtained by putting as many particles as possible into state ϕ_1 and for the diagram $[n_1 n_2]$ this is n_1, with n_2 particles in state ϕ_2, so that $\lambda = n_1 - n_2$. Combining this with the value for $\lambda + 2\mu$ gives $n_1 = \lambda + \mu$, $n_2 = \mu$ which demonstrates the equivalence

$$(\lambda\mu) \equiv \boxed{\lambda + \mu} \\ \boxed{\mu}$$

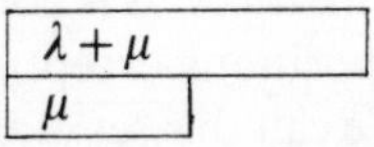

Thus the octet (11) corresponds to the Young diagram ⊟ and the decuplet (30) to ☐☐☐ . The rules given in section 11.6 for multiplying SU_3 representations are now special cases of equation (18.13). In particular, equation (11.11) follows from equation (17.29), taking account of the equivalences in SU_3.

For the group SU_4 which was used in discussing nuclear structure in chapter 12 we may similarly relate the labels $(P P' P'')$ to the partition. In this case a three-rowed partition $[n_1 n_2 n_3]$ is sufficient. Recall that P, P' and P'' relate to

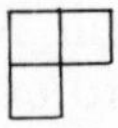

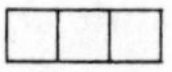

maximum values of S_z, T_z and Y_{zz} which have explicit matrices

$$S_z = \frac{1}{2}\begin{pmatrix} 1 & 0 & 0 & 0 \\ 0 & 1 & 0 & 0 \\ 0 & 0 & -1 & 0 \\ 0 & 0 & 0 & -1 \end{pmatrix}, \quad T_z = \frac{1}{2}\begin{pmatrix} 1 & 0 & 0 & 0 \\ 0 & -1 & 0 & 0 \\ 0 & 0 & 1 & 0 \\ 0 & 0 & 0 & -1 \end{pmatrix}$$

$$Y_{zz} = \frac{1}{2}\begin{pmatrix} 1 & 0 & 0 & 0 \\ 0 & -1 & 0 & 0 \\ 0 & 0 & -1 & 0 \\ 0 & 0 & 0 & 1 \end{pmatrix}$$

in the original four-dimensional space of $p^\uparrow, n^\uparrow, p^\downarrow, n^\downarrow$ in the notation of section 12.1. From these matrices we see that the combinations $S_z + T_z$, $S_z - Y_{zz}$ and $T_z - Y_{zz}$ are the counting operators for the differences between the number of particles in states ϕ_1, ϕ_2 and ϕ_3, respectively, and the number in state ϕ_4. Since, for a three-rowed partition, we do not need to put any particles into state ϕ_4, it follows that $P + P' = n_1$, $P - P'' = n_2$ and $P' - P'' = n_3$. Referring to the examples in equation (12.6) we have the relations

$$D^{(\frac{3}{2}\frac{3}{2}\frac{3}{2})} \equiv U^{[3]}, \quad D^{(\frac{3}{2}\frac{1}{2}\frac{1}{2})} \equiv U^{[21]}, \quad D^{(\frac{1}{2}\frac{1}{2}-\frac{1}{2})} = U^{[111]}$$

which agree with the assignments in equation (12.5).

18.8 The infinitesimal operators of U_N

Returning now to the group U_N we note that in the original N-dimensional space there are N^2 infinitesimal operators corresponding to the N^2 independent Hermitian $N \times N$ matrices. It is convenient to take N of these to be diagonal, with zero in all positions except for one diagonal matrix element which has the value $+1$. We call this set of operators H_i with $i = 1$ to N. The remaining $N(N-1)$ operators may be combined, as for the operators $T\pm$, $U\pm$, $V\pm$ of (11.2), to form $\frac{1}{2}N(N-1)$ pairs of raising and lowering operators E_{ij} and E_{ji} which are zero except for $+1$ in the off-diagonal positions ij and ji, respectively. They have the effect of shifting a particle from state ϕ_i to ϕ_j, so that $E_{ji}\phi_k = \delta_{ik}\phi_j$.

We now investigate the matrices of these operators in an arbitrary irreducible representation $U^{(\alpha)}$. In the first place, the operators H_i commute with each other and are the infinitesimal operators of the string $U_1 \times U_1 \times \ldots \times U_1$ of N subgroups U_1 referring to each dimension. Thus, using the results of section 18.3, we see that the matrices $H_i^{(\alpha)}$ of H_i in the representation $U^{(\alpha)}$ are diagonal in the basis chosen in section 18.4 with values

r_i in the notation used there. The set of numbers $(r_1 r_2 \ldots r_N)$ is called the 'weight' of the basis vector. For example the eight basis vectors given in equation (18.12) have the following weights, in the same order,

$$(210)(120)(201)(111)(021)(111)(102)(012) \qquad (18.21)$$

Notice that the weights do not provide a unique labelling system whereas the sequence of Young diagrams described in section 18.4 does. It is convenient to order the possible weights and we say that $(r'_1\, r'_2 \ldots r'_N)$ is greater than $(r_1, r_2 \ldots r_N)$ if $r'_1 > r_1$. For the case $r'_1 = r_1$ the ordering is done by the values of r'_2 and r_2 and so on. Thus the greatest weight in the set (18.21) is (210). It can be seen from the definition of r_1 that, in an arbitrary irreducible representation $U^{(\alpha)}$ where $\alpha \equiv [n_1\, n_2 \ldots]$, the greatest weight is the same as the partition $r_1 = n_1, r_2 = n_2, \ldots$, etc. Thus the greatest weight serves as a label for the representation $U^{(\alpha)}$, a result which is a generalisation of the use of the greatest $m(=j)$ to label the irreducible representations $D^{(j)}$ of $\mathscr{R}_3$.

The matrices of the raising and lowering operators may be obtained by a generalisation of the method of subsection 7.4.2 making use also of the chain of subgroups. We shall not give any details.

18.9 The complex conjugate representations of U_N and SU_N

To every representation $U^{(\alpha)}$ of U_N there is a corresponding complex conjugate representation $U^{(\alpha)*}$ obtained by taking the complex conjugates of all the matrix elements of $U^{(\alpha)}$. Thus in particular for the infinitesimal operators this implies that the set of weights in $U^{(\alpha)*}$ are the negatives of those in $U^{(\alpha)}$. Immediately we see that $U^{(\alpha)*}$ cannot coincide with any of the representations $U^{(\alpha)}$ defined in section 18.1 because they necessarily have positive weights.

One consequence of this is that the representations $U^{(\alpha)}$ described by all partitions α of any n are not complete. However it may be shown that the complete set of irreducible representations of U_N is given by $(\det U)^{-l}U^{(\alpha)}$, where l is any positive integer. From the arguments given in section 18.6 it is clear that the inclusion of the simple factor $(\det U)^{-l}$ produces another representation and if the weights of $U^{(\alpha)}$ are given by $(r_1, r_2, \ldots, r_N)$ then the weights of $(\det U)^{-l}U^{(\alpha)}$ are given by $(r_1 - l, r_2 - l, \ldots, r_N - l)$. To see this we need to write $U = 1 + ia_i H_i$ for an infinitesimal transformation by H_i, where a_i is the corresponding small parameter. Then $(\det U)^{-l} = (1 + ia_i)^{-l} \approx 1 - ila_i$ but, by definition of the infinitesimal operator $H_i^{(\alpha)}$ in the representation $U^{(\alpha)}$, we have $U^{(\alpha)} = 1 + ia_i H_i^{(\alpha)}$ so that for small a_i,

$$(\det U)^{-l}U^{(\alpha)} = 1 + ia_i(H_i^{(\alpha)} - l) \qquad (18.22)$$

which gives the desired result.

Making use of this larger set of irreducible representations we can now show the equivalence

$$\mathrm{U}^{(\alpha)*} \equiv (\det \mathrm{U})^{-n_1}\mathrm{U}^{(\beta)} \tag{18.23}$$

for the complex conjugate representation where, as usual, α denotes the partition $\alpha = [n_1 n_2 \ldots n_N]$ and $\beta = [n_1 - n_N, n_1 - n_{N-1}, \ldots, n_1 - n_2, 0]$. In terms of Young diagrams, β may be obtained quickly from α by removing the diagram α from the rectangular diagram with n_1 columns and N rows, as indicated in figure 18.1. (Remember that some of the n_i may be zero and the first row of β is the last row of the figure, etc.)

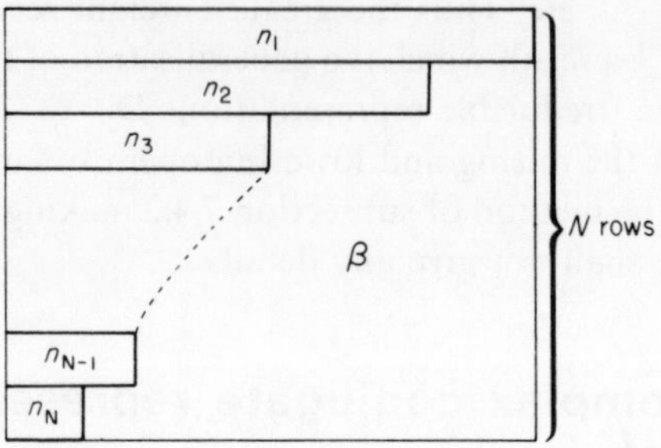

Figure 18.1

Before justifying this equivalence we take a few examples.

$N = 2$ $\mathrm{U}^{[1]*} \equiv (\det \mathrm{U})^{-1}\mathrm{U}^{[1]}$, $\mathrm{U}^{[2]*} \equiv (\det \mathrm{U})^{-2}\mathrm{U}^{[2]}$, $\mathrm{U}^{[11]*} \equiv (\det \mathrm{U})^{-1}\mathrm{U}$
$\mathrm{U}^{[21]*} \equiv (\det \mathrm{U})^{-2}\mathrm{U}^{[1]}$
$N = 3$ $\mathrm{U}^{[1]*} \equiv (\det \mathrm{U})^{-1}\mathrm{U}^{[11]}$, $\mathrm{U}^{[2]*} \equiv (\det \mathrm{U})^{-2}\mathrm{U}^{[22]}$, $\mathrm{U}^{[11]*} \equiv (\det \mathrm{U})^{-1}\mathrm{U}$
$\mathrm{U}^{[21]*} \equiv (\det \mathrm{U})^{-2}\mathrm{U}^{[21]}$

The expression (18.23) is not unique because from the arguments in section 18.6, the addition of a full column to β and the inclusion of an extra factor $(\det \mathrm{U})^{-1}$ causes no change. The equivalence (18.23) may be justified by showing that each side of the equation has the same set of weights. For example, the maximum weight on the left is $(-n_N, -n_{N-1}, \ldots, -n_2, -n_1)$ corresponding to the minimum weight in $\mathrm{U}^{(\alpha)}$, namely $(n_N, n_{N-1}, \ldots, n_2, n_1)$. Thus the maximum weight of $\mathrm{U}^{(\beta)}$ will be $(n_1 - n_N, n_1 - n_{N-1}, \ldots, n_1 - n_2, 0)$ as stated below (18.23). Finally, we use a result that the set of weights defines the representation.

For the group SU_N the property $\det \mathrm{U} = 1$ leads to the much simpler equivalence $\mathrm{U}^{(\alpha)*} \equiv \mathrm{U}^{(\beta)}$, where β is related to α as before. Remembering also the equivalences described in section 18.6 we see that for SU_2, $\mathrm{U}^{(n)*} \equiv U^{(n)}$ so that all representations of SU_2 and therefore $\mathcal{R}_3$ are self-conjugate. For SU_3, using the $(\lambda\mu)$ notation, we have the general result

$$(\lambda\mu)^* \equiv \boxed{\begin{array}{l}\lambda+\mu \\ \mu\end{array}}^{\,*} \equiv \boxed{\begin{array}{l}\lambda+\mu \\ \lambda\end{array}} \equiv (\mu\lambda)$$

so that in particular $(10)^* = (01)$, and (11) is self-conjugate.

18.10 The use of the group U_N in classifying many-particle wave functions

Because of the way in which we have introduced the group U_N, through products of the kind Φ in equation (18.2), it should come as no surprise that the group U_N has a role to play when constructing atomic wave functions for several valence electrons. Consider n valence electrons in single-particle states ϕ_{lm} with fixed l and the usual range of possible values of $m = l, (l-1), \ldots, -l$. From the arguments of section 18.1 it is clear that the product wave functions with permutation symmetry described by a partition $\alpha = [n_1 n_2 \ldots]$ of n will also transform according to the irreducible representation $U^{(\alpha)}$ of the group U_{2l+1} of unitary transformations among the $(2l+1)$ single-particle states ϕ_{lm}. Although the Pauli principle demands that the wave function be totally antisymmetric with respect to the permutation of particles, the partition α refers only to the orbital coordinates. Thus α itself need not be the partition $[11 \ldots 1]$ but it must be capable of yielding this partition when combined with the spin part of the wave function. This problem was discussed in subsection 8.6.4 and in section 17.10, where it was shown that the spin part must transform according to the adjoint representation $\tilde{\alpha}$ of the group $\mathscr{S}_n$ of particle permutations in the spin coordinates. (Remember that $\tilde{\alpha}$ is related to α by the interchange of rows and columns in the Young diagram.) However, the spin part of the wave function is itself a product of the kind (18.2) with $N = 2$ so that the spin part of the wave function transforms according to the representation $U^{(\tilde{\alpha})}$ of U_2. Thus the Young diagram $\tilde{\alpha}$ may have two rows at most and hence the orbital partition α has two columns at most and, of course, $2l+1$ rows at most.

We have seen in sections 18.6 and 18.7 the relation between representations of U_2, SU_2 and $\mathscr{R}_3$ so that $\tilde{\alpha}$ immediately determines the spin S of the system of n particles. If we write $\tilde{\alpha} = [\tilde{n}_1, \tilde{n}_2]$ then $S = \frac{1}{2}(\tilde{n}_1 - \tilde{n}_2)$. Thus the label α of the representation $U^{(\alpha)}$ of U_{2l+1} is already specified when n and S are given and in a sense this new label α is superfluous. A further problem is to deduce the possible values of total orbital angular momentum L which may be associated with given n and S. However, since L is the representation label for the group $\mathscr{R}_3$ we are asking how the representation $U^{(\alpha)}$ of U_{2l+1} reduces on restriction to its subgroup $\mathscr{R}_3$,

$$U^{(\alpha)} \dot{=} \sum_L m_L D^{(L)} \tag{18.24}$$

(The coefficient m_L should not be confused with the state label m.)

But this is a familiar group-theoretical problem which may be answered in various ways. In fact, a method for deducing the coefficients m_L was developed in subsection 8.6.4 using the group $\mathscr{S}_n$, without any reference to U_N. An alternative method is now available using the set of weights of $U^{(\alpha)}$. If we label our N single-particle states by $m = l, l-1, \ldots, -l$, in that order, then the total angular momentum projection operator L_z is given by $L_z = \sum_{m=-l}^{l} mH_m$ in terms of the diagonal operators H_i introduced in section 18.8. Thus the values of M are given simply in terms of the weights, $M = \sum_{m=-l}^{l} mr_m$. For example, in the eight-dimensional representation [21] of U_3, the set of weights (18.21) lead to the following set of M-values: 2, 1, 1, 0, -1, 0, -1, -2. From the known multiplet structure of $D^{(L)}$, i.e. $M = L, L-1, \ldots, -L$, we therefore conclude that for the group U_3, the reduction (18.24) becomes $U^{[21]} = D^{(2)} \dot{+} D^{(1)}$. This method is essentially using the group characters of U_N which we discuss in detail later in section 18.11; see problem 18.5 for another example. A third alternative method for deducing the coefficients m_L, which is less tedious for large l, is explained in problem 18.6.

As an example of this method of classifying states, let us return to the simple problem of three p-electrons ($l = 1$) discussed in subsection 8.6.4. Table 18.2 lists first the possible partitions α of $n = 3$, followed in column two by the adjoint partitions $\tilde{\alpha}$. Notice that the partition $\alpha = [3]$ must be excluded since the corresponding $\tilde{\alpha} = [111]$ has more than two rows. The value of S follows directly from $S = \frac{1}{2}(\tilde{n}_1 - \tilde{n}_2)$. The values of L for $\alpha = [21]$ were deduced above and the same technique shows that the one-dimensional representation [111] has the single weight (111), implying that $M = 0$ only and hence that $L = 0$.

Table 18.2

Orbital symmetry and U_3 label α	*Spin symmetry and U_2 label $\tilde{\alpha}$*	S	L
[111]	[3]	$\frac{3}{2}$	0
[21]	[21]	$\frac{1}{2}$	2, 1

The role of the group U_N in atomic multiplets discussed above may be extended immediately to the nuclear supermultiplets which were introduced in chapter 12 using also the interpretation of the SU_4 labels $(PP'P'')$ which was described in section 18.8. We give no details. As remarked in section 12.1 the spin dependence of the nuclear force is sufficiently strong that the SU_4 symmetry is strongly broken and the jj-coupling approximation makes a better first approximation (see subsection 8.6.1 for a mention of jj-coupling in atoms). In this case each particle carries a definite total angular momentum j, which includes both spin and orbital contributions, and the usual isospin of $\frac{1}{2}$. When

n valence nucleons are considered it is clear that the group U_{2j+1} takes the place of U_{2l+1}. The reduction from U_{2j+1} to $\mathscr{R}_3$ gives the values of J as in equation (18.24). The association between J and isospin T is analogous to the association between L and S in the atomic case; for a given representation $U^{(\alpha)}$ of U_{2j+1} the isospin part of the wave function must have adjoint symmetry $\tilde{\alpha}$ giving $T = \frac{1}{2}(\tilde{n}_1 - \tilde{n}_2)$.

18.10.1 The use of subgroups of U_N

The introduction of the groups U_{2l+1} and U_{2j+1} into these problems of atomic and nuclear structure is in a sense disappointing because they carry no new physical information. The representation labels α are, as we have seen, equivalent to the spin, supermultiplet or isospin labels, depending on the system. However, they may be used as a first step in defining a new group which, depending on the nature of the interaction between particles, may carry useful physical information. To illustrate this idea, consider three electrons in the atomic f-shell, i.e. $l = 3$. In the reduction (18.24) corresponding to $\alpha = [21]$ the non-zero values of m_L are given by $m_1 = m_6 = m_7 = m_8 = 1$, $m_2 = m_3 = m_4 = m_5 = 2$. Unlike the case shown in table 18.2 there are now L-values for which $m_L > 1$, so that the quantum numbers S, L, M_S and M_L are no longer sufficient to define the possible states. Of course physically this problem is resolved in perturbation theory by diagonalising the Coulomb interaction numerically. A 2×2 matrix occurs for $L = 2$, 3, 4 and 5. From the group-theoretical point of view there is a possibility of finding a labelling system for these pairs of states if one can find—see Racah (1965) in the bibliography—a new group $\mathscr{G}$ which is a subgroup of U_{2l+1} and which contains $\mathscr{R}_3$ as a subgroup. One may then carry out the restriction from U_7 to $\mathscr{R}_3$ in two steps $U_7 \to \mathscr{G} \to \mathscr{R}_3$. In this way the basis vectors (wave functions) would carry also a representation label for the group $\mathscr{G}$. In some, but not necessarily all, cases the pairs of states referred to above will carry different labels and therefore be distinguished by their properties under this intermediate group $\mathscr{G}$. The introduction of such a group $\mathscr{G}$ may be useful on two levels. It may simply be used to provide a convenient, systematic labelling scheme within which to set up the matrix of the interaction. It may also be significant physically, if the interaction has approximate invariance with respect to $\mathscr{G}$. In this case the use of a basis labelled by irreducible representations of $\mathscr{G}$ will approximately diagonalise the energy matrix and the labels may be associated with physical states.

To find the intermediate group $\mathscr{G}$ we must impose restrictions on the unitary transformations without excluding any of the $\mathscr{R}_3$ transformations. A systematic way of doing this is first to write down the commutation relations of the infinitesimal operators of U_{2l+1}. One then searches for a subset of the operators of U_{2l+1} which contains the operators of $\mathscr{R}_3$ and which is closed under commutation. By this we mean that the commutator of any pair in the subset gives a linear combination of operators in the subset. From the general definitions of section 7.2 and from equation (7.7) in particular, such a subset defines a group which is necessarily a subgroup of U_{2l+1} and which contains $\mathscr{R}_3$ as a subgroup. By comparing the structure constants obtained for $\mathscr{G}$ in this way with those of all known groups one may identify $\mathscr{G}$. This technique shows that, for arbitrary l, the group $\mathscr{R}_{2l+1}$ may be chosen for $\mathscr{G}$ but that, for the small l of interest in physical problems, very few other possibilities exist. The more direct way to introduce $\mathscr{R}_{2l+1}$ is to restrict the unitary transformations U by the condition that the two-particle function

$$\Phi = \sum_i \phi_i(1)\,\phi_i(2) \tag{18.25}$$

in the notation of section 18.1, should be invariant. This implies that

$$\Phi = \mathrm{T(U)}\Phi = \sum_{i,j,k} U_{ji}\,U_{ki}\,\phi_j(1)\,\phi_k(2)$$

so that

$$\sum_i U_{ji}\,U_{ki} = \delta_{jk}$$

In other words, $U_{ki} = (\mathrm{U}^{-1})_{ik}$ but since U is unitary this implies that U is a real orthogonal matrix, which defines the group $\mathscr{R}_{2l+1}$. To show that the physical $\mathscr{R}_3$ is contained in this group $\mathscr{R}_{2l+1}$ we must find a basis ϕ_i for the $(2l+1)$ states with angular momentum l such that the function Φ defined in equation (18.25) is invariant under rotations. One sees immediately that the usual m-basis ψ_m would not suffice. However if we define a new basis

$$\phi_m^+ = [\psi_m + (-1)^m \psi_{-m}]/2^{\frac{1}{2}}$$
$$\phi_m^- = i[\psi_m - (-1)^m \psi_{-m}]/2^{\frac{1}{2}} \text{ with } \phi_0 = \psi_0$$

then we have

$$\begin{aligned}\Phi &= \sum_{m>0} [\phi_m^+(1)\,\phi_m^+(2) + \phi_m^-(1)\,\phi_m^-(2) + \phi_0(1)\,\phi_0(2)] \\ &= \sum_{m>0} (-1)^m [\psi_m(1)\,\psi_{-m}(2) + \psi_{-m}(1)\,\psi_m(2)] + \psi_0(1)\,\psi_0(2) \\ &= \sum_m (-1)^m \psi_m(1)\,\psi_{-m}(2)\end{aligned} \tag{18.26}$$

This expression is recognised as the S-state ($L = 0$) of the two particles with the usual sign conventions for the ψ_m (see subsection A.4.2), and is therefore invariant under rotations.

We shall not go into any detail here concerning the irreducible representations of $\mathscr{R}_{2l+1}$ except to remark that they are denoted by a set of l integers

$(r_1 r_2 \ldots r_l)$ and we give in table 18.3 a few examples of the reductions for the case $l = 3$. It is seen that the new $\mathscr{R}_7$ label has succeeded in distinguishing the two $L = 3$ states for $n = 3$ and $S = \frac{1}{2}$ but has failed to do so for the pairs of states with $L = 2$, 4 and 5.

Table 18.3

n	U_7	$\mathscr{R}_7$	$\mathscr{R}_3$ (L)
1	[1]	(100)	3
2	[2]	(000)	0
		(200)	2, 4, 6
	[11]	(110)	1, 3, 5
3	[21]	(100)	3
		(210)	1, 2, 2, 3, 4, 4, 5, 5, 6, 7, 8
	[111]	(111)	0, 2, 3, 4, 6

In the *jj*-coupling problem where the group U_{2j+1} is encountered, one can carry out a similar search (Racah, 1965) for a group $\mathscr{G}$ which contains $\mathscr{R}_3$ and is contained in U_{2j+1}. The result of such a search leads to what is known as the 'symplectic group' Sp_{2j+1}. One might have expected to find $\mathscr{R}_{2j+1}$ by the same arguments as before but this is not the case. The last step in arriving at equation (18.26) assumed that $(-1)^m = (-1)^{-m}$ which is only true for integer m and hence for integer l. The group Sp_{2j+1} may be identified by its infinitesimal operators, as outlined earlier, but the most direct way to visualise the group is to note that there is still only one invariant two-particle state in *jj*-coupling, namely the state with $J = 0$, which is given as in equation (18.26) by

$$\Phi = \sum_{m=-j}^{j} (-1)^{j-m} \psi_m(1) \psi_{-m}(2)$$

$$= \sum_{m>0} (-1)^{j-m} [\psi_m(1) \psi_{-m}(2) - \psi_{-m}(1) \psi_m(2)] \quad (18.27)$$

Notice that Φ is now antisymmetric under particle permutation so that it cannot be written in the form (18.25) by any choice of basis. The set of matrices which leaves this state Φ invariant may then be taken as the definition of the symplectic group in $(2j+1)$ dimensions. Its irreducible representations are described by a set of $(j+\frac{1}{2})$ integers, very like the group $\mathscr{R}_{2l+1}$. Again we give no details except to quote some examples for the case $j = \frac{5}{2}$ in table 18.4.

The word 'seniority' is sometimes used to describe the representations of $\mathscr{R}_{2l+1}$ or Sp_{2j+1}. One says that a state has seniority v if the smallest number of particles for which that representation occurs is $n = v$. Thus for example the two $L = 3$ states with $S = \frac{1}{2}$ (i.e. [21]) for three particles shown in table 18.3 will have seniorities $v = 1$ and 3, respectively, for (100) and (210). In table 18.4

Table 18.4

n	U_6	Sp_6	$\mathscr{R}_3(J)$
1	[1]	(100)	$\frac{5}{2}$
2	[2]	(200)	1, 3, 5
	[11]	(000)	0
		(110)	2, 4
3	[21]	(100)	$\frac{5}{2}$
		(210)	$\frac{1}{2}, \frac{3}{2}, \frac{5}{2}, (\frac{7}{2})^2, \frac{9}{2}, \frac{11}{2}, \frac{13}{2}$
	[111]	(100)	$\frac{5}{2}$
		(111)	$\frac{3}{2}, \frac{9}{2}$

one also sees that, for odd n and each U_6 symmetry, there is a state with $v = 1$ which necessarily has the same spin $J = \frac{5}{2}$ as a single particle. For even n there is always a state with seniority $v = 0$ and hence $J = 0$.

From the physical point of view, the group $\mathscr{R}_{2l+1}$ has significance in describing the levels of the configuration l^n if the perturbing interaction between pairs of valence electrons exhibits degeneracies appropriate to the group. In other words, for the case of $l = 3$ illustrated in table 18.3 we would need to find the $L = 2, 4$ and 6 states for $n = 2$ at about the same energy and the states with $L = 1, 3$ and 5 lying together at some other energy. In practice with the Coulomb forces this does not happen since the states with high L are depressed, see subsection 8.6.5. Thus, in atoms, the group $\mathscr{R}_{2l+1}$ is useful only as a means of setting up a systematic framework in which to diagonalise the perturbation.

In nuclei, however, the strong spin – orbit force leads to *jj*-coupling and the attractive force between valence nucleons then depresses the state with low J. This is the reverse of the atomic situation since the force between electrons is repulsive. In fact, the short-range attractive nuclear force not only depresses the $J = 0$ state but also leaves the $J = 2$ and 4 states, shown in table 18.4 with labels [11] (10), close together in energy. Hence in nuclei, the group Sp_{2j+1} has real physical significance. As a result, the ground states of nuclei would be expected to be described by irreducible representations of Sp_{2j+1}. Because in the two-particle system the invariant (000) lies lowest in energy one might expect the ground state for general n to contain as many such pairs as possible, consistent with the Pauli principle. This may be verified in a more detailed model which shows that for odd n the ground state has seniority $v = 1$, the representation (100), while, for even numbers of neutrons and protons separately, the ground state has $v = 0$ with representation (000). These conclusions agree with, and hence provide justification for, the simple single-particle nuclear shell-model which assumes that all pairs of neutrons and protons couple to $J = 0$ leaving the spin of the nucleus equal to that of the last odd nucleon. (See also Section 19.2.)

The groups U_{2l+1} and U_{2j+1} are not symmetry groups of the Hamiltonian in the way that the group $\mathscr{R}_3$ was, in chapter 7. The operators of U_{2l+1} are defined only within the space of the configurations l^n. Even within this space the operators of U_{2l+1} do not commute with the residual interaction between electrons but in a very crude approximation they might be assumed to do so. If one were to assume that, in the states of the two-particle configuration l^2, all symmetric states (i.e. even L and $S = 0$) had the same energy and all antisymmetric states (i.e. odd L and $S = 1$) had another common value for their energy then it would follow that the Hamiltonian must be invariant under U_{2l+1}. This provides some physical justification for the group although in practice the splitting of the energies for different L is large. The same remarks apply to the nuclear structure problems mentioned above and in section 12.1.

18.11 Characters

In the next two sections of this chapter we return to the mathematical properties of the group U_N, calculating the characters of the irreducible representations and describing the integration over the group volume. Little practical use is made of the results but they are relevant to some of the proofs we have omitted and they provide another link with our treatment of the group $\mathscr{R}_3$ in chapter 7.

The first step in deducing the character is to identify the classes of U_N, since the character of a representation is a class property, see section 4.9. Given any unitary matrix U it is possible to bring it to diagonal form W by a unitary transformation V: $\mathrm{VUV}^{-1} = \mathrm{W}$. Hence U is in the same class as the diagonal matrix W and we need only consider the characters for the diagonal matrices. Since U is also unitary the diagonal matrix elements have the form $\exp(-i\theta)$ so that only n real parameters $\theta_1, \theta_2, \ldots, \theta_n$ lying between 0 and 2π are needed to define the diagonal unitary matrix. (For the group SU_N there is the additional constraint $\theta_1 + \theta_2 + \ldots + \theta_N = 0$.) Hence, although U_N is a group with n^2 parameters the character depends on only n of them. This feature was present in the group $\mathscr{R}_3$ discussed in chapter 7, where the character was a function of the rotation angle only and was independent of the other two parameters defining the axis of rotation.

Consider now the representation $\mathrm{U}^{(\alpha)}$. For the diagonal group element U the matrix of $\mathrm{U}^{(\alpha)}$ in the basis described in section 18.4 will also be diagonal and the matrix element corresponding to a basis vector with weight $(r_1 r_2 \ldots r_n)$ will be simply

$$\exp\left(-i \sum_{j=1}^{N} r_j \theta_j\right)$$

Thus the character of $\mathrm{U}^{(\alpha)}$ is given by

$$\chi^{(\alpha)} = \sum_{r_1 r_2 \ldots r_N} \exp\left(-i \sum_{j=1}^{N} r_j \theta_j\right) \tag{18.28}$$

where the sum runs over all the weights belonging to the representation α, as described in section 18.4. With the help of some rather elaborate algebra this sum may be given in closed form, as the quotient of two determinants,

$$\chi^{(\alpha)} = \begin{vmatrix} \varepsilon_1^{n_1+N-1} & \varepsilon_1^{n_2+N-2} & \cdots & \varepsilon_1^{n_N} \\ \varepsilon_2^{n_1+N-1} & \varepsilon_2^{n_2+N-2} & \cdots & \varepsilon_2^{n_N} \\ \vdots & & & \vdots \\ \varepsilon_N^{n_1+N-1} & \cdot & \cdots & \varepsilon_N^{n_N} \end{vmatrix} \div \begin{vmatrix} \varepsilon_1^{N-1} & \varepsilon_1^{N-2} & \cdots & 1 \\ \varepsilon_2^{N-1} & \varepsilon_2^{N-2} & \cdots & 1 \\ \vdots & & & \vdots \\ \varepsilon_N^{N-1} & \cdot & \cdots & 1 \end{vmatrix} \tag{18.29}$$

where $\varepsilon_j = \exp(-i\theta_j)$.

As a simple illustration of this general result let us take $N = 2$ and the partition $\alpha = [n]$ with only one row. The possible weights are simply $(n, 0)$, $(n-1, 1), \ldots, (0, n)$ so that from equation (18.28)

$$\begin{aligned}\chi^{(n)} &= \exp(-in\theta_1) + \exp[-i(n-1)\theta_1 - i\theta_2] + \ldots + \exp(-in\theta_2) \\ &= \exp[-\tfrac{1}{2}in(\theta_1+\theta_2)] \sin\{\tfrac{1}{2}(n+1)(\theta_1-\theta_2)\}/\sin\tfrac{1}{2}(\theta_1-\theta_2)\end{aligned}$$

a result which also follows from equation (18.29). On restricting to the group SU_2, putting $\theta_1 + \theta_2 = 0$, this reduces to the familiar expression (7.42) with $n = 2j$.

18.12 Group integration and orthogonality

From the general theory of chapter 4 the characters of irreducible representations of U_N should have orthogonality relations when integrated over the group parameters. Since the character is a class function it is necessary to integrate only over the parameters θ_i, which distinguish the classes. Thus from equation (4.25) and the remarks in section 7.1 we expect a relation of the kind

$$\int \chi^{(\alpha)*}(\boldsymbol{\theta})\, \chi^{(\beta)}(\boldsymbol{\theta})\, \rho(\boldsymbol{\theta})\, \mathrm{d}\boldsymbol{\theta} = \delta_{\alpha\beta} V \tag{18.30}$$

where $\boldsymbol{\theta}$ is an abbreviation for the set $\theta_1, \theta_2 \ldots \theta_N$ and similarly $\mathrm{d}\boldsymbol{\theta} \equiv \mathrm{d}\theta_1 \mathrm{d}\theta_2 \ldots \mathrm{d}\theta_N$, the range of integration being from 0 to 2π for each angle θ_i. The volume V is defined by $V = \int \rho(\boldsymbol{\theta})\mathrm{d}\boldsymbol{\theta}$ and it remains to determine the appropriate weight factor $\rho(\boldsymbol{\theta})$ using the results of appendix 4.3. Before giving the derivation we quote the result, $\rho(\boldsymbol{\theta}) = |\Delta|^2$, where Δ is the denominator in equation (18.29).

To obtain this result we start from equation (A.4.15), the object being to calculate the Jacobian $(\partial \boldsymbol{c}/\partial \boldsymbol{a})_{\boldsymbol{a}=0}$, where $\boldsymbol{a}$ and $\boldsymbol{c}$ refer to the N^2 parameters of the unitary transformations and $\mathrm{U}(\boldsymbol{c}) = \mathrm{U}(\boldsymbol{a})\,\mathrm{U}(\boldsymbol{b})$. For an arbitrary unitary transformation U we take N of the N^2 parameters to be the angles θ_i obtained as in section 18.11 when U is diagonalised and the remaining $N^2 - N$ parameters to define the matrix which brings U to diagonal form. Without loss of generality we may take U($\boldsymbol{b}$) to be diagonal (this defines the basis) with matrix elements $U_{ii}(\boldsymbol{b}) = \varepsilon_i$ in the notation of the previous section. Since we are only interested in the limit $\boldsymbol{a} \to 0$ we need consider only small $\boldsymbol{a}$ for which the arbitrary U($\boldsymbol{a}$) differs from the identity by a skew-Hermitian matrix

$$\mathrm{U}(\boldsymbol{a}) = \begin{pmatrix} 1 - ia_{11} & a_{12} - ia_{21} & \dots \\ -a_{12} + ia_{21} & 1 - ia_{22} & \\ \vdots & & \end{pmatrix}$$

where the N^2 parameters a_{ij} are real and independent. By ordinary matrix multiplication, U($\boldsymbol{c}$) is then given by

$$\mathrm{U}(\boldsymbol{c}) = \begin{pmatrix} (1 - ia_{11})\varepsilon_1 & (a_{12} - ia_{21})\varepsilon_2 & \dots \\ (-a_{12} + ia_{21})\varepsilon_1 & (1 - ia_{22})\varepsilon_2 & \\ \vdots & & \end{pmatrix}$$

Since U($\boldsymbol{c}$) is nearly diagonal, it is easily written in the form $\mathrm{U} = \mathrm{V}^{-1}\mathrm{W}\mathrm{V}$, where W is diagonal, and we find

$$\mathrm{V}(\boldsymbol{c}) = \begin{pmatrix} 1 & \left(\dfrac{a_{12} + ia_{21}}{\varepsilon_1/\varepsilon_2 - 1}\right) & \dots \\ \left(\dfrac{-a_{12} + ia_{21}}{\varepsilon_2/\varepsilon_1 - 1}\right) & 1 & \\ \vdots & & \end{pmatrix},$$

$$\mathrm{W}(\boldsymbol{c}) = \begin{pmatrix} (1 - ia_{11})\varepsilon_1 & 0 & \dots \\ 0 & (1 - ia_{22})\varepsilon_2 & \\ \vdots & & \end{pmatrix}$$

ignoring second-order terms in the a_{ij}. The matrix V is not uniquely determined by the equation $\mathrm{U} = \mathrm{V}^{-1}\mathrm{W}\mathrm{V}$ since it may be multiplied by any diagonal matrix and we have made use of this freedom by taking the diagonal matrix elements to be $+1$. If we now take as the N^2 parameters for U($\boldsymbol{c}$) the N angles θ'_i given by W($\boldsymbol{c}$), i.e. $\theta'_i = \theta_i + a_{ii}$ and the real and imaginary parts of the off-diagonal matrix elements of V($\boldsymbol{c}$), namely

$$c_{12} = a_{12}\,\mathscr{R}\{(\varepsilon_1/\varepsilon_2 - 1)^{-1}\} - a_{21}\,\mathscr{I}\{(\varepsilon_1/\varepsilon_2 - 1)^{-1}\}$$
$$c_{21} = a_{12}\,\mathscr{I}\{(\varepsilon_1/\varepsilon_2 - 1)^{-1}\} + a_{21}\,\mathscr{R}\{(\varepsilon_1/\varepsilon_2 - 1)^{-1}\}$$

then the Jacobian $(\partial \boldsymbol{c}/\partial \boldsymbol{a})$ is easily calculated. Since $\partial\theta'_i/\partial a_{jk} = \delta_{ij}\delta_{jk}$ the first

N rows and columns of the determinant of $(\partial \boldsymbol{c}/\partial \boldsymbol{a})$ corresponding to the θ_i' and a_{ii} is just the unit matrix. The remaining part of the determinant is a product of $\frac{1}{2}N(N-1)$ factors of the type

$$\begin{vmatrix} \partial c_{12}/\partial a_{12} & \partial c_{12}/\partial a_{21} \\ \partial c_{21}/\partial a_{12} & \partial c_{21}/\partial a_{21} \end{vmatrix} = |\varepsilon_1 - \varepsilon_2|^{-2}$$

Thus, finally, the weight factor is given by

$$\rho(\boldsymbol{\theta}) = \left(\frac{\partial \boldsymbol{c}}{\partial \boldsymbol{a}}\right)^{-1}_{\boldsymbol{a}=0}$$

$$= |\prod_{i<j}^{N} (\varepsilon_i - \varepsilon_j)|^2 = |\Delta|^2$$

since the product is the same as the determinant in the denominator of equation (18.29).

The orthogonality relation (18.30) may now be verified for the characters $\chi^{(\alpha)}$ given in equation (18.29) and this also leads to proofs of irreducibility and completeness using a technique similar to that in section 4.12. Notice that the weight factor $\rho(\boldsymbol{\theta})$ exactly cancels with the denominators of χ^* and χ in the integrand of (18.30).

18.13 The groups SU_2 and $\mathscr{R}_3$

We now consider in more detail the special case of SU_2 which was first introduced in section 10.1 to describe isospin. In that section we argued briefly that SU_2 had three infinitesimal operators with the same commutation relations as those of $\mathscr{R}_3$ and hence we were able to take over all the representation theory developed in chapter 7 for $\mathscr{R}_3$. Here we describe more carefully the relation between the parameters of the SU_2 matrices and the rotation parameters. The fact that this relation is two-to-one rather than one-to-one, a homomorphism rather than an isomorphism, throws light on the double-valued representations of $\mathscr{R}_3$. The use of SU_2 also suggests a new (Cayley – Klein) set of parameters to describe rotations and these are most convenient in deducing the parameters of a product of two rotations.

18.13.1 The parameters of SU_2

Let us denote an orthonormal pair of basis vectors in a two-dimensional space by $\boldsymbol{e}_1$ and $\boldsymbol{e}_2$, although we stress that they do *not* refer to the x- and y-axes in physical space. A typical group element of U_2 is thus given by a 2×2 unitary matrix in this basis and it is soon verified that the group postulates are satisfied. For example, the product of two unitary matrices is itself unitary. An arbitrary 2×2 matrix with complex elements contains 8 parameters but the unitary condition imposes four real equations to be satisfied leaving 4 parameters to describe the general group element of U_2. It is convenient to write the general element as

$$\mathrm{U} = \exp(i\phi)\begin{pmatrix} \alpha & \beta \\ \gamma & \delta \end{pmatrix} \tag{18.31}$$

with the parameters satisfying $\alpha\delta - \beta\gamma = 1$. From the unitary condition $\mathrm{UU}^{\dagger} = 1$ it is clear that $|\det \mathrm{U}| = 1$ and the form (18.31) exhibits U as the product of a matrix with determinant $= +1$ and a phase factor. From the unitary condition we have the relations $\alpha\alpha^* + \beta\beta^* = 1$, $\gamma\gamma^* + \delta\delta^* = 1$, $\alpha\gamma^* + \beta\delta^* = 0$, $\gamma\alpha^* + \delta\beta^* = 0$, the last two of which may be regarded either as a single complex equation or two real equations. Taking these equations together with the condition $\alpha\delta - \beta\gamma = 1$ leads to the conclusion $\delta = \alpha^*$, $\gamma = -\beta^*$ so that

$$\mathrm{U} = \exp(i\phi)\begin{pmatrix} \alpha & \beta \\ -\beta^* & \alpha^* \end{pmatrix}$$

with the one remaining condition $\alpha\alpha^* + \beta\beta^* = 1$.

The set of matrices U with $\phi = 0$ and hence with determinant $= +1$ from a subgroup of U_2 which is called the 'unimodular' or 'special unitary' group and is denoted by SU_2. In fact we may write $U_2 = U_1 \times SU_2$ as the product of SU_2 with the Abelian, one-parameter group U_1 which multiplies by the phase factor $\exp(i\phi)$ and is seen to be isomorphic with $\mathscr{R}_2$. It will therefore be sufficient to study the group SU_2 which has only three parameters. Henceforth we shall consider only SU_2 with elements

$$\mathrm{U} = \begin{pmatrix} \alpha & \beta \\ -\beta^* & \alpha^* \end{pmatrix} \tag{18.32}$$

and the condition $\alpha\alpha^* + \beta\beta^* = 1$. We now introduce three convenient real parameters in place of the two complex numbers α, β with one real condition. The notation that we use may seem rather strange but it is chosen to simplify the discussion in subsection 18.13.2 of the connection between SU_2 and $\mathscr{R}_3$. Without loss of generality we may write

$$\alpha = \cos\tfrac{1}{2}a - ik_z \sin\tfrac{1}{2}a, \qquad \beta = -(k_y + ik_x)\sin\tfrac{1}{2}a \tag{18.33}$$

with $\boldsymbol{k} = (k_x, k_y, k_z)$ any unit vector and $0 \leqq a \leqq 2\pi$, see problem 18.8. The three real parameters are a and the two angles required to fix the unit vector $\boldsymbol{k}$. As a further simplification we define $a_x = ak_x$, $a_y = ak_y$ and $a_z = ak_z$ and then the matrix U is determined by the three real parameters a_q which lie in the range $\sum_q a_q^2 \leqq 4\pi^2$, i.e. the vector $\boldsymbol{a} = (a_x, a_y, a_z)$ lies inside a sphere of radius 2π.

18.13.2 Infinitesimal operators and irreducible representations of SU_2

To find the infinitesimal operators corresponding to the three parameters a_q we must study U close to the unit operator, in other words for small a. Then we have $\alpha = 1 - \frac{1}{2}iak_z = 1 - \frac{1}{2}ia_z$ and $\beta = -\frac{1}{2}a_y - \frac{1}{2}ia_x$ giving

$$\mathrm{U} = 1 - \tfrac{1}{2}a_x\begin{pmatrix} 0 & i \\ i & 0 \end{pmatrix} - \tfrac{1}{2}a_y\begin{pmatrix} 0 & 1 \\ -1 & 0 \end{pmatrix} - \tfrac{1}{2}a_z\begin{pmatrix} i & 0 \\ 0 & -i \end{pmatrix}$$

so that the three infinitesimal operators are simply $-is_q$ in the notation of equation (8.15) where s_q are the familiar spin matrices for $s = \frac{1}{2}$.

We therefore conclude that the commutation relations of the infinitesimal operators of SU_2 are the same as those for the group $\mathscr{R}_3$ since the spin matrices are infinitesimal operators of $\mathscr{R}_3$ in the representation $\mathrm{D}^{(\frac{1}{2})}$. Because the irreducible representations of $\mathscr{R}_3$ were deduced in section 7.4 from these commutation relations, it follows that the irreducible representations of SU_2 will be the same as those of $\mathscr{R}_3$. However we shall see in subsection 18.13.3 that whereas the half-integer representations of $\mathscr{R}_3$ were double-valued they will be single-valued representations of SU_2. Indeed, the representation $\mathrm{D}^{(\frac{1}{2})}$ is identical with the group elements themselves, the 2×2 matrices (18.32).

18.13.3 Connection between the groups $\mathscr{R}_3$ and SU_2

The fact that two groups like $\mathscr{R}_3$ and SU_2 have the same commutation relations for their infinitesimal operators, the same set of structure constants in the language of section 7.2, does not mean that the two groups are necessarily isomorphic (one-to-one correspondence between group elements). To study this point it is necessary to go beyond the infinitesimal operations to the group elements for finite values of the parameters. Consider first the group $\mathscr{R}_3$. For rotations about the z-axis we have seen in section 7.3 and equation (7.6) that the finite rotation is related to the infinitesimal operator by an exponential $\mathrm{R}_z(a) = \exp(a\mathrm{X}_z)$. In this relation there is nothing special about the z-axis so that for a rotation $\mathrm{R}_{\boldsymbol{k}}(a)$ about an arbitrary axis $\boldsymbol{k}$ we may also write

$$\mathrm{R}_{\boldsymbol{k}}(a) = \exp\left(\sum_q a_q \mathrm{X}_q\right) = \exp(a\boldsymbol{k}.\boldsymbol{X}) \qquad (18.34)$$

where in the notation of equation (7.22), $a_q = ak_q$ with k_q the component of $\boldsymbol{k}$ and we have introduced the vector operator $\mathbf{X} = (\mathrm{X}_x, \mathrm{X}_y, \mathrm{X}_z)$. In making this apparent jump from the group $\mathscr{R}_2$ to $\mathscr{R}_3$ we are saying only that an arbitrary rotation is a member of the one-parameter subgroup $\mathscr{R}_2$ of rotations about the axis $\boldsymbol{k}$ and is hence generated from the appropriate small change $\sum_q a_q \mathrm{X}_q$ in the same way that the rotation about the z-axis was generated from $a\mathrm{X}_z$ in section 7.2.

The operator expression (18.34) may be applied in any representation and for the two-dimensional representation $D^{(\frac{1}{2})}$ it gives a very simple explicit way of deducing the matrices $D^{(\frac{1}{2})}(a_x, a_y, a_z)$ for a finite rotation from the matrices (8.15) already deduced for the infinitesimal operators. Remembering the difference $X_q = -iJ_q$ between the infinitesimal operators X_q and the angular momentum operators J_q, equation (8.15) gives

$$X_x = -\tfrac{1}{2}i\begin{pmatrix} 0 & 1 \\ 1 & 0 \end{pmatrix}, \quad X_y = \tfrac{1}{2}\begin{pmatrix} 0 & -1 \\ 1 & 0 \end{pmatrix}, \quad X_z = -\tfrac{1}{2}i\begin{pmatrix} 1 & 0 \\ 0 & -1 \end{pmatrix} \quad (18.35)$$

from which we see that $X_q^2 = -\frac{1}{4}$ and $X_pX_q + X_qX_p = 0$ for $p \neq q$. Thus the scalar product in the exponent of equation (18.34) has the property

$$(\boldsymbol{k}.\mathbf{X})^2 = \sum_{q,p} k_q X_q k_p X_p = -\tfrac{1}{4}\sum_q k_q^2 = -\tfrac{1}{4}$$

using the normalisation of the vector $\boldsymbol{k}$. Thus the representation matrix for $j = \frac{1}{2}$ is

$$\begin{aligned} D^{(\frac{1}{2})}(\boldsymbol{k}, a) &= \exp(a\boldsymbol{k}.\mathbf{X}) \\ &= 1 + a(\boldsymbol{k}.\mathbf{X}) + \tfrac{1}{2}a^2(\boldsymbol{k}.\mathbf{X})^2 + \tfrac{1}{6}a^3(\boldsymbol{k}.\mathbf{X})^3 + \tfrac{1}{24}a^4(\boldsymbol{k}.\mathbf{X})^4 + \ldots \\ &= \{1 - \tfrac{1}{2}(a^2/4) + \tfrac{1}{24}(a^4/16) + \ldots\} + (\boldsymbol{k}.\mathbf{X})\{a - \tfrac{1}{6}(a^3/4) + \ldots\} \\ &= \cos\tfrac{1}{2}a + 2(\boldsymbol{k}.\mathbf{X})\sin\tfrac{1}{2}a \qquad (18.36) \end{aligned}$$

and using the matrices (18.35) for the X_q this becomes

$$D^{(\frac{1}{2})}(\boldsymbol{k}, a) = \begin{pmatrix} \cos\frac{1}{2}a - ik_z\sin\frac{1}{2}a & (-k_y - ik_x)\sin\frac{1}{2}a \\ (k_y - ik_x)\sin\frac{1}{2}a & \cos\frac{1}{2}a + ik_z\sin\frac{1}{2}a \end{pmatrix} \quad (18.37)$$

This 2×2 matrix is identical with (18.32)—if we identify the rotation parameters $\boldsymbol{k}$ and a with the SU_2 parameters $\boldsymbol{k}$ and a introduced in equation (18.33). The correspondence is not one-to-one however. To produce all unitary matrices the unit vector $\boldsymbol{k}$ may point in any direction and the angle $\frac{1}{2}a$ must cover the interval $0 \leqq \frac{1}{2}a \leqq \pi$ (Notice that it is not necessary to allow $\frac{1}{2}a$ to lie between π and 2π, i.e. for a to lie between 2π and 4π, since this merely changes the sign of $\sin\frac{1}{2}a$ which is the same as a change in sign of the vector $\boldsymbol{k}$.) However to produce all rotations the angle a need only cover the interval $0 \leqq a \leqq \pi$ since $R_{\boldsymbol{k}}(\pi + a) = R_{-\boldsymbol{k}}(\pi - a)$. Thus two unitary transformations with their a-values differing by π will correspond to the same rotation. The groups $\mathcal{R}_3$ and SU_2 are said to be homomorphic. The correspondence may be made one-to-one only if the group $\mathcal{R}_3$ is extended, abstractly, to include rotations through angles from 0 to 4π. The name 'universal covering group' is used to describe such an extension.

We note that the double group which was introduced in section 7.6 with elements $R_{\boldsymbol{k}}(a)$ and $\bar{E}R_{\boldsymbol{k}}(a)$ where $0 \leqq a \leqq \pi$ is isomorphic with the group SU_2 through the correspondence

$$R_{\boldsymbol{k}}(a) \leftrightarrow D^{(\frac{1}{2})}(\boldsymbol{k}, a)$$
$$\bar{E}R_{-\boldsymbol{k}}(a) \leftrightarrow D^{(\frac{1}{2})}(\boldsymbol{k}, 2\pi - a)$$

The matrix (18.37) illustrates clearly that the half-integer representations are not continuous representations of $\mathscr{R}_3$. As one rotates through an angle $a = 2\pi$ the physical system returns to its starting point but the matrix (18.37) is changed by a factor -1. In the covering group as a increases to 4π the matrix (18.37) does return to its original value and continuity is restored. Thus the half-integer representations are continuous as representations of SU_2.

18.13.4 Explicit formula for the parameters of a product of rotations

$$\cos \tfrac{1}{2}c = \cos \tfrac{1}{2}a \cos \tfrac{1}{2}b - \boldsymbol{k}.\boldsymbol{l} \sin \tfrac{1}{2}a \sin \tfrac{1}{2}b \tag{18.38}$$
$$(\sin \tfrac{1}{2}c)\boldsymbol{m} = (\sin \tfrac{1}{2}a \cos \tfrac{1}{2}b)\boldsymbol{k} + (\sin \tfrac{1}{2}b \cos \tfrac{1}{2}a)\boldsymbol{l} + (\sin \tfrac{1}{2}a \sin \tfrac{1}{2}b)\boldsymbol{k} \wedge \boldsymbol{l}$$

The four real numbers $\cos \frac{1}{2}a$, $k_x \sin \frac{1}{2}a$, $k_y \sin \frac{1}{2}a$ and $k_z \sin \frac{1}{2}a$ are sometimes called the Cayley–Klein parameters of the rotation $R_{\boldsymbol{k}}(a)$. The formulae (18.38) are the equivalent for the group $\mathscr{R}_3$ of the relation $c = a + b$ for combining rotations in $\mathscr{R}_2$.

The form (18.36) may be used to deduce the angle and axis of the product of two rotations. Suppose $R_m(c) = R_{\boldsymbol{k}}(a)R_l(b)$, then from equation (18.36) we have

$$\begin{aligned} D^{(\frac{1}{2})}(\boldsymbol{m}, c) &= (\cos \tfrac{1}{2}a + 2\boldsymbol{k}.\mathbf{X} \sin \tfrac{1}{2}a)(\cos \tfrac{1}{2}b + 2\boldsymbol{l}.\mathbf{X} \sin \tfrac{1}{2}b) \\ &= (\cos \tfrac{1}{2}a \cos \tfrac{1}{2}b - \boldsymbol{k}.\boldsymbol{l} \sin \tfrac{1}{2}a \sin \tfrac{1}{2}b) \\ &\quad + 2\{(\sin \tfrac{1}{2}a \cos \tfrac{1}{2}b)\boldsymbol{k} + (\sin \tfrac{1}{2}b \cos \tfrac{1}{2}a)\boldsymbol{l} + (\sin \tfrac{1}{2}a \sin \tfrac{1}{2}b)\boldsymbol{k} \wedge \boldsymbol{l}\}.\mathbf{X} \end{aligned}$$

Equating this to $(\cos \frac{1}{2}c + 2\boldsymbol{m}.\mathbf{X} \sin \frac{1}{2}c)$ we deduce the angle c and axis $\boldsymbol{m}$ from the two equations

18.13.5 Examples of SU_2 basis vectors

Let us introduce the coordinates ξ, η of an arbitrary vector $\boldsymbol{e}$ in the two-dimensional space of the group SU_2 so that from equation (3.38) the transformation of functions is given by the equation

$$T(U)\psi(\xi, \eta) = \psi(\bar{\xi}, \bar{\eta})$$

with

$$\bar{\xi} = \alpha^*\xi - \beta\eta$$
$$\bar{\eta} = \beta^*\xi + \alpha\eta \tag{18.39}$$

from equations (3.39) and (18.32). Consider the transformation of the $(2j+1)$ functions defined by

$$\xi^{2j}, \xi^{2j-1}\eta, \xi^{2j-2}\eta^2, \ldots, \xi\eta^{2j-1}, \eta^{2j} \tag{18.40}$$

Since (18.39) is a linear transformation it is clear that this set of functions will form an invariant space and thus provide a representation of SU_2 with dimension $(2j+1)$. For the particular unitary transformation corresponding to a rotation of angle a about the z-axis, the parameters α and β are given by $\alpha = \exp(-\frac{1}{2}ia)$ and $\beta = 0$. In this case the transformation (18.39) is very simple and the character of the representation provided by the set of functions (18.40) is given by

$$(\alpha^*)^{2j} + (\alpha^*)^{2j-1}\alpha + \ldots + \alpha^{2j} = \exp(iaj) + \exp[ia(j-1)] + \ldots + \exp(-iaj)$$

Comparison with section 7.4.3 shows this to be just the character of the irreducible representation $D^{(j)}$ of $\mathscr{R}_3$. Hence we conclude that the set (18.40) provides a basis for the representation $D^{(j)}$ of SU_2. In particular, the three functions ξ^2, $\xi\eta$ and η^2 provide a basis for the vector representation $D^{(1)}$.

Bibliography

More details of the group U_N may be found in Boerner (1963), see bibliography to chapter 4, or Littlewood (1950), see chapter 17 bibliography. The spectroscopic applications introduced in section 18.10 are discussed further by Judd (1963), see chapter 8 bibliography, in atomic structure, while the nuclear structure applications are reviewed by

Hecht, K. T. (1973). *Symmetry in Nuclei*: Annual reviews of nuclear science (Annual Reviews Inc., Palo Alto, California)

Much of the early work on the use of the unitary groups and their subgroups in spectroscopy was done by Racah and some of this is described in

Racah, G. (1965). Group theory and spectroscopy, *Ergebn. exakt. Naturw.*, **37**, 28

Problems

18.1 Construct product functions belonging to the representations [3], [21] and [111] of U_3, as suggested in example (4) of section 18.2.

18.2 Use the method of section 18.4 to label the basis vectors of the following representations: (a) [3] of U_3, (b) [21] of U_4.

18.3 Reduce the direct product $[21] \times [2]$ of U_3. How does this result simplify if, instead of U_3, one is using (a) the group SU_3 (use the notation (λ, μ)), (b) the group SU_2?

18.4 Deduce the weights of the basis vectors in part (a) of problem 2 and hence show that the reduction (18.24) for this case is $\mathrm{U}^{[3]} = \mathrm{D}^{(3)} \dot{+} \mathrm{D}^{(1)}$.

18.5 Find the L-values for the totally antisymmetric states of two and three d-particles. (There is one antisymmetric state for each combination of different m-values of the particles. Hence list the number of independent states for each value of $M = \Sigma m$ and so deduce the possible values of L.)

18.6 Reduce the products $[1] \times [1]$, $[1] \times [11]$ and $[1] \times [2]$ for the group U_5. Hence, knowing the reduction of product representations (7.44) of $\mathscr{R}_3$ and the results of the previous problem, deduce by subtraction the L-values of the $[2]$, $[3]$ and $[21]$ representations of two and three d-particles.

18.7 Follow the method of problems 5 and 6 to list the possible combinations of J and T for three nucleons in a $j = \frac{5}{2}$ shell.

18.8 Show that there is a one-to-one correspondence between the parameters $\boldsymbol{k}$ and a of equation (18.33), with $0 \leqslant a \leqslant 2\pi$ and $\boldsymbol{k}$ a unit vector, and the two complex parameters α, β with the condition $\alpha\alpha^* + \beta\beta^* = 1$.

19

Two Familiar 'Accidental' Degeneracies—the Oscillator and Coulomb Potentials

The appearance of degeneracies in the spectrum of energy levels as a consequence of the existence of a group of symmetry operations on the Hamiltonian of the system, has been central to our discussions of symmetry in quantum mechanics. However, as we explained in section 5.3, the full degeneracies will be understood only if the full symmetry group has been identified. A degeneracy may always happen by chance or by design. For example a numerical parameter in the Hamiltonian may be adjusted until two energy levels cross and this is usually called an 'accidental' degeneracy. If however one finds what appear to be systematic accidental degeneracies, not just in a single level but in many levels, then it is usually a sign that the degeneracies are not accidental, but are due to the existence of some hitherto unsuspected symmetry operations which enlarge the symmetry group. In such a situation one should strictly not use the word 'accidental'. In this chapter we describe two famous examples (see Jauch and Hill, 1940, in the bibliography) of such accidental degeneracies which are not strictly accidental but are due to a larger symmetry group. Both examples relate to the motion of a single particle in a spherically symmetric potential so that one expects the usual $(2l+1)$-fold degeneracies due to rotational symmetry as described in sections 7.5 and 8.1. For general forms of the radial dependence of the potential $V(r)$ this is all the degeneracy one finds, but for two particular cases $V(r)\propto r^2$ and $V(r)\propto r^{-1}$, the detailed solution of the Schrodinger equation is found to lead to additional degeneracies of a systematic kind. These two cases are well known as the harmonic oscillator and the Coulomb potential and they both have important roles to play in physics. The oscillator is of general importance in describing small departures from an equilibrium position and is also of importance as a first approximation to the motion of individual nucleons in a nucleus, the origin being at the centre of mass of the nucleus. The Coulomb potential describes the motion of the electron in the hydrogen atom. We shall show that the symmetry groups in the two cases are U_3 and $\mathcal{R}_4$, respectively, both of which contain the obvious rotation group $\mathcal{R}_3$ as a subgroup. As a straightforward generalisation, we show that the harmonic oscillator in n-dimensions has symmetry group U_n.

19.1 The three-dimensional harmonic oscillator for one particle

It is conventional to write the oscillator potential as $V(r)=\frac{1}{2}M\omega^2r^2$, where $\omega/2\pi$ is the classical frequency of oscillation for a particle of mass M. In quantum mechanics we must solve the Schrodinger equation

$$(-\hbar^2\nabla^2/2M+\tfrac{1}{2}M\omega^2r^2)\,\psi(r,\theta,\phi)=E\psi(r,\theta,\phi)$$

For convenience, let us measure energies in units of $\hbar\omega$ and distances in units of $(\hbar/M\omega)^{\frac{1}{2}}$ which we call the oscillator 'length parameter' and denote by b. In these units, the Schrodinger equation becomes $\frac{1}{2}(-\nabla^2+r^2)\psi=E\psi$ and the Hamiltonian is

$$\mathrm{H}=\tfrac{1}{2}(-\nabla^2+r^2) \tag{19.1}$$

This Hamiltonian is clearly spherically symmetric, a fact which is expressed through the three commutation relations $[\mathrm{H},\mathrm{L}_q]=0$, where $q=x, y$ or z and $\mathrm{L}_z=-i(x\partial/\partial y-y\partial/\partial x)$, etc., are the infinitesimal rotation operators, see sections 5.6 and 8.2. We shall presently construct a total of nine operators which all commute with H and which are then shown to be the infinitesimal operators of a group U_3. It is convenient to begin by defining three operators

$$\mathrm{a}_x=(x+\partial/\partial x)/\sqrt{2},\quad \mathrm{a}_y=(y+\partial/\partial y)/\sqrt{2},\quad \mathrm{a}_z=(z+\partial/\partial z)/\sqrt{2}$$

and their Hermitian adjoints

$$\mathrm{a}_x^\dagger=(x-\partial/\partial x)/\sqrt{2},\quad \mathrm{a}_y^\dagger=(y-\partial/\partial y)/\sqrt{2},\quad \mathrm{a}_z^\dagger=(z-\partial/\partial z)/\sqrt{2} \tag{19.2}$$

(Recall that $\mathrm{p}_x=-i\hbar\,\partial/\partial x$ is Hermitian so that the Hermitian adjoint of $\partial/\partial x$ is

$-\partial/\partial x$.) One immediately verifies the commutation relations

$$[a_q, a_{q'}] = [a_q^\dagger, a_{q'}^\dagger] = 0, \quad [a_q, a_{q'}^\dagger] = \delta_{q,q'} \tag{19.3}$$

$$[a_q, H] = a_q, \quad [a_q^\dagger, H] = -a_q^\dagger \tag{19.4}$$

using the explicit form (19.1) for H. The Hamiltonian may also be written

$$H = \sum_q (a_q^\dagger a_q + \tfrac{1}{2}) \tag{19.5}$$

This algebraic technique is often used in quantum mechanics textbooks to solve the Schrodinger equation for the oscillator because from (19.4) we may conclude that if ψ is an eigenfunction with energy E then the functions $a_q\psi$ are also eigenfunctions of H with energy $(E-1)$. In other words, a_q reduces the energy by one unit and similarly $a_q^\dagger$ increases the energy by one unit. The wave function ψ_0 of the lowest energy level must satisfy the conditions $a_q\psi_0 = 0$ so that from (19.5) the lowest eigenvalue has the value $\frac{3}{2}$. Using the explicit differential form for the a_q these conditions pose simple differential equations which lead to the explicit solution $\psi_0 = \exp(-\frac{1}{2}r^2)$, apart from normalisation. The excited states then appear at integer intervals and the wave functions corresponding to an excitation N are given by the set of functions

$$(a_x^\dagger)^{N_x}(a_y^\dagger)^{N_y}(a_z^\dagger)^{N_z}\psi_0 \tag{19.6}$$

where N_x, N_y and N_z are any integers satisfying $N_x+N_y+N_z = N$. In particular, for $N = 1$ there is a three-fold degeneracy, for $N = 2$ a six-fold degeneracy and in general a degeneracy of order $\frac{1}{2}(N+1)(N+2)$. The possible values of N_x, N_y and N_z are shown in table 19.1 for small N. One sees immediately that these degeneracies are not of the kind $(2l+1)$ which were

Table 19.1

N	1	2	3
N_x	1 0 0	2 0 0 1 1 0	3 0 0 2 2 1 1 0 0 1
N_y	0 1 0	0 2 0 1 0 1	0 3 0 1 0 2 0 2 1 1
N_z	0 0 1	0 0 2 0 1 1	0 0 3 0 1 0 2 1 2 1
l	1	2, 0	3, 1

expected. They must therefore be the sum of several $(2l+1)$-fold degeneracies and the appropriate values of l are shown in the last row of table 19.1. To see how these l-values are deduced we notice that the three operators $a_q^\dagger$ transform like the vector representation $D^{(1)}$ of the group $\mathcal{R}_3$. Thus, since ψ_0 is spherically symmetric, the excited states (19.6) with fixed N will transform like the symmetrised product $D^{(1)} \times D^{(1)} \times \ldots \times D^{(1)}$ with N factors, as defined in appendix 3.1. Only the symmetrised product may occur because the $a_q^\dagger$ commute with each other. There is no scope for any antisymmetry with only a single particle. The formulae of appendix 3.1 for the character of symmetrised products together with the standard formula (7.42) for the $\mathscr{R}_3$ characters give the reduction of this product and hence the resulting values of l, as shown in the last row of table 19.1. In fact one may deduce generally that $l = N$, $N-2, \ldots, 1$ or 0 depending on whether N is odd or even, see problem 19.2.

Having established in this explicit way that the three-dimensional harmonic oscillator has a greater degeneracy than expected on the basis of spherical symmetry we now return to the problem of finding the larger symmetry group. From the commutation relations (19.4) one may verify directly that, for any q and q', $[a_q^\dagger a_{q'}, H] = 0$. This result may also be seen from the fact that, whereas a_q reduces the eigenvalue by one unit, $a_q^\dagger$ increases it by the same amount so that the product $a_q a_{q'}$ cannot change the eigenvalue but merely transforms within the vector space of each set of degenerate eigenfunctions. Thus we have found a set of nine operators $a_q^\dagger a_{q'}$ which all commute with the Hamiltonian H and from these may be constructed a set of unitary symmetry operators

$$U = \exp\left(\sum_{q,q'} c_{qq'} a_q^\dagger a_{q'}\right)$$

provided that the coefficients $c_{qq'}$ satisfy the skew-Hermitian condition $c^*_{qq'} = -c_{q'q}$. This condition leaves the freedom of nine real numbers in the coefficients $c_{qq'}$ and so we have a nine-parameter set of unitary transformations which commute with the Hamiltonian H. To confirm that this is in fact the group U_3 we consider its effect on the set of three operators $a_q^\dagger$, finding

$$(a_s^\dagger)' = U a_s^\dagger U^{-1} = \sum_{s'} (\exp C)_{s's} a_{s'}^\dagger \tag{19.7}$$

where C is the matrix $c_{qq'}$. To obtain this result we use the operator identity

$$e^{A} B e^{-A} = B + [A, B] + \tfrac{1}{2!}[A,[A,B]] + \tfrac{1}{3!}[A,[A,[A,B]]] + \ldots$$

together with the relation

$$[a_q^\dagger a_{q'}, a_s^\dagger] = \delta_{q's} a_q^\dagger$$

which follows from equation (19.3). The significance of the result (19.7) is that, for skew-Hermitian C, it is the most general unitary transformation in the three-dimensional space of the operators $a_q^\dagger$. Thus the operators U are in one-to-one correspondence with the matrices $\exp C$ of the group U_3. In this sense, the matrix of the operator $a_q^\dagger a_{q'}$ is given by $(a_q^\dagger a_{q'})_{ts} = \delta_{q's}\delta_{qt}$.

The infinitesimal operators are the nine independent skew-Hermitian combinations of the operators $a_q^\dagger a_{q'}$, corresponding to the nine skew-Hermitian 3×3 matrices described in section 11.4. For some purposes it is convenient to take linear combinations which are irreducible tensor operators with respect to rotations, see subsection 7.4.6. Since both $a_q^\dagger$ and a_q transform like a vector, i.e. the representation $D^{(1)}$, the set of nine products $a_q^\dagger a_{q'}$ transforms like the product representation

$$D^{(1)} \times D^{(1)} = D^{(0)} \dot{+} D^{(1)} \dot{+} D^{(2)}$$

using the familiar rule (7.44) for its reduction. The invariant $D^{(0)}$ is essentially the Hamiltonian, since from equation (19.5), $\sum_q \overset{\dagger}{a}_q a_q = H - \frac{3}{2}$

The vector operators $D^{(1)}$ are the angular momentum operators L_q since

$$L_z = -i(x\,\partial/\partial y - y\,\partial/\partial x) = -i(\overset{\dagger}{a}_x a_y - \overset{\dagger}{a}_y a_x), \text{ etc.}$$

The remaining five independent combinations may now be written as a tensor operator of rank 2 (quadrupole), like a spherical harmonic $Y_q^{(2)}$. In the conventional notation of subsection 7.4.6 we write

$$\begin{aligned}
Q_0^{(2)} &= 2\overset{\dagger}{a}_z a_z - \overset{\dagger}{a}_x a_x - \overset{\dagger}{a}_y a_y, \\
Q_1^{(2)} &= \sqrt{\tfrac{3}{2}}(-\overset{\dagger}{a}_z a_x - \overset{\dagger}{a}_x a_z - i\overset{\dagger}{a}_y a_z - i\overset{\dagger}{a}_z a_y) \\
Q_{-1}^{(2)} &= \sqrt{\tfrac{3}{2}}(\overset{\dagger}{a}_z a_x + \overset{\dagger}{a}_x a_z - i\overset{\dagger}{a}_y a_z - i\overset{\dagger}{a}_z a_y) \\
Q_2^{(2)} &= \sqrt{\tfrac{3}{2}}(\overset{\dagger}{a}_x a_x - \overset{\dagger}{a}_y a_y + i\overset{\dagger}{a}_x a_y + i\overset{\dagger}{a}_y a_x), \\
Q_{-2}^{(2)} &= \sqrt{\tfrac{3}{2}}(\overset{\dagger}{a}_x a_x - \overset{\dagger}{a}_y a_y - i\overset{\dagger}{a}_x a_y - i\overset{\dagger}{a}_y a_x)
\end{aligned} \quad (19.8)$$

Since H has this larger symmetry group U_3 one expects each eigenfunction to be labelled by an irreducible representation of U_3. We first note that $U_3 = U_1 \times SU_3$ following the argument given in section 10.4. In the present problem the infinitesimal operator for U_1 is simply the invariant $\sum_q \overset{\dagger}{a}_q a_q = H - \frac{3}{2}$ and the eight remaining traceless operators L_q and $Q_p^{(2)}$ describe SU_3. Thus the U_1 representation is labelled by N and it remains to identify the SU_3 representation corresponding to each energy level. Recalling the study of SU_3 operators in section 11.6 it is seen from the matrices (11.2) that we may associate the operators $\frac{1}{3}(\overset{\dagger}{a}_x a_x + \overset{\dagger}{a}_y a_y - 2\overset{\dagger}{a}_z a_z)$ with Y and $\frac{1}{2}(\overset{\dagger}{a}_x a_x - \overset{\dagger}{a}_y a_y)$ with T_z so that we may relate the numbers N_x, N_y and N_z used above to the numbers Y and M_T used in chapter 11 by the equations

$$\tfrac{1}{3}(N_x + N_y - 2N_z) = Y, \quad \tfrac{1}{2}(N_x - N_y) = M_T \quad (19.9)$$

The diagrams in figure 11.6 then show immediately that the three eigenfunctions with $N = 1$ belong to the representation (10), those with $N = 2$ belong to (20) and those with $N = 3$ belong to (30). As an illustration, in figure 19.1 we reproduce from figure 11.6 the diagram for $D^{(30)}$ showing the values of $(N_x N_y N_z)$ corresponding to each lattice point. Because the products (19.6) are symmetric in the N factors $\overset{\dagger}{a}_q$ and thus belong to the U_3 representation $[N]$, see section 18.7, it follows generally that the set of eigenfunctions with energy $(N + \frac{3}{2})$ belongs to the irreducible representation $(N0)$.

The question of which values of angular momentum l occur for given N is, group theoretically, the question of restricting from the group SU_3 to its subgroup $\mathscr{R}_3$. We stress that this is a different process from the restriction from SU_3 to SU_2 described in section 11.5. The infinitesimal operators of the

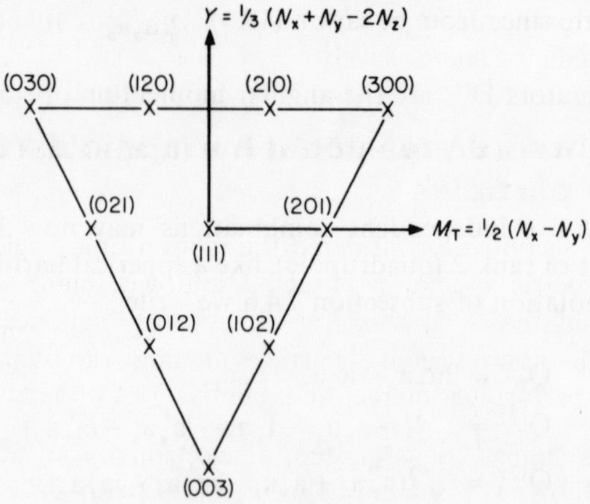

Figure 19.1

physical rotations $\mathscr{R}_3$ are the operators L_q, see equation (19.7), while the operators for the SU_2 subgroup in the xy-plane would be

$$T_+ = a_x^\dagger a_y, \; T_- = a_y^\dagger a_x, \; T_z = \tfrac{1}{2}(a_x^\dagger a_x - a_y^\dagger a_y) \qquad (19.10)$$

It is clear that, for example, T_+ is a 'raising operator' which reduces N_y by one unit and increases N_x by one unit, thus moving one step to the right in figures like figure 19.1. One soon verifies, using equation (19.3), that the three operators (19.10) satisfy the standard commutation relations (7.30) of SU_2. The operators defined in equation (19.10) do not, of course, have anything to do with isospin but we use the same notation to emphasise the mathematical connection with chapter 11. The angular momentum L_z may now be written simply as

$$\begin{aligned} L_z &= -i(a_x^\dagger a_y - a_y^\dagger a_x) = -i(T_+ - T_-) \\ &= -i(T_x + iT_y - T_x + iT_y) \\ &= 2T_y \end{aligned} \qquad (19.11)$$

Hence the set of eigenvalues of L_z within a representation $(\lambda\mu)$ of SU_3 is the same as the set of eigenvalues of $2T_y$, which is necessarily the same as the set of eigenvalues of $2T_z$, which is given by the set of values of $2M_T = N_x - N_y$. These may be deduced immediately from the figures like figure 19.1. Knowing the eigenvalues of L_z enables us finally to deduce the possible values of L. For example, figure 19.1 tells us that the representation (30) contains the following eigenvalues for L_z,

$$-3, \; -1, \; 1, \; 3, \; -2, \; 0, \; 2, \; -1, \; 1, \; 0$$

which implies that $l = 3$ and $l = 1$. In general one deduces that $l = N, N-2,$

$N-4, \ldots, 1$ or 0 for the representation $(N0)$, which is the familiar result for the l-values in an oscillator energy level.

19.2 The three-dimensional harmonic oscillator for many particles

In the preceding section we considered the motion of a single particle in a spherically symmetric oscillator potential and we found additional degeneracies beyond those expected for an arbitrary spherically symmetric potential. Consider now a system of particles moving in an oscillator potential and subject to a perturbing interaction potential $\sum_{i<j} V(r_{ij})$ between particles. This situation is similar to the system of electrons in an atom which we described in section 8.6. There is was seen to lead to an LS coupling result, although in our present discussion the spin need not be considered. From the group theory point of view the total angular momentum L reflects the fact that the wave function transforms like the representation $D^{(L)}$ of the group $\mathscr{R}_3$ of simultaneous rotations of all particles and is additional to the labels l which describe the behaviour of the single-particle wave functions under separate rotations. The Hamiltonian, including the perturbation $\sum_{i<j} V(r_{ij})$ is invariant under the group $\mathscr{R}_3$ of simultaneous rotations. Let us now study this process of extension from one to many particles for the group U_3, following the steps taken for $\mathscr{R}_3$. Just as we define the total angular momentum operators $L_q = \sum_i L_q(i)$ as sums over particles i, so we can define the nine total U_3 operators as $\sum_i a_q^\dagger(i) a_{q'}(i)$. It is clear that the commutators of these operators are the same as those for the single-particle operators since operators for different particles commute. Hence they describe the group U_3 of simultaneous U_3 transformations on all particles, which contains the group of simultaneous rotations, described by the total angular momentum L, as a subgroup. As with the single-particle operators, the nine U_3 operators may be taken as $H = \sum_i H(i)$, where $H(i)$ is the oscillator Hamiltonian for particle i, $L_q = \sum_i L_q(i)$ the total angular momentum and the five components of the quadrupole operator $Q_p^{(2)} = \sum_i Q_p^{(2)}(i)$. From general theory it follows that if the perturbing potential $\sum_{i<j} V(r_{ij})$ commutes with these nine operators then the eigenfunctions of the system are labelled by irreducible representations of U_3, in other words by N which determines the unperturbed oscillator energy and a label $(\lambda\mu)$ of SU_3. We shall not go into detail regarding the possible $(\lambda\mu)$ which appear with each N, except to remark that the procedure is similar to the problem of deducing the possible values of L in an atomic configuration which we described in subsection 8.6.4. In such a many-particle system, one no longer has only the simple representations with $\mu = 0$ which arose for a single particle.

A perturbation which is invariant under SU_3 could be constructed from the Casimir operators which are, by definition, invariant. For the group of simultaneous SU_3 transformations, the Casimir operator C_2 defined in section 11.10 will involve both one- and two-body parts. In terms of the operators L_q and $Q_p^{(2)}$ it may be written as

$$C_2 = \tfrac{1}{2}(\mathbf{L}.\mathbf{L}) + \tfrac{1}{6}(\mathbf{Q}^{(2)}.\mathbf{Q}^{(2)}) = \tfrac{1}{2}\sum_{i,j}(\mathbf{L}(i).\mathbf{L}(j)) + \tfrac{1}{6}\sum_{i,j}(\mathbf{Q}^{(2)}(i).\mathbf{Q}^{(2)}(j)) \tag{19.12}$$

Since the eigenvalues of C_2 are known, see equation (11.21), and the eigenvalues of $(\mathbf{L}.\mathbf{L})$ are simply $L(L+1)$, it follows that the eigenvalues of the quadrupole term $(\mathbf{Q}^{(2)}.\mathbf{Q}^{(2)})$ may be deduced. The two-body part of this is sometimes called the 'quadrupole force' and has been used as a model for understanding the development of deformations and rotational motion in nuclei—see Harvey (1968) in the bibliography.

The interesting general aspect of this use of SU_3 is the way in which the symmetry is extended from the single-particle to the many-body system.

19.3 The harmonic oscillator in *n* dimensions

In section 19.1 we chose to discuss the three-dimensional harmonic oscillator because of its obvious physical significance in the real three-dimensional space of the physical world. However from the algebraic point of view the fact that the number of dimensions was three was not important. We could equally well have started with operators $\nabla^2 = \sum_{q=1}^{n} \partial^2/\partial r_q^2$ and $r^2 = \sum_{q=1}^{n} r_q^2$ defining an n-dimensional oscillator. The extension from three to n dimensions is straightforward leading to the conclusion that the symmetry group is U_n.

In particular the two-dimensional oscillator has degeneracies corresponding to irreducible representations of SU_2 which, as we have seen in section 18.13, are the same as those of $\mathcal{R}_3$. Hence the two-dimensional oscillator, with energies $(N+1)$, has degeneracies corresponding to an angular momentum-like label $\tfrac{1}{2}N$, the order of the degeneracy being $2(\tfrac{1}{2}N)+1 = N+1$. The pair of operators $a_x^\dagger$ and $a_y^\dagger$ in this case transform like the representation $D^{(\frac{1}{2})}$ of the group SU_2.

19.4 The symmetry group of the Coulomb potential

The Hamiltonian for a particle of charge $-e$ in a Coulomb potential e/r, like the electron in the hydrogen atom, is given by (see section 8.5)

$$H = p^2/2M - e^2/r = -\hbar^2\nabla^2/2M - e^2/r \tag{19.13}$$

If we measure length in units of $\hbar^2/Me^2$ (the Bohr radius) and energy in units of $e^4/2\hbar^2$ ($= Rh$, where R is the Rydberg constant), then the Hamiltonian takes the form

$$\mathrm{H} = -(\nabla^2 + 2/r) \tag{19.14}$$

and the Schrodinger equation is given as usual by $\mathrm{H}\psi = E\psi$, with E the energy and $\psi(\boldsymbol{r})$ the wave function. It is well known that the energy levels are labelled by an integer $n = 1, 2, 3, \ldots$, with energy $-n^{-2}$ and that for given n the angular momentum takes the values $l = 0, 1, 2, \ldots, (n-1)$. Thus there is a greater degeneracy than one would expect from the obvious spherical symmetry.

Because it is spherically symmetric, the Hamiltonian will again commute with the three infinitesimal operators L_q of $\mathscr{R}_3$. Although it is by no means obvious, some detailed but straightforward algebra shows that H also commutes with the three components of the vector operator

$$\mathbf{A} = \tfrac{1}{2}\{(\nabla \wedge (\boldsymbol{r} \wedge \nabla)) - ((\boldsymbol{r} \wedge \nabla) \wedge \nabla)\} + \boldsymbol{r}/r \tag{19.15}$$

In terms of physical operators this may be written

$$\mathbf{A} = -[\{(\mathbf{p} \wedge \mathbf{L}) - (\mathbf{L} \wedge \mathbf{p})\}/2M - e^2\boldsymbol{r}/r]/e^2$$

where the quantity in the square bracket has been called the Runge–Lentz vector and is known in the classical Coulomb problem to be a constant of the motion. The existence of these three further Hermitian symmetry operators A_q suggests that, together with the L_q, they may be the infinitesimal operators of some continuous group which contains $\mathscr{R}_3$. We therefore study the commutation relations between the six operators A_q and L_q to see firstly if they satisfy relations of the general type (7.7) and secondly if the structure constants are those of a well-known Lie group.

Since the three operators A_q form a vector their commutation relations with the rotation operators L_q are simply

$$[\mathrm{L}_x, \mathrm{A}_x] = 0, \quad [\mathrm{L}_x, \mathrm{A}_y] = i\mathrm{A}_z, \quad [\mathrm{L}_x, \mathrm{A}_z] = -i\mathrm{A}_y, \text{ etc.} \tag{19.16}$$

see equation (7.26) and subsection 7.4.6. From the definition (19.15) the commutator of A_q with $\mathrm{A}_{q'}$ may be calculated, giving ultimately

$$[\mathrm{A}_x, \mathrm{A}_y] = (\nabla^2 + 2/r)(x\,\partial/\partial y - y\,\partial/\partial x) = -i\,\mathrm{H}\mathrm{L}_z, \text{ etc.} \tag{19.17}$$

Thus the commutator is not given precisely in the form (7.7) as a sum of the symmetry operators L_q and $\mathrm{A}_{q'}$ but involves also the Hamiltonian H. However, since H commutes with **A** and **L** we may incorporate the factor $-\mathrm{H}$ into the operators by defining

$$\mathbf{A}' = (-\mathrm{H})^{-\frac{1}{2}}\mathbf{A}$$

so that

$$[\mathrm{A}'_x, \mathrm{A}'_y] = i\mathrm{L}_z, \text{ etc.} \tag{19.17a}$$

The use of $-\mathrm{H}$ rather than H in the definition of $\mathbf{A}'$ will be convenient in considering bound states, for which the eigenvalues of H are negative. In this case $\mathbf{A}'$ is Hermitian but it becomes skew-Hermitian for positive energies. Thus for negative energies the operators $\mathbf{L}$ and $\mathbf{A}'$ define unitary transformations $\exp\{-i(\boldsymbol{a}.\mathbf{L})-i(\boldsymbol{c}.\mathbf{A}')\}$ where $\boldsymbol{a}$ and $\boldsymbol{c}$ are real vector parameters. The six infinitesimal operators are $-i\mathbf{L}$ and $-i\mathbf{A}'$. The minus sign here ensures that the rotation parameters $\boldsymbol{a}$ are the same as those defined in subsection 7.4.1. We shall now identify the commutation relations (19.16) and (19.17a) as those for the group $\mathscr{R}_4$.

19.4.1 The groups $\mathscr{R}_4$ and $\mathscr{L}$

The rotation group $\mathscr{R}_4$ in four dimensions is defined as the set of (real) orthogonal 4×4 matrices with determinant of $+1$. If R denotes such a matrix we may write $\mathrm{R} = 1+\mathrm{M}$ where the matrix elements of M are small if R is close to the identity. The orthogonality condition $\mathrm{R}^{\dagger}\mathrm{R} = 1$ implies that, for small M, $\mathrm{M}^{\dagger}+\mathrm{M} = 0$ so that the infinitesimal operator M is skew-symmetric and may be written

$$\mathrm{M} = \begin{pmatrix} 0 & -a_z & a_y & c_x \\ a_z & 0 & -a_x & c_y \\ -a_y & a_x & 0 & c_z \\ -c_x & -c_y & -c_z & 0 \end{pmatrix} = \sum_q (a_q \mathrm{X}_q + c_q \mathrm{Z}_q) \qquad (19.18)$$

This defines the six independent infinitesimal operators X_q, Z_q of the group where the notation X_q follows that used in subsection 7.4.1 for the group $\mathscr{R}_3$, exhibiting the subgroup $\mathscr{R}_3$ of $\mathscr{R}_4$ obtained by putting $c_q = 0$. The commutation relations follow from the definitions in equation (19.18),

$$\begin{gathered} [\mathrm{X}_x, \mathrm{X}_y] = \mathrm{X}_z, \text{ etc.} \\ [\mathrm{X}_x, \mathrm{Z}_x] = 0,\ [\mathrm{X}_x, \mathrm{Z}_y] = \mathrm{Z}_z,\ [\mathrm{X}_x, \mathrm{Z}_z] = -\mathrm{Z}_y, \text{ etc.} \\ [\mathrm{Z}_x, \mathrm{Z}_y] = \mathrm{X}_z, \text{ etc.} \end{gathered} \qquad (19.19)$$

where the others follow from cyclic rearrangement of indices. Comparison with equations (19.16) and (19.17a) shows that $\mathbf{X}$ and $\mathbf{Z}$ have the same commutation relations as the infinitesimal symmetry operators $-i\mathbf{L}$ and $-i\mathbf{A}'$.

Thus, so far as infinitesimals are concerned, we can identify the symmetry group of the bound states with $\mathscr{R}_4$. A more careful study of the range of the parameters would be necessary to establish that the finite symmetry operations could be put into one-to-one correspondence (isomorphism) with $\mathscr{R}_4$. (In fact, the $\mathscr{R}_4$ invariance of H may be shown explicitly by mapping the momentum $\boldsymbol{p}$ on to a point which lies on a unit sphere in a four-dimensional space and has coordinates

$$\xi = 2p_0p_x/(p_0^2+p^2), \quad \eta = 2p_0p_y/(p_0^2+p^2)$$
$$\zeta = 2p_0p_z/(p_0^2+p^2), \quad \chi = (p_0^2-p^2)/(p_0^2+p^2)$$

where $p_0 = (-E)^{-\frac{1}{2}}$. If the Schrodinger equation is written as an integral equation in momentum space it exhibits an invariance with respect to rotation in this four-dimensional space.)

For positive energy states it is more convenient to define $\mathbf{A}'' = (\mathrm{H})^{-\frac{1}{2}}\mathbf{A}$ instead of $\mathbf{A}'$, so that $\mathbf{A}''$ is Hermitian with the commutation relation (19.17a), replaced by

$$[\mathrm{A}''_x, \mathrm{A}''_y] = -i\mathrm{L}_z, \text{ etc.} \tag{19.17b}$$

The commutation relations of the infinitesimal symmetry operators $-i\mathbf{L}$ and $-i\mathbf{A}''$ now differ from those given in equation (19.19) for the group $\mathscr{R}_4$. However, they now agree with the commutation relations (15.32) for the Lorentz group $\mathscr{L}$. This result is to be expected since the Lorentz group is a four-dimensional rotation group with a sign change in one component of the metric and this corresponds to the change in the sign of H.

19.4.2 The classification of states of the Coulomb potential

Having found the symmetry group it now follows from the general theory that the energy levels may be classified by irreducible representations. We therefore face the task of finding the possible irreducible representations of the group $\mathscr{R}_4$ but, fortunately, this may be done very quickly by making use of a (local) isomorphism between the groups $\mathscr{R}_4$ and $\mathscr{R}_3 \times \mathscr{R}_3$. To understand this we define new infinitesimal operators

$$\mathbf{F} = \tfrac{1}{2}(\mathbf{X}+\mathbf{Z}) \text{ and } \mathbf{G} = \tfrac{1}{2}(\mathbf{X}-\mathbf{Z})$$

which is equivalent to the use of $(\boldsymbol{a}+\boldsymbol{c})$ and $(\boldsymbol{a}-\boldsymbol{c})$ as parameters in equation (19.18). Then, from equation (19.19),

$$[\mathrm{F}_x, \mathrm{F}_y] = \mathrm{F}_z, \quad [\mathrm{G}_x, \mathrm{G}_y] = \mathrm{G}_z, \text{ etc.} \tag{19.20}$$

with all components of $\mathbf{F}$ commuting with all components of $\mathbf{G}$. Thus the operators $\mathbf{F}$ and $\mathbf{G}$ separately satisfy the same commutation relations as $\mathbf{X}$ and therefore describe $\mathscr{R}_3$ groups. Since they commute with each other it follows that together they describe the product group $\mathscr{R}_3 \times \mathscr{R}_3$ and hence we have established an isomorphism for the infinitesimals of $\mathscr{R}_4$ and $\mathscr{R}_3 \times \mathscr{R}_3$. We may therefore use the known irreducible representations $\mathrm{D}^{(j)}$ of $\mathscr{R}_3$ with $j = 0, \frac{1}{2}, 1, \frac{3}{2}, \ldots$, to conclude that the irreducible representations of $\mathscr{R}_4$ are labelled by a pair $j_1 j_2$ of such indices (see section 4.21 for representations of a product group). The irreducible representations of $\mathscr{R}_4$ are therefore denoted by $\mathrm{D}^{(j_1 j_2)}$, where j_1 and j_2 refer to the two $\mathscr{R}_3$ groups. The operators $(\mathbf{F}.\mathbf{F})$ and $(\mathbf{G}.\mathbf{G})$ provide two Casimir operators with values $-j_1(j_1+1)$ and $-j_2(j_2+1)$, respectively (see section 7.5), and the dimension of $\mathrm{D}^{(j_1 j_2)}$ is $(2j_1+1)(2j_2+1)$.

In studying the oscillator in section 19.1 we saw that only some of the representations of SU_3 could be realised with only a single particle and a similar situation occurs with the Coulomb problem. The restriction in this case comes about because $(\mathbf{A}'.\mathbf{L}) = (\mathbf{L}.\mathbf{A}') = 0$, which follows directly from the definitions of $\mathbf{L}$ and $\mathbf{A}'$, using some detailed algebra. Thus if we construct the symmetry operators $-\frac{1}{2}i(\mathbf{L} \pm \mathbf{A}')$ corresponding to $\mathbf{F}$ and $\mathbf{G}$ it is clear that both Casimir operators reduce to the same expression $-\frac{1}{4}\{(\mathbf{L}.\mathbf{L}) + (\mathbf{A}'.\mathbf{A}')\}$. Hence the only possible representations are those with $j_1 = j_2$ namely $\mathrm{D}^{(jj)}$ with $j = 0, \frac{1}{2}, 1, \frac{3}{2}, \ldots$. Some more algebra shows that the Casimir operators simplify further, giving

$$(\mathbf{F}.\mathbf{F}) = (\mathbf{G}.\mathbf{G}) = -\tfrac{1}{4}\{(\mathbf{L}.\mathbf{L}) + (\mathbf{A}'.\mathbf{A}')\} = \tfrac{1}{4}(1 + \mathrm{H}^{-1})$$

In a representation $\mathrm{D}^{(jj)}$ this Casimir operator has the value $-j(j+1)$ so that the corresponding value of the energy is given by

$$E = \langle \mathrm{H} \rangle = -(2j+1)^{-2} \tag{19.21}$$

with a degeneracy of $(2j+1)^2$. In the standard theory of the hydrogen atom it is of course conventional to use an integer $n = (2j+1)$ to label the energies so that $j = 0, \frac{1}{2}, 1, \frac{3}{2}, \ldots$, corresponds to $n = 1, 2, 3, 4, \ldots$, and the energy formula (19.21) reduces to the more familiar expression $E = -n^{-2}$ in the energy units introduced at the beginning of section 19.4.

To deduce which angular momenta l occur at each energy involves the reduction

$$\mathrm{D}^{(jj)} = \sum_l c_l \mathrm{D}^{(l)} \tag{19.22}$$

of the irreducible representation $\mathrm{D}^{(jj)}$ of $\mathscr{R}_4$ following the restriction to the subgroup $\mathscr{R}_3$ of physical rotations. Notice that it is the operator $\mathbf{X} = \mathbf{F} + \mathbf{G}$ which describes these rotations. The problem of deducing the non-zero coefficients in the series (19.22) is now exactly the same as the vector coupling of two angular momenta $l = j + j$ which was described in subsection 7.4.4. Thus from equation (7.44) we conclude that $l = 0, 1, 2, \ldots, 2j(= n-1)$, which is the familiar result for the hydrogen atom.

For the positive energy states we simply remark that the Lorentz group has no finite-dimensional unitary irreducible representations, see subsection 15.2.5, and this is consistent with the well-known continuum of states which occurs for positive energy.

The technique described in section 19.2 for extending the use of the group U_3 to a system of particles may also be applied to a system of particles moving in a Coulomb potential with an $\mathscr{R}_4$ symmetric interaction. However, this does not seem to have much relevance to any recognised physical problem.

Bibliography

The symmetries of the oscillator and Coulomb potentials for a single particle were discussed by

Jauch, J. M. and Hill, E. L. (1940). *Phys. Rev.*, **57**, 641

The exploitation of the oscillator symmetry in the nuclear many-body problem is reviewed by

Harvey, M. (1968). *Advances in Nuclear Physics* 1. (Plenum, New York)

More recent work on the Coulomb symmetries is described by

Englefield, M. J. (1972). *Group Theory and the Coulomb Problem* (Wiley-Interscience, New York)

Problems

19.1 Show that the conditions $a_q \psi_0 = 0$, with a_q defined by equation (19.1), lead to the solution $\psi_0 = A \exp(-\frac{1}{2}r^2)$.

19.2 Justify the result quoted in section 19.1, that on restriction to the subgroup $\mathscr{R}_3$, the totally symmetric representation $[N]$ of SU_3 reduces into a sum of representations $D^{(l)}$, where $l = N, N-2, N-4, \ldots, 1$ or 0. (Follow the technique of problem 18.5 by taking symmetric products of N factors, each of which has $m = 1$, 0 or -1. Then show that there is only one product with $\Sigma m = N$ or $N-1$, that there are two products with $\Sigma m = N-2$, and $N-3$, three with $N-4$ and $N-5$, etc.)

20

A Miscellany

Having described systematically the theory of symmetry and its applications to a wide variety of physical systems we find that there are a number of related topics which, usually because they would have drawn attention away from the main argument, have so far been omitted. These topics, most of which are not connected with each other, are collected together here. Each section of this chapter is self-contained and the order of sections is arbitrary. The first two sections have immediate physical relevance, while the next two are concerned with general mathematical questions and the last with a point of mathematical detail.

20.1 Non-invariance groups

Hitherto we have been concerned exclusively with symmetry groups $\mathscr{G}$, which by definition leave the Hamiltonian invariant. We now investigate some groups which do not have this property but which nevertheless are of some interest. They are often called non-invariance or dynamical groups. Their significance is that they bring together into a single representation eigenfunctions corresponding to *different* energies, so that the spectrum and transition probabilities may be expressed in terms of the group operators. Hence these dynamical quantities may be deduced from the group theory. The application of these ideas has so far been limited to simple systems.

As an illustration, we consider the one-dimensional harmonic oscillator. In the notation of section 19.1, the Hamiltonian may be written

$$H = \tfrac{1}{2}(x^2 - d^2/dx^2) = a^\dagger a + \tfrac{1}{2} \tag{20.1}$$

and the energies are well known to be given by $(n+\frac{1}{2})$ in the usual units of $\hbar\omega$, where $n = 0, 1, 2, \ldots$. We now construct the three Hermitian operators

$$K_1 = \tfrac{1}{4}(a^2 + a^{\dagger 2}), \qquad K_2 = \tfrac{1}{4}i(a^2 - a^{\dagger 2}), \qquad K_3 = \tfrac{1}{2}H \tag{20.2}$$

and from the commutation relations (19.3) we find that

$$[K_1, K_2] = -iK_3, \qquad [K_3, K_1] = iK_2, \qquad [K_3, K_2] = -iK_1 \tag{20.3}$$

It may now be seen that these are just the commutation relations of a Lorentz group $\mathscr{L}_3$ in three dimensions. Such a group may be constructed by removing one of the space dimensions (z) from the usual Lorentz group discussed in section 15.2. Its infinitesimal operators are then X_z, Y_x and Y_y and their commutation relations are given in equations (15.32),

$$[Y_x, Y_y] = -X_z, \qquad [X_z, Y_x] = Y_y, \qquad [X_z, Y_y] = -Y_x \tag{20.4}$$

These agree with equations (20.3) if we associate K_1, K_2, K_3 with iY_x, iY_y and iX_z. Again, the factors of i are necessary here because the infinitesimal operators for the unitary transformations generated by the Hermitian operators (20.2) must include a factor i, see section 7.2. Hence the non-invariance group defined by the operators (20.2) has the same commutation relations as $\mathscr{L}_3$ and is therefore (locally) isomorphic with it. We shall not pursue the question of the global transformations, i.e. the question of the range of the group parameters. The infinitesimal properties are sufficient to determine the representations if one is not concerned with questions of many-valuedness.

We now study the unitary irreducible representations of $\mathscr{L}_3$ following the procedure used in subsection 7.4.2 for $\mathscr{R}_3$. First choose a basis in which the operator K_3, and hence the energy, is diagonal. We write $K_3\phi_n = \frac{1}{2}(n+\frac{1}{2})\phi_n$, where for convenience the eigenvalues are expressed in the familiar form of the oscillator energies. There is no loss of generality here since, in this general discussion of the representations of $\mathscr{L}_3$, the number n is, as yet, quite arbitrary and is not restricted to be an integer. The remaining group operators K_1 and K_2 then couple eigenfunctions with different energy. In fact, if we define $K_\pm = K_1 \pm iK_2$ then

$$[K_3, K_\pm] = \pm K_\pm, \qquad [K_+, K_-] = -2K_3 \tag{20.5}$$

showing that $K_\pm$ are raising and lowering operators in the energy. In detail, if $H\phi_n = (n+\frac{1}{2})\phi_n$ then

$$H(K_\pm\phi_n) = 2K_3K_\pm\phi_n = 2K_\pm(K_3 \pm 1)\phi_n = (n+\tfrac{1}{2}\pm 2)(K_\pm\phi_n) \quad (20.6)$$

showing that the operators $K_\pm$ raise and lower the energy by two units of $\hbar\omega$. The Casimir operator for $\mathscr{L}_3$, corresponding to J^2 for the group $\mathscr{R}_3$, is now given by

$$C = K_1^2 + K_2^2 - K_3^2 = \tfrac{1}{2}(K_+K_- + K_-K_+) - K_3^2 \quad (20.7)$$

with a significant change of sign in the third component.

If we now follow the steps used in subsection 7.4.2 to construct the finite dimensional unitary irreducible representations of $\mathscr{R}_3$ we are led to a contradiction because the expression for the normalisation constants A_n defined by the equation

$$\phi_{n+2} = A_n K_+ \phi_n \quad (20.8)$$

takes the form $|A_n|^2 < 0$. Thus we conclude that there are no finite dimensional unitary irreducible representations of $\mathscr{L}_3$ except for the trivial identity representation. (The same conclusion was reached in subsection 15.2.4. for the group $\mathscr{L}$.) We therefore explore the possibility of infinite dimensional representations. This amounts to releasing the constraints that the possible values of n in the representation are bounded above and below.

Let us first release only the upper bound so that we assume the existence of a least $n = n_0$ which implies that

$$K_-\phi_{n_0} = 0 \quad (20.9)$$

The value of the Casimir operator in this representation is found by writing equation (20.7) as $C = K_+K_- + K_3 - K_3^2$ and then operating on ϕ_{n_0} to give the value

$$C = \tfrac{1}{16}(1+2n_0)(3-2n_0) \quad (20.10)$$

This value is then valid for all basis vectors ϕ_n in the representation. Starting with ϕ_{n_0} we now use the raising operator K_+ to generate the set of ϕ_n, where $n = n_0 + 2t$ with t an integer. (Remember from equation (20.5) that K_+ increases the value of K_3 by 1 and hence the value of n by 2.) To ensure that the representation is unitary, the infinitesimal operators K_1, K_2 and K_3 must have Hermitian matrices. This implies that n, and therefore n_0, must be real. It also implies that $K_+^\dagger = K_-$ and so from equation (20.8)

$$\begin{aligned} |A_n|^{-2} &= (\phi_n, K_-K_+\phi_n) = (\phi_n, (C + K_3^2 + K_3)\phi_n) \\ &= \tfrac{1}{16}\{(1+2n_0)(3-2n_0) + (1+2n)(5+2n)\} \\ &= \tfrac{1}{4}(n+n_0+1)(n-n_0+2) \end{aligned} \quad (20.11)$$

To avoid contradiction, this expression must be $\geqq 0$ for $n \geqq n_0$ which leads to the limitation $n_0 \geqq -\frac{1}{2}$, with the value $n_0 = -\frac{1}{2}$ producing the identity representation. For $n_0 > -\frac{1}{2}$ and $n > n_0$ the expression (20.10) will not vanish, so that for each n_0 we have an infinite dimensional unitary irreducible representation $T^{(n_0)}$. However, not all of these representations can be realised in the oscillator problem because, if we use the explicit form (20.2) for the group operators and make use of the commutation relations (19.3), the Casimir operator (20.7) reduces to a constant, $C = 3/16$. Putting this value into the expression (20.10) leads to the two possibilities $n_0 = 0$ or $n_0 = 1$. The eigenfunctions must therefore belong to $T^{(0)}$ with $n = 0, 2, 4, \ldots$, or to $T^{(1)}$ with $n = 1, 3, 5, \ldots$. This accounts for the entire spectrum of the one-dimensional oscillator within two irreducible representations of the non-invariance group $\mathscr{L}_3$. The process by which the value of the Casimir operator limits the possible representations has been met before, in subsection 19.4.2.

The representations $T^{(n_0)}$ derived above are not the only unitary irreducible representations of $\mathscr{L}_3$. In the first place one could retain an upper bound to the possible values of K_3 in the representation. This would lead to a kind of mirror image of $T^{(n_0)}$ with values of K_3 extending down to $-\infty$. It is also possible to generate representations without either upper or lower bounds for K_3. However, none of these representations is relevant to the oscillator problem since they would contain states with unbounded negative energy.

The method used here to generate the non-invariance group $\mathscr{L}_3$ of the one-dimensional oscillator may be applied to the more complicated three-dimensional examples of the oscillator and the Coulomb potential. In the latter case, all eigenfunctions fall into a single irreducible representation of the group $\mathscr{L}_5$, which is like a five-dimensional rotation group with a change in sign of one component in the metric. In this case the symmetry group $\mathscr{R}_4$ is contained as a subgroup within the non-invariance (or dynamical) group $\mathscr{L}_5$.

The choice of dynamical group for a given system is not, however, unique. It should contain the symmetry group and hence account for the degeneracies and also contain operators which couple eigenfunctions. The spectrum of energies should emerge as the allowed values of one of the group operators. From this point of view the concept of the dynamical group has been of interest in the theory of elementary particles. Here the masses of different particles provide a spectrum with apparently unrelated values. One would like to find a dynamical group which brings them together within a single representation and hence relates the masses to some group operators.

On a more practical level the non-invariance groups may be used to deduce simple formulae for transition matrix elements between eigenfunctions. Thus in the simple one-dimensional oscillator we have, from the definitions of H and K_1, the identity $x^2 \equiv H + 2K_1$ so that the matrix elements of x^2 follow from those of the group operators H and K_1 which are known for the irreducible representations using equations (20.8) and (20.11). But, x^2 is the kind of operator involved in electromagnetic transitions of quadrupole type.

20.2 The Jahn–Teller effect and spontaneously broken symmetries

The Jahn–Teller effect is concerned with symmetries which occur following an approximate separation of the Hamiltonian. Because the separation is only approximate there are terms which break the symmetry. The word 'spontaneous' is sometimes used to distinguish this effect from the symmetry breaking caused by the addition of an external perturbation which we discussed in section 5.8. Although the idea is a general one, it is in the structure of molecules that the Jahn–Teller effect was first described and in which it is most clearly seen. More recently the same idea has been used in the theory of elementary particles. To help visualisation we shall present the theory in the language of molecules but its generality will be apparent. Brief mention of the application to elementary particles will be made at the end of the section.

20.2.1 The adiabatic approximation

A molecule is composed of nuclei and electrons interacting via the usual electrical forces and we denote the coordinates of the nuclei and electrons symbolically by $\boldsymbol{R}$ and $\boldsymbol{r}$, respectively. Because the nuclei are more than a thousand times heavier than the electrons and interact with the same forces as the electrons one expects the nuclei to move much more slowly than the electrons. The crucial approximation is first to calculate the orbital motion of the electrons on the assumption that the nuclei are fixed, and then to calculate the equilibrium positions and the rotational and vibrational motion of the nuclei taking account of consequent changes in the electron energies. In general, one calls this an 'adiabatic' approximation, although in molecules it is more often referred to as the Born–Oppenheimer method.

In more detail let us write the full Hamiltonian as

$$\mathrm{H}(\boldsymbol{R},\boldsymbol{r}) = \mathrm{T}_N(\boldsymbol{R}) + \mathrm{T}_e(\boldsymbol{r}) + \mathrm{V}(\boldsymbol{R},\boldsymbol{r}) \tag{20.12}$$

where T_N and T_e denote the kinetic energies of nuclei and electrons, respectively, and V denotes the potential energy of interaction between the nuclei, between electrons and between electrons and nuclei. In the adiabatic approximation one first solves the Schrodinger equation

$$\{\mathrm{T}_e(\boldsymbol{r}) + \mathrm{V}(\boldsymbol{R},\boldsymbol{r})\}\psi_n(\boldsymbol{R},\boldsymbol{r}) = E_n(\boldsymbol{R})\psi_n(\boldsymbol{R},\boldsymbol{r}) \tag{20.13}$$

for the electrons, keeping $\boldsymbol{R}$ fixed. We have used the symbol n to label the eigenvalues although in practice n will need to be a composite label because of the many dimensions of the electron coordinates $\boldsymbol{r}$. Next, one seeks an approximate eigenfunction Ψ of the Hamiltonian (20.12) by writing $\Psi = \psi_n(\boldsymbol{R},\boldsymbol{r})\Phi_n(\boldsymbol{R})$. Substitution into the Schrodinger equation $\mathrm{H}(\boldsymbol{R},\boldsymbol{r})\Psi = E\Psi$ then leads to the equation

$$\{\mathrm{T}_N(\boldsymbol{R}) + E_n(\boldsymbol{R})\}\Phi_n(\boldsymbol{R}) = E\Phi_n(\boldsymbol{R}) \tag{20.14}$$

if we neglect the derivatives of $\psi_n(\boldsymbol{R},\boldsymbol{r})$ with respect to $\boldsymbol{R}$. This neglect really defines the adiabatic approximation in its simplest form. Knowing the electronic energies $E_n(\boldsymbol{R})$ for any fixed $\boldsymbol{R}$ from equation (20.13) enables us in principle to solve equation (20.14) and so complete the solution.

In practice the solution of equation (20.14) is obtained by continuing with the idea of slow motion of the nuclei. To find the lowest energy one first neglects the kinetic energy $\mathrm{T}_N(\boldsymbol{R})$ and simply minimises the function $E_0(\boldsymbol{R})$ with respect to $\boldsymbol{R}$, i.e. for each component R_i of $\boldsymbol{R}$:

$$\partial E_0(\boldsymbol{R})/\,\partial R_i = 0 \tag{20.15}$$

This provides the equilibrium positions $\boldsymbol{R} = \boldsymbol{R}_0$ of the nuclei. Of course, it only fixes their relative positions and the inclusion of $\mathrm{T}_N(\boldsymbol{R})$ contributes a rotational energy. Allowing an expansion of the potential function $E_0(\boldsymbol{R})$ about $\boldsymbol{R}_0$ we can also generate vibrations about the equilibrium position, as described in chapter 6. In this chapter, however, we are interested only in the static equilibrium position.

20.2.2 The role of symmetry

The full Hamiltonian $\mathrm{H}(\boldsymbol{R},\boldsymbol{r})$ is necessarily invariant under all rotations of nuclei and electrons together, since the interactions depend only on relative distances. One therefore has the familiar result that the overall wave function Ψ has definite angular momentum J which in the present problem will relate to the rotational motion. However, there is nothing new about this general result which has been discussed earlier.

The present interest in symmetry concerns the potential $\mathrm{V}(\boldsymbol{R},\boldsymbol{r})$ which for fixed $\boldsymbol{R}$ governs the electronic motion. Regarded as a function of the electron coordinates $\boldsymbol{r}$, it will not be invariant under all rotations of $\boldsymbol{r}$ because the nuclear coordinates $\boldsymbol{R}$ are fixed at their equilibrium values $\boldsymbol{R}_o$. However, if the equilibrium arrangement of nuclei has symmetry with respect to a point group $\mathscr{G}$ then $\mathrm{V}(\boldsymbol{R}_0,\boldsymbol{r})$ must have the same symmetry. When the molecule contains several identical atoms, as in the examples quoted in chapter 6, one can reasonably expect to find such symmetry. The consequences of the symmetry will appear both in the vibrational spectrum, as described in chapter 6, and also in the electronic energy levels E_n which will have characteristic degeneracies corresponding to irreducible representations $\mathrm{T}^{(\alpha)}$ of $\mathscr{G}$, see section 14.4.

Let us now look a little more closely at the consistency of equations (20.13) and (20.15) for a symmetrical equilibrium configuration. We shall find that in many cases the distribution of electrons is sufficiently unsymmetrical that the equilibrium position moves away from the symmetrical one—the Jahn–Teller effect. Differentiating the Schrodinger equation (20.13) with respect to R_i leads to the result

$$\partial E_0(\boldsymbol{R})/\,\partial R_i = \langle \psi_0 |\, \partial \mathrm{V}(\boldsymbol{R},\boldsymbol{r})/\,\partial R_i \,| \psi_0 \rangle \tag{20.16}$$

so that from equation (20.15) these matrix elements should vanish in the equilibrium position $\boldsymbol{R} = \boldsymbol{R}_0$. Let us now consider the significance of the vanishing of these matrix elements using the selection rule technique described in section 5.4. As we have seen in detail in chapter 6, the $3N$ coordinates R_i of the N nuclei of a molecule may be defined such that they belong to definite irreducible representations $T^{(\gamma)}$ of $\mathcal{G}$. If R_i is a symmetrical coordinate, belonging to the identity representation $T^{(1)}$, then since V is invariant, so also is the operator $\partial V/\partial R_i$. Hence, no matter to which representation $T^{(\alpha)}$ the wave function ψ_0 belongs, there is no symmetry reason why the matrix element should vanish. However the value of any symmetrical coordinate may be varied indefinitely without destroying the symmetry, so that the vanishing of the matrix element may be achieved in this way and simply determines the size and the other free parameters of the symmetrical system. For the remaining non-symmetrical coordinates no such freedom exists since a non-zero value for any of them implies a departure from symmetry. Hence if the matrix elements (20.16) are to vanish they must do so for reasons of symmetry. Since V is invariant, the set of representations $T^{(\gamma)}$ to which the derivatives $\partial V/\partial R_i$ belong is the same as the set to which the coordinates belong. Thus we require the vanishing of (20.16) for all $T^{(\gamma)}$, other than $T^{(1)}$, which occur for the coordinates $\boldsymbol{R}$. (One should exclude here the rotational and translational coordinates, see section 6.5, since V is necessarily independent of these.) From the selection rule arguments of section 5.4 this means that $T^{(\alpha)}$ must not occur in the reduction of the products $T^{(\gamma)} \times T^{(\alpha)}$ and in terms of characters this condition becomes

$$\sum_{G_a} \chi^{(\alpha)*}(G_a)\chi^{(\gamma)}(G_a)\chi^{(\alpha)}(G_a) = 0$$

$$\sum_{G_a} |\chi^{(\alpha)}(G_a)|^2 \chi^{(\gamma)}(G_a) = 0 \tag{20.17}$$

For any one-dimensional (unitary) representation $T^{(\alpha)}$, we have $|\chi^{(\alpha)}(G_a)|^2 = 1$ for each element G_a so that (20.17) is always satisfied because of the orthogonality of $\chi^{(\gamma)}$ with the identity representation. However, for all representations with dimensions greater than one it is found that except for linear molecules there is at least one $T^{(\gamma)}$ for which (20.17) is not satisfied. Thus if there is a degeneracy in the electronic ground state then the minimum energy condition (20.15) is not satisfied in the symmetrical position and so the lowest energy is obtained in a non-symmetrical position of equilibrium in which there will generally be no degeneracies. It is interesting to note that in the case of a one-dimensional representation $T^{(\alpha)}$ the electron density $|\psi_0|^2$ is invariant since $|\chi^{(\alpha)}(G_a)|^2 = 1$ (This is true even when $T^{(\alpha)}$ is not the identity and ψ_0 is itself not invariant.) Intuitively one would expect the symmetry to be unbroken in this situation, while for representations with greater dimension no such argument is generally possible.

As an example, consider the ammonia molecule described in section 6.5, where it was found that the six internal coordinates belonged to representations A_1 and E, each appearing twice. For the sake of argument let us suppose that the electron wave function belongs to the two-dimensional representation E giving a degeneracy. Then the matrix elements (20.16) corresponding to the two symmetrical A_1-type coordinates will not vanish for symmetry reasons but can be made to do so by choice of the bond angle ϕ and the NH bond length. For the E-type coordinates the use of the known characters shows that equation (20.17) is not satisfied when $\mathrm{T}^{(\alpha)} = \mathrm{T}^{(\gamma)} = E$ and hence the symmetrical position is not a position of equilibrium.

In practice it is not trivial to find an observable example of the Jahn–Teller effect. This is because the electronic ground states of molecules are usually symmetrical and therefore non-degenerate. Excited states should, however, demonstrate the effect and probably the best example is seen in the photo-electron spectrum of methane which indicates (see Sturge, 1967, in the bibliography) that, in the final ionised state of methane, the molecule is distorted from the regular tetrahedron.

We have ignored spin in the discussion above. It may be shown that, although in principle any spin degeneracy (beyond the two-fold time-reversal degeneracy for an odd number of electrons) leads to a Jahn–Teller symmetry breaking, the effect is very small.

20.2.3 Spontaneous symmetry breaking

There is a very interesting symmetry argument in the Born–Oppenheimer approximation for molecules which occurs in many other physical systems and is sometimes referred to as spontaneous symmetry breaking. The complete Hamiltonian has the full $\mathscr{R}_3$ symmetry because it depends only on the relative interactions of the constituent electrons and nuclei. However, in finding an approximate solution we made use of a subgroup of $\mathscr{R}_3$, the point group $\mathscr{G}$ appropriate to the equilibrium arrangement of the nuclei. In this sense, the symmetry was broken from $\mathscr{R}_3$ to $\mathscr{G}$ and would be restored only when the rotational motion of the molecule is included, i.e. in addition to the motion of the electrons and the vibration of the nuclei one must also allow the entire system to rotate. In a macroscopic crystal, however, the symmetry group $\mathscr{G}$ acquires greater significance because, with a macroscopic moment of inertia, the energy quanta for rotational motion become very small.

For a molecule, the restriction from $\mathscr{R}_3$ to a point group $\mathscr{G}$ was perhaps natural because of the distinction between electrons and nuclei. However, the same principle occurs in other physical systems. For example, in the structure of nuclei the constituent nucleons are all identical but there is strong evidence that they acquire a non-spherical equilibrium shape which then rotates. The number of nucleons is sufficently large, of the order of 100, that the subgroup is not a point group but the continuous group $\mathscr{R}_2$ together with two-fold rotations about all axes perpendicular to the axis of $\mathscr{R}_2$—a group denoted by D_∞ (the limit of D_n). Unlike a crystal, there is no macroscopic assembly of nuclei in which to see the D_∞ symmetry but one may infer the symmetry from the properties of the rotational levels of nuclei.

Another more sophisticated example occurs in the theory of superconductivity. Here, one is concerned not with rotational symmetry but with the conservation of the number of electrons. This is such an obvious symmetry of a non-relativistic system that one does not usually mention it. The group concerned is the unitary group in one dimension with a single parameter α and group operators $\exp(i\alpha N)$, where N is the number operator. The essence of the theory is to construct, in a particularly simple form, a trial wave function which breaks the number symmetry, i.e. which is a superposition of states with different particle number. For a large number of electrons interacting mainly in time-reversed pairs of single-particle states, this proves to be a good approximation. For a small number of particles one would have to recover a state with definite particle number (the quantity corresponding to angular momentum in the previous example) and this might be achieved by the action of a number projection operator on the symmetry-breaking trial wave function. Again, in a macroscopic system, the symmetry breaking solution acquires significance and leads to an explanation of the phenomenon of superconductivity whereby electric current passes without resistance. (Excitations from the symmetry breaking state are not possible until the energy passes a certain energy gap, whereas for free electrons there are excitations at infinitesimally low energy.)

As a final example, we mention briefly the use of symmetry breaking in the relativistic field theory of elementary particles. It arises in attempts to unify the theories of electromagnetic and weak (β-decay) interactions. Because of the short range of the weak interactions the relevant field particles (vector mesons) must have finite mass, in contrast to the photon, and this introduces divergencies in the field theory which cannot (apparently) be removed. For zero-mass field particles such difficulties do not occur and one is able to construct a unified Lagrangian which is invariant under a set of gauge transformations (see subsection 16.3.5) and which offers hope of relating various coupling constants that occur in the weak and electromagnetic interactions. The vital step of introducing a finite mass for the vector mesons is now achieved by the device of symmetry breaking. It is supposed that the vacuum is not an invariant (nor does it belong to any irreducible representation) of the full gauge symmetry group but is invariant only under some subgroup. This introduces, into the Lagrangian, terms which are equivalent to assigning a mass to some of the vector mesons. By suitable choice of the gauge group and its subgroup under which the vacuum is invariant, one may arrange that the photon preserves its zero mass while the vector mesons acquire mass. The introduction of mass by this device avoids the divergencies referred to earlier. The mechanism by which the vacuum achieves broken symmetry is a little obscure but seems to involve the introduction of an additional field of scalar particles, some of which conspire to provide the third component needed by the vector mesons in acquiring mass! (Note from subsection 16.3.7 that the photon has only two states $m = \pm 1$, whereas a finite mass particle with $s = 1$ needs $m = \pm 1$ and $m = 0$.)

20.3 Normal subgroups, semi-direct products and little groups

In the early parts of this book we limited our study of the theory of groups to those properties which were vital in understanding the physical applications. There are many fascinating properties, even of finite groups, which we have not mentioned. Here we introduce the idea of the normal subgroup and describe its use in finding representations. In fact this provides a general background for the introduction of little groups which we have used in an *ad hoc* fashion in obtaining representations of the space groups in chapter 14 and the Euclidean and Poincaré groups in chapter 15.

For the direct product of two groups defined in section 2.5 the characters and representations are obtained trivially from those of the two separate groups, as described in section 4.21. Remember that in the direct product $\mathscr{G} = \mathscr{H} \times \mathscr{K}$ the elements of $\mathscr{H}$ must commute with those of $\mathscr{K}$. We now define what is meant by saying that a group $\mathscr{G}$ is a 'semi-direct product', written $\mathscr{G} = \mathscr{H} \wedge \mathscr{K}$. The elements of $\mathscr{G}$ must be the set of products $\mathrm{G}_{ia} = \mathrm{H}_i\mathrm{K}_a$, where H_i and K_a denote, respectively, elements of two subgroups $\mathscr{H}$ and $\mathscr{K}$ and, although the H_i need not commute with the K_a, the relation

$$\mathrm{K}_a\mathrm{H}_i\mathrm{K}_a^{-1} = \mathrm{H}_j \tag{20.18}$$

must be satisfied where H_j is another element of $\mathscr{H}$. (It is possible to give a more general definition of a normal subgroup in which $\mathscr{H}$ is simply a subgroup of $\mathscr{G}$ for which a relation of the kind $\mathrm{G}_a\mathrm{H}_i\mathrm{G}_a^{-1} = \mathrm{H}_j$ exists for all G_a in $\mathscr{G}$. The factorisation $\mathrm{G} = \mathrm{HK}$ of the elements of $\mathscr{G}$ does not then necessarily occur and although the factor group may still be defined, it is not necessarily a subgroup of $\mathscr{G}$.) This definition implies that the elements conjugate to any H_i with respect to any element of $\mathscr{G}$ will all lie in $\mathscr{H}$. Note that the definition (20.18) is not symmetrical between the two subgroups $\mathscr{H}$ and $\mathscr{K}$. The group $\mathscr{H}$ is called a 'normal' (or invariant or self-conjugate) subgroup of $\mathscr{G}$. The group $\mathscr{K}$ is called the 'factor' (or quotient) group of $\mathscr{G}$ with respect to $\mathscr{H}$, a relation often expressed by the notation $\mathscr{K} = \mathscr{G}/\mathscr{H}$. If g, h and k denote the orders (number of elements) of $\mathscr{G}$, $\mathscr{H}$ and $\mathscr{K}$ then clearly $g = hk$ and k is called the 'index' of $\mathscr{H}$ in $\mathscr{G}$.

As examples of semi-direct product groups among the finite groups there is the tetrahedral group, see section 9.3, which may be written as $T = D \wedge C_3$ and the simpler example $D_4 = C_4 \wedge C_2$. A careful study of the elements of T (or D_4) and their multiplication table is necessary to convince oneself of these relations. The space groups of section 14.9 which were formed by including a group $\mathscr{T}$ of discrete translations with a point group $\mathscr{G}$ are semi-direct products $\mathscr{T} \wedge \mathscr{G}$ with the translations forming the normal subgroup because of equation (14.72). In a similar way the Euclidean group of section 15.1 is given as $\mathscr{E}_3 = \mathscr{T}_3 \wedge \mathscr{R}_3$ and the Poincaré group of section 15.4 as $\mathscr{P} = \mathscr{T}_4 \wedge \mathscr{L}$, where $\mathscr{T}_3$ and $\mathscr{T}_4$ denote the translation groups in three-space and space-time, respectively.

Let us now see how a knowledge of this semi-direct product structure $\mathscr{G} = \mathscr{H} \wedge \mathscr{K}$ of a group can help us to find its irreducible representations. For simplicity we limit our discussion to the case when the normal subgroup $\mathscr{H}$ is Abelian (the generalisation is straightforward) so that its irreducible representations are one-dimensional denoted by $T^{(\lambda)}$. Since $\mathscr{H}$ is a subgroup of $\mathscr{G}$ the basis vectors of an irreducible representation T of $\mathscr{G}$ may be chosen to belong to definite irreducible representations of $\mathscr{H}$ so that, denoting these vectors by $|\lambda\rangle$ we have, for any H in $\mathscr{H}$,

$$T(H)|\lambda\rangle = T^{(\lambda)}(H)|\lambda\rangle \tag{20.19}$$

We now choose a particular $|\lambda\rangle$ and use the elements K_a of $\mathscr{K}$ to generate from it the set of vectors denoted by

$$|\lambda a\rangle = T(K_a)|\lambda\rangle \tag{20.20}$$

Each of these new vectors must itself belong to one of the representations of $\mathscr{H}$ because from equations (20.18), (20.19) and (20.20)

$$T(H)|\lambda a\rangle = T(H)T(K_a)|\lambda\rangle = T(K_a)T(H')|\lambda\rangle = T^{(\lambda)}(H')|\lambda a\rangle \tag{20.21}$$

where $H' = K_a^{-1}HK_a$. However, notice that the representation of $\mathscr{H}$ defined by this equation is not necessarily $T^{(\lambda)}$ since it associates with the group element H the matrix element $T^{(\lambda)}(H')$ for a different element H′. Let us therefore denote this representation of $\mathscr{H}$ by $T^{(\lambda_a)}$. Consider first the simplest possibility, that the set of representations $T^{(\lambda_a)}$, as G_a runs through the elements of $\mathscr{K}$, are all inequivalent. In this case the vectors $|\lambda a\rangle$ must be linearly independent and provide a basis for a k-dimensional irreducible representation of $\mathscr{G}$. The explicit form for the representation is quickly found by operating on $|\lambda a\rangle$ with the general group element G = HK,

$$\begin{aligned} T(HK)|\lambda a\rangle &= T(H)T(K)T(K_a)|\lambda\rangle = T(H)T(K_b)|\lambda\rangle \\ &= T(K_b)T(H')|\lambda\rangle = T^{(\lambda)}(H')|\lambda b\rangle \end{aligned} \tag{20.22}$$

where we have defined $K_b = KK_a$ and $H' = K_b^{-1}HK_b$. Thus the matrix elements of T(HK) are zero except for the numbers $T^{(\lambda)}(H')$ coupling rows a with the appropriate columns b and these numbers are known from the irreducible representations $T^{(\lambda)}$ of the subgroup $\mathscr{H}$.

Some modification is necessary when any of the representations $T^{(\lambda_a)}$ are equivalent to $T^{(\lambda)}$. Given λ let us denote by $\tilde{K}_a$ the set of elements of $\mathscr{K}$ for which this equivalence holds. We now show that this set forms a subgroup of $\mathscr{K}$ which we denote by $\tilde{\mathscr{K}}$. It is generally referred to as the 'little group', relative to $\mathscr{G}$, $\mathscr{H}$ and λ. We shall not verify that the set $\tilde{K}_a$ satisfy all the group postulates but only the multiplication law. Given that $\tilde{K}_a$ and $\tilde{K}_b$ belong to the set so that

$$T^{(\lambda)}(\tilde{K}_a^{-1}H\tilde{K}_a) = ST^{(\lambda)}(H)S^{-1} \text{ and } T^{(\lambda)}(\tilde{K}_b^{-1}H\tilde{K}_b) = RT^{(\lambda)}(H)R^{-1}$$

for some fixed S and R, independent of H, we have for $\tilde{K}_b\tilde{K}_a$

$$T^{(\lambda)}(\tilde{K}_a^{-1}\tilde{K}_b^{-1}H\tilde{K}_b\tilde{K}_a) = T^{(\lambda)}(\tilde{K}_a^{-1}H'\tilde{K}_a) = ST^{(\lambda)}(H')S^{-1} = SRT^{(\lambda)}(H)R^{-1}S^{-1}$$

where again $H' = \tilde{K}_b^{-1}H\tilde{K}_b$. Thus the multiplication law is satisfied. The set of vectors $|\lambda a\rangle$ which transform equivalently to a given λ must therefore form an invariant space under the little group $\tilde{\mathscr{K}}$ and so we may choose them to transform according to definite irreducible representations $T^{(\alpha)}$ of $\tilde{\mathscr{K}}$. Thus the basis vectors will carry both labels λ and α and also a row label i if $T^{(\alpha)}$ has dimension greater than one. To generate the irreducible representations of $\mathscr{G}$ we start from one such set of vectors $|\lambda\alpha i\rangle$ with fixed λ and α. It is a general property of any group $\mathscr{K}$ of order k that given a subgroup $\tilde{\mathscr{K}}$ of order $\tilde{k}$ any element of $\mathscr{K}$ may be written in the form $K = M_c\tilde{K}$, where M_c is one of a set of $k/\tilde{k}$ elements of $\mathscr{K}$ (this is Lagrange's theorem, see problem 2.4). Because of this result the representation T of $\mathscr{G}$ may be generated by operating on the vectors $|\lambda\alpha i\rangle$ with the set of $k/\tilde{k}$ elements M_c, $T(M_c)|\lambda\alpha i\rangle = |\lambda\alpha i, c\rangle$. The representation is labelled $T^{(\lambda,\,\alpha)}$ and has dimension $s_\alpha k/\tilde{k}$ with its matrix elements being found as in the derivation of equation (20.22), i.e.

$$\begin{aligned}
T(HK)|\lambda\alpha i, c\rangle &= T(H)T(K)T(M_c)|\lambda\alpha i\rangle = T(H)T(K')|\lambda\alpha i\rangle \\
&= T(K')T(H')|\lambda\alpha i\rangle = T(K')T^{(\lambda)}(H')|\lambda\alpha i\rangle \\
&= T^{(\lambda)}(H')T(M_d)T(\tilde{K}')|\lambda\alpha i\rangle = T^{(\lambda)}(H')\sum_j T_{ji}^{(\alpha)}(\tilde{K}')T(M_d)|\lambda\alpha j\rangle \\
&= T^{(\lambda)}(H')\sum_j T_{ji}^{(\alpha)}(\tilde{K}')|\lambda\alpha j, d\rangle \qquad (20.23)
\end{aligned}$$

where the new symbols K', H', M_d, $\tilde{K}'$ and d are defined by the equations $K' = KM_c$, $H' = K'^{-1}HK'$, $K' = M_d\tilde{K}'$. Thus the representation is given in terms of the matrix elements of the representations of the subgroups $\mathscr{H}$ and $\tilde{\mathscr{K}}$.

The question arises whether each choice of λ leads to a different irreducible representation of $\mathscr{G}$ and the answer is generally 'no', because if some of the $T^{(\lambda_a)}$ are not equivalent to $T^{(\lambda)}$ then the same representation of $\mathscr{G}$ would have been obtained by starting from any of these $T^{(\lambda_a)}$ instead of $T^{(\lambda)}$. The set of representations $T^{(\lambda_a)}$ are said to be in the same 'orbit'. In constructing all irreducible representations of $\mathscr{G}$ one need only choose one λ from each orbit. (The concept of orbit is closely related to that of the 'star of $\boldsymbol{k}$' in subsection 14.9.1, since $\boldsymbol{k}$ corresponds to λ. Representations $T^{(\boldsymbol{k}_i)}$ of the translation group, where $\boldsymbol{k}_i$ is in the star of $\boldsymbol{k}$, will be in the same orbit.)

As a simple example of this procedure let us find the representations of the semi-direct product group $D_4 = C_4 \wedge C_2$. We first note geometrically that the C_2 axis must be perpendicular to the C_4 axis and that the product elements fall into the five classes of D_4 as follows: E; C_4^2; C_4, C_4^3; C_2, $C_4^2C_2$; C_4C_2, $C_4^3C_2$. There are four irreducible representations $T^{(\lambda)}$ of C_4 from which to begin, see table A.1 of volume 1. Starting with the identity representation A of C_4 it is clear that the little group here must be the factor group C_2 itself, since for the identity representation the matrix elements $T^{(\lambda)}(H) = 1$ are the same for all H. Thus to each irreducible representation $T^{(\alpha)}$ of C_2, and there are two of these (A and B in the notation of table A.1), we get a one-dimensional representation of D_4. From equation (20.23) and using the character table for C_2 one sees that this provides the representations of D_4 which are labelled A_1 and A_2 in table A.1. Turning now to the next representation B of C_4 the little group is again seen to be C_2 so that two more representations B_1 and B_2 of D_4 are produced. Finally if we take the first of the pair of representations of C_4 labelled by E, the little group can no longer contain the element C_2 because $C_2^{-1}C_4C_2 = C_4^3$ and the matrix elements of C_4 and C_4^3 are not the same for the representations E of C_4. Thus the little group reduces trivially to the identity and we have a two-dimensional representation ($k/\tilde{k} = 2$) of D_4 given by equation (20.22) and labelled by E in table A.1. The use of the second of the pair of E representations of C_4 leads to the same representation of D_4 because the pair belong to the same orbit.

20.4 The classification of Lie groups

A systematic listing of the finite point groups was given in chapter 9 but for the continuous Lie groups introduced in chapter 7, we have so far considered only those examples which have occurred in particular physical problems. The object of this section is to find a systematic listing of Lie groups so that in any new symmetry problem one is in a position to recognise the group responsible.

We begin by defining a few new terms. If a group has no invariant subgroup it is called 'simple'. If it has no Abelian invariant subgroup it is called 'semi-simple', so that the simple groups form a subset of the semi-simple groups. The word 'non-semi-simple' is sometimes used for groups which have an Abelian invariant subgroup. As we have seen in the preceding section the non-semi-simple groups may be described as semi-direct products so we restrict our attention to semi-simple groups. Furthermore it may be shown that if a Lie group is semi-simple but not simple then it may be written as a direct product of simple groups. Thus we shall, later on, restrict our attention further to the classification of the simple Lie groups only.

The discussion starts from the set of r infinitesimal operators X_p together with their commutations relations, see section 7.2,

$$[X_q, X_p] = \sum c_{qp}^t X_t \qquad (20.24)$$

(A set of operators with this law of 'multiplication' is often called a Lie 'algebra'.) If the matrix

$$g_{qs} = \sum_{p,t} c^t_{qp} c^p_{st} \tag{20.25}$$

is formed from the structure constants c^t_{qp} then the (Cartan) criterion for the group to be semi-simple is that det $g \neq 0$. (It is not difficult to deduce this criterion if we notice that the existence of an Abelian invariant subgroup implies that a subset $X_{i'}$ of the X_i satisfy the relations

$$[X_{q'}, X_{p'}] = 0, \qquad [X_{q'}, X_t] = \sum_{s'} c^{s'}_{q't} X_{s'}$$

where we use a prime to denote the members of the subset). For any given group there is much freedom in defining the X_p because any real linear combination of the X_p is itself an infinitesimal operator, and in trying to classify the different Lie groups we shall naturally choose a convenient set. We first find the largest set of mutually commuting infinitesimal operators, denoting them by H_i. The number of operators H_i is called the 'rank' of the group and denoted by l. Necessarily $1 \leqq l \leqq r$ since any operator commutes with itself. One may then choose the remaining operators E_{α} to be 'eigenoperators' of the H_i, in the sense that

$$[H_i, E_{\alpha}] = \alpha_i E_{\alpha} \tag{20.26}$$

for some set of 'eigenvalues' α_i. That the E_{α} may be chosen in this way to be eigenvectors of all the H_i at the same time follows from the fact that the H_i commute—a familiar result in ordinary eigenvector theory. Given the structure constants for any set of X_p one can search to find the H_i and hence construct the H_i and E_{α}. The set of l eigenvalues α_i is conveniently denoted by a vector $\boldsymbol{\alpha} = (\alpha_1\, \alpha_2 \ldots \alpha_l)$ in l dimensions. It is called a 'root vector' and it can be shown that for semi-simple groups there is no degeneracy, i.e. no two operators E have the same non-zero root vector. (One may of course regard the H_i themselves as eigenoperators with $\boldsymbol{\alpha} = 0$, in which special case there is a degeneracy of order l). Thus the root vector $\boldsymbol{\alpha}$ is a sufficient label for the E_{α}.

To complete the commutation relations among the new set of operators H_i, E_{α} we need to study $[E_{\alpha}, E_{\beta}]$ but by rewriting the double commutator (Jacobi identity) we have

$$\Big[H_i, [E_{\alpha}, E_{\beta}]\Big] = \Big[[H_i, E_{\alpha}], E_{\beta}\Big] + \Big[E_{\alpha}, [H_i, E_{\beta}]\Big] = (\alpha_i + \beta_i)[E_{\alpha}, E_{\beta}]$$

so that the commutator $[E_{\alpha}, E_{\beta}]$ is itself an eigenoperator of the H_i with root vector $\boldsymbol{\alpha} + \boldsymbol{\beta}$. Thus if $\boldsymbol{\alpha} + \boldsymbol{\beta} \neq 0$ we may write

$$[E_{\alpha}, E_{\beta}] = N_{\alpha\beta} E_{\alpha+\beta} \tag{20.27}$$

with some normalisation constant which depends on the definition of the E_{α}. When $\boldsymbol{\alpha} + \boldsymbol{\beta} = 0$ the commutator $[E_{\alpha}, E_{\beta}]$ commutes with the H_i and must therefore be a linear combination of them so that we may write

$$[\mathrm{E}_{\boldsymbol{\alpha}}, \mathrm{E}_{-\boldsymbol{\alpha}}] = \sum_i \alpha^i \mathrm{H}_i \tag{20.28}$$

defining the constants α^i which again depend on the choice of H_i and the normalisation of $\mathrm{E}_{\boldsymbol{\alpha}}$. In fact we can conveniently make $\alpha^i = \alpha_i$. (To justify this step one first chooses the H_i such that $g_{ij} = \delta_{ij}$ by using a Schmidt process because $g_{ik} = \sum_{\alpha} \alpha_i \alpha_k$ has the form of a scalar product. Next, one defines $c_{pqs} = \sum_t g_{pt} c^t_{qs}$ and shows it to be antisymmetric in its three indices. Hence we have

$$c_{k\alpha-\alpha} = \sum_t g_{kt} c^t_{\alpha-\alpha} = c^k_{\alpha-\alpha} = \alpha^k$$

and also

$$c_{k\alpha-\alpha} = c_{-\alpha k\alpha} = \sum_t g_{-\alpha t} c^t_{k\alpha} = g_{-\alpha\alpha} c^{\alpha}_{k\alpha} = \alpha_k \, g_{\alpha-\alpha}$$

Thus α^k is proportional to α_k and a choice of magnitude of the $\mathrm{E}_{\boldsymbol{\alpha}}$ will then lead to the equality.)

In classifying the Lie groups one may first use the rank l and for each value of l find the possible sets of root vectors $\boldsymbol{\alpha}$ in l-dimensional space. We shall see that these vectors must satisfy some rather stringent conditions so that there are only a few solutions. The first property of the roots is that if $\boldsymbol{\alpha}$ is a root vector then so is $-\boldsymbol{\alpha}$. (This can be seen by constructing the matrix elements $g_{\boldsymbol{\alpha\beta}}$ from the definition (20.25) using the vanishing of certain structure constants implied by equations (20.26)–(20.28). It is seen that for given $\boldsymbol{\alpha}$, all matrix elements vanish unless $\boldsymbol{\beta} = -\boldsymbol{\alpha}$ so that, unless a root $-\boldsymbol{\alpha}$ exists, the entire row $\boldsymbol{\alpha}$ of the matrix g vanishes, implying that $\det g = 0$ which violates Cartan's criterion of semi-simplicity.) This enables us to divide the roots into *positive* and negative, according to whether the first component $\alpha_1 > 0$ or $\alpha_1 < 0$. If $\alpha_1 = 0$ then the sign of the second component α_2 is used to decide whether the root is positive or negative and so on. The ordering of the H_i and hence of the α_i is arbitrary. The number $\frac{1}{2}(r-l)$ of positive root vectors is generally greater than l so that they are not linearly independent. For a basis one may continue to use the l vectors $(1, 0, 0 \ldots)$, $(0, 1, 0 \ldots)$, etc., but it is more convenient to use a basis of vectors each of which is itself a positive root vector and in particular a basis of what are called 'simple positive roots'. Such a root is defined to have the property that it cannot be written as the sum of two other positive roots. It may be shown that there are just l simple positive roots and that they are linearly independent. A further property is that if $\boldsymbol{\alpha}$ and $\boldsymbol{\beta}$ are two simple positive roots then it follows that $\boldsymbol{\beta}-\boldsymbol{\alpha}$ cannot be a root of any kind. (For suppose $\boldsymbol{\beta}-\boldsymbol{\alpha} = \gamma$, with γ a positive root, then $\boldsymbol{\beta} = \boldsymbol{\alpha}+\gamma$ which contradicts the definition of $\boldsymbol{\beta}$ as a 'simple' positive root. A similar argument disposes of the possibility that γ is negative).† However, there may be roots of the form $\boldsymbol{\beta}+\boldsymbol{\alpha}$ and indeed there will

† The symbols γ and ξ, like $\boldsymbol{\alpha}$ and $\boldsymbol{\beta}$, represent vectors and should have been printed in bold in this section.

generally be strings of roots $\beta+\alpha$, $\beta+2\alpha$, . . . , $\beta+n\alpha$, which terminate at some integer n, i.e. $\beta+(n+1)\alpha$ is not a root. The value of n may be related to the vectors by the equation

$$n = -2(\alpha.\beta)/(\alpha.\alpha) \tag{20.29}$$

where the scalar product is defined as $\alpha.\beta = \sum_i \alpha_i\beta_i$. This general result is deduced from a recurrence relation as follows. If m is an integer $\leqq n$ then, from the Jacobi identity,

$$\left[E_{\beta+m\alpha}, [E_\alpha, E_{-\alpha}]\right] = \left[[E_{\beta+m\alpha}, E_\alpha], E_{-\alpha}\right] + \left[E_\alpha, [E_{\beta+m\alpha}, E_{-\alpha}]\right]$$

i.e.

$$\sum_i \alpha_i[E_{\beta+m\alpha}, H_i] = N_{\beta+m\alpha,\alpha}[E_{\beta+m\alpha+\alpha}, E_{-\alpha}] + N_{\beta+m\alpha,-\alpha}[E_\alpha, E_{\beta+m\alpha-\alpha}]$$

and so

$$-\sum_i \alpha_i(\beta_i+m\alpha_i)E_{\beta+m\alpha} = (N_{\beta+m\alpha,\alpha}N_{\beta+m\alpha+\alpha,-\alpha} - N_{\beta+m\alpha,-\alpha}N_{\beta+m\alpha-\alpha,\alpha})E_{\beta+m\alpha}$$

and if, for brevity, we define $A_m = N_{\beta+m\alpha,\alpha}N_{\beta+m\alpha+\alpha,-\alpha}$ then we have

$$\alpha.\beta+m\alpha.\alpha = -A_m + A_{m-1} \tag{20.30}$$

Now since, as explained above, $\beta-\alpha$ is not a root we have $N_{\beta-\alpha} = 0$ so that $A_{-1} = 0$ and from recurrence relation (20.30) we may deduce

$$-A_m = (m+1)\alpha.\beta + \tfrac{1}{2}m(m+1)\alpha.\alpha \tag{20.31}$$

If n denotes the termination of the string, as defined above, then $N_{\beta+n\alpha,\alpha} = 0$ so that $A_n = 0$ and hence from equation (20.31) we deduce the relation (20.29).

From the definition of the scalar product it follows (Schwartz inequality) that $(\alpha.\beta)^2 \leqq (\alpha.\alpha)(\beta.\beta)$ and hence from equation (20.29), and the corresponding equation $p = -2(\alpha.\beta)/(\beta.\beta)$ for the β-string $\alpha+\beta$, $\alpha+2\beta$, . . ., $\alpha+p\beta$, where p is again an integer,

$$-(\alpha.\beta)/(\alpha.\alpha)^{\frac{1}{2}}(\beta.\beta)^{\frac{1}{2}} = +(\tfrac{1}{4}np)^{\frac{1}{2}} \leqq 1 \tag{20.32}$$

This may be said to define the angle between α and β. From the same two equations one has the ratio of the lengths

$$(\beta.\beta)/(\alpha.\alpha) = n/p \tag{20.33}$$

The values of n (and p) are strictly limited by equation (20.32) which implies that $np = 0, 1, 2$ or 3. (The value 4 is not allowed since this would mean that $\alpha = -\beta$ contradicting the definition of α and β as both positive roots.) Hence we are able to enumerate the possible sets of simple positive roots and, from these, all roots are constructed by forming all possible strings. In some cases it is possible to build β-strings on roots $\beta + m\alpha$ although multiples like $m(\beta+\alpha)$ with $m > 1$ are not allowed.

The enumeration is done very concisely by forming what are known as 'Dynkln diagrams'. Each simple positive root is represented by a point. For each pair of such roots the quantity np (which determines the angle between them) is signified by joining the corresponding points with that number np of straight lines, drawn close together. The relative lengths of two roots joined in this way is sometimes denoted by placing the relative values of $\alpha.\alpha$ over each point. In fact these are very limited because if $np = 1$ then $n = p = 1$ and from equation (20.33) the lengths are equal. If $np = 2$ one is $\sqrt{2}$ times the other, while if $np = 3$ one is $\sqrt{3}$ times the other. The task of drawing all possible Dynkin diagrams is greatly simplified by noting the following rules which follow from the equations we have derived above:

(1) Only connected diagrams need be considered because if a diagram splits into two unconnected parts then, because there are no connecting lines, the roots in one part are orthogonal ($\alpha.\beta = 0$) to those in the other and this implies that the group is a direct product and not 'simple'.

(2) There can be no loops. For example, suppose α, β and γ were to form a triangle of single lines then, from equation (20.32) with $np = 1$, $\tilde{\alpha}.\tilde{\beta} = \tilde{\beta}.\tilde{\gamma} = \tilde{\gamma}.\tilde{\alpha} = -\frac{1}{2}$, where for brevity we write $\tilde{\alpha} = \alpha/(\alpha.\alpha)^{\frac{1}{2}}$, etc. Now since $\tilde{\alpha}$, $\tilde{\beta}$ and $\tilde{\gamma}$ have to be linearly independent it must be possible to write $\tilde{\alpha} = b\tilde{\beta} + c\tilde{\gamma} + \xi$, where ξ is orthogonal to $\tilde{\beta}$ and $\tilde{\gamma}$ and is non-zero. This is simply the projection of $\tilde{\alpha}$ on to the subspace defined by $\tilde{\beta}$ and $\tilde{\gamma}$ with ξ lying in the orthogonal complement space. The coefficients b and c are then given by the equations $\tilde{\beta}.\tilde{\alpha} = b + c\tilde{\beta}.\tilde{\gamma}$ and $\tilde{\gamma}.\tilde{\alpha} = b\tilde{\gamma}.\tilde{\beta} + c$ and inserting the value $-\frac{1}{2}$ for each scalar product this gives $\xi.\xi = 0$, a contradiction. Larger loops are excluded by a similar argument and the use of double lines only sharpens the contradiction by giving $\xi.\xi < 0$.

(3) There can be at most three lines radiating from any point. Suppose there were roots $\alpha_1, \alpha_2, \ldots \alpha_p$ all connected to a root β then no two of the roots α_i could be connected to each other without violating rule (2) and so the roots α_i are mutually orthogonal $\alpha_i.\alpha_j = 0$ for $i \neq j$. Thus if as in (2) we were to write $\tilde{\beta} = \sum_{i=1}^{p} a_i\tilde{\alpha}_i + \xi$ with $\xi.\tilde{\alpha}_i = 0$ for all i, then the coefficients are given by $a_i = \tilde{\beta}.\tilde{\alpha}_i$ and

$$\xi.\xi = 1 - \sum_{i=1}^{p} a_i^2 < 1 - \tfrac{1}{4}p$$

But once again $\xi.\xi > 0$ so that $p \leqq 3$.

(4) Rule (3) excludes diagrams containing any of the following pieces:

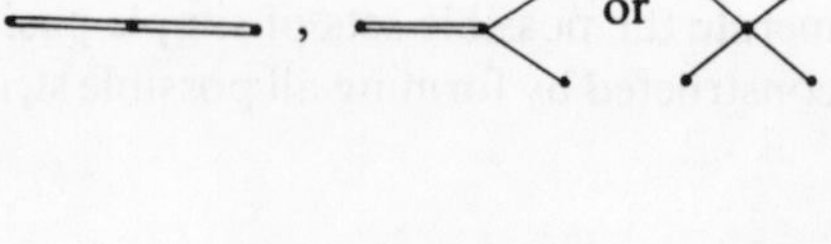

The arguments in rule (3) may be extended to show that if any number of single lines are inserted into these pieces, for example

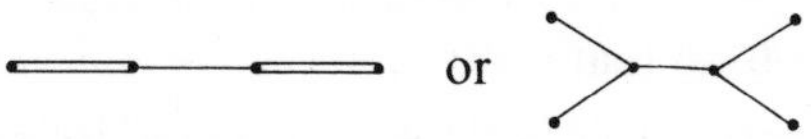

then the same contradiction arises. One therefore concludes that no Dynkin diagram may contain more than one double-line connection

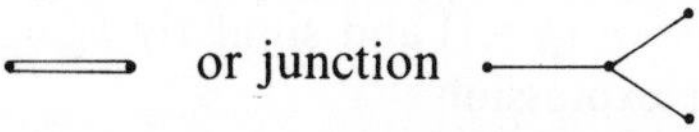

nor may it contain both a double line and a junction.

We are now in a position to list the only four types of diagrams which may exist:

(a) A chain of single lines

(b) A chain with one double-line connection and $p+q+2=l$

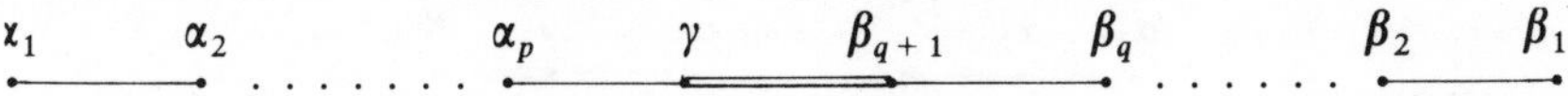

(The unsymmetrical notation is for convenience in the algebra below.)

(c) A chain with one junction and p, q and r roots in each of the three legs with $p+q+r+1=l$

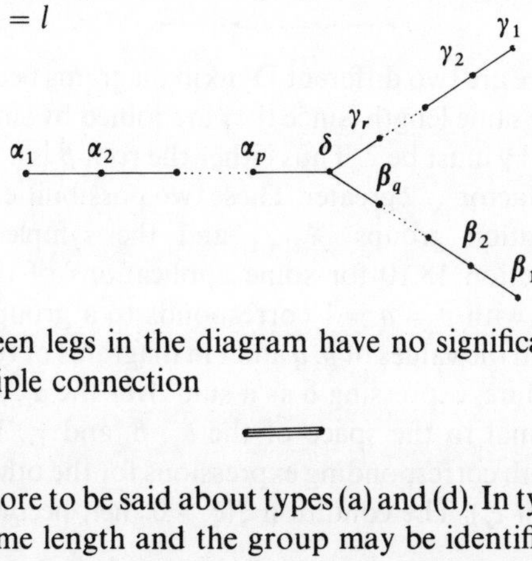

The angles between legs in the diagram have no significance.

(d) A single triple connection

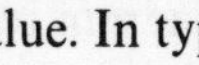

There is little more to be said about types (a) and (d). In type (a) all the simple roots have the same length and the group may be identified with the special unitary group SU_{l+1}. To see this equivalence one must use the diagram to construct the commutation relations of the infinitesimal operators and then compare with the relations appropriate to the group SU_{l+1}, see section 18.8. The rank l may take any integer value. In type (d) one may not add any more roots since this would imply more than three lines at one of the points. Thus in type (d) there is only one group, with rank $l=2$, which is conventionally called G_2. The simple roots have lengths in the ratio $\sqrt{3}$:1.

In type (b) we must ask where the double connection may lie in the chain, i.e. what are the values for p and q, having chosen $p \geq q$ without loss of generality. As before, we write

$$\tilde{\gamma} = \sum_i^p a_i \tilde{\alpha}_i + \sum_i^{q+1} b_i \tilde{\beta}_i + \xi$$

with $\xi.\tilde{\alpha}_i = \xi.\tilde{\beta}_i = 0$, so that

$$\tilde{\alpha}_j.\tilde{\gamma} = \sum_i a_i(\tilde{\alpha}_i.\tilde{\alpha}_j) = a_j - \tfrac{1}{2}(a_{j+1} + a_{j-1})$$

with a similar result for $\tilde{\beta}_j.\tilde{\gamma}$. However $\tilde{\alpha}_j.\tilde{\gamma} = 0$ except for $\tilde{\alpha}_p.\tilde{\gamma} = -\frac{1}{2}$ so that we can deduce $a_p = -p/(p+1)$ and similarly $b_q = -\sqrt{(2)}q/(q+1)$. Using these numbers in the expression

$$\xi.\xi = 1 - \sum_i a_i \tilde{\alpha}_i.\tilde{\gamma} - \sum_i b_i \tilde{\beta}_i.\tilde{\gamma} = 1 - a_p \tilde{\alpha}_p.\tilde{\gamma} - b_{q+1}\tilde{\beta}_{q+1}.\tilde{\gamma}$$

$$= 1 + \tfrac{1}{2}a_p + b_{q+1}/\sqrt{2}$$

reduces the condition $\xi.\xi > 0$ to the result $pq < 2$. Thus either $q = 0$ with any p or $p = q = 1$. Diagrams of type (b) may therefore be of the general form

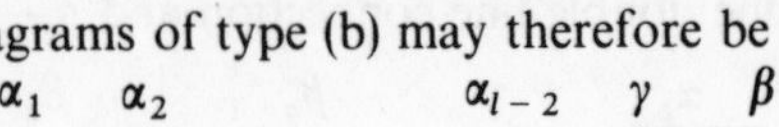

for any l or of the particular form, for $l = 4$,

In the first case there are two different Dynkin diagrams because although the α_i and γ all have the same length (since they are joined by single lines) the ratio of (length)^2 of β and γ must be 2. Thus either the root β is a factor $\sqrt{2}$ smaller than all others or a factor $\sqrt{2}$ greater. These two possibilities may be identified with the odd rotation groups $\mathscr{R}_{2l+1}$ and the symplectic groups Sp_{2l}, respectively (see section 18.10 for some applications of these groups). The particular diagram with $p = q = 1$ corresponds to a group known as F_4.

The limitations on the values of p, q and r in diagrams of type (c) are deduced by the same procedure, expressing δ as a sum over the α_i, β_i and γ_i with ξ its projection orthogonal to the space of the α_i, β_i and γ_i. In this case again $a_p = -p/(p+1)$ with corresponding expressions for the other coefficients and $\xi.\xi = 1 + \frac{1}{2}(a_p + b_q + c_r)$. The condition $\xi.\xi > 0$ then becomes

$$p/(p+1) + q/(q+1) + r/(r+1) < 2 \tag{20.34}$$

Because of the symmetry of the diagram we may take $p \geqq q \geqq r$ without loss of generality and $r \geqq 1$ or else the diagram reduces to type (a). Starting with the smallest values $q = r = 1$ the condition (20.34) gives $p/(p+1) = 1$ which is satisfied for all p and gives the general diagram

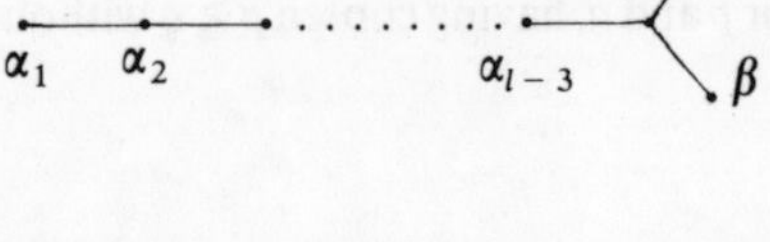

which corresponds to the even rotation groups $\mathscr{R}_{2l}$. Moving on to th
value of q, namely $q = 2$, $r = 1$, the condition (20.34) becomes p
which is satisfied only if $p = 2$, 3 or 4. Greater values of q and r
solution. Thus there are just three more particular groups, referred t
and E_8 with the Dynkin diagrams

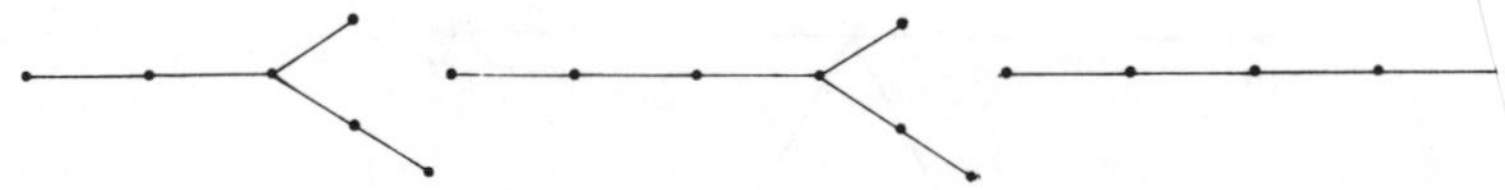

It is an amusing coincidence that the inequality (20.34) (sometimes ca
Diophantine equation) is essentially the same, when $r = 1$, as equation
which arose in classifying the point groups. Hence the enumeration o
groups of type (c) is in one-to-one correspondence with the listing of the p
groups.

Two groups which are isomorphic or homomorphic and so have the san
structure constants, may be identified by having the same Dynkin diagram.
Thus, for example, the groups $\mathscr{R}_6$ and SU_4 both have the diagram

The groups $\mathscr{R}_3$ and SU_2 are represented, almost trivially, by a single point. The group $\mathscr{R}_4$ does not appear in the classification above because it has the same structure constants as the direct product $\mathscr{R}_3 \times \mathscr{R}_3$ and is not therefore a 'simple' group. This structure is in fact suggested by trying to put $l = 2$ in the $\mathscr{R}_{2l}$ diagram which would lead to two unconnected dots—the diagram expected for $\mathscr{R}_3 \times \mathscr{R}_3$.

To find all roots and hence the commutation relations, given the Dynkin diagram one must construct the strings described earlier in this section. We illustrate the procedure with the group SU_3 described in detail in sections 11.6 and 18.7. The Dynkin diagram is

which implies that $l = 2$ with two equal roots satisfying $\tilde{\alpha}.\beta = -\frac{1}{2}$. Hence from equation (20.29) the string contains only $\alpha + \beta$ and of course there are also the corresponding three negative roots, making six in all. Since $l = 2$ in this case, we can simply draw all the roots in two dimensions and the scalar product $\tilde{\alpha}.\beta = -\frac{1}{2}$ implies an angle of 120° giving the picture shown in figure 20.1. Notice that, because of the angle of 120°, the root $\alpha + \beta$ has the same length as α and β. This picture of course agrees with figure 11.3 for the six infinitesimal operators $T_\pm$, $U_\pm$, $V_\pm$ in the notation of chapter 11. (The relative scale of the two axes is different in the two figures by the factor $\frac{1}{2}\sqrt{3}$ discussed in section 11.6.) Finally, to deduce the commutation relations (20.26)–(20.28) we must choose a basis and hence define H_1 and H_2. We shall take axis 2 along α with axis 1 perpendicular to it, since this is consistent with α and β being

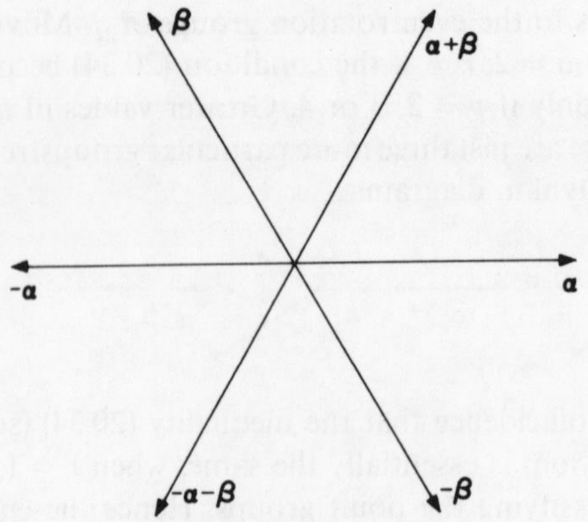

Figure 20.1

simple positive roots. With the vectors taken of unit length this gives

$$[H_2, E_\alpha] = E_\alpha, \qquad [H_2, E_\beta] = -\tfrac{1}{2}E_\beta, \qquad [H_2, E_{\alpha+\beta}] = \tfrac{1}{2}E_{\alpha+\beta}$$

$$[H_1, E_\alpha] = 0, \qquad [H_1, E_\beta] = \tfrac{1}{2}(3)^{\frac{1}{2}}E_\beta, \qquad [H_1, E_{\alpha+\beta}] = \tfrac{1}{2}(3)^{\frac{1}{2}}E_{\alpha+\beta}$$

together with

$$[E_\alpha, E_{-\alpha}] = H_2, \qquad [E_\beta, E_{-\beta}] = -\tfrac{1}{2}H_2 + \tfrac{1}{2}(3)^{\frac{1}{2}}H_1,$$

$$[E_{\alpha+\beta}, E_{-\alpha-\beta}] = \tfrac{1}{2}H_2 + \tfrac{1}{2}(3)^{\frac{1}{2}}H_1$$

The remaining commutation relations are given by equation (20.27) but there is freedom in fixing the normalisation constants because the relative magnitudes of the operators E are not yet defined. In general one may do this so that the operators H are Hermitian while $E_\alpha^\dagger = -E_{-\alpha}$ and the constants N are real. This enables one to deduce generally that $N_{-\alpha-\beta} = -N_{\alpha\beta}$ and, by considering the double commutator $\Big[[E_\alpha, E_\beta], E_{-\alpha-\beta}\Big]$ that $N_{\alpha\beta} = N_{\beta,-\alpha-\beta}$. Using also the trivial relation $N_{\alpha\beta} = -N_{\beta\alpha}$ we can then determine the constants $N_{\alpha\beta}$ from equation (20.31) apart from phase. In the SU_3 example this gives $N_{\alpha\beta} = \sqrt{\frac{1}{2}}$ so that

$$[E_\alpha, E_\beta] = \sqrt{(\tfrac{1}{2})}E_{\alpha+\beta}, \qquad [E_{\alpha+\beta}, E_{-\beta}] = \sqrt{(\tfrac{1}{2})}E_\alpha,$$

$$[E_{\alpha+\beta}, E_{-\alpha}] = -\sqrt{(\tfrac{1}{2})}E_\beta, \text{ etc.}$$

It is soon verified that all these commutation relations agree with those given in equations (11.3) with the correspondences

$$H_2 = T_z, \qquad H_1 = \tfrac{1}{2}\sqrt{(3)}Y, \qquad E_\alpha = T_+/\sqrt{2},$$

$$E_\beta = U_+/\sqrt{2}, \qquad E_{\alpha+\beta} = V_-/\sqrt{2}$$

In most of this section we have discussed the infinitesimal operators X_p or the more convenient linear combinations H_i and $E_{\boldsymbol{\alpha}}$. The finite group elements are generated as in section 7.2 as exponentials of real linear combinations of the X_p, although it is possible to define what is known as the complex extension of a Lie group by allowing complex coefficients of the X_p. In a unitary representation the X_p must be skew-Hermitian, see section 7.2, so that from each Hermitian operator H_i one may construct a corresponding infinitesimal operator by including a factor $\sqrt{-1}$. To each pair $E_{\pm\boldsymbol{\alpha}}$, one has a pair of skew-Hermitian infinitesimal operators $i(E_{\boldsymbol{\alpha}}+E_{-\boldsymbol{\alpha}})$ and $(E_{\boldsymbol{\alpha}}-E_{-\boldsymbol{\alpha}})$. Note that $E_{\boldsymbol{\alpha}}$ is not strictly an infinitesimal operator. The simplest example of this is the group $\mathscr{R}_3$ where, see chapter 7, the three infinitesimal operators are

$$X_x = -iJ_x = -\tfrac{1}{2}i(J_+ + J_-), \qquad X_y = -iJ_y = -\tfrac{1}{2}(J_+ - J_-) \text{ and } X_z = -iJ_z$$

with J_z playing the role of the only H operator and the raising and lowering operators $J_{\pm}$ corresponding to $E_{\pm\boldsymbol{\alpha}}$ as is appropriate for a group of rank $l = 1$.

The simple positive roots and Dynkin diagrams may also be used to deduce the irreducible representations of the Lie groups, generalising the method that we have used in subsection 7.4.2 and section 18.8.

20.5 The rotation matrices

The irreducible representation matrices $D^{(j)}_{m'm}(R)$ for an element R of the group $\mathscr{R}_3$ were essentially defined in chapter 7 through the expressions (7.39) and (7.40) for the matrix elements of the infinitesimal operators **J** and the expression

$$T(R) = \exp \boldsymbol{a}.\mathbf{X} = \exp(-i\boldsymbol{a}.\mathbf{J}) \tag{20.35}$$

which relates the finite rotation operator to the infinitesimal operators. Here the rotation is parameterised by the vector $\boldsymbol{a}$ as in section 7.4. One often refers to the $D^{(j)}_{m'm}(R)$ as the rotation matrices. Although we have used the properties of these matrices from time to time we have not tried to calculate them as functions of the parameters $\boldsymbol{a}$ except for the special case of $j = \tfrac{1}{2}$ in subsection 18.13.3. As this example might suggest, the use of the parameters $\boldsymbol{a}$ is not very convenient and it is usual to parameterise the rotation by what are known as the three Euler angles α, β and γ. (The Euler angles α, β and γ should not be confused with the matrix elements α and β of the SU_2 matrix (18.32) for which the same notation was unfortunately used.) To explain this new parameterisation we note that an arbitrary rotation is defined by the position of a 'new' set of axes x', y' and z', obtained by rotating the original set x, y and z. To do this we introduce the usual polar angles (like θ and ϕ for a point $\boldsymbol{r}$) for the z'-axis relative to the original set and call them, conventionally, β and α with the usual range $0 \leqq \beta \leqq \pi$ and $0 \leqq \alpha \leqq 2\pi$. In other words β is the angle between the z- and z'-axes and α the angle between the x-axis and the projection of the z'-axis on to the xy-plane, see figure 20.2. It remains to define the position of the

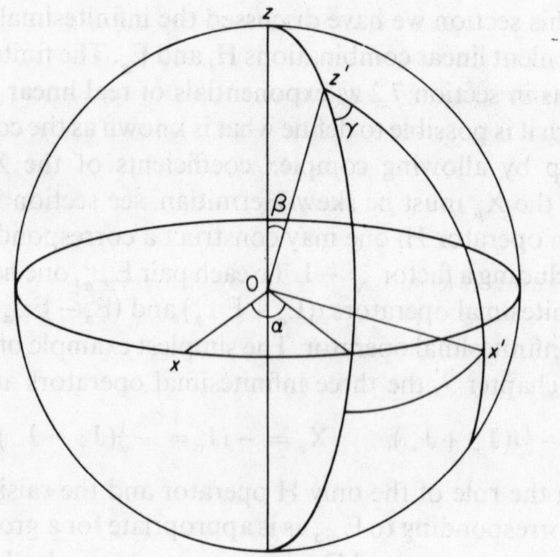

Figure 20.2

x'-axis (and hence automatically the y'-axis) and this is done by giving the angle γ between the planes Ozz' and $Oz'x'$, as shown in the figure. This arbitrary rotation is conveniently expressed as the product of three simple rotations about the original axes. We first note that if $\gamma = 0$ the rotation is achieved by the product $R_z(\alpha)R_y(\beta)$. Here the β-rotation carries the x-axis to a latitude of β-south while the α-rotation gives it a longitude of α, in terrestrial notation. (The order of these rotations is important since otherwise the β-rotation would have to be about the axis obtained from Oy by the rotation $R_z(\alpha)$. For the general case $\gamma \neq 0$ we must *first* carry out a γ-rotation about the z-axis giving the general rotation as

$$R = R_z(\alpha)R_y(\beta)R_z(\gamma) \qquad (20.36)$$

(We could equally well have used a *final* rotation of γ about the z'-axis but we shall soon see the advantage of having all rotations in (20.36) relating to the same, original set of axes.)

From the factorisation (20.36) the representation operator (20.35) becomes

$$T(R) = \exp(-i\alpha J_z)\exp(-i\beta J_y)\exp(-i\gamma J_z)$$

and we recall the definition of the rotation matrix, using the notation $|jm\rangle$ for the basis vectors

$$D^{(j)}_{m'm}(\alpha, \beta, \gamma) = \langle jm' | T(R) | jm \rangle$$

Hence, using the fact that J_z is diagonal in this basis, we have the immediate simplification

$$D^{(j)}_{m'm}(\alpha . \beta, \gamma) = \exp[-i(\alpha m' + \gamma m)] \langle jm' | \exp(-i\beta J_y) | jm \rangle \qquad (20.37)$$

The remaining matrix element may be found using the relation $J_y = (J_+ - J_-)/2i$ and the formula (7.40) for the matrix elements of $J_\pm$. As a first step in deriving the general matrix element we first deduce the matrix for $j = \frac{1}{2}$. In this particular case the matrix of J_y was given in equation (8.15)

$$J_y = \tfrac{1}{2}\begin{pmatrix} 0 & -i \\ i & 0 \end{pmatrix}$$

so that $J_y^2 = \frac{1}{4}$ and, as in subsection 18.13.3, the series for $\exp(-i\beta J_y)$ simplifies

$$\exp(-i\beta J_y) = (1 - \tfrac{1}{4}\beta^2 + \ldots) - iJ_y(\beta - \tfrac{1}{24}\beta^3 + \ldots) = \cos\tfrac{1}{2}\beta - 2iJ_y \sin\tfrac{1}{2}\beta$$

The complete matrix is therefore given as

$$D^{(\frac{1}{2})}(\alpha,\beta,\gamma) = \begin{pmatrix} \exp[-\frac{1}{2}i(\alpha+\gamma)]\cos\frac{1}{2}\beta & -\exp[\frac{1}{2}i(\gamma-\alpha)]\sin\frac{1}{2}\beta \\ \exp[\frac{1}{2}i(\alpha-\gamma)]\sin\frac{1}{2}\beta & \exp[\frac{1}{2}i(\alpha+\gamma)]\cos\frac{1}{2}\beta \end{pmatrix} \tag{20.38}$$

By equating this to the matrix (18.37) we can relate the Euler angles to the previous parameters $\boldsymbol{a}$. Hence we can show that the weight function in the group integration, see appendix 4.3, is given by $\rho(\alpha,\beta,\gamma) = \sin\beta$.

The general matrix element may be deduced from equation (20.38) taking $|jj\rangle = |\frac{1}{2}\frac{1}{2}\rangle_1 |\frac{1}{2}\frac{1}{2}\rangle_2 \ldots |\frac{1}{2}\frac{1}{2}\rangle_{2j}$ as the product of $2j$ factors, like the wave function of $2j$ particles with spin $j = \frac{1}{2}$ and $m = \frac{1}{2}$. Then $|jm\rangle$ has $j+m$ spins up and $j-m$ spins down and will be a sum over the different ways of assigning the spins to the particles. The number of ways is given by the binomial coefficient $\binom{2j}{j-m}$. Including the normalisation constants and using equation (20.37) gives

$$D^{(j)}_{m'm}(\alpha,\beta,\gamma) = \exp[-i(\alpha m' + \gamma m)]\binom{2j}{j-m'}^{-\frac{1}{2}}\binom{2j}{j-m}^{-\frac{1}{2}}$$
$$\times \sum_{m_i', m_i} \langle m_1' m_2' \ldots | \exp(-i\beta J_y) | m_1 m_2 \ldots \rangle$$

where m_i denotes the spin projection $\pm\frac{1}{2}$ of particle i and the sum is restricted by the constraints $\sum_i m_i = m$, $\sum_i m_i' = m'$. Because of the symmetry of the operator and the wave functions we may include only one term on the right and multiply by the number of terms. Thus

$$D^{(j)}_{m'm}(\alpha,\beta,\gamma) = \exp[-i(\alpha m' + \gamma m)]\binom{2j}{j-m'}^{-\frac{1}{2}}\binom{2j}{j-m}^{\frac{1}{2}}$$
$$\times \sum_{m_i'} \langle m_1' m_2' \ldots | \exp(-i\beta J_y) | \overbrace{+ + \ldots +}^{j+m} \overbrace{- - \ldots -}^{j-m} \rangle \tag{20.39}$$

where the first $j+m$ particles on the right have $m = +\frac{1}{2}$. Since the operator is a product of corresponding operators for each particle, each matrix element in

(20.39) is a product of $2j$ matrix elements of $\exp(-i\beta J_y)$ taken from the $D^{(\frac{1}{2})}$ matrix (20.38). For each particle whose spin projection is the same on left and right there is a factor $\cos\frac{1}{2}\beta$, while for those which differ there is a factor $\pm\sin\frac{1}{2}\beta$ corresponding to the two cases $\langle -|\;\;|+\rangle$ and $\langle +|\;\;|-\rangle$, respectively. The only relevant parameter in the sum over m_i' is the number x of particles in the first $j+m$ which have spin $+\frac{1}{2}$. Thus, including the binomial coefficients $\binom{j+m}{x}$ and $\binom{j-m}{j+m'-x}$ to account for the number of ways of arranging the spins in this way gives finally

$$D^{(j)}_{m'm}(\alpha,\beta,\gamma)=\exp[-i(\alpha m'+\gamma m)]\binom{2j}{j-m'}^{-\frac{1}{2}}\binom{2j}{j-m}^{\frac{1}{2}}\sum_x\binom{j+m}{x}\binom{j-m}{j+m'-x}$$

$$\times(-1)^{j+m'-x}(\cos\tfrac{1}{2}\beta)^{2x-m-m'}(\sin\tfrac{1}{2}\beta)^{2j-2x+m+m'} \qquad (20.40)$$

a result which simplifies a little when the explicit forms are inserted for the binomial coefficients.

Bibliography

Some more discussion of dynamical groups may be found in Englefield (1972), in the bibliography to chapter 19, and in

Wybourne, B. G. (1974). *Classical Groups for Physicists* (Wiley-Interscience, New York)

The Jahn–Teller effect is described in some detail in

Sturge, M. D. (1967). Jahn–Teller effects in solids, in *Solid State Physics*, vol. 20 (Academic Press, New York) and for an experimental verification of the effect, see

Dixon, R. N. (1971). *Molec. Phys.*, **20**, 113

Spontaneous symmetry breaking is reviewed by

Guralnik, G. S., Hagen, C. R. and Kibble, T. W. B. (1968). Broken symmetries and the Goldstone theorem, in *Advances in Particle Physics*, vol. 2 (Interscience, New York)

and although they concentrate on elementary particle theory, there is a section on non-relativistic systems. See also the review by

Beg, M. A. B. and Sirlin, A. (1974). Gauge theories of weak interactions *A. Rev. nucl. Sci.*, **24**

A more rigorous account of the use of normal subgroups in constructing irreducible representations is given in Lomont (1959), in the bibliography to chapter 15.

The structure of Lie groups and their classification is described with mathematical rigour in

Gilmore, R. (1974). *Lie Groups, Lie Algebras and some of their Applications* (Wiley-Interscience, New York)

For further reading on the representations of Lie groups see Boerner (1963), in the bibliography to chapter 4; Littlewood (1950) in the chapter 17 bibliography; and Wybourne (1974) above.

The bibliography to chapter 7, especially Brink and Satchler (1968), may be consulted for further reading on the subject of rotation matrices.

Problems

20.1 Show that D_3 is the semi-direct product group $C_3 \wedge C_2$. Hence deduce the character table for D_3 by following the method of section 20.3.

20.2 Draw the root diagram for the group G_2 introduced in section 20.4.

Appendix 3*: Topics in Representation Theory

Some useful but more advanced properties of group representations are collected here rather than in chapter 4 of volume 1.

A.3.1 Symmetrised products of representations

The direct product $T^{(\alpha)} \times T^{(\beta)}$ of two representations of a group $\mathcal{G}$ was defined in section 4.17 and a simple formula (4.43) was deduced for its character. This would extend naturally to a product $T = T^{(\alpha)} \times T^{(\beta)} \times \ldots$ of n terms and in the present section we are concerned with the special case when all the factors are equivalent $\alpha = \beta = \ldots$. To discuss this representation it is helpful to construct a set of basis vectors from products of functions, as in section 4.17. Let ϕ_i with $i = 1, 2, \ldots, s_\alpha$ denote a set of functions transforming like the irreducible representation $T^{(\alpha)}$ so that the set of $(s_\alpha)^n$ products $\phi_i(1)\,\phi_j(2)\ldots\phi_k(n)$ provide a basis for T

$$T\phi_i(1)\phi_j(2)\ldots\phi_k(n) = \sum_{i',j',\ldots,k'} T^{(\alpha)}_{i'i}T^{(\alpha)}_{j'j}\ldots T^{(\alpha)}_{k'k}\phi_{i'}(1)\phi_{j'}(2)\ldots\phi_{k'}(n)$$

* Appendices 1 and 2 appear at the end of volume 1.

The index p in the factors $\phi_i(p)$ serves to label the factors and is relevant in the definition of scalar product, namely

$$\begin{aligned}(\phi_{i'}(1)\phi_{j'}(2)\ldots\phi_{k'}(n),\ \phi_i(1)\phi_j(2)\ldots\phi_k(n))\\ = (\phi_{i'}(1),\ \phi_i(1))(\phi_{j'}(2),\ \phi_j(2))\ldots(\phi_{k'}(n),\ \phi_k(n))\\ = \delta_{i'i}\delta_{j'j}\ \ldots\ \delta_{k'k}\end{aligned}$$

showing that the set of products is orthonormal given that the ϕ_i are orthonormal. (In physical applications, p will label the different particles of a system while i labels the possible states of any of the particles.) It is convenient to introduce a more concise notation, writing

$$|ij\ldots k\rangle \equiv \phi_i(1)\phi_j(2)\ldots\phi_k(n)$$

where the index p has been dropped but is inferred by the ordering of the labels in $|ij\ldots k\rangle$. The scalar product is then written as $\langle i'j'\ldots k'|ij\ldots k\rangle$. (This notation is familiar in quantum mechanics.)

Let us now consider permutations P of the n indices p, defined for example by

$$P_{12}|ij\ldots k\rangle = \phi_i(2)\phi_j(1)\ldots\phi_k(n) = |ji\ldots k\rangle \qquad \text{(A.3.1)}$$

The set of all such permutations form the symmetric group $\mathscr{S}_n$ described in chapter 17 and it is clear from equation (A.3.1) that the vector space L of the products $|ij\ldots k\rangle$ will be invariant under the group $\mathscr{S}_n$. In fact, the permutations commute with the operations of $\mathscr{G}$ so that L provides a basis for a representation W of the product group $\mathscr{G}\times\mathscr{S}_n$. If we denote the irreducible representations of the groups $\mathscr{G}$, $\mathscr{S}_n$ and $\mathscr{G}\times\mathscr{S}_n$ by $T^{(\gamma)}$, $V^{(\lambda)}$ and $T^{(\gamma)}\times V^{(\lambda)}$, respectively, then the reduction of the representation W may be written as

$$W = \dot{\sum_{\gamma,\lambda}} m_{\gamma\lambda} T^{(\gamma)}\times V^{(\lambda)} \qquad \text{(A.3.2)}$$

Thus it is possible to choose a basis for L in which the basis vectors are labelled by γ and λ, describing their transformation properties with respect to both $\mathscr{G}$ and $\mathscr{S}_n$. If G_a, P and G_aP denote arbitrary elements of the groups $\mathscr{G}$, $\mathscr{S}_n$ and $\mathscr{G}\times\mathscr{S}_n$, then the character equation corresponding to the reduction (A.3.2) is

$$\chi(G_aP) = \sum_{\gamma,\lambda} m_\gamma\lambda\chi^{(\gamma)}(G_a)\chi^{(\lambda)}(P) \qquad \text{(A.3.3)}$$

using the result (4.66).

In practice, we are often interested in one of the subspaces in the reduction $L = \sum_\lambda L_\lambda$, where L_λ contains all the basis vectors of L which transform according to a particular irreducible representation $V^{(\lambda)}$ of $\mathscr{S}_n$. This space L_λ provides a representation T_λ of $\mathscr{G}$ which from equation (A.3.2) reduces into irreducible representations of $\mathscr{G}$ according to

$$T_\lambda = \dot{\sum_\gamma} m_{\gamma\lambda} T^{(\gamma)}$$

and its character is therefore given by

$$\chi_\lambda(G_a) = \sum_\gamma m_{\gamma\lambda}\chi^{(\gamma)}(G_a)$$

By using the orthogonality (4.25a) of characters of $\mathscr{S}_n$ this is given from equation (A.3.3) by

$$\chi_\lambda(G_a) = \sum_\gamma m_{\gamma\lambda}\chi^{(\gamma)}(G_a) = \frac{1}{n!}\sum_P \chi^{(\lambda)*}(P)\chi(G_aP) \tag{A.3.4}$$

where the sum runs over the $n!$ permutations P of $\mathscr{S}_n$. The procedure for finding χ_λ will be first to calculate $\chi(G_aP)$ and then to use equation (A.3.4) with the known $\chi^{(\lambda)}$ from the character table for the symmetric group. Once χ_λ is found, the integers $m_{\gamma\lambda}$ follow from the usual orthogonality of characters of $\mathscr{G}$

$$m_{\gamma\lambda} = \frac{1}{g}\sum_a \chi^{(\gamma)*}(G_a)\chi_\lambda(G_a) \tag{A.3.5}$$

where g is the number of elements in $\mathscr{G}$.

We now calculate the $\chi(G_aP)$ for a few simple permutations and leave the deduction of a general formula until the end of the section. Consider first the identity P = E which, from the definition of a character, gives

$$\begin{aligned}\chi(G_aE) &= \sum_{i,j,\ldots,k} \langle ij\ldots k|T(G_a)|ij\ldots k\rangle \\ &= \sum_{i,j,\ldots,k} T^{(\alpha)}_{ii}(G_a)T^{(\alpha)}_{jj}(G_a)\ldots T^{(\alpha)}_{kk}(G_a) \\ &= \{\sum_i T^{(\alpha)}_{ii}(G_a)\}^n = \{\chi^{(\alpha)}(G_a)\}^n \end{aligned} \tag{A.3.6}$$

thus expressing $\chi(G_aE)$ in terms of the known irreducible characters of $\mathscr{G}$. In a similar way, for the permutation P_{12} we have, using equation (A.3.1),

$$\begin{aligned}\chi(G_aP_{12}) &= \sum_{i,j,\ldots,k} \langle ij\ldots k|T(G_a)|ji\ldots k\rangle \\ &= \sum_{i,j,\ldots,k} T^{(\alpha)}_{ij}(G_a)T^{(\alpha)}_{ji}(G_a)\ldots T^{(\alpha)}_{kk}(G_a) \\ &= \sum_{i,\ldots,k} T^{(\alpha)}_{ii}(G_a^2)\ldots T^{(\alpha)}_{kk}(G_a) \\ &= \chi^{(\alpha)}(G_a^2)\{\chi^{(\alpha)}(G_a)\}^{n-2} \end{aligned} \tag{A.3.7}$$

which involves just the irreducible characters again, since G_a^2 is simply another element of $\mathscr{G}$. For the more complicated permutation $\binom{123}{231}$ of three objects, in the notation of section 2.2(10), a similar argument shows that

$$\chi(G_a(\begin{smallmatrix}1 & 2 & 3\\ 2 & 3 & 1\end{smallmatrix})) = \chi^{(\alpha)}(G_a^3)\{\chi^{(\alpha)}(G_a)\}^{n-3} \qquad \text{(A.3.8)}$$

With these results we are in a position to deduce all the $\chi_\lambda(G_a)$ for the examples $n = 2$ and $n = 3$. Firstly for $n = 2$ there are only two group elements E and P_{12} and there are two irreducible representations corresponding to symmetric or antisymmetric basis vectors. From the characters given in table 4.5 and equations (A.3.4) to (A.3.7) we have

$$\chi_{\text{sym}}(G_a) = \tfrac{1}{2}[\{\chi^{(\alpha)}(G_a)\}^2 + \chi^{(\alpha)}(G_a^2)]$$

and (A.3.9)

$$\chi_{\text{antisym}}(G_a) = \tfrac{1}{2}[\{\chi^{(\alpha)}(G_a)\}^2 - \chi^{(\alpha)}(G_a^2)]$$

For $n = 3$ we may take the characters from table 4.2 because of the isomorphism between $\mathscr{S}_3$ and D_3 (see section 2.3). There are three classes, given by E; P_{12}, P_{23}, P_{31}; $(\begin{smallmatrix}1&2&3\\2&3&1\end{smallmatrix})$, $(\begin{smallmatrix}1&2&3\\3&1&2\end{smallmatrix})$ and the three irreducible representations are usually described as (1) totally symmetric, (2) totally antisymmetric, and (3) mixed symmetry (two-dimensional). In this case, we find as before

$$\begin{aligned}
\chi_{\text{sym}}(G_a) &= \tfrac{1}{6}[\{\chi^{(\alpha)}(G_a)\}^3 + 3\chi^{(\alpha)}(G_a^2)\chi^{(\alpha)}(G_a) + 2\chi^{(\alpha)}(G_a^3)]\\
\chi_{\text{antisym}}(G_a) &= \tfrac{1}{6}[\{\chi^{(\alpha)}(G_a)\}^3 - 3\chi^{(\alpha)}(G_a^2)\chi^{(\alpha)}(G_a) + 2\chi^{(\alpha)}(G_a^3)] \qquad \text{(A.3.10)}\\
\chi_{\text{mixed}}(G_a) &= \tfrac{1}{6}[2\{\chi^{(\alpha)}(G_a)\}^3 - 2\chi^{(\alpha)}(G_a^3)]
\end{aligned}$$

Notice that there has been no need to specify the group $\mathscr{G}$ although, finally, to obtain numbers from these expressions, one must look up the values of the irreducible characters $\chi^{(\alpha)}$ of $\mathscr{G}$.

It is possible to obtain a general formula for the characters $\chi(G_aP)$ by using the result, discussed in section 17.1, that any permutation may be written as a product of 'cycles' of various lengths. If P contains n_1 cycles of length 1, n_2 cycles of length 2, and so on, then by a continuation of the method used for the simple permutations above, one finds that

$$\chi(G_aP) = \prod_i \{\chi^{(\alpha)}(G_a^i)\}^{n_i} \qquad \text{(A.3.11)}$$

A.3.2 The use of a subgroup in reducing product representations

The way in which a product of two representations of a group $\mathscr{G}$ reduces into irreducible pieces was described in section 4.17 and in particular the integer coefficients m_γ in the reduction (4.44)

$$T^{(\alpha)} \times T^{(\beta)} = \dot{\sum} m_\gamma T^{(\gamma)}$$

were deduced from equation (4.45) using the tables of characters. There is an alternative way of deducing these coefficients if the corresponding coefficients are known for a subgroup $\mathscr{H}$ of $\mathscr{G}$. Let us denote the irreducible representations of $\mathscr{H}$ by $T^{(\tilde{\alpha})}$, $T^{(\tilde{\beta})}$, etc., and suppose that we know the coefficients $m_{\tilde{\gamma}}^{\tilde{\alpha}\tilde{\beta}}$ in the reduction

$$T^{(\tilde{\alpha})} \times T^{(\tilde{\beta})} = \dot{\sum_{\tilde{\gamma}}} m_{\tilde{\gamma}}^{\tilde{\alpha}\tilde{\beta}} T^{(\tilde{\gamma})} \tag{A.3.12}$$

and also that we know the coefficients $n_{\alpha\tilde{\alpha}}$ for the reduction (4.49) of $T^{(\alpha)}$ on restriction from $\mathscr{G}$ to its subgroup $\mathscr{H}$,

$$T^{(\alpha)} = \dot{\sum_{\tilde{\alpha}}} n_{\alpha\tilde{\alpha}} T^{(\tilde{\alpha})}$$

Combining these three equations we have

$$\begin{aligned} T^{(\alpha)} \times T^{(\beta)} &= \dot{\sum_{\tilde{\alpha},\tilde{\beta},\tilde{\gamma}}} n_{\alpha\tilde{\alpha}} n_{\beta\tilde{\beta}} T^{(\tilde{\alpha})} \times T^{(\tilde{\beta})} \\ &= \sum_{\tilde{\alpha},\tilde{\beta},\tilde{\gamma}} n_{\alpha\tilde{\alpha}} n_{\beta\tilde{\beta}} m_{\tilde{\gamma}}^{\tilde{\alpha}\tilde{\beta}} T^{(\tilde{\gamma})} \end{aligned} \tag{A.3.13}$$

and also

$$\begin{aligned} T^{(\alpha)} \times T^{(\beta)} &= \dot{\sum_{\gamma}} m_{\gamma} T^{(\gamma)} \\ &= \dot{\sum_{\gamma\tilde{\gamma}}} m_{\gamma} n_{\gamma\tilde{\gamma}} \chi T^{(\tilde{\gamma})} \end{aligned} \tag{A.3.14}$$

so that, equating the right-hand sides of equations (A.3.13) and (A.3.14), we have for each $\tilde{\gamma}$

$$\sum_{\tilde{\alpha},\tilde{\beta}} n_{\alpha\tilde{\alpha}} n_{\beta\tilde{\beta}} m_{\tilde{\gamma}}^{\tilde{\alpha}\tilde{\beta}} = \sum_{\gamma} m_{\gamma} n_{\gamma\tilde{\gamma}} \tag{A.3.15}$$

The only unknowns in this set of equations (A.3.15) are the required coefficients m_{γ} and, in many cases, the equations are sufficient to enable us to deduce them.

To illustrate the method, we use the same example as in section 4.17, the product $T^{(3)} \times T^{(3)}$ for the group D_3, using now the subgroup C_3 as described in section 4.18. Thus equation (A.3.13) becomes

$$\begin{aligned} T^{(3)} \times T^{(3)} &= (\tau^{(2)} \dot{+} \tau^{(3)}) \times (\tau^{(2)} \dot{+} \tau^{(3)}) \\ &= 2\tau^{(1)} \dot{+} \tau^{(2)} \dot{+} \tau^{(3)} \end{aligned}$$

Comparing with the known reductions $T^{(3)} = \tau^{(2)} \dot{+} \tau^{(3)}$, $T^{(1)} = T^{(2)} = \tau^{(1)}$ from section 4.18 we are able to deduce that

$$T^{(3)} \times T^{(3)} = T^{(3)} \dot{+} m_1 T^{(1)} \dot{+} m_2 T^{(2)}$$

where $m_1 + m_2 = 2$. This example also illustrates the limitations of the method, i.e. it does not always provide a complete solution. It cannot in this example tell us that $m_1 = m_2 = 1$ but only that $m_1 + m_2 = 2$. Nevertheless, the method is increasingly useful in the continuous groups where the characters of the larger group $\mathscr{G}$ are more difficult to handle than those of the subgroup $\mathscr{H}$.

A.3.3 Class multiplication

The methods used in section 4.15 for finding the irreducible characters were satisfactory for groups where the number of classes was small. In this section we derive additional relations between the characters which are sufficient to determine them for any finite group. We first introduce the sum of all group elements in a class $\mathscr{C}_i$ which we denote by the same symbol $\mathscr{C}_i$ and which is called a 'class operator':

$$\mathscr{C}_i = \sum_{\mathrm{G}_a \text{ in } \mathscr{C}_i} \mathrm{G}_a \tag{A.3.16}$$

We next show that the product of two such sums must itself contain all the elements of a given class the same number of times, so that we can write

$$\mathscr{C}_i \mathscr{C}_j = \sum_{\substack{\mathrm{G}_a \text{ in } \mathscr{C}_i \\ \mathrm{G}_b \text{ in } \mathscr{C}_j}} \mathrm{G}_a \mathrm{G}_b = \sum_k c_{ijk} \mathscr{C}_k \tag{A.3.17}$$

To prove this result, write

$$\mathscr{C}_i \mathscr{C}_j = n_b \mathrm{G}_b + n_c \mathrm{G}_c + \ldots \tag{A.3.18}$$

where G_b and G_c are two elements in the same class $\mathscr{C}_i$. For any element G_a in the group we can write

$$\mathrm{G}_a \mathscr{C}_i \mathrm{G}_a^{-1} = \mathscr{C}_i \tag{A.3.19}$$

since for any G in $\mathscr{C}_i$ the element $\mathrm{G}_a \mathrm{G} \mathrm{G}_a^{-1}$ is also in $\mathscr{C}_i$ and is different for each choice of G. It therefore follows that

$$\begin{aligned} \mathscr{C}_i \mathscr{C}_j &= \mathrm{G}_a \mathscr{C}_i \mathrm{G}_a^{-1} \mathrm{G}_a \mathscr{C}_j \mathrm{G}_a^{-1} = \mathrm{G}_a \mathscr{C}_i \mathscr{C}_j \mathrm{G}_a^{-1} \\ &= n_b \mathrm{G}_a \mathrm{G}_b \mathrm{G}_a^{-1} + n_c \mathrm{G}_a \mathrm{G}_c \mathrm{G}_a^{-1} + \ldots \end{aligned} \tag{A.3.20}$$

By choosing G_a such that $\mathrm{G}_a \mathrm{G}_b \mathrm{G}_a^{-1} = \mathrm{G}_c$ and comparing (A.3.20) with (A.3.18) we see that $n_b = n_c$ which justifies the expression (A.3.17).

We now choose some irreducible representation $\mathrm{T}^{(\alpha)}$ of $\mathscr{G}$ and construct the matrix sums

$$\mathrm{T}_i^{(\alpha)} = \sum_{\mathrm{G}_a \text{ in } \mathscr{C}_i} \mathrm{T}^{(\alpha)}(\mathrm{G}_a) \tag{A.3.21}$$

Equation (A.3.19) is now written in the form $\mathrm{G}_a \mathscr{C}_i = \mathscr{C}_i \mathrm{G}_a$ which, in the matrix representation $T^{(\alpha)}$, becomes $T^{(\alpha)}(G_a)T_i^{(\alpha)} = T_i^{(\alpha)}T^{(\alpha)}(G_a)$. Since this equation is satisfied for all G_a in $\mathscr{G}$ it follows from Schur's first lemma that $T_i^{(\alpha)}$ is a constant times the unit matrix, $T_i^{(\alpha)} = \lambda_i^{(\alpha)}1$.

Equating traces in equation (A.3.21) now gives $s_\alpha \lambda_i^{(\alpha)} = c_i \chi_i^{(\alpha)}$, so that

$$T_i^{(\alpha)} = \frac{c_i}{s_\alpha}\chi_i^{(\alpha)}1 \tag{A.3.22}$$

where c_i is the number of elements in the class $\mathscr{C}_i$. Writing (A.3.17) in matrix form, we have

$$T_i^{(\alpha)}T_j^{(\alpha)} = \sum_k c_{ijk} T_k^{(\alpha)}$$

and using (A.3.22) this gives a relation between characters,

$$c_i c_j \chi_i^{(\alpha)} \chi_j^{(\alpha)} = s_\alpha \sum_k c_{ijk} \chi_k^{(\alpha)} \tag{A.3.23}$$

We note that the coefficients c_{ijk} appearing in equation (A.3.23) are known from the group multiplication table via equation (A.3.17). Thus we have derived a set of equations (A.3.23) for all i and j which can be used in deducing the characters.

Appendix 4: Some Results Pertaining to the Group $\mathscr{R}_3$

The first two sections in this appendix contain some useful properties of the spherical harmonics, which follow directly from our study of the group $\mathscr{R}_3$ in chapter 7. The last section discusses group integration generally and then deduces the necessary weight function for the group integrals in $\mathscr{R}_3$.

A.4.1 An integral over three spherical harmonics

The Wigner – Eckart theorem may be used to evaluate a useful integral. From equation (7.53), regarding $Y^{(l_1)}_{m_1}(\theta, \phi)$ as an operator,

$$\int_{\phi=0}^{2\pi}\int_{\theta=0}^{\pi} Y^{(l)*}_{m}(\theta,\phi)Y^{(l_1)}_{m_1}(\theta,\phi)Y^{(l_2)}_{m_2}(\theta,\phi)\sin\theta \mathrm{d}\theta \mathrm{d}\phi$$
$$= C(l_1 l_2 l, m_1 m_2 m)\,\langle l||\mathbf{Y}^{(l_1)}||l_2\rangle \tag{A.4.1}$$

using the fact that $\mathscr{R}_3$ is simply reducible so that t is not required and also that the Clebsch–Gordan coefficients C are real. This result may be used to expand the product $Y^{(l_1)}_{m_1}Y^{(l_2)}_{m_2}$, regarded as a single function, in the form of equation

(7.49). We have

$$Y^{(l_1)}_{m_1}(\theta,\phi)\,Y^{(l_2)}_{m_2}(\theta,\phi)=\sum_{lm}C(l_1l_2l,m_1m_2m)\langle l\|\mathbf{Y}^{(l_1)}\|l_2\rangle Y^{(l)}_m(\theta,\phi) \quad \text{(A.4.2)}$$

making use of equation (7.50) and (A.4.1). To find the value of the reduced matrix element we first invert equation (A.4.2) using the orthogonality of the Clebsch–Gordan coefficients, see section 4.17,

$$\langle l\|\mathbf{Y}^{(l_1)}\|l_2\rangle Y^{(l)}_m(\theta,\phi)=\sum_{m_1m_2}C(l_1l_2l,m_1m_2m)\,Y^{(l_1)}_{m_1}(\theta,\phi)Y^{(l_2)}_{m_2}(\theta,\phi) \quad \text{(A.4.3)}$$

Then, since the reduced matrix element $\langle l\|\mathbf{Y}^{(l_1)}\|l_2\rangle$ is independent of θ and ϕ, we may insert any convenient values for θ and ϕ in equation (A.4.3). By taking $\theta=0$, the spherical harmonics simplify enormously, becoming independent of ϕ,

$$Y^{(l)}_m(0,\phi)=\delta_{m,0}\left(\frac{2l+1}{4\pi}\right)^{\frac{1}{2}}P_k(\cos 0)=\left(\frac{2l+1}{4\pi}\right)^{\frac{1}{2}}\delta_{m,0} \quad \text{(A.4.4)}$$

giving

$$\langle l\|\mathbf{Y}^{(l_1)}\|l_2\rangle=\left(\frac{(2l_1+1)(2l_2+1)}{4\pi(2l+1)}\right)^{\frac{1}{2}}C(l_1l_2l,000) \quad \text{(A.4.5)}$$

The integral (A.4.1) is finally given by

$$\int_{\phi=0}^{2\pi}\int_{\theta=0}^{\pi}Y^{(l)*}_m(\theta,\phi)\,Y^{(l_1)}_{m_1}(\theta,\phi)\,Y^{(l_2)}_{m_2}(\theta,\phi)\sin\theta\,\mathrm{d}\theta\,\mathrm{d}\phi$$

$$=\left(\frac{(2l_1+1)(2l_2+1)}{4\pi(2l+1)}\right)^{\frac{1}{2}}C(l_1l_2l,000)C(l_1l_2l,m_1m_2m) \quad \text{(A.4.6)}$$

It is interesting to note that this integral vanishes unless l_1, l_2 and l satisfy triangular conditions, see subsection 7.4.4. It also vanishes unless l_1+l_2+l is even, because of parity.

A.4.2 The spherical harmonic addition theorem

Consider the products of spherical harmonics of the coordinates of *two* particles $Y^{(l_1)}_{m_1}(\theta_1\phi_1)Y^{(l_2)}_{m_2}(\theta_2\phi_2)$. In the way described in section 4.17 and subsection 7.4.4, using equation (4.46) it is possible to form an invariant by summing such products when $l_1=l_2$, for then it is possible to have $J=0$ in equation (7.44). The invariant may be written as

$$f^{(0)}_0=\sum_{m_1}C(l_1l_10,m_1-m_10)Y^{(l_1)}_{m_1}(\theta_1\phi_1)Y^{(l_1)}_{-m_1}(\theta_2\phi_2) \quad \text{(A.4.7)}$$

making use of the fact that, for invariance under the subgroup $\mathscr{R}_2$, necessarily $m_1 + m_2 = 0$. Notice that although $f_0^{(0)}$ is an invariant under rotations of the system it will depend on the relative positions of the two particles. In fact we shall now show that $f_0^{(0)}$ is a Legendre polynomial of the angle θ_{12} between the radius vectors to the two particles. To show this we note that since $f_0^{(0)}$ is invariant it is unaffected by a rotation of the system which brings particle 1 on to the z-axis. In this position, $\theta_1 = 0$ and $\theta_2 = \theta_{12}$ so that using equation (A.4.4) the equation (A.4.7) reduces to

$$f_0^{(0)} = C(l_1 l_1 0, 000)\left(\frac{2l_1+1}{4\pi}\right)P_{l_1}(\cos\theta_{12})$$

where we have also used the fact that when $m = 0$, the spherical harmonic reduces to a Legendre polynomial. The Clebsch–Gordan coefficients in equation (A.4.7) have a simple form (see problem 7.14)

$$C(l_1 l_1 0, m_1 - m_1 0) = (-1)^{l_1 - m_1}/(2l_1+1)^{\frac{1}{2}}$$

giving finally for equation (A.4.7)

$$\sum_m (-1)^m Y_m^{(l)}(\theta_1 \phi_1) Y_{-m}^{(l)}(\theta_2 \phi_2) = \left(\frac{2l+1}{4\pi}\right) P_l(\cos\theta_{12}) \qquad \text{(A.4.8)}$$

This result is known as the spherical harmonic addition theorem and is used for example in analysing the interaction potential between two electrons into factors which depend on the coordinates of the separate electrons, see appendix 5.1.

A.4.3 Group integration

In section 7.1 we remarked that the group sum $\sum_{a=1}^{g}$, which occurred in the orthogonality relations for irreducible representations of a finite group, would be replaced by an integral over the parameters $a_1, a_2, \ldots, a_r$ with some weight function $\rho(a_1, a_2, \ldots, a_r)$. In the particular case of the group $\mathscr{R}_2$ we saw in equation (7.14) that the orthogonality was given with a weight function $\rho(a) = 1$. To deduce the weight function for the group $\mathscr{R}_3$ it is necessary to study more carefully the properties which it must possess. In this section we first consider the general problem and then deduce the weight function for $\mathscr{R}_3$. This enables us to write down the orthogonality relations for the irreducible representations and characters of $\mathscr{R}_3$.

The essential property of the finite sum

$$\sum_{a=1}^{g} f(\mathrm{G}_a) \qquad \text{(A.4.9)}$$

where f is some function depending on the group element G_a, is that the sum is unchanged if, throughout the sum, G_a is replaced by the element $G_c = G_a G_b$ for some fixed G_b. This property was used repeatedly in chapter 4 and its proof in section 2.9 is simple. From the properties of a group, as G_a runs through the elements once then so does G_c for fixed G_b so that the same terms appear in the sum (A.4.9) but in a different order. It is this property which needs to be explored for continuous groups, namely that $\rho(\boldsymbol{a})$ must be chosen to ensure that, for any function $f(\boldsymbol{a})$ depending on the group elements $G(\boldsymbol{a})$,

$$\int_{\boldsymbol{a} \text{ in } \mathscr{G}} f(\boldsymbol{a})\rho(\boldsymbol{a})\mathrm{d}\boldsymbol{a} = \int_{\boldsymbol{a} \text{ in } \mathscr{G}} f(\boldsymbol{c})\rho(\boldsymbol{a})\mathrm{d}\boldsymbol{a} \tag{A.4.10}$$

where $\boldsymbol{c}$ denotes the parameters of the group element

$$G(\boldsymbol{c}) = G(\boldsymbol{a})G(\boldsymbol{b}) \tag{A.4.11}$$

for any fixed $\boldsymbol{b}$. Here we use the notation $\boldsymbol{a}$ for the set of parameters $a_1, a_2, \ldots, a_r$, while $\mathrm{d}\boldsymbol{a}$ is an abbreviation for the volume element $\mathrm{d}\boldsymbol{a} = \mathrm{d}a_1 \mathrm{d}a_2 \ldots \mathrm{d}a_r$. Now trivially

$$\int_{\boldsymbol{a} \text{ in } \mathscr{G}} f(\boldsymbol{a})\rho(\boldsymbol{a})\mathrm{d}\boldsymbol{a} = \int_{\boldsymbol{c} \text{ in } \mathscr{G}} f(\boldsymbol{c})\rho(\boldsymbol{c})\mathrm{d}\boldsymbol{c} \tag{A.4.12}$$

but if we use equation (A.4.11) for fixed $\boldsymbol{b}$ then $\boldsymbol{c}$ is a function of the parameters $\boldsymbol{a}$ and $\boldsymbol{b}$, so that introducing the Jacobian

$$\frac{\partial \boldsymbol{c}}{\partial \boldsymbol{a}} = \begin{vmatrix} \dfrac{\partial c_1}{\partial a_1} & \dfrac{\partial c_1}{\partial a_2} & \cdots & \dfrac{\partial c_1}{\partial a_r} \\ \vdots & & & \vdots \\ \dfrac{\partial c_r}{\partial a_1} & & \cdots & \dfrac{\partial c_r}{\partial a_r} \end{vmatrix} \tag{A.4.13}$$

we may change the integration variable from $\boldsymbol{c}$ to $\boldsymbol{a}$. Notice that if $\boldsymbol{b}$ is fixed and $\boldsymbol{c}$ runs over the group then $\boldsymbol{a}$ also runs over the group so that equation (A.4.12) becomes

$$\int_{\boldsymbol{a} \text{ in } \mathscr{G}} f(\boldsymbol{a})\rho(\boldsymbol{a})\mathrm{d}\boldsymbol{a} = \int_{\boldsymbol{a} \text{ in } \mathscr{G}} f(\boldsymbol{c})\rho(\boldsymbol{c})\frac{\partial \boldsymbol{c}}{\partial \boldsymbol{a}}\mathrm{d}\boldsymbol{a}$$

Comparing this with the required equation (A.4.10) shows that the weight function ρ must satisfy the condition

$$\rho(\boldsymbol{c})\frac{\partial \boldsymbol{c}}{\partial \boldsymbol{a}} = \rho(\boldsymbol{a}) \tag{A.4.14}$$

for all $\boldsymbol{a}$. Assuming that such a ρ can be found, we may choose any convenient value of $\boldsymbol{a}$ for evaluating $\rho(\boldsymbol{c})$ and by taking $\boldsymbol{a} = 0$ we have

$$\rho(\boldsymbol{c}) = \rho(0) \Bigg/ \left(\frac{\partial \boldsymbol{c}}{\partial \boldsymbol{a}}\right)_{\boldsymbol{a}=0} \tag{A.4.15}$$

The constant $\rho(0)$ is unimportant and is generally taken as $\rho(0) = 1$. To show that the choice (A.4.15) is sufficient to ensure that equation (A.4.14) is satisfied is left as an exercise.

In the finite groups the group sum invariably entered in the form

$$\frac{1}{g}\sum_{a=1}^{g} f(\mathrm{G}_a) \tag{A.4.16}$$

The division by g, the number of group elements, ensures that if f is the constant function $f(\mathrm{G}_a) = 1$ for all a then the sum also takes the value unity. For a continuous group the number g must be replaced by the group volume defined as

$$V = \int_{\boldsymbol{a} \text{ in } \mathscr{G}} \rho(\boldsymbol{a})\mathrm{d}\boldsymbol{a}$$

It is then clear that the integral

$$\frac{1}{V}\int_{\boldsymbol{a} \text{ in } \mathscr{G}} f(\boldsymbol{a})\rho(\boldsymbol{a})\mathrm{d}\boldsymbol{a} \tag{A.4.17}$$

will take the value unity if f is the constant function $f(\boldsymbol{a}) = 1$. Both definitions (A.4.16) and (A.4.17) may therefore be regarded as averaging procedures over the group. It may now be seen that the proofs of chapter 4 are equally valid if the finite average (A.4.16) is replaced by the continuous average (A.4.17). Of course, this assumes that the integral (A.4.17), or group volume, is finite. Such groups, which include the rotation and unitary groups, are called 'compact'. Although most of the groups of physical interest fall into this category, there are some which do not, such as the Lorentz and translation groups discussed in chapter 15.

For the group $\mathscr{R}_2$ the functional relation between the parameters a, b and c of equation (A.4.11) is simply $c = a + b$ so that trivially $\partial c/\partial a = 1$. The volume is then $\int_0^{2\pi}\mathrm{d}a = 2\pi$, and this justifies the orthogonality relation (7.14) as a special case of equation (4.25).

In the group $\mathscr{R}_3$ the relation between $\boldsymbol{c}$, $\boldsymbol{a}$ and $\boldsymbol{b}$ is not so simple and we make use of the vector representation of these rotations. Let us choose the z-axis in the direction of the axis of rotation of $\mathrm{R}(\boldsymbol{b})$ which gives to $\mathrm{R}(\boldsymbol{b})$ the simple matrix

$$\mathrm{R}(\boldsymbol{b}) = \begin{pmatrix} \cos b & -\sin b & 0 \\ \sin b & \cos b & 0 \\ 0 & 0 & 1 \end{pmatrix}$$

For $\mathrm{R}(\boldsymbol{a})$ we must then take an arbitrary direction but since the Jacobean is evaluated as $a \to 0$ we may treat the rotation angle as small and for its matrix use the unit operator plus the infinitesimal operator from equation (7.24)

$$\mathrm{R}(\boldsymbol{a}) \approx \begin{pmatrix} 1 & -a_z & a_y \\ a_z & 1 & -a_x \\ -a_y & a_x & 1 \end{pmatrix}$$

Hence the matrix of the product is

$$\mathrm{R}(\boldsymbol{c}) = \mathrm{R}(\boldsymbol{a})\mathrm{R}(\boldsymbol{b}) \approx \begin{pmatrix} \cos b - a_z \sin b & -\sin b - a_z \cos b & a_y \\ a_z \cos b + \sin b & -a_z \sin b + \cos b & -a_x \\ -a_y \cos b + a_x \sin b & a_y \sin b + a_x \cos b & 1 \end{pmatrix} \tag{A.4.18}$$

Having found the matrix of $\mathrm{R}(\boldsymbol{c})$ it remains to deduce the parameters $\boldsymbol{c}$ from the matrix. The angle c is found by equating the trace of the matrix $\mathrm{R}(\boldsymbol{c})$ to the known trace $(1+2\cos c)$ for a rotation through angle c, giving $\cos c = \cos b - a_z \sin b$ which, remembering that a_z is small, implies $c = b + a_z$. To find the direction of $\boldsymbol{c}$ we use the fact that the vector $\boldsymbol{c}$ will be unchanged by the rotation $\mathrm{R}(\boldsymbol{c})$,

$$\mathrm{R}(\boldsymbol{c})\boldsymbol{c} = \boldsymbol{c} \tag{A.4.19}$$

We must take care in using equation (A.4.19) since the form (A.4.18) for the matrix of $\mathrm{R}(\boldsymbol{c})$ is good only to first order in $\boldsymbol{a}$. However from equation (A.4.19) and the unitarity of the rotations we have also $\mathrm{R}^{\dagger}(\boldsymbol{c})\boldsymbol{c} = \boldsymbol{c}$ so that $\{\mathrm{R}(\boldsymbol{c}) - \mathrm{R}^{\dagger}(\boldsymbol{c})\}\boldsymbol{c} = 0$, which gives explicitly the three equations

$$\begin{aligned} -2(\sin b + a_z \cos b)c_y + [a_y(1+\cos b) - a_x \sin b]c_z &= 0 \\ 2(\sin b + a_z \cos b)c_x - [a_x(1+\cos b) + a_y \sin b]c_z &= 0 \\ [-a_y(1+\cos b) + a_x \sin b]c_x + [a_y \sin b + a_x(1+\cos b)]c_y &= 0 \end{aligned}$$

Hence the components c_x, c_y, c_z of $\boldsymbol{c}$ are in the ratio

$$\{a_y \sin b + a_x(1+\cos b)\} : \{-a_x \sin b + a_y(1+\cos b)\} : 2\{\sin b + a_z \cos b\},$$

which to leading order is the same as

$$\tfrac{1}{2}\{a_y + a_x(1+\cos b)/\sin b\} : \tfrac{1}{2}\{-a_x + a_y(1+\cos b)/\sin b\} : 1$$

Taking into account the magnitude $c = b + a_z$ deduced earlier we have finally and again to first order in $\boldsymbol{a}$,

$$c_x = \tfrac{1}{2}b\{a_y + a_x(1+\cos b)/\sin b\},\ c_y = \tfrac{1}{2}b\{-a_x + a_y(1+\cos b)/\sin b\},$$
$$c_z = b + a_z$$

The Jacobian is now evaluated directly

$$\frac{\partial \boldsymbol{c}}{\partial \boldsymbol{a}} = \begin{vmatrix} \tfrac{1}{2}b(1+\cos b)/\sin b & \tfrac{1}{2}b & 0 \\ -\tfrac{1}{2}b & \tfrac{1}{2}b(1+\cos b)/\sin b & 0 \\ 0 & 0 & 1 \end{vmatrix} = \tfrac{1}{2}b^2(1+\cos b)/\sin^2 b$$

In the limit $\boldsymbol{a} \to 0$ we may write $b = c$ so that the required weight function is

$$\rho(c) = \frac{2\sin^2 c}{c^2(1+\cos c)} = \frac{2(1-\cos c)}{c^2} \tag{A.4.20}$$

The group volume defined earlier is then

$$V = \int_{\boldsymbol{a} \text{ in } \mathscr{G}} \frac{2(1-\cos a)}{a^2} \mathrm{d}a_x \mathrm{d}a_y \mathrm{d}a_z$$

Transforming to polar coordinates for the vector $\boldsymbol{a}$, and integrating over angle, gives

$$V = \int_{a=0}^{\pi} \frac{2(1-\cos a)}{a^2} a^2 \mathrm{d}a \iint \mathrm{d}\Omega = 8\pi^2$$

The group average (A.4.17) is then

$$\frac{1}{4\pi^2} \int_{\boldsymbol{a}} f(\boldsymbol{a})(1-\cos a) \mathrm{d}a \mathrm{d}\boldsymbol{\Omega} \tag{A.4.21}$$

For a function $f(\boldsymbol{a})$ which is independent of the angle of $\boldsymbol{a}$, and this would be true for any class function like the character, the average becomes

$$\frac{1}{\pi} \int_{a=0}^{\pi} f(a)(1-\cos a) \mathrm{d}a \tag{A.4.22}$$

Using this average to replace the finite sum in equation (4.25a) then gives the orthogonality relation for characters of $\mathscr{R}_3$,

$$\frac{1}{\pi} \int_{a=0}^{\pi} \chi_a^{(j_1)} \chi_a^{(j_2)} (1-\cos a) \mathrm{d}a = \delta_{j_1 j_2} \tag{A.4.23}$$

a result which may be verified from the explicit formula (7.42) for $\chi_a^{(j)}$. It should however be noticed that the orthogonality is not valid for the half-integer representations which are double-valued. Orthogonality for these double-valued representations may be recovered by extending the range of the rotation angle to 2π. Over this range the representation is single-valued. Further discussion of this enlargement of the group $\mathscr{R}_3$ is given in section 7.6 and in section 18.13.3.

If the Euler angles α, β and γ are used as parameters for the rotation instead of a_1, a_2 and a_3 then it may be shown, see section 20.5, that the weight function is $\rho(\alpha, \beta, \gamma) = \sin \beta$ so that the average becomes

$$\frac{1}{8\pi^2} \int_{\gamma=0}^{2\pi} \int_{\beta=0}^{\pi} \int_{\alpha=0}^{2\pi} f(\alpha, \beta, \gamma) \sin \beta \, \mathrm{d}\alpha \mathrm{d}\beta \mathrm{d}\gamma \tag{A.4.24}$$

The orthogonality relation for matrix elements of the irreducible representations then takes the form

$$\frac{1}{8\pi^2}\int_0^{2\pi}\int_0^{\pi}\int_0^{2\pi} D^{(j_1)*}_{m_1'm_1}(\alpha,\beta,\gamma)D^{(j_2)}_{m_2'm_2}(\alpha,\beta,\gamma)\sin\beta\,\mathrm{d}\alpha\,\mathrm{d}\beta\,\mathrm{d}\gamma$$

$$= \delta_{j_1j_2}\delta_{m_1'm_2'}\delta_{m_1m_2}(2j_1+1)^{-1} \quad \text{(A.4.25)}$$

using equation (4.23). Again, for half-integer j the range of the parameters must be doubled and this may be achieved in a variety of ways, for example by allowing α to extend up to 4π.

Appendix 5: Techniques in Atomic Structure Calculations

Some detailed calculations of the ordering of atomic energy levels for the configurations p^2 and p^3 are given in the first section, to reinforce the more qualitative discussion in chapter 8. The second section returns to the theory of angular momentum and the group $\mathscr{R}_3$ and introduces the more intricate problems encountered when more than two angular momenta are coupled together. Some of these ideas are used in section A.5.3 to calculate atomic transition strengths. Some more details of the effects of symmetry in a crystal field, which was introduced in section 9.9 of the first volume, are given in the last two sections.

A.5.1 Term energies for p^2 and p^3 configurations

Two valence p-electrons

We first deduce the energies of the three terms ^3P, ^1S and ^1D of two electrons in a shell with $l = 1$ (see subsection 8.6.4) by using the simplest method, that of the 'diagonal sum'. A more sophisticated method which requires the knowledge of tabulated coefficients is described in section A.5.2. We make use of the fact that since the Coulomb repulsion e^2/r_{12} is invariant under rotation of all particles the energies are independent of M_L and diagonal in L. Thus we may select any convenient value of M_L. The matrix elements of the Coulomb repulsion are most easily calculated in the product basis $m_1 m_2$ rather than the coupled basis $L M_L$. Furthermore we know that the trace of a matrix is independent of the basis. Let us denote the required term energies by E_L and the diagonal matrix elements in the product basis by $E(m_1 m_2)$. Then considering separately the matrix for each value of M we are able to deduce a set of equations relating the E_L to the $E(m_1 m_2)$.

Taking first the maximum $M = 2$ for which there is only one basis state we have directly $E_D = E(1\,1)$. For $M = 1$ there are two basis states and we have $E_P + E_D = E(1\,0) + E(0\,1)$. For $M = 0$ there are three basis states giving $E_S + E_P + E_D = E(1\,-1) + E(0\,0) + E(-1\,1)$. It remains only to calculate the diagonal matrix elements

$$E(m_1 m_2)$$

$$= \iint \mathrm{d}\boldsymbol{r}_1 \mathrm{d}\boldsymbol{r}_2 u_{nl}^2(r_1) u_{nl}^2(r_2) Y_{m_1}^{(l)*}(\theta_1\phi_1) Y_{m_2}^{(l)*}(\theta_2\phi_2) Y_{m_1}^{(l)}(\theta_1\phi_1) Y_{m_2}^{(l)}(\theta_2\phi_2)(e^2/r_{12})$$

We do this for arbitrary l since no more work is required. The interaction $(1/r_{12})$ is separated into parts depending on each electron by first expanding it in Legendre polynomials of $\cos\theta_{12}$, where θ_{12} is the angle between $\boldsymbol{r}_1$ and $\boldsymbol{r}_2$, and then using the spherical harmonic addition theorem (A.4.8). Finally, the angular integrals are carried out using equation (A.4.6). Thus expanding

$$e^2/r_{12} = \sum_{k=0}^{\infty} v_k(r_1, r_2) P_k(\cos\theta_{12})$$

and writing for the radial integral

$$F^{(k)} = \iint r_1^2 r_2^2 \mathrm{d}r_1 \mathrm{d}r_2 u_{nl}^2(r_1) u_{nl}^2(r_2) v_k(r_1, r_2)$$

we have

$$E(m_1 m_2) = \sum_{k\,(\text{even})=0}^{2l} F^{(k)} C^2(kll,000) C(kll,0m_1m_1) C(kll,0m_2m_2) \quad \text{(A.5.1)}$$

The upper limit on k has come about because of the vector coupling of k, l and l. The coefficients C vanish otherwise. The restriction to even k results from consideration of parity in the single-particle integral (A.4.6). The vector coupling coefficients C all take the value unity when $k = 0$ so that in the case of $l = 1$ we have the simple formula

$$E(m_1 m_2) = F^{(0)} + F^{(2)} C^2(211,000) C(211,0m_1m_1) C(211,0m_2m_2)$$

Using the known values of the coupling coefficients (see problem 7.8) we can now deduce $E(m_1 m_2)$ and hence E_L in terms of the two radial integrals $F^{(0)}$ and $F^{(2)}$,

$$E_P = F^{(0)} - \tfrac{1}{5}F^{(2)}, \qquad E_D = F^{(0)} + \tfrac{1}{25}F^{(2)}, \qquad E_S = F^{(0)} + \tfrac{2}{5}F^{(2)} \quad \text{(A.5.2)}$$

From its definition one sees that the integral $F^{(k)}$ is positive since $v_k(r_1, r_2)$ has the explicit form $v_k(r_1, r_2) = r_<^k / r_>^{k+1}$, where $r_<$ and $r_<^k$ denote the lesser and greater of r_1 and r_2. Without calculating the value of $F^{(2)}$, which would demand knowledge of the radial wave functions $u_{nl}(r)$, we can see that the term energies satisfy Hund's rule. In fact we may deduce the ratio of the excitation energies of the ^1S and ^1D terms above the ground state ^3P term $(E_S - E_P)/(E_D - E_P) = 2.5$, which is to be compared with the observed ratio of 2.1 in the carbon ($Z = 6$) atom which has two valence electrons in the $2p$-shell. The small discrepancy is due to the admixture of higher states such as that obtained by placing one valence electron in the $3p$-shell. We have, after all, only been using first-order perturbation theory.

Three valence p-electrons

The energies of the three possible terms ^4S, ^2P and ^2D, see subsection 8.6.4, may be calculated by a natural extension of the method given for two particles using a product basis, $m_1 m_2 m_3$, but this method soon becomes laborious as the number of electrons increases beyond three and a more sophisticated method known as the 'fractional parentage' method is generally used. The basic idea is simple and we shall use it here.

Any antisymmetric function $\Psi_{SL}(1\,2\,3)$ of three particles with the same nl must of necessity be antisymmetric in particles numbered 1 and 2. It must therefore be possible to write

$$\Psi_{SL}(1\,2\,3) = \sum_{\Phi} a_\Phi \{\Phi(1\,2)\psi(3)\}_{SLM_SM_L} \quad \text{(A.5.3)}$$

where Φ runs over all the terms for two valence electrons and the curly bracket denotes the vector coupling of Φ to the single particle wave function of electron number 3 to give total S and total L.

We wish to calculate the term energies

$$F_{SL} = \left(\Psi_{SL}(1\,2\,3) \Big| \sum_{i<j}^{3} e^2/r_{ij} \Big| \Psi_{SL}(1\,2\,3) \right)$$

but since Ψ is antisymmetric, the contribution from each pair of electrons is the same and the sum is equal to three times the contribution of any particular pair, for example electrons numbered 1 and 2. Thus using also equation (A.5.3)

$$\begin{aligned} F_{SL} &= 3\sum_{\Phi} |a_\Phi|^2 (\Phi(1\,2)|e^2/r_{12}|\Phi(1\,2)) \\ &= 3\sum_{\Phi} |a_\Phi|^2 E_\Phi \end{aligned} \quad \text{(A.5.4)}$$

where E_Φ denotes the term energies for the two-particle system. In deriving equation (A.5.4) we have integrated over the coordinates of particle number 3 which is trivial and gives a factor unity from normalisation since the operator is now independent of particle 3. We have also introduced the coupling coefficients implied in the expression (A.5.3) and carried out the sum over the M_S and M_L values of Φ. These sums again give a factor unity from the normalisation of the coupling coefficients and the fact that E_Φ is independent of these M-values.

Knowing the two-electron term energies from the previous section one needs only to deduce the 'fractional parentage coefficients' a_Φ to obtain the three-electron term energies F_{SL}. Some elaborate methods have been developed for this purpose and extensive tables have been published. Here we shall deduce the coefficients by an elementary method. From the normalisation of Ψ the coefficients must be normalised $\sum_\Phi |a_\Phi|^2 = 1$ and for the purpose of using (A.5.4) the phase of a_Φ is not relevant. The coefficients are conveniently presented in table A.4—with Ψ labelling the rows and Φ the

Table A.4

$\Psi \backslash \Phi$	^3P	^1D	^1S
^4S	1	0	0
^2D	α	β	0
^2P	γ	δ	ε

columns. The zero entries in the table follow directly from the triangular conditions on vector coupling, i.e. a total $S = \frac{3}{2}$ cannot be produced by coupling the single particle spin of $\frac{1}{2}$ of electron number 3 to the 'parent' spin $S = 0$ and a total $L = 2$ cannot be produced by coupling $l = 1$ to the ^1S parent. Use of the normalisation condition completes the first row and gives the energy of the ground state term as

$$F(^4S) = 3E_p = 3F^{(0)} - (3/5)F^{(2)} \qquad \text{(A.5.5a)}$$

using the results (A.5.2). To find the second row we use the result (8.44) noting that equation (A.5.4) is valid for any invariant two-body interaction and hence for $\mathcal{M}^r$ in (8.44). Since $\mathrm{P}^r_{ij} = -1$ in the ^3P term and $+1$ in the ^1D this gives

$$3(-\alpha^2 + \beta^2) = 3 - \tfrac{9}{4} - \tfrac{1}{2}(\tfrac{3}{2}) = 0$$

which combined with the normalisation $\alpha^2 + \beta^2 = 1$ gives $\alpha^2 = \beta^2 = \frac{1}{2}$. Using these values for α^2 and β^2 we deduce the energy of the ^2D term,

$$F(^2D) = \tfrac{3}{2}E_P + \tfrac{3}{2}E_D = 3F^{(0)} - \tfrac{6}{25}F^{(2)} \qquad \text{(A.5.5b)}$$

The same argument applied to the third row gives

$$3(-\gamma^2 + \delta^2 + \varepsilon^2) = 3 - \tfrac{9}{4} - \tfrac{1}{2}(\tfrac{3}{2})$$

which together with the normalisation gives $\gamma^2 = \frac{1}{2}$, $\delta^2 + \varepsilon^2 = \frac{1}{2}$. To find δ^2 and ε^2 we use the two-body operator $\sum_{i<j} [\mathbf{l}(i) + \mathbf{l}(j)]^2$ in precise analogy with the corresponding spin operator used in deriving equation (8.43). The corresponding expression is

$$\sum_{i<j} [\mathbf{l}(i) + \mathbf{l}(j)]^2 = \mathbf{L}^2 - t(2-t)l(l+1)$$

which when applied to the ^2P term, using equation (A.5.4), gives $3(2\gamma^2 + 6\delta^2) = 2 + 6$. Knowing $\gamma^2 = \frac{1}{2}$ this gives $\delta^2 = 5/18$, $\varepsilon^2 = 4/18$, completing the third row of the table and giving for the energy of the ^2P term

$$F(^2P) = \tfrac{3}{2}E_P + \tfrac{5}{6}E_D + \tfrac{4}{6}E_S = 3F^0 \tag{A.5.5c}$$

From the three term energies (A.5.5) we may again deduce the ratio of excitation energies

$$\frac{F(^2P) - F(^4S)}{F(^2D) - F(^4S)} = 1.67$$

which is to be compared with the observed ratio 1.5 in nitrogen ($Z = 7$) with three valence $2p$-electrons.

This example illustrates the method of fractional parentage which is used for more complex atoms and also in nuclear physics. More systematic methods for calculating the coefficients of fractional parentage are available, making use of other groups, notably the group U_{2l+1} of unitary transformations in the $(2l + 1)$ dimensional space of the wave functions ψ_{lm} for a single particle and its various subgroups, see section 18.10.

A.5.2 Recoupling coefficients (6*j*- and 9*j*-symbols)

We have seen how the Clebsch – Gordan (or vector-coupling) coefficients play a vital role in the construction of wave functions and the calculation of matrix elements. These coefficients are calculated entirely from the group properties of $\mathcal{R}_3$ and are independent of any details of the physical system other than its symmetry. When more than two angular momenta are coupled together one naturally encounters products of Clebsch – Gordan coefficients and certain sums of products occur sufficiently frequently that it is worth while introducing a symbol to denote them and tabulating numerical values for them—see Brink and Satchler (1968) and Rotenberg *et al.* (1959) in the bibliography to chapter 7, for further details of the recoupling coefficients. It is clear that unlimited complexity may be achieved by coupling more and more angular momenta together but, in practice, it is only the first one or two steps along this path which are of much interest. The processes which we develop in this section are applicable to most groups but have only been developed extensively for the group $\mathcal{R}_3$. For the Abelian group $\mathcal{R}_2$ these processes are trivial.

The product representation $D^{(j_1)} \times D^{(j_2)}$ reduces simply, as given by equation (7.44), so that there is a unique basis vector which transforms irreducibly with given jm, provided $|j_1 - j_2| \leq j \leq (j_1 + j_2)$. The Clebsch–Gordan coefficients $C(j_1 j_2 j,\ m_1 m_2 m)$ are defined as the coefficients for the expansion of this function in the product basis $m_1 m_2$. The more elaborate product representation $D^{(j_1)} \times D^{(j_2)} \times D^{(j_3)} \times D^{(j_4)}$ will not reduce simply and in general a given irreducible representation $D^{(j)}$ may occur several times in its reduction. Hence the reduction is not unique and a single label jm will not uniquely specify the basis functions of the reduced representation. The reduction may be carried out in two parts, first reducing separately the two products

$$D^{(j_1)} \times D^{(j_2)} = \sum_{j_{12} = |j_1 - j_2|}^{(j_1 + j_2)} D^{(j_{12})}$$

and

$$D^{(j_3)} \times D^{(j_4)} = \sum_{j_{34} = |j_3 - j_4|}^{(j_3 + j_4)} D^{(j_{34})} \tag{A.5.6}$$

and finally reducing the product

$$D^{(j_{12})} \times D^{(j_{34})} = \sum_{j = |j_{12} - j_{34}|}^{(j_{12} + j_{34})} D^{(j)} \tag{A.5.7}$$

Each of these steps is unique and defines a set of basis vectors which we denote by $|j_{12} j_{34}, jm\rangle$. An alternative set of basis vectors may be defined by taking the products in a different order, for example $D^{(j_1)} \times D^{(j_3)}$ and $D^{(j_2)} \times D^{(j_4)}$ followed by $D^{(j_{13})} \times D^{(j_{24})}$ would define a set $|j_{13} j_{24}, jm\rangle$. The transformation between these two sets is usually written as

$$|j_{12} j_{34}, jm\rangle = \sum_{j_{13} j_{24}} [(2j_{12}+1)(2j_{34}+1)(2j_{13}+1)(2j_{24}+1)]^{\frac{1}{2}} \times \begin{Bmatrix} j_1 & j_2 & j_{12} \\ j_3 & j_4 & j_{34} \\ j_{13} & j_{24} & j \end{Bmatrix} |j_{13} j_{24}, jm\rangle \tag{A.5.8}$$

which defines the $9j$-symbol $\begin{Bmatrix} \cdot & \cdot & \cdot \\ \cdot & \cdot & \cdot \\ \cdot & \cdot & \cdot \end{Bmatrix}$. Since functions with different j or m are orthogonal it follows that the sum (A.5.8) is restricted to fixed j and m and it is easily shown, using the raising operator J_+, that the coefficients are independent of m. From their method of construction it is clear that any of the basis vectors on either side of equation (A.5.8) may be written as a sum of vectors $|m_1 m_2 m_3 m_4\rangle$ in the simple product basis with coefficients which are products of three Clebsch–Gordan coefficients. Hence using the orthogonality of these coefficients, equation (A.5.8) leads to an expression for the $9j$-

symbol as a sum over products of six Clebsch–Gordan coefficients. Fortunately, there are tables of 9j-symbols! The reason for extracting the square root factor in equation (A.5.8) is because the 9j-symbol so defined has extensive symmetry relations. A reflection in either diagonal leaves it unchanged, while the exchange of any two rows or columns induces a factor $(-1)^p$, where p is the sum of all nine j-values in the symbol.

In an extension of the Wigner–Eckart theorem (7.53) the matrix elements of a coupled operator in a coupled system are also given in terms of a 9j-symbol. Consider a system with two components, like two particles, or the orbital and spin angular momenta of a single particle. We distinguish the components by indices 1 and 2 and write a coupled wave function as $|j_1 j_2 jm\rangle$. We take irreducible sets $\mathrm{R}^{(k_1)}_{q_1}$ and $\mathrm{S}^{(k_2)}_{q_2}$ of operators (see section 7.4.6) in each component and couple them to form an irreducible set with respect to simultaneous rotations

$$\mathrm{T}^{(K)}_Q = \sum_{q_1 q_2} C(k_1 k_2 K, q_1 q_2 Q)\mathrm{R}^{(k_1)}_{q_1}\mathrm{S}^{(k_2)}_{q_2} \tag{A.5.9}$$

$\mathrm{R}^{(k_1)}_{q_1}$ is a unit operator so far as the second component is concerned and vice versa. Using the Wigner–Eckart theorem and the definition (A.5.8) of the 9j-symbol one then finds

$$\begin{aligned}\langle j_1 j_2 jm|\mathrm{T}^{(K)}_Q|j'_1 j'_2 j'm'\rangle &= (-1)^{2K} C(j'Kj, m'Qm)\,\langle j_1 j_2 j||\mathrm{T}^{(K)}||j'_1 j'_2 j'\rangle \\ &= (-1)^{2K} C(j'Kj, m'Qm)[(2j'+1)(2K+1) \\ &\quad \times (2j_1+1)(2j_2+1)]^{\frac{1}{2}} \\ &\quad \times \begin{Bmatrix} j_1 & j_2 & j \\ j'_1 & j'_2 & j' \\ k_1 & k_2 & K \end{Bmatrix} \langle j_1 j_2||\mathbf{R}^{(k_1)}\mathbf{S}^{(k_2)}||j'_1 j'_2\rangle\end{aligned} \tag{A.5.10}$$

This formula may be derived by inserting all the Clebsch–Gordan coefficients which appear on the left of equation (A.5.10) when the various couplings are uncoupled and the Wigner–Eckart theorem is used in each component. The resulting sum is then seen to be identical with that appearing in equation (A.5.8). The result should not be unexpected since the separation of the two components in (A.5.10) has much in common with the transformation (A.5.8) using the correspondence

$$(j_1 j_2 j_3 j_4 j_{12} j_{34} j_{13} j_{24} j) \to (j_1 j_2 j'_1 j'_2 j j' k_1 k_2 K)$$

The importance of equation (A.5.10) is that the dependence of the matrix element on K, j and j' is given explicitly in terms of known functions and does not depend on the detailed definition of the operators. If, in the product basis $|j_1 j_2 m_1 m_2\rangle$, the wave function separates then so does the reduced matrix element

$$\langle j_1 j_2||\mathbf{R}^{(k_1)}\mathbf{S}^{(k_2)}||j'_1 j'_2\rangle = \langle j_1||\mathbf{R}^{(k_1)}||j'_1\rangle\langle j_2||\mathbf{S}^{(k_2)}||j'_2\rangle \tag{A.5.11}$$

There are several special cases of these results which are in fact the ones most frequently encountered. When one of the entries in a 9j-symbol vanishes two other pairs of entries must be the same because of triangular conditions, leaving only six independent j-values. In this case one writes

$$\begin{Bmatrix} a & b & e \\ c & d & e \\ f & f & 0 \end{Bmatrix} = \frac{(-1)^{b+c+e+f}}{[(2e+1)(2f+1)]^{\frac{1}{2}}} \begin{Bmatrix} a & b & e \\ d & c & f \end{Bmatrix} \tag{A.5.12}$$

and refers to $\{\vdots \;\vdots\; \vdots\}$ as a 6j-symbol. Again the reason for extracting the factor in the definition (A.5.12) is because this leads to greater symmetry in the 6j-symbol. It is unchanged by the exchange of any pair of columns or by the exchange of any two numbers in the top row with those immediately below them in the bottom row. Because of the symmetry of the 9j-symbol there is an expression similar to (A.5.12) for any 9j-symbol with a zero in any position.

By setting $j_4 = 0$, the equation (A.5.8) gives the transformation between the two sets of irreducible basis functions for a system of three j-values

$$|j_{12}j_3, jm\rangle = \sum_{j_{13}} (-1)^{j_{12}+j_{13}+j_2+j_3}[(2j_{12}+1)(2j_{13}+1)]^{\frac{1}{2}} \times \begin{Bmatrix} j_1 & j_{12} & j_2 \\ j & j_{13} & j_3 \end{Bmatrix} |j_{13}j_2, jm\rangle \tag{A.5.13}$$

The result (A.5.10) may be specialised in two way. First, by taking $S^{(k_2)}_{q_2} = 1$, the unit operator, so that $k_2 = 0$, we obtain

$$\langle j_1 j_2 jm | R^{(k_1)}_{q_1} | j_1' j_2' j' m'\rangle = (-1)^{j_1+j_2+j'-k_1} C(j'k_1 j, m' q_1 m)\delta_{j_2 j_2'} \times [(2j'+1)(2j_1+1)]^{\frac{1}{2}} \begin{Bmatrix} j & j' & k_1 \\ j_1' & j_1 & j_2 \end{Bmatrix} \langle j_1 \| \mathbf{R}^{(k_1)} \| j_1'\rangle \tag{A.5.14}$$

in which the dependence on the total angular momenta j and j' is given entirely by known functions.

As a second specialisation, set $K = 0$ so that $k_1 = k_2$ and the operator $T^{(0)}_0$ is now an invariant, giving

$$\langle j_1 j_2 jm | T^{(0)}_0 | j_1' j_2' j' m'\rangle = \delta_{jj'}\delta_{mm'}(-1)^{j_1'+j_2+j-k_1}\left(\frac{(2j_1+1)(2j_2+1)}{(2k_1+1)}\right)^{\frac{1}{2}} \times \begin{Bmatrix} j_1 & j_1' & k_1 \\ j_2' & j_2 & j \end{Bmatrix} \langle j_1 j_2 \| \mathbf{R}^{(k_1)}\mathbf{S}^{(k_1)} \| j_1' j_2'\rangle \tag{A.5.15}$$

This formula gives the j-dependence of the matrix element of the invariant $T_0^{(0)}$ through a $6j$-symbol.

The explicit form of the invariant operator is from equation (A.5.9)

$$T_0^{(0)} = \sum_{q_1} (-1)^{k_1 - q_1}(2k_1+1)^{-\frac{1}{2}} R_{q_1}^{(k_1)} S_{-q_1}^{(k_1)}$$

putting in the known values for the Clebsch–Gordan coefficients. It is fairly common practice, however, to write

$$(\mathbf{R}^{(k_1)}.\mathbf{S}^{(k_1)}) = (-1)^{k_1}(2k_1+1)^{\frac{1}{2}} T_0^{(0)} = \sum_{q_1} (-1)^{q_1} R_{q_1}^{(k_1)} S_{-q_1}^{(k_1)}$$

and to refer to $(\mathbf{R}^{(k_1)}.\mathbf{S}^{(k_1)})$ as the scalar product of the two irreducible sets of operators $R_{q_1}^{(k_1)}$ and $S_{q_1}^{(k_1)}$. In particular for the angular momentum operators which have $k = 1$,

$$(\mathbf{J}.\mathbf{J}) = -J_{+1}J_{-1} - J_{-1}J_{+1} + J_0 J_0 = J_x^2 + J_y^2 + J_z^2$$

which agrees with the usual notion of a scalar product of two vectors. Care must be taken to avoid errors of $(-1)^{k_1}(2k_1+1)^{\frac{1}{2}}$ due to these two ways of expressing the invariant.

Some of the results obtained earlier in this chapter may be obtained directly from the formulae derived above rather than by the use of equivalent operators. For example, equations (8.28) and (8.39) are particular cases of equation (A.5.15) while equation (A.5.14) will be used in the next section to deduce the ratios of transition strengths.

A.5.3 Transition strengths

We have already discussed selection rules for the emission and absorption of electric dipole radiation in sections 5.4 and 8.1. In an LS-coupling situation for a many-electron atom they are given by

$$S' = S, \qquad J' = J, J \pm 1, \qquad L' = L \pm 1 \tag{A.5.16}$$

with the usual exclusion of $0 \to 0$ transitions in L or J. Here we have denoted the initial and final states by SLJ and $S'L'J'$, respectively. These rules follow immediately from the fact that the dipole operator is invariant in spin space and a vector operator in position space. The Wigner–Eckart theorem may now be used to deduce the ratios of transition strengths between two terms for different J and J'. In fact we need the extension of that theorem given by equation (A.5.14). Making the correspondence

$$(j_1 j_2 j_1' j_2' j j' m m' k_1) \to (L S L' S J J' M M' 1)$$

and denoting the dipole operator by $V_q^{(1)}$ we have

$$\langle LSJM|V_q^{(1)}|L'SJ'M'\rangle = (-1)^{L+S+J'-1}C(J'1J, M'qM) \times[(2L+1)(2J'+1)]^{\frac{1}{2}}\begin{Bmatrix} J & J' & 1 \\ L' & L & S \end{Bmatrix}\langle LS||V^{(1)}||L'S\rangle$$

The transition strength is usually defined to be the sum of squares of the matrix elements of $V_q^{(1)}$ summed over the possible projections M and M' of initial and final states. From normalisation of the Clebsch–Gordan coefficients

$$\sum_{M'} C^2(J'1J, M'qM) = 1$$

so that the strength is given by

$$S(J,J') = (2J+1)(2L+1)(2J'+1)\begin{Bmatrix} J & J' & 1 \\ L' & L & S \end{Bmatrix}^2 \langle LS||V^{(1)}||L'S\rangle^2 \tag{A.5.17}$$

Thus without any detailed knowledge of the wave functions we deduce that for fixed L and L', the dependence on J and J' is given by

$$S(J,J') \propto (2J+1)(2J'+1)\begin{Bmatrix} J & J' & 1 \\ L' & L & S \end{Bmatrix}^2$$

This result has been known as the Hönl–Kronig intensity rule. A simple sum rule may be obtained for the total intensity summed over final states J'. From equation (A.5.13) the $6j$-symbols must satisfy the normalisation condition

$$\sum_{j_{12}} (2j_{12}+1)(2j_{13}+1)\begin{Bmatrix} j_1 & j_{12} & j_2 \\ j & j_{13} & j_3 \end{Bmatrix}^2 = 1$$

giving the J-dependence of the summed strengths as

$$\sum_{J'} S(J,J') \propto (2J+1)$$

which is another well-known empirical rule.

For quadrupole transitions the strengths are given in just the same way by an equation like (A.5.17) but with $k_1 = 2$ rather than $k_1 = 1$.

When an energy level with angular momentum J is split into $(2J+1)$ levels by a magnetic field as described in section 8.5 for the hydrogen atom and illustrated in figure 8.1(c) the relative strengths of transitions between states with different M may be related using the formulae above. As an example consider radiation polarised in the xy-plane so that the dipole operator has $q = \pm 1$ implying that $M' = M \mp 1$. Then, omitting the summations carried out in arriving at equation (A.5.17) the strengths are given by

$$S(J,J',M,M') = C^2(J'1J, M'\pm 1M)(2L+1)(2J'+1) \times\begin{Bmatrix} J & J' & 1 \\ L' & L & S \end{Bmatrix}^2 \langle LS||V^{(1)}||L'S\rangle^2$$

Thus for example the ratio of strengths for the two transitions $1s_{\frac{1}{2}} \to 2p_{\frac{3}{2}}$ and $1s_{\frac{1}{2}} \to 2p_{\frac{1}{2}}$, shown in figure 8.1(c), both with $M = -\frac{1}{2}$ and $M' = +\frac{1}{2}$, is

$$\frac{C^2(\frac{3}{2}\,1\,\frac{1}{2},\frac{1}{2}\,-1\,-\frac{1}{2}) \times 4 \times \begin{Bmatrix} \frac{1}{2} & \frac{3}{2} & 1 \\ 1 & 0 & \frac{1}{2} \end{Bmatrix}^2}{C^2(\frac{1}{2}\,1\,\frac{1}{2},\frac{1}{2}\,-1\,-\frac{1}{2}) \times 2 \times \begin{Bmatrix} \frac{1}{2} & \frac{1}{2} & 1 \\ 1 & 0 & \frac{1}{2} \end{Bmatrix}^2} - \frac{1}{2}$$

where the values of the coefficients are taken from Rotenberg *et al.* (1959) in the bibliography to chapter 7. Because of the presence of the Clebsch–Gordan coefficients this differs from the ratio of 2 obtained from equation (A.5.17) for the total strengths from $1s_{\frac{1}{2}}$ to $2p_{\frac{3}{2}}$ and $2p_{\frac{1}{2}}$, respectively.

A.5.4 The crystal field potential

The results of subsection 9.9.2 do not depend on the detailed form of the crystal field potential but only on its symmetry which is determined by the crystal structure. However, this told us only the manner in which the multiplets would split but did not tell us anything about the ordering of the split levels or their energy spacings. If we now want to calculate such details of the states in the crystal field we will need to evaluate matrix elements of the crystal field potential in the states which we have found by symmetry arguments. In this section we study the crystal field potential and in the following section methods are given for evaluating the matrix elements.

The potential due to the surrounding atoms or ions will have a form which is invariant under all the point group symmetry operators and will therefore transform according to the identity representation. For the region in which we are interested it will also be a solution to Laplace's equation and can therefore be expanded in spherical harmonics as

$$V_c = \sum_{kq} A_q^{(k)} r^k Y_q^{(k)}(\theta, \phi) \tag{A.5.18}$$

Since rotations can only mix spherical harmonics of the same k the contribution to V_c from each k must also transform according to the identity representation of the point group. This places very strong restrictions on the coefficients $A_q^{(k)}$ which we illustrate by taking the symmetry group O.

From the formula (7.42) for the character of $D^{(k)}$ and using table 9.5 we soon find that for $k = 1, 2, 3$ and 5 the representation $D^{(k)}$ contains no invariant under the group O and for $k = 4$ there is just one.

By defining the z-axis to be an axis of greatest symmetry we may also restrict the possible values of q which occur in the expression (A.5.18). For example in the group O, the four-fold rotational symmetry about the z-axis implies that the values of q must have the form $q = 4n$, with n an integer. Thus the only surviving coefficients with k < 6 are $A_0^{(0)}$, $A_0^{(4)}$, $A_4^{(4)}$ and $A_{-4}^{(4)}$ and, since there is only one fourth-order invariant, the coefficients $A_0^{(4)}$, $A_4^{(4)}$ and $A_{-4}^{(4)}$ must be related. To make the potential invariant under a four-fold rotation about the x- or y-axes requires that $A_{-4}^{(4)} = A_4^{(4)} = (\frac{5}{14})^{\frac{1}{2}} A_0^{(4)}$, see problem A.8. Hence the potential for a cubic field has the form

$$V_c = A_0^{(0)} + A_0^{(4)} r^4 \{ Y_0^{(4)} + (\tfrac{5}{14})^{\frac{1}{2}} (Y_4^{(4)} + Y_{-4}^{(4)}) \} + \text{terms with } k \geqq 6 \quad (A.5.19)$$

In this particular case it is equally easy to write down an expression for V in powers of x, y and z which has the required symmetry. The terms must be even in x, y and z and be symmetric with respect to permutation of x, y and z. The series must therefore take the form

$$V_c = A_0^{(0)} + \alpha(x^2 + y^2 + z^2) + \beta(x^4 + y^4 + z^4) + \gamma(x^2 y^2 + y^2 z^2 + z^2 x^2) + \text{powers} \geqq 6$$

The potential must also satisfy Laplace's equation $\nabla^2 V_c = 0$ giving $\alpha = 0$ and $\gamma = -3\beta$, a result which is seen to be identical with equation (A.5.19) if the explicit formula (7.48) for the spherical harmonics is used.

It is possible to calculate numerical values for the non-zero coefficients $A_q^{(k)}$ for a particular model, e.g. that the potential is due to point charges located at the neighbouring lattice sites, but these models do not take into account the polarisation of the ions and exchange effects. It is usual therefore to regard the coefficient $A_q^{(k)}$ as undetermined parameters which are fixed by comparing predictions with experiments. This procedure is meaningful since only a few terms in the series (A.5.18) will give non-vanishing matrix elements for electron states of definite angular momentum, because of the restrictions (8.3) derived from the triangle rule of vector coupling. This means that there are just a few parameters $A_q^{(k)}$ to be chosen to fit consistently all the data available from the range of experiments on specific heats, magnetic susceptibilities, optical absorption and paramagnetic resonance.

For the cubic field at the vanadium ion in vanadium bromate the potential will be given by the expression (A.5.19). No terms involving $k > 4$ need be considered since we are dealing with d-electrons and the single particle matrix elements are of the form $\langle d | Y_q^{(k)} | d \rangle$ which vanish by the triangle rule for $k > 4$. Since the constant $A_0^{(0)}$ gives the same contribution in all states, the crystal field splittings in vanadium bromate are given in terms of the single parameter $A_0^{(4)}$.

A.5.5 The use of symmetry to deduce ratios of splittings

The calculation of the crystal field splittings in terms of the parameters $A_q^{(k)}$ is in general a complicated numerical problem involving the radial wave functions of the electrons and details of the many-electron wave functions. However, it is possible to deduce relations between some of the splittings by the use of symmetry alone. This is done by using the Wigner–Eckart theorem or, what is really the same thing, by the use of equivalent operators, see equations (4.62), (7.53) and subsection 7.4.7.

We illustrate the technique by calculating the ratio of the energy differences between the three split components A_2, T_2 and T_1 of the F-level in the second column of figure 9.9. The potential in this case is given by equation (A.5.19) and, as shown above, the terms with $k \geqq 6$ do not contribute. Furthermore, the $\mathscr{R}_3$ invariant term $A_0^{(0)}$ contributes the same amount to each component and may therefore be ignored in calculating energy differences. Thus the differences are both proportional to $A_0^{(4)}$ and the symmetry property of the operator is defined as $k = 4$, with respect to $\mathscr{R}_3$ and (invariant) A_1 with respect to the group O. Using the notation $V(k = 4, A_1)$ for this part of V_c we need to find the matrix elements $\langle L = 3, \mathrm{T}^{(\alpha)} | V(k = 4, A_1) | L = 3, \mathrm{T}^{(\alpha)} \rangle$ for $\mathrm{T}^{(\alpha)} = A_2, T_2$ and T_1. The form of this matrix element is very similar to that of equation (7.53) where the Wigner–Eckart theorem for the group $\mathscr{R}_3$ was used. The difference is that here the group O is used to label the rows of the representations of $\mathscr{R}_3$ instead of the group $\mathscr{R}_2$. In other words, operators and wave functions are now labelled by L and $\mathrm{T}^{(\alpha)}$ rather than by L and M.

The required coupling coefficients for use in the Wigner–Eckart theorem in this basis are not generally available so that it is usual to express both operators and wave functions in the familiar M-basis. For the operator, this has already been done in equation (A.5.19) and we may write

$$V(k = 4, A_1) = V_0^{(4)} + (\tfrac{5}{14})^{\frac{1}{2}}(V_4^{(4)} + V_{-4}^{(4)}) \tag{A.5.20}$$

We deliberately use the notation $V_q^{(4)}$ rather than $Y_q^{(4)}$ to emphasise that the actual potential is summed over all electrons. Thus, whereas $Y_q^{(4)}$ must refer to a specific electron, the expression $V_q^{(4)}$ stands for the sum of such terms. It will of course have the same rotation properties and that is all that concerns us at the moment. Expressions for a typical wave function

$$|L = 3, T^{(\alpha)}\rangle = \sum_M c_M^{(\alpha)} |L = 3, M\rangle$$

in the M-basis are easily deduced and for practical purposes the coefficients $c_M^{(\alpha)}$ have been tabulated. In this example we shall deduce them by setting up the 7×7 matrix of the operator (A.5.20) in the M-basis for $L = 3$ and then diagonalising. From the reduction $\mathrm{D}^{(3)} = A_2 \dot{+} T_1 \dot{+} T_2$ we know that the resulting eigenvalues must contain two three-fold degeneracies.

From the m-dependence of the operator (A.5.20) it is clear that the term $V_0^{(4)}$ contributes only on the diagonal of the matrix, while the other two terms change M by four units. Thus, we see that the 7×7 matrix breaks up into three 2×2 matrices with $M = \pm 2$, $M = +1$ and -3 and $M = -1$ and $+3$, respectively, while $M = 0$ is uncoupled and is therefore an eigenvector. We thus need to calculate only a few matrix elements of the kind $\langle L = 3, M' | V_q^{(4)} | L = 3, M \rangle$ which are related, according to the Wigner–Eckart theorem by

$$\langle L = 3, M' | V_q^{(4)} | L = 3, M \rangle = C(343, MqM') \langle L = 3 \| V^{(4)} \| L = 3 \rangle$$

Since we are only interested in ratios, the reduced matrix element $\langle L=3||V^{(4)}||L=3\rangle$ may be ignored and the coupling coefficients $C(343, MqM')$ may be found in tables. In this way one finds the eigenvectors given in table A.5 and the eigenvalues, with a constant factor extracted, in the last column. (We are interested only in ratios here.) The crystal field in this particular salt has a sign for $A_0^{(4)}$ which leads to the representation A_2 coming lowest. The ratio of the splittings, deduced from the table, is shown in figure 9.9.

Table A.5

Representation of O	*Wave function*	*Energy shift*
A_2	$\{\vert L=3, M=2\rangle - \vert L=3, M=-2\rangle\}2^{-\frac{1}{2}}$	-6
T_1	$\{\vert L=3, M=2\rangle + \vert L=3, M=-2\rangle\}2^{-\frac{1}{2}}$	
	$\{3^{\frac{1}{2}}\vert L=3, M=\pm 3\rangle - 5^{\frac{1}{2}}\vert L=3, M=\mp 1\rangle\}8^{-\frac{1}{2}}$	-1
T_2	$\{5^{\frac{1}{2}}\vert L=3, M=\pm 3\rangle + 3^{\frac{1}{2}}\vert L=3, M=\mp 1\rangle\}8^{-\frac{1}{2}}$	
	$\vert L=3, M=0\rangle$	$+3$

The use of the coupling coefficients C (343, MqM') may be avoided by constructing equivalent operators $\mathrm{L}_q^{(4)}$ from products $\mathbf{L}\times\mathbf{L}\times\mathbf{L}\times\mathbf{L}$ of the angular momentum operators. Since there is only one such operator with $q=\pm 4$ we may take $\mathrm{L}_{\pm 4}^{(4)} = (\mathrm{L}_\pm)^4$ as a fourth power of the raising or lowering operators. The remaining operator $\mathrm{L}_0^{(4)}$ may now be deduced either by successive use of equation (7.52),

$$\mathrm{L}_0^{(4)} = 24(70)^{\frac{1}{2}}\Big[\mathrm{L}_-,\Big[\mathrm{L}_-,\big[\mathrm{L}_-,[\mathrm{L}_-,(\mathrm{L}_+)^4]\big]\Big]\Big]$$

or by various short-cut methods, see problem A.9. The final equivalent operator is then given by

$$\mathrm{L}_0^{(4)} + (\tfrac{5}{14})^{\frac{1}{2}}(\mathrm{L}_4^{(4)} + \mathrm{L}_{-4}^{(4)}) = (\tfrac{5}{14})^{\frac{1}{2}}\{14\mathrm{L}_z^4 - 12\mathrm{L}^2\mathrm{L}_z^2 + \tfrac{6}{5}(\mathrm{L}^2)^2$$
$$-\tfrac{12}{5}\mathrm{L}^2 + 10\mathrm{L}_z^2 + \mathrm{L}_+^4 + \mathrm{L}_-^4\} \quad \text{(A.5.21)}$$

and within states with $L=3$ we may write $\langle \mathbf{L}^2\rangle = 12$ giving

$$\mathrm{L}_0^{(4)} + (\tfrac{5}{14})^{\frac{1}{2}}(\mathrm{L}_4^{(4)} + \mathrm{L}_{-4}^{(4)}) = (\tfrac{5}{14})^{\frac{1}{2}}\{14\mathrm{L}_z^4 - 134\mathrm{L}_z^2 + 144 + \mathrm{L}_+^4 + \mathrm{L}_-^4\}$$

In the M-basis this operator may be evaluated directly using equation (7.40) and $\langle \mathrm{L}_z\rangle = M$ without the need to look up values for coupling coefficients. Of course it leads to the same result as presented in table A.5.

Finally, we remark that the formula (A.5.21) may also be used to deduce the splitting of each J-multiplet shown in the third column of figure 9.8. It is necessary only to write $\mathbf{J}^2$ for $\mathbf{L}^2$ and J_z for L_z. The relative strengths of the splitting in different J-multiplets may be deduced with the help of equation (A.5.14).

Problems on appendices 4 and 5

A.1 Show that the choice $\rho(\boldsymbol{c}) = \rho(0)/(\partial \boldsymbol{c}/\partial \boldsymbol{a})_{\boldsymbol{a}=0}$ is sufficient to ensure that equation (A.4.14) is satisfied.

A.2 Use the orthogonality relation (A.4.25) to show that the generalised projection operator (transfer operator) for the group $\mathscr{R}_3$ may be written in the form

$$\mathrm{P}^{(j)}_{m'm} = (2j+1)\int D^{(j)}_{m'm}(\alpha,\beta,\gamma)\,\mathrm{T}(\alpha,\beta,\gamma)\sin\beta\,\mathrm{d}\alpha\,\mathrm{d}\beta\,\mathrm{d}\gamma/8\pi^2$$

where $\mathrm{T}(\alpha,\beta,\gamma)$ is the rotation operator.

A.3 By elementary arguments show that an alternative form for the simple projection operator $\mathrm{P}^{(j)}$ is

$$\mathrm{P}^{(j)} = \prod_{j'\neq j}\{\mathbf{J}^2 - j'(j'+1)\}\Big/\prod_{j'\neq j}\{j(j+1)-j'(j'+1)\}$$

where $\prod$ denotes the infinite product over $j' = 0, \frac{1}{2}, 1, \ldots,$ excluding $j' = j$.

A.4 Calculate the coupling coefficients required in the derivation of equation (A.5.2). (Use the method of question 7.8.)

A.5 In question 7.12, the ratios between matrix elements of a tensor operator of degree 2, in states with $l = 1$, were calculated from the Wigner–Eckart theorem. Deduce the same ratios by using the equivalent operator method of section 7.4.7 (Start with the equivalent operator $\mathrm{L}^{(2)}_2 = \mathrm{L}_+\mathrm{L}_+$ and construct the other components from equation (7.52) with equations (7.28) and (7.30). Then use equation (7.40) to find the matrix elements.)

A.6 Use equation (A.5.14) to show that the matrix elements of the dipole operator $\mathrm{L}_0 + g\mathrm{S}_0$ in LS-coupling are given by the formula

$$\langle LSJ'M|\,\mathrm{L}_0 + g\mathrm{S}_0\,|LSJM\rangle = gM\delta_{J'J} + (1-g)(-1)^{L+S+J+1}$$
$$\times C(J1J', M0M)\begin{Bmatrix} J' & J & 1 \\ L & L & S\end{Bmatrix}[L(L+1)(2L+1)(2J+1)]^{\frac{1}{2}}$$

(Write $\mathrm{S}_0 = \mathrm{J}_0 - \mathrm{L}_0$ and use the result of question 7.13 for the reduced matrix element of an angular momentum operator.)

A.7 Use equation (A.5.15) to deduce the result (A.5.2). Treat $P_k(\cos\theta_{12})$ as a scalar product $[\mathbf{Y}^{(k)}(1).\mathbf{Y}^{(k)}(2)]$ because of the addition theorem (A.4.8) and take the reduced matrix elements of $\mathbf{Y}^{(k)}$ from equation (A.4.5). You will need the following coefficients:

$$C(211, 000) = -(\tfrac{1}{3})^{\frac{1}{2}},\quad \begin{Bmatrix} 1 & 1 & 2 \\ 1 & 1 & 0\end{Bmatrix} = \tfrac{1}{3},\quad \begin{Bmatrix} 1 & 1 & 2 \\ 1 & 1 & 1\end{Bmatrix} = \tfrac{1}{6},\quad \begin{Bmatrix} 1 & 1 & 2 \\ 1 & 1 & 2\end{Bmatrix} = \tfrac{1}{30}$$

A.8 Show that, if the potential V_c of equation (A.5.18) is to be invariant under the group O, then the coefficients must satisfy the relations $A^4_{-4} = A^4_4 = (\frac{5}{14})^{\frac{1}{2}}A^4_0$. (Consider two-fold and four-fold rotations about the x-axis, using $Y^{(4)}_{\pm 4} = N(x \pm iy)^4$, $Y^{(4)}_0 = N(\frac{2}{35})^{\frac{1}{2}}(35z^4 - 30z^2r^2 + 3r^4)$.)

A.9 In subsection A.5.5. we derived an expression (A.5.21)for the operator equivalent for $V(k = 4, A_1)$. Here, we suggest a short-cut method to achieve the same result. The operator we require must be a fourth-order polynomial in the operators L_x, L_y and L_z. However, we know that $\mathrm{L}_4^{(4)} = \mathrm{L}_+^4$ and that, since $\mathrm{L}_0^{(4)}$ has $q = 0$, it must have the form $\mathrm{L}_0^{(4)} = C(\mathbf{L}^4 + \alpha\mathbf{L}^2\mathbf{L}_z^2 + \beta\mathbf{L}_z^4 + \gamma\mathbf{L}^2 + \delta\mathbf{L}_z^2)$. The coefficients α, β, γ and δ may be found by demanding that $\mathrm{L}_0^{(4)}$ has zero matrix elements in all states with $L < 2$. This is a necessary condition for a tensor operator of degree $k = 4$. The choice of states $L = 1$, $M = 0$; $L = 1$, $M = 1$; $L = \frac{1}{2}$, $M = \frac{1}{2}$; $L = \frac{3}{2}$, $M = \frac{1}{2}$ is sufficient to give the four coefficients. To find the correct relative magnitude of $\mathrm{L}_0^{(4)}$ and $\mathrm{L}_4^{(4)}$ we must make use of the symmetry group O and choose the constant C so that in the complete expression $\mathrm{L}_0^{(4)} + (\frac{5}{15})^{\frac{1}{2}}(\mathrm{L}_4^{(4)} + \mathrm{L}_{-4}^{(4)})$ the coefficients of L_z^4 and L_x^4 are the same.

A.10 Deduce the relative splitting for given J in column three of figure 9.8 by using an equivalent operator like (A.5.21) for the crystal field.

A.11 With the method suggested in the previous question one cannot deduce the relative splitting in different J due to the crystal field. Use equation (A.5.14), together with the table of Rotenberg *et al.* (1959) in the bibliography to chapter 7, to find this relative splitting.

Appendix 6: Solutions to Problems in Volume 2

Chapter 14

14.4 See figure S.3 for the Brillouin zone. The little groups are C_{4v} at the points Γ and M, C_{2v} at X, and C_{1h} at Δ, Σ and Z. As $k \to 0$, Δ_1 is compatible with Γ_1, Γ_3 and Γ_5, and Δ_2 is compatible with Γ_2, Γ_4 and Γ_5. As $k \to \pi/a$, Δ_1 is compatible with X_1 and X_4, while Δ_2 is compatible with X_2 and X_3. (The irreducible representations of the little group C_{4v} at Γ are denoted by Γ_i, where $i = 1$ to 5 corresponds to the order in which the representations are listed in the character tables in appendix 1. The same convention is used at the other points.)

14.5 The eigenstates are $\Phi^{(A)} = \psi_1 + \psi_2 + \psi_3 + \psi_4$, $\Phi^{(B_2)} = \psi_1 + \psi_4 - \psi_3 - \psi_2$, $\Phi^{(E)} = \psi_1 - \psi_4$, $\Phi^{(E)} = \psi_2 - \psi_3$, the last two being degenerate. The energies all contain the constant $h^2\pi^2/2Ma^2 + V_{00}$ and in addition, $V_{11} + 2V_{01}$ for A_1, $V_{11} - 2V_{01}$ for B_2 and $-V_{11}$ for the E-doublet, where

$$V_{pq} = v_c^{-1} \int V(x, y) \exp\{(px + qy)i\pi/a\} \mathrm{d}x\mathrm{d}y$$

and $\psi_1 = \exp\{(x + y)i\pi/a\}$ $\psi_2 = \exp\{(x - y)i\pi/a\}$,
$\psi_3 = \exp\{(-x + y)i\pi/a\}$ and $\psi_4 = \exp\{(-x - y)i\pi/a\}$.

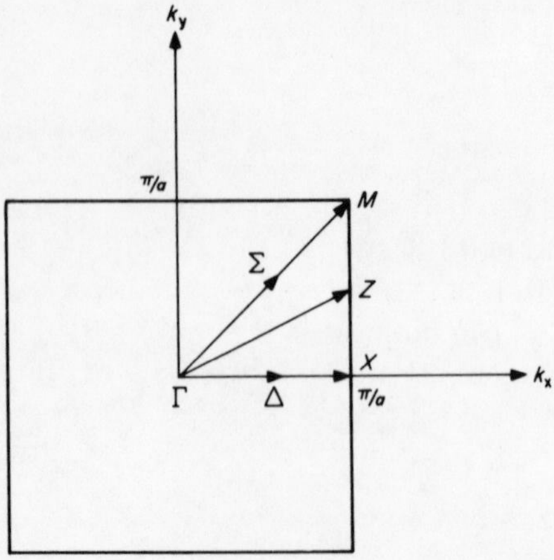

Figure S.3

Chapter 17

17.1 (1 2 4)(3 6)(5)

17.4 Dimension is five: (2 2 1 1 1), (2 1 2 1 1), (2 1 1 2 1), (1 2 2 1 1), (1 2 1 2 1).

17.5

$$P_{12} = \begin{pmatrix} 1 & 0 & 0 \\ 0 & 1 & 0 \\ 0 & 0 & -1 \end{pmatrix}, \quad P_{23} = \begin{pmatrix} 1 & 0 & 0 \\ 0 & -\frac{1}{2} & \sqrt{\frac{3}{4}} \\ 0 & \sqrt{\frac{3}{4}} & \frac{1}{2} \end{pmatrix}, \quad P_{34} = \begin{pmatrix} -\frac{1}{3} & \sqrt{\frac{8}{9}} & 0 \\ \sqrt{\frac{8}{9}} & \frac{1}{3} & 0 \\ 0 & 0 & 1 \end{pmatrix}$$

Chapter 18

18.1 For $L^{[3]}$; $|111\rangle, |222\rangle, |333\rangle$ and the symmetrised products formed from $|112\rangle, |113\rangle, |221\rangle, |223\rangle, |331\rangle, |332\rangle$ and $|123\rangle$. For $L^{[111]}$; the antisymmetrised product formed from $|123\rangle$. The orthogonal complement then belongs to $L^{[21]}$. (Or use the $\mathscr{S}_3$ projection operators $P_i^{[21]}$.)

18.2 (a) $\begin{array}{|c|c|c|}\hline 1&1&1\\\hline\end{array}$ $\begin{array}{|c|c|c|}\hline 1&1&2\\\hline\end{array}$ $\begin{array}{|c|c|c|}\hline 1&2&2\\\hline\end{array}$ $\begin{array}{|c|c|c|}\hline 2&2&2\\\hline\end{array}$ $\begin{array}{|c|c|c|}\hline 1&1&3\\\hline\end{array}$

$\begin{array}{|c|c|c|}\hline 1&2&3\\\hline\end{array}$ $\begin{array}{|c|c|c|}\hline 2&2&3\\\hline\end{array}$ $\begin{array}{|c|c|c|}\hline 1&3&3\\\hline\end{array}$ $\begin{array}{|c|c|c|}\hline 2&3&3\\\hline\end{array}$ $\begin{array}{|c|c|c|}\hline 3&3&3\\\hline\end{array}$

(b) There are eight as in equation (18.12), six of the kind $\begin{array}{|c|c|}\hline 1&1\\\hline 4\\\cline{1-1}\end{array}$

where the first row is given in table 18.1 and finally

$\begin{array}{|c|c|}\hline 1&4\\\hline 2\\\cline{1-1}\end{array}$ $\begin{array}{|c|c|}\hline 1&4\\\hline 3\\\cline{1-1}\end{array}$ $\begin{array}{|c|c|}\hline 2&4\\\hline 3\\\cline{1-1}\end{array}$ $\begin{array}{|c|c|}\hline 1&4\\\hline 4\\\cline{1-1}\end{array}$ $\begin{array}{|c|c|}\hline 2&4\\\hline 4\\\cline{1-1}\end{array}$ $\begin{array}{|c|c|}\hline 3&4\\\hline 4\\\cline{1-1}\end{array}$

18.3

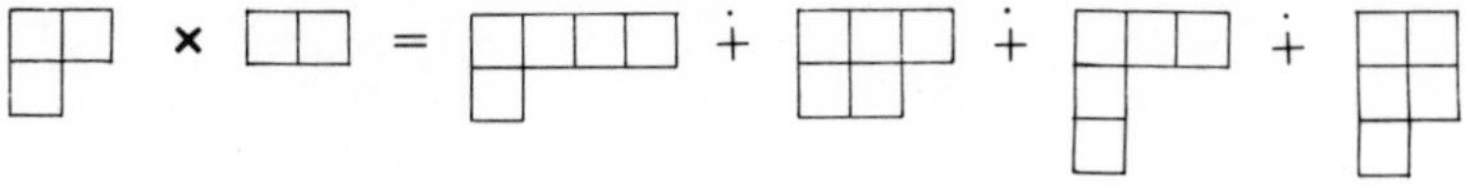

(a) $(11) \times (20) = (31) \dot{+} (12) \dot{+} (20) \dot{+} (01)$. (b) $D^{(\frac{1}{2})} \times D^{(1)} = D^{(\frac{3}{2})} \dot{+} D^{(\frac{1}{2})}$

18.4 (3 0 0)(2 1 0)(1 2 0)(0 3 0)(2 0 1)(1 1 1)(0 2 1)(1 0 2)(0 1 2)(0 0 3). Thus $M = 3, 2, 1, 0, 1, 0, -1, -1, -2, -3$ and so $L = 3$ or $L = 1$.

18.5 $L = 3$ and $L = 1$ in both cases.

18.6 For $[2]$, $L = 4, 2$ or 0. For $[3]$, $L = 6, 4, 3, 2$ or 0. For $[21]$, $L = 5, 4, 3, 2$ (twice) and 1.

18.7 $T = \frac{3}{2}$ with $J = \frac{9}{2}, \frac{5}{2}, \frac{3}{2}$. $T = \frac{1}{2}$ with $J = \frac{13}{2}, \frac{11}{2}, \frac{9}{2}, \frac{7}{2}$(twice), $\frac{5}{2}$(twice), $\frac{3}{2}, \frac{1}{2}$.

Chapter 20

20.2 See figure S.4.

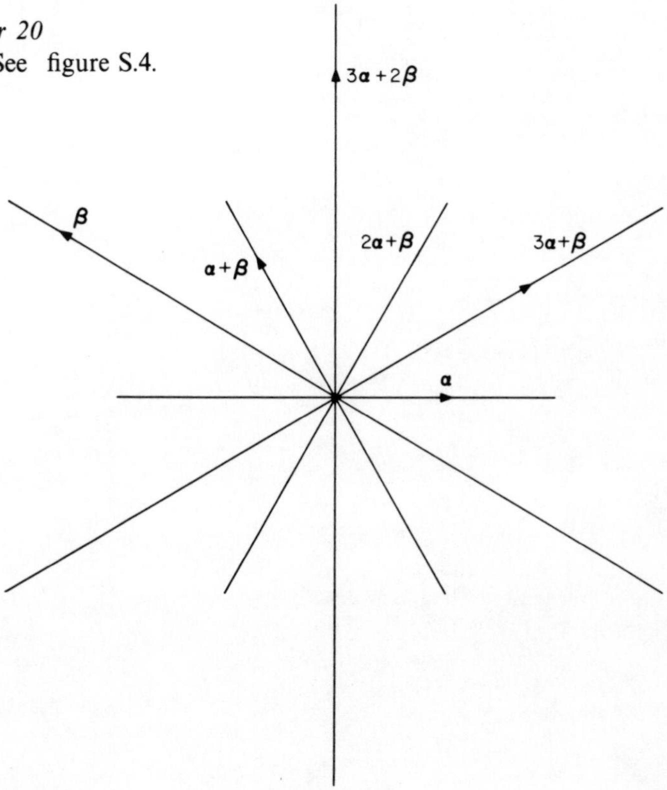

Figure S.4

Appendices 4 and 5

A.10 See A.11.

A.11 The shifts in the nine levels in the third column of figure 9.8 are given by $0, -66, 132, -28, -4, 36, (-49 \pm 5\sqrt{721}), 196$ in arbitrary units, with the figure roughly to scale.

18.3

(a) 111 × 210 = (31) + (21) + (20) + (30); (b) D[2] × D[1] = D[3] + D[2]

18.4 (3)(0) + (0)(1)(2)(0)(1)(0)(2)(0)(1)(1)(0)(2)(1)(0)(2)(0)(1)(0)(0). [illegible] Thus [illegible]

18.5 $L = 2$ and $\chi = 1$ in both cases.

18.6 For [2], $Z = 4, 2$, or 0. For [31], $L = 5, 4, 3, 2$, or 0. For [21], $L = 5, 4, 3$, (twice) and 1.

18.7 [illegible] twice), [illegible] twice), [illegible]

Chapter 20

20.1 See figure 5.4.

Figure 5.4

Appendices 4 and 5

A.10 See A.11.

A.11 The shifts in the nine levels in the third column of figure 9.4 are given by $Q_1 = 66$, [illegible] in arbitrary units, with the figure roughly to scale.

Index to Volumes 1 and 2*

* Pages 1–280 refer to volume 1 and pages 281–557 refer to volume 2